Celtic Music

Celtic Music
A Complete Guide

JUNE SKINNER SAWYERS

DA CAPO PRESS

A CIP record for this book is available from the Library of Congress.

ISBN 0-306-81007-7
First Da Capo Press Edition 2001

Designed by Cynthia Young
Set in 11 point Sabon by Perseus Publishing Services

Published by Da Capo Press
A Member of the Perseus Books Group
http://www.dacapopress.com

1 2 3 4 5 6 7 8 9—05 04 03 02 01

For Terry, who gave me love

Contents

Chronology

1014   Brian Boru, the Irish high king, killed at the Battle of Clontarf; ended Viking control in Ireland.

1169   The Norman Conquest.

1366   Statutes of Kilkenny passed, restricting Irish laws, language, and customs. Among other things, the statutes forbade the Anglo-Irish minority, which held power, from intermarrying with the native Irish population.

1601   Lord Mountjoy defeats Hugh O'Neill and "Red" Hugh O'Donnell at the Battle of Kinsale, symbolizing the end of the old Gaelic order and the beginning of a new Anglo-Irish dominance based in Dublin.

1607   Flight of the Earls. Ulster chiefs go into voluntary exile to the safety of the continent.

1615 (circa)   Mary MacLeod is born on the Isle of Harris.

1649   Cromwell arrives in Ireland at the head of a 30,000-troop garrison, takes Dublin, and lays siege to Drogheda.

1660   Roderick Morison, last of the Highland harpers, is born on the Isle of Lewis.

1670   Turlough O Carolan, the last of the Irish harpers, is born in County Meath.

1688   The Glorious Revolution brings the Protestant William of Orange to the English throne.

1690   William defeats the Catholic James II at the Battle of the Boyne.

1691   Flight of the Wild Geese. The last of the Irish nobility leaves Ireland following the signing of the Treaty of Limerick to join French and Spanish armies on the continent.

1695   Catholic Penal Laws go into effect in Ireland, whose purpose is to force Irish Catholics to abandon their religion and accept the Protestant faith.

1707   Act of Union between Scotland and England.

1721   Thomas Percy is born.

1727   Niel Gow is born in Inver, near Dunkeld.

1742   Handel's *Messiah* premieres at Mr. Neal's New Musick Hall in Dublin.

1746   Battle of Culloden. The defeat of the Highland army led to the disarming of the clans and the prohibition of Highland dress.

1759   Robert Burns is born in Alloway.

1760   Joseph MacDonald's *A Compleat Theory of the Scots Highland Bagpipe* is published.

1765   The first edition of Thomas Percy's *Reliques of Ancient English Poetry* is published.

1773   Edward Bunting is born.

1773   The *Hector* arrives in Pictou, Nova Scotia, bringing the first shipload of Highland Scots to Canada.

1782–
1820   The first major period of the Highland Clearances, a Westminster government policy in which the Highland poor were forcibly evicted to make way for more profitable sheep farms.

1786   Robert Burns's first volume of poetry, *Poems, Chiefly in the Scottish Dialect*, is published.

1792   Belfast Harp Festival.

1796   Edward Bunting's *General Collection of the Ancient Music of Ireland* is published.

1798   1798 Rising in Ireland.

1800   Act of Union between Great Britain and Ireland. The Irish parliament is abolished.

1802   The first two volumes of Sir Walter Scott's *Minstrelsy of the Scottish Borders* is published.

1808   Thomas Moore's *Irish Melodies* is published.

1810   Sir Walter Scott's *Lady of the Lake* is published.

1815   Captain Simon Fraser's *The Airs and Melodies Peculiar to the Highlands of Scotland* is published.

1821   Mary MacPherson is born.

1825   Francis James Child is born in Boston.

1829   Catholic Emancipation in Ireland. Irish Catholics gain the right to sit in the British Parliament.

1840–
1854   The second major period of the Highland Clearances.

1843   Scots fiddler James Scott Skinner is born in Banchory.

1847   The worst year of the Irish Famine.

1848   Francis O'Neill is born in County Cork.

1891   An Comunn Gaidhealach (The Highland Organization)
        is formed in Oban.

1893   Douglas Hyde founds the Gaelic League in Ireland.

1903   Francis O'Neill's *Music of Ireland* is published.

1908   Jeannie Robertson is born.

1915   Ewan MacColl is born.

1916–   Cecil Sharp spends forty-six weeks collecting folksongs
1918   in Appalachia.

1919   Cecil Sharp publishes *English Folksongs from the
        Southern Appalachians.*

1931   The Clarsach Society is formed.

1931   Séan Ó Riada (John Reidy) is born.

1940   *The Cape Breton Collection of Scottish Melodies for the
        Violin* is published.

1951   The School of Scottish Studies is established in
        Edinburgh.

1953   Jord Cochevelou, the father of Breton harpist Alan
        Stivell, unveils his harp prototype to the public.

1955   Séan Ó Riada becomes musical director of the Abbey
        Theatre in Dublin.

1960   Séan Ó Riada commissioned to write the score for the
        documentary *Mise Eire (I Am Ireland)* using traditional
        Irish music as its foundation.

1972   Institute of Cornish Studies established at the University
        of Exeter.

1972   Planxty is formed.

1975   The Bothy Band is formed.

1975   The Chieftains turn professional.

1983   Sabhal Mor Ostaig, the Gaelic College in Skye, is established.

1983   The Welsh Music Information Centre opens in Cardiff.

1985   The Scottish Music Information Centre, which promotes the works of Scottish and Scottish-based composers of all periods, is founded in Glasgow.

1990   Carnegie-Mellon University in Pittsburgh becomes the first institution of higher learning in the United States to offer a bachelor of arts in bagpipe playing.

1990   The College of Piping and Celtic Performing Arts opens in Summerside, Prince Edward Island.

1994   *Riverdance* premieres in Dublin.

1996   Balnain House of Highland Music in Inverness opens.

1998   The Chieftains celebrate thirty-five years together.

Preface

I've had a lifelong interest in folk and traditional music. It is only fairly recently though that what is now referred to as Celtic music captured my imagination. How ironic, given that I am a native Scot.

I approach the subject of Celtic music not as a musician but as someone who views the topic from a historical and sociological perspective. I am not so much interested in the intricacies and technicalities of what makes the music as much as the reasons why the music sounds the way it does and how it came to be at this point in its history. Above all, it is the emotional pull of the music that draws me, and I suspect many others, in. I search here for the bigger picture, for the human element behind the musical notes.

The book is organized in roughly chronological fashion with some thematic overlap. Thus, I begin with a definition of what Celtic music is before turning to its ancient roots. Next I explore the rich instrumental tradition of the Celtic lands, with a particular emphasis on the fiddle and the dance music that this "devil's box" so greatly inspired.

The bagpipe deserves a separate chapter all its own, if only for the richness and astonishing complexity of the pibroch, the classical music of the Highland bagpipe, as well as the often overlooked history of the other members of the bagpipe family. Chapter 5 is devoted to various categories of Celtic-language song—and isn't it reassuring to learn that new songs are being written in a Celtic language every day—while chapter 6 discusses an entirely different style of song—the ballad, which, as it turns out, is not particularly Celtic but nevertheless earns its place in the Celtic pantheon because of its monumental influence and importance.

I then travel across the Atlantic to the New World to examine the Celtic roots of Southern music, especially the "high lonesome sound" of bluegrass, arguably the most "Celtic" of American music. The New World theme continues in chapter 8 with a discussion of the emigrant song tradition and, in particular, Irish-American popular song.

Finally, the last two chapters bring the music up to date with discussions of a new Celtic subgenre, Celtic rock. I close on a universal note by discussing the exciting cross-fertilization that is currently taking place within the tradition, as musicians on both sides of the Atlantic leave their tightly confined boxes behind, casting musical boundaries to the wind, to march head-on into the great musical unknown.

It promises to be an exhilarating ride. I hope you enjoy it.

June Skinner Sawyers
Chicago
September 2000

Acknowledgments

Many people were of invaluable assistance during the writing of this book. In particular I wish to thank Nicholas Carolan in Dublin, Mícheál Ó Súilleabháin in Limerick, and the staff of the Scottish Music Centre in Glasgow for providing essential background information. Rob Gibson, an expert on Scottish music and politics and a fine singer to boot, was more than generous with both his time and knowledge. Thanks also to the members of Cowboy Celtic, particularly David Wilkie and Denise Withnell; Talitha MacKenzie; Mark Howard; Colin Hynd; as well as the staffs and publicists of Green Linnet, Shanachie, Hannibal, and Greentrax records, especially Ian Green. Additional thanks to Andy Mitchell of Ullapool for permission to quote from his song "Indiana."

The Cape Breton–based *Am Bráighe*, a quarterly newspaper, is an invaluable source of information on Gaelic Nova Scotia. Kudos to editor Frances MacEachen and her staff for their fine work. The pages *of Irish Music Magazine, Scottish World, The Living Tradition, Taplas,* the now-defunct *Keltic Fringe* newsletter, and *Dirty Linen* were also very useful.

I recommend anyone interested in Celtic music to consult the work of the many scholars and writers listed in the bibliography, particularly Robert Cantwell, P. J. Curtis, and Mark J. Prendergast. The latter provided especially useful background information for the Celtic rock chapter. As always, the writing of John Purser is a joy to read.

The inspiration for this book came from years of listening to, thinking, writing, and lecturing about Celtic music. An earlier version of the country-Celtic connection, for example, appeared in obscure pamphlets. I now welcome the opportunity here to offer my thoughts and musical suggestions to a, presumably, larger audience. In addition, my students at the Newberry Library in Chicago offered valuable feedback and insights. I thank them for supporting a type of music that must, at times, have seemed quite alien and mysterious.

I would like to thank my agent Caroline Carney for her support and encouragement. I would also like to thank my editors Andrea Schulz and Jane Snyder for their good-natured professionalism and attention to detail. They helped make the editing process fun.

Finally, warm words of praise must go to the musicians themselves who have given the world the greatest of gifts—music.

I

What Is Celtic Music?

Reels, Songs, and More

I believe that perhaps the main problem in the world today is that so many people have been uprooted. They have been cut off from their roots and have lost their identities and sense of connections to the world. Celtic culture can reconnect us because its roots go right back to the beginning of western civilization. In other cultures the lines have been broken, especially by imperialism. I believe this is why younger Europeans who do not live in the Celtic countries feel something deep inside whenever they hear Celtic music.

—ALAN STIVELL, BRETON HARPER

Celtic music seems to be everywhere or, at the very least, an approximation of it. But not only music. Look around you and you'll witness a procession of Celtic-themed novels, travel narratives, movies, theatrical productions, and poetry. From the memoirs of Frank McCourt and the poetry of Seamus Heaney to the plays of Brian Friel and the freedom-loving patriots of *Braveheart*, we seem to be smack in the middle of a modern Celtic renaissance—but one that encompasses all of the Celtic lands. Even the

mysterious sounds of the uilleann pipes, once only heard within traditional circles, are broadcast in television advertisements.

What's going on here?

And just what exactly is this chameleon-like thing called Celtic?
What is Celtic music? What does one mean by Celtic?

THE WORD *CELTIC* is thrown about quite a lot nowadays. Indeed,
one could even say that, in light of present-day trends, most everything seems to be classified as Celtic in a not-always-too-subtle attempt to join the Celtic bandwagon. Some, especially traditional
musicians, cringe at the very sound of the word.

And it's true that a substantial part of the current Celtic "scene"
has little to do with authentic Celtic tradition. Even those who
purport to play some form or another of Celtic music seem to have
forgotten their roots. Packaging of traditional music is common-
place. Quite often the musical mingling of completely different cultures, such as African or Cajun, seems a bit forced, contrived, artificial. Yet, in the right hands—as we shall see in chapter 10—
musical cross-fertilization can be a quite healthy and exhilarating
experience, for musician and listener alike.

Credit for the "Celtification" of pop, as *Entertainment Weekly*
once put it, must go to firstly, the decade-old chart success of the
ethereal-voiced Irish songbird, Enya, and, more recently, the phenomenon that is known as *Riverdance*, which has grossed more
than $300 million worldwide at last count, and is still going strong.

At last count, Enya's *Shepherd's Moon* has sold more than three
million units worldwide since its release in 1992. Another recording, *Watermark*, sold more than 1.25 million units in the U.S.
alone. No stranger to traditional music—she is a member of the
Brennon family of Clannad fame—she insists that she not only has
not forgotten her roots, but rather that her heritage is fully incorporated into her music.

But the biggest reason for the resurgence of interest in Celtic music is the phenomenal success of the television series *Roots* in the

1970s and, prior to that, the folk music revival of the 1960s. By transforming a shameful period of American history into a small-screen masterpiece that most anyone could empathize with, *Roots* made the distant past both engrossing and entertaining—something worthy of discussion and reflection. The folk boom tapped into a deep-seated need on the part of many people around the world to explore their musical roots. Add to all this the amazing Irish-American cultural renaissance currently going strong and you have a potent and volatile mix that bodes extremely well for the future.

The recent spate of what is frequently classified as Celtic music—the synthesized, drum-kit variety—must be separated from the traditional melodies of groups like the Chieftains. Some of the latest Celtic music—especially the so-called Celtic compilations—has a sterile, electronic quality, which can offer huge crossover potential, but is so far removed from authentic Celtic culture as to render it virtually meaningless. Cindy Byram, publicity director for Shanachie Entertainment, pejoratively dismissed it as "Celtic muzak" while Dublin singer-songwriter Susan McKeown complained that "Celtic seems to have become this handy catchphrase used to describe ethereal, high-pitched vocals dripping with synthesizers." As many musicians know, it is so, so difficult to incorporate modern elements into a very old music without disturbing its essence. In order to change the tradition, you must first be thoroughly a part of it; you must live and breathe it. Only then can you know what needs "fixing" and what should or should not be touched.

The best of Celtic music transcends cultural barriers and artificial distinctions and—like the best of music anytime, anywhere—can bring people together. Part of the global beat, it is also a music that is, for many people, comfortably familiar, even if they don't know much about its history. Call it comfort music if you want—music that soothes the soul just as easily as it feeds a hungry heart.

What exactly makes Celtic music distinctive from other types of music in the world?

First of all, let's define what we mean by *Celtic*. What, for instance, are the Celtic lands?

Today, there are six modern Celtic nationalities divided into two groups. The Irish, the Scots, and Manx form one group, referred to as "Q" Celtic; the Welsh, Bretons, and Cornish, or "P" Celtic, form the other. (Sometimes the Galicians in Spain are also included, especially in a cultural context.)

An increasing number of people in these lands are aware of having cultural links with one another. Sometimes these can be the haziest and most tenuous of connections; other times the knowledge is deep and firmly rooted, and the links strong.

What they all have in common are Celtic origins—that is, they speak, or at one time spoke, a Celtic language, either Irish Gaelic, Scots Gaelic, Manx, Welsh, Cornish, or Breton.

Is *Celtic music* a synonym for *traditional music*? Sometimes yes, sometimes no. In our entertainment-driven world, it all comes down to packaging. If a record label decides that a recording that contains some examples of traditional music would do better in the marketplace if it has the word *Celtic* on it, then it is given the label of *Celtic*. So be it.

At the same time, use the word *Celtic* around a traditional musician and responses can range from open hostility to weary resignation. Quite frankly, *Celtic music* is a marketing term that I am using, for the purposes of this book, as a matter of convenience, knowing full well the cultural baggage that comes with it. In the present context, it includes both songs and music—traditional and contemporary—of the English-speaking Irish and Scots and their Celtic cousins as well as the Celtic language–speaking Gaels (that is, speakers of Irish Gaelic in Ireland and Scots Gaelic in Scotland) and their Celtic cousins, whether in their native lands and in the broader Celtic diaspora.

Which leads to the question, What is traditional music, and does the term apply to music from all the Celtic lands?

Although a very broad term, essentially *traditional music* refers to music that is oral and belongs to a living popular tradition. Every Celtic land has its own traditions, customs, and musical peccadilloes. For convenience's sake, let's use Ireland as an example.

In Ireland much of the traditional-music repertoire dates from the eighteenth and nineteenth centuries, although some tunes are earlier in origin. It is music of rural origin. Most of the instrumental music consists of dance music—jigs, reels, and hornpipes. Slower pieces form only a small proportion of the repertoire. Of the instruments, strings, winds, and reeds dominate, especially the fiddle, tin whistle, flute, uilleann pipes, concertina, and accordion.

The traditional singing style is usually unaccompanied. To compensate for the lack of musical instruments, singers developed an elaborate style known as ornamentation, a complex technique that embellishes the melody through the nuances and inflections of the human voice. In effect, the human voice became the instrument.

CHARACTERISTICS

The indigenous music of the Celtic-speaking peoples share some common features, some common traits and characteristics, such as ornamentation (varying notes in a song or piece of music), a cyclical way of seeing things where the beginning becomes the end and the end the beginning, a wonderful sense of improvisation set against the fixed dictates of tradition, and the intermingling emotions of joy and sadness. Yet several musical forms are unique to a specific Celtic country, whether Welsh choirs, Irish *sean-nós* (pronounced "shan-nose"), Hebridean *waulking* songs, or Breton *kan ha diskan*.

The piping tradition is of course very strong in the Celtic lands. But what kind of pipes are we referring to? Scotland has the Lowland pipes, the Border pipes, the small pipes, and, the best known, the Highland pipes. Ireland has the uilleann pipes. Northumbria in the north of England the Northumbrian small pipes, Brittany, the *biniou*, and Galicia, the *gaita*.

The classical music of the Highland bagpipes, said noted Scottish-music critic and historian John Purser, is "profoundly bound up with the history of the Celtic peoples of Scotland (and Ireland), intimately related to the Gaelic vocal tradition, and closely related to unique forms of fiddle music and *clarsach* music."

After all the techniques are checked off, the quality that the music of the Celtic lands most commonly shares is something a lot more intangible and certainly less quantifiable—a feeling or quality that evokes emotions of sadness or joy, sorrow or delight. Some of Celtic music's qualities, it is true, derive from the modal scales of traditional music, but others are hard to pin down. All share, for lack of a better word, a Celtic spirit, a unique bond with one another that transcends time, distance, and political units.

Celtic Identity

Is there a common Celtic identity among the people of the Celtic lands? The words of the late Celtic historian Robert O'Driscoll may help to place the issue of Celtic identity in perspective. In his opinion, the Celts' perception of the world embodies a "belief in the aristocracy of the imagination and the honoured place of the poet; their strong feeling for the supernatural . . . , and a veneration for nature in all its manifestations; their ritual expression of grief, their sense of the sacredness of place and of a communion between the living and the dead; and, most of all, their view of themselves as the guardians of a tradition that was older than any that their conquerors could claim." Apply these qualities to music and you're left with more of a common feeling rather than a common sound.

"Music has always given the Scots their identity," Aly Bain, fiddler with the Boys of the Lough, told his biographer Alastair Clark, "but when I was a kid, nobody knew what our music was, so the identity wasn't there. Our identity is always going to hinge on our music and our culture, and if you don't preserve it then we will just become another European satellite."

One definition of what constitutes Celtic music would be music, either songs or tunes, created by the Celtic-speaking peoples: the Irish-speaking people of the Republic of Ireland, the Scottish Gaels of the Highlands and Islands, the Welsh speakers of Wales, the Breton speakers of Brittany, and, if one could find them, the few Manx and Cornish speakers of the Isle of Man and Cornwall, respectively.

Another definition of Celtic music—admittedly a very broad one that will probably grossly offend the purists—is the indigenous music of the Celtic lands. This definition would include music of Ireland, Scotland, Wales, Brittany, the Isle of Man, and Cornwall, as well as music that has traveled from these lands to other shores with its Celtic roots inevitably changed or altered yet its essential Celtic spirit intact. For the purposes of this book, it is the latter definition that I am embracing. For example, chapter 6 will discuss the rich ballad tradition of Scotland even though, according to the first definition, virtually none of these ballads are strictly speaking Celtic (there are a few exceptions). Rather they belong to the English- and Scots-speaking Lowland traditions with nary a Celtic word among them. At the same time, the Irish ballad tradition is for all intents and purposes an English-speaking tradition, since there are very few ballads in the Irish tongue.

Alas, things can get rather sticky.

At this point, then, I would like briefly to address the characteristics and traits that make Celtic music—the ingredients, if you will, of the Celtic musical cauldron—country by country.

Ireland

Irish music has its roots in the bardic tradition. As early as the twelfth century—when the Normans came to Ireland—music was established as an essential part of Irish life. In early Ireland, the Irish aristocracy encouraged music by an extensive system of patronage.

This all changed as continuous English invasions wracked the island. Eventually, in the early 1600s, harpers and pipers were forbidden from creating their music. During Cromwell's reign, for example, all harpers, pipers, and wandering musicians had to obtain letters from local authorities before allowed to travel through the country.

By the eighteenth century the laws against musicians had become less stringent—so much so that by 1792 the organizers of the Belfast Harp Festival asked a young folk music collector named Edward Bunting to transcribe the airs played by the last of the Irish harpers. In the process, Bunting's collection of Irish tunes became—and remains to this day—one of the most important sources in Irish-music history.

Unfortunately, by this time Bunting had been trained in the classical mode of the Continent, the Europe of Mozart and Beethoven. When taking down his notes, then, Bunting forced what was essentially a modal tradition to conform to the major and minor key system of classical music. The rhythms of Irish music are closely connected with the rhythms of Irish poetry—poetry in the Irish language.

Despite Continental influences, though, traditional Irish music never really died. The people in the countryside continued to keep it alive during the centuries with their love songs (the most common), vision poems (called *aisling*), laments, drinking songs, and work songs. The vision poems are unique to Ireland and Irish music. In a dream or vision, the writer or poet, sees a vision—usually a woman—coming down from the sky. He describes her appearance and asks her to identify herself. She says she is Ireland—the personification of Ireland—who is grieving because her native land has been subjected to so much pain and invasions from foreigners. These vision poems were written chiefly in the eighteenth century as part of the oral tradition.

As English gradually became the dominant language in the country, the itinerant ballad singers who wandered the countryside or on the city streets came to sing English-language songs that were based on Irish poetry and followed Irish rhythms. During the changeover from English to Irish, many songs were lost, and others lost their distinctive Irish qualities. Still, they retained much of the Irish character in both their subject matter and their robust sense of humor.

IRISH TRADITIONAL MUSIC ARCHIVE

The archive, located in a substantial brick-brown building on Merrion Square in the heart of Dublin, currently holds more than ten thousand hours of sound recordings, three thousand ballad sheets, and three thousand photographs, making it the premier research center for traditional Irish music in the world.

Highlights of its collections include:

- Sound recordings: from cylinders and reel-to-reel tapes to cassettes and CDs.
- Printed items: ballad sheets, chapbooks, sheet music, song collections, dance collections, periodicals, programs, catalogs, postcards, leaflets, posters, and newspaper clippings.
- Visual items: drawings, prints, photographs, microfilm, and videocassettes.

Its special collections include:

- Breandán Breathnach Collection: Breathnach, a traditional-Irish music scholar, died in 1985; his collection includes sound recordings, music manuscripts, printed items, and personal papers.
- Aidan O'Hara Collection: Sound recordings made 1975 to 1979 in areas of Irish settlememt in Newfoundland.
- Alun Evans Collection: Sound recordings made from 1968 to 1974 of the Donegal fiddler John Doherty.
- Willie Clancy Summer School Collection: Sound recordings, photographs, and videotapes from the 1980s and 1990s.
- Séan Ó Riada Collection: Sound recordings relating primarily to Ó Riada's radio and concert work in the 1960s.
- Leslie Shepard Collection: Ballad sheets, chapbooks, and books of the eighteenth through twentieth centuries.

Ornamentation is a typically Irish—and indeed, pan-Celtic—trait that can apply to songs and tunes. When applied to singing, *ornamentation* means slightly varying the notes or stopping and prolonging them. The singer may stretch certain syllables. For example, the word *country*—two syllables—may be turned into *coun-ter-ie*, with three syllables, if the song demands it. In traditional Irish song, it is the words that are of paramount importance.

A distinctive style of traditional Irish singing is known as *seann-nós,* a highly ornamented way of singing that owes much to the ancient bardic tradition, when poems were transmitted orally from generation to generation.

The musical traditions of Ireland and Scotland are very much alike. But it is interesting to note that certain songs are common in Scotland but not in Ireland. Labor or occupational songs, for example, which are very common in Scotland, are rare in Ireland. Scotland has the *waulking* song or the rowing song, but no comparable body of songs exists in Ireland.

The changeover from Irish to English led to a type of song that combined both languages. Called macaronic, these songs were composed with phrases or lines alternating in Irish and English.

Irish music falls into primarily two broad categories: songs and dance tunes. Of the latter, marches constitute the largest class.

The jig is the oldest surviving form of dance music. It is found in three forms: the single jig (in 6/8 and sometimes 12/8 time); the double jig (in 6/8 time); and the slip jig (in 9/8 time). It has been suggested that the jig is of Italian origin and may have come to Ireland via Italy through the harpers. Most Irish jigs are of native origin, although some have been borrowed from England. Many reels, which date back to the mid-eighteenth century, are of Scottish origin. Names have been changed to reflect the change in locale. "The Duke of Gordon's Rant" from Scotland is known in Ireland, for example, as "Lord Gordon's Reel" or "The Perthshire Hunt" became "The Boyne Hunt" in Ireland. (The dance tradition is discussed at length in chapter 3.)

The vast bulk of the airs and tunes that we know today were composed during the last three hundred years, most during the latter half of the eighteenth century and the early years of the nineteenth.

The traditional musician begins with the bare bones of a tune—the skeleton of a tune, if you will—then, through the combination of a mastery of technique (the use of decorations, slides, sudden stops, and so on), much skill, and even more passion makes it his or her own.

Important instruments within the Irish tradition are the harp, the fiddle, the uilleann or union pipes, the tin whistle and the flute.

Scotland

The music of Scotland is the by-product of two, perhaps three, distinctive cultures: the Anglo-Saxon culture in the Lowlands, the

Celtic culture in the Highlands and Islands, and the Norse influence in Shetland and Orkney.

But even there things are not as simple as you might think. Scots Gaelic—the language of the Gael—is spoken in the Highlands and Islands (as is English) but there are varieties of Gaelic. There's the Gaelic as found on Skye, the Gaelic in Lewis, the Gaelic on Barra. Each region has its own dialect, its own idiomatic differences. It's my understanding that the various Gaelic speakers can understand one another—it's just that each one thinks his or her Gaelic is the best!

Similarly, the Lowlands has its own set of linguistic variations. Two languages are spoken—English and Scots. Although many people still consider Scots a dialect of English, many more believe it should be considered a language all its own. Scots is a version of northern English speech that emerged in the fourteenth century and remains very much alive today. Scots is the language of the home, a "secret" language that the most modern Scots use, in one degree or another, on a daily level. It even had its own "golden age"—the second half of the fifteenth century, when gifted poets like Robert Henryson and William Dunbar lived and worked; they were among the greatest in medieval Scotland.

No less than Jean Redpath, Scotland's foremost singer of traditional songs, has called Scots "a pretty colorful language. There are things you can say in Scots that there's no way you can translate directly into English.

"There's also something a little more intangible. That's a sticky one because there have been volumes written on whether or not we are talking about merely a regional dialect or an expression of a different people, a different culture, a different emotional outlook. It's almost an ideology."

The Lowland Scots heard in the Borders is different from the Lowland Scots of a native of Glasgow or Ayrshire, while the Scots heard in the northeast of Scotland, called the Doric, is completely different. These differences were more pronounced in the past than they are today, of course. Modern communications has tended to diminish—but not eradicate—differences in speech and accent.

Scotland has a great ballad and song tradition. Songs unique to Scotland include *waulking songs* (work songs) within the Gaelic tradition. These occupational songs are very rhythmic and were sung when women shrank newly woven cloth. *Bothy ballads* from the northeast of Scotland were songs about the life and living conditions of farm laborers under the bothy system.

Generally speaking, the Scots singing style is not as ornamented as the Irish. Traditional singing is usually performed unaccompanied. But Scottish singers in the Highlands and Islands have over the years developed vocal techniques that emulate instruments, especially the bagpipes. *Mouth music*, for example, consists of nonsense syllables sung rapidly in a rhythmic manner. They are essentially dance tunes without the aid of instruments; indeed, they developed when instruments such as the pipes were forced underground during times of repression.

The traditional dance music of the Highlands refers to bagpipe and fiddle music, while Lowland Scotland has contributed the gentler country dance tunes. A uniquely Scottish dance tune is the *strathspey,* which is actually a slow reel. The counties of Angus, Perth, and Fife in the Scottish heartland were known for the quality—and quantity—of their Scottish country dance bands. Musicians like Jimmy Shand and Ian Powrie hailed from this part of Scotland.

The Highland bagpipe consists of a chanter and three drones attached to a bag filled with air by the mouth through a blow-pipe. The melody is played on the chanter while the drones provide the fixed notes. Rhythm and expression are achieved by timing and the use of grace notes. The latter can range from very short notes to complicated strings of notes.

Much of traditional Scots music was written under patronage, commissioned by clan chiefs. Highland chiefs, for example, often hired bards to write songs and poems for special occasions. Similarly, they usually had their own piper. The MacCrimmons, one of the renowned Highland piping families, revolutionized bagpipe music by developing the *piobaireachd,* the classical music of the Highland bagpipe.

Bagpipes have been popular in western Europe through the Middle Ages and into the sixteenth century. Traditionally, pipers tended to be shepherds or humble village musicians. In the Gaidhealtachd—the Gaelic-speaking areas of Scotland—the pipers fulfilled more important functions, playing in battles and at funerals. It's hard to say when the bagpipe first became popular in the Highlands, but the scholar and former professor of Celtic at the University of Glasgow Derek Thomson theorizes that circa 1400 is as accurate a date as any.

In the eighteenth century the British government outlawed the wearing of tartan. Until recently many historians also assumed that the pipes were also banned. Recent scholarship, though, especially the seminal work of John G. Gibson, seems to refute that erroneous assumption. Rather, Gibson maintains that one of the major reasons for the popular decline of piping was the mass emigration that took place in the Highlands during the nineteenth century. By then, the bagpipe played a prominent role in the formation of the military band.

Wales

The Anglo-Saxons called Wales "the land of the foreigners" or the land of the *weahlas*—hence, Wales. In the eighth century Offa, the ruler of the kingdom of Mercia, built a stone wall, nearly 150 miles long—Offa's Dyke—to mark the boundary between England and Wales, from the River Severn to the River Dee.

The native Welsh—the survivors of the British Celts who had been pushed westward until they had no place left to go—called their country "the land of comrades" or, in Welsh, Cymru.

After many battles and conflicts between the two countries, Wales was formally annexed to the English crown in 1284. In 1400 the great Welsh leader Owen Glyndwr (or Glendower), drove out the English and united Welsh under one rule. Glyndwr's reign proved to be short-lived, however.

Henry VIII tried to bring Wales under English rule; his Act of Annexation proclaimed that no one who spoke the Welsh tongue could hold political office, nor could he own land.

Henry's attempt at forced cultural conformity notwithstanding, Wales continues to have its own body of Welsh songs—sacred songs are an especially important part of the Welsh heritage—and music, although perhaps the most distinctive feature of the country's musical heritage is the Welsh choir. Still, in recent years there has been a resurgence of interest in the music of the Welsh triple harp. Much of the credit must go to Robin Huw Bowen, whose passion and commitment to the instrument is evident in almost everything he does.

Brittany

A series of miracle plays formed the core of Breton literature in the sixteenth century. In 1532 Brittany signed a treaty with France in which the kings of France became dukes of Brittany. France agreed to respect Brittany's political and administrative rights. In 1789 all of this came to nought when the French National Assembly abolished the treaty and forcibly annexed Brittany.

The Breton revival began in the nineteenth century. Strong connections with Wales, in particular, were aggressively fostered, while the ongoing Celtic renaissance in Ireland added considerably to the momentum.

Breton music consists of mostly dance music. The oldest form of accompaniment for dance in Brittany is provided by two musicians playing the *bombarde* (an early form of the oboe), although its sound more closely resembles the trumpet and the *biniou* (a one-droned, mouth-blown bagpipe). Both musicians play the same melodic line, but without harmonies, except for the drone from the *biniou* (pitched an octave above the Scottish Highland pipes). The two players are referred to as *sonerion*.

Traditional Breton music is played in twelve different modes or combinations of specific notes, which numerous scholars have called a legacy from ancient Greek music. It is this quality that gives Breton music its distinctly minor—and, I might add, typically Celtic—sound.

The Breton language is spoken chiefly in lower Brittany. Breton, according to Lois Kuter, an expert on Breton culture, is still spoken by approximately five hundred thousand people, or 16 percent, of the population of Brittany as their first language.

Alan Stivell, the famous Breton harper, when discussing the various commonalities between the Celtic countries, made some thoughtful and enlightening remarks:

Brittany is a Celtic nation like Scotland, Ireland, Cornwall, and Wales. The Breton language is the most spoken Celtic language in the world. Although Brittany is a part of France, the French are a Latin people, and the Bretons are Celts. Brittany is a kind of bridge between continental Europe and the British Isles. Breton music is a Celtic music. The rhythms and intervals in all Celtic musics are very similar. While other Europeans favor a diatonic scale, Celts have a tendency to go back to a pentatonic scale. The way an Irishman swings in a reel and a Breton swings in a gavotte (dance) are very close.

My music is primarily Celtic, and Celtic music is a part of the unconscious of all Western peoples. Celtic culture has much in common with all non-imperial cultures throughout the world—with American Indians, with Tibetans, with the Eskimos. But the commonality with American Anglo-Saxons is obvious, since the musics have Celtic roots. The Celtic culture in an American mind is something completely unconscious.

Traditional Breton songs are unaccompanied and sung in unison while most ballads are sung solo. As with dance, song repertoires vary from region to region.

Perhaps the best-known Breton instrument is the Celtic harp, a small harp whose golden age in Brittany as well as in the other Celtic countries came during the Middle Ages. There was a great deal of musical exchange among the harpers of Brittany, Wales, Scotland, and Ireland. The renaissance of the Celtic harp in Brittany can be traced to the 1950s, when Alan Stivell's father began to reconstruct the ancient Breton harp.

Cornwall

The Saxons pushed the Celts west toward the western edge of the British peninsula to an area now called Cornwall. The Saxons called the land *Kern-weahlas* (Cornish foreigners), or sometimes "the land of the West Welsh." Celts occupied the area as far east as Exeter until the tenth century when they were forced back. In 930 A.D. Athelstan, the grandson of Alfred the Great, attacked Cornwall and brought it under English control, driving the Celts out of Exeter.

Cornish literature consists of chiefly late medieval works. During what came to be known as the period of Middle Cornish, literature flourished, mostly in the form of miracle plays. The most important of these was the *Ordinalia*, a cycle of three religious plays based on biblical themes and reportedly written between 1275 and 1450. Another play, *Bewnans Meriasek* (Life of Meriasek) is reportedly the oldest surviving life of a Celtic saint in any British Celtic language.

In 1549 the first Act of Uniformity was passed, demanding the English language be used in all church services throughout Cornwall. The handwriting was on the wall. Not long after, the Cornish, vastly outnumbered and isolated in their peninsular kingdom, had little choice but to succumb to the demands of the majority culture. Still, stubborn outposts of resistance remained.

By as early as 1600, central Cornwall was already primarily an English-speaking area. Fifty years later Cornish as a living language was confined to the far western corners of the peninsula. Although the last monoglot (monolingual) Cornish speakers died in the seventeenth century, remnants of the Cornish tongue and Cornish dialect, especially in the form of rhymes and proverbs, persevered. After all, folk memories live on much longer than legislation.

In 1928 the first Cornish Gorsedd (festival), modeled along the lines of the Welsh Gorsedd, was held. It has been held annually ever since. In recent years there has been a resurgence of interest in the ancient Cornish tongue. Cornish classes are being held, and, in 1972 the Institute of Cornish Studies was established at the University of Exeter.

Cornwall, like the Isle of Man, has a strong carol tradition. Although carols are usually associated with Christmas, in Cornwall the term has come to refer to any dance tune customarily played or sung at a feast, whether it be pagan or Christian. Traditional Cornish carols are thought to be descendants of street dances. Some towns and villages in Cornwall, such as Padstow, have carols that are unique to that town.

Because of the loss of the Cornish language many years ago, few traditional Cornish songs have been passed along through the generations. Indeed, many songs and dances disappeared when the Methodists made a concerted effort to sweep away what they called "devil music." Similar conditions existed in Wales. Some dance and march tunes, though, became incorporated into Sunday school sessions.

The Cornish equivalent of the well-known Irish and Scottish gathering known as a *ceilidh,* pronounced kaylee (spellings vary; the Irish tend to use *ceili*, the Scots *ceilidh*), is the *troyll* (pronounced "troil" or "trall"). These informal parties were usually held in Cornish fishing villages and celebrated a good catch. The fisherfolk would bring out their fiddles and concertinas and a handmade drum similar to the Irish *bodhran*, but called the *croder croghen* in Cornwall. Music and dancing would take place and all manner of gaiety broke out all over. *Troylls* continued to be held in Cornwall into this century.

A few years back a local Cornish musician by the name of Mervyn Davey and his brothers formed a folk group called Bucca. This irrepressible bunch of musicians and proud sons of Cornwall resurrected the Cornish bagpipe and the Cornish hand drum. They even included contemporary examples of Cornish tunes and songs, sung chiefly in Cornish.

Isle of Man

The Manx have, like the other Celtic peoples, a rich heritage of native music and song. The themes of Manx folk songs are typically Celtic in nature: You'll find supernatural tales, love songs, work songs, historical ballads, lullabies, and nature poetry. In Man, as in Wales, there is a great body of popular sacred music known as Manx carols or *Carvalyn Gailckagh*.

The Isle of Man is the oldest self-governing Celtic nation in the world, since it has had home rule status since 1866. Although Man is not part of the United Kingdom, the seat of government in Westminster legislates over the island. The last native Manx speaker died in 1974. Yet like Cornwall, the Isle of Man has experienced a revivalist movement.

According to folk legend, the island was named after Manannan Mac Lir, the Celtic ocean god. Original inhabitants were Celts who spoke Brythonic, or "P" Celtic—the tongue of the Welsh and Cornish. In the fourth century the Goidelic branch, or "Q" Celtic—the Irish and Scots—gained domination and held sway until the English tongue took over.

The Manx established their own parliament which they called the Thingvollr, meaning "Parliament Field" (as evidenced by the name, Norse influences were very strong on the island). Today the parliament uses a simpler variation of the name, the Tynwald. Scotland ruled Mannin for over twenty years until Edward I annexed it. It changed hands over the years between the Scots and the English.

When Manx home rule was introduced in 1866 more than half of the population spoke Manx—although people in power spoke English, and English quickly became the lingua franca of the land. The Education Act of 1872 required that English be taught in all of the island's schools, which assured the quick decline of the native Manx tongue.

According to a 1921 census, only 896 people on the island spoke Manx and of that amount, only 19 were monoglot (knowing or using only one language). By 1971 only 284 people remained who were able to speak the language.

The oldest Manx carols date from the early years of the eighteenth century. Although these were originally composed as Christmas songs and sung in churches on St. Mary's Eve (Christmas Eve), Methodist preachers encouraged their parishioners to sing the songs throughout the year. The carols were usually very long—oftentimes more than sixty verses—and were devotional in nature. Toward the end of the eighteenth century, through the considerable influence of the Methodist Church, religious carols replaced secular folk songs. By World War II the tradition of singing secular folk songs had all but died out.

Today, the island is undergoing a revival of interest in the language. In the early 1980s bilingual street signs began to appear in some towns. There was a revival of interest in Manx music and Manx dancing. And in 1983 the first film ever made in the Manx language premiered: *Ny Kirree fo Niaghtey (The Sheep Under the Snow)*, which is also the name of a traditional Manx lament about the loss of more than two thousand sheep during a severe winter storm. The events form the basis of the novel *Song of Mannin*, by Mona Douglas.

Galicia

Located on the northwestern tip of Spain, Galicia—geographically, at least—is like the rest of the Celtic lands: hilly and rainy.

Galicia lost its Celtic language when Celtic tribes from the British Isles emigrated in the fifth to seventh centuries in what is now Galicia and Asturias; they quickly assimilated with the native Latinized population. Yet the Galician language, Gallego, a Romance language and a separate branch from the Celtic language on the Indo-European family tree, includes a number of Celtic root words. Galicia can even boast its own bagpipes, called the *gaita*.

There is a joy in grief.
—OLD GAELIC SAYING

Celtic music can be many things to many people and often means many things to many people. I imagine that the people who bought the best-selling soundtrack of the motion picture *Titanic,* which features wispy Enya-like vocals and lighter-than-the-wind Celtic doodlings, did not particularly care if the music they heard was traditional or not. All they knew was that it affected them, deeply, by tapping into their unspoken yearnings.

People who had no previous interest in Celtic music or whose only knowledge of it was a few Clancy Brothers recordings, the easy listening piano musings of Phil Coulter, or, perhaps, an old ticket stub from *Riverdance* responded in droves. And they were responding to what could have been. The wistful, timeless quality of the music affects people on an unspoken level, barely acknowledged.

And maybe the deep feeling that the music evokes is the secret to both its longevity and modern appeal. It makes us feel something. Whether sadness or mirth—or, in typically Celtic fashion, both at the same time—it brings out our humanity.

What follows is a musical road map to the Celtic lands—an examination of its past, an assessment of its present, a glimpse into its future. It is a music for all time.

RECOMMENDED LISTENING

Canu Cymru/Music of Wales (Sain). A representative sampling of Welsh musical traditions, including male choirs, the triple harp, hymn-singing, rock, and contemporary folk. Features such well-known Welsh artists as acclaimed opera singer Bryn Terfel, harpist Eleanor Bennett, folk group 4 Yn y Bar, contemporary singer Sian James, boy treble Aled Jones, and the contemporary folk of Dafydd Iwan and Ar Log.

Celtic Connections (The Living Tradition). Highlights from various Celtic Connections festivals, the emphasis here is from the Irish and Scots traditions. Artists featured include Dervish, Dougie Maclean, Aly Bain, Iron Horse, Déanta, Brian McNeill, Catherine-Ann MacPhee, Old Blind Dogs, Alasdair Fraser and Paul Machlis, Altan, Boys of the Lough, Cherish the Ladies, The Cast, and Wolfstone.

Celtic Graces: A Best of Ireland (Hemisphere). A compilation from three major Irish labels, Tara, Gael-Linn, and Mulligan, this CD features a representative sampling of the best of Irish music over the last few decades. Highlights include Davy Spillane's "Midnight Walker," the Bothy Band's "The Maids of Mitchelstown" and "The Maid of Coolmore," Paul Brady's "Arthur McBride," Clannad's "Eirigh Suas a Stoirin" (Rise Up My Love), and Planxty's "The Pursuit of Farmer Michael Hayes."

Her Infinite Variety: Celtic Women in Music and Song (Green Linnet). A two-CD set featuring some of the finest female singers and musicians from the Celtic lands and throughout the Celtic diaspora. Includes

Mairéad Ni Mhaonaigh of Altan, Karen Matheson of Capercaillie, Tríona Ní Dhomhnaill, Liz Carroll, Cherish the Ladies, Déanta, Eileen Ivers, Joanie Madden, Niamh Parsons, Sharon Shannon, Síleas, and June Tabor. Liner notes by Fiona Ritchie, host of the popular radio show "The Thistle and Shamrock."

The Music and Song of Greentrax: The Best of Scottish Music (Greentrax). A two-CD set of the independent Scottish record label's best artists—traditional and contemporary. Features Ceolbeg, Shooglenifty, Mairi MacInnes, Hamish Moore, Eric Bogle, Seelyhoo, Gordon Duncan, Deaf Shepherd, Sheena Wellington, Brian McNeill, Catherine-Ann MacPhee, Jean Redpath, the Whistlebinkies, and Dougie Pincock.

Traditional Music of Scotland (Green Linnet). Excellent sampling of Scots traditional music by the likes of Capercaillie ("Iain Ghlinn' Cuiach"), John Cunningham ("Archibald McDonald of Keppoch"), the Tannahill Weavers ("Are Ye Sleeping Maggie?"), and Andy M. Stewart ("Land o' the Leal").

Women of the World: Celtic (Putumayo). Fine sampling by leading female vocalists of the Celtic world, including Maire Brennan of Clannad, Maighréad Ní Dhomhnaill, Mary Black, Karen Matheson of Capercaillie, Connie Dover, Maura O'Connell, and Fiona Joyce. A similar compilation, *Her Infinite Variety: Celtic Women in Music & Song* (Green Linnet), features a two-CD set. The line-up here includes women-led groups (Déanta, Niamh Parsons and the Loose Connection, Altan, Capercaillie) and all-women groups or duos (Cherish the Ladies, Síleas), as well as solo artists (Eileen Ivers, Sharon Shannon, Liz Carroll).

2

From Ancient Roots

Bardic Heroes, Traveling Harpers,
and the Classical Connection

Three things come without asking: fear, jealousy, and love.

–OLD GAELIC SAYING

And this race of men from the plains were all the harder, for hard land had borne them.

–LUCRETIUS

Listening to the traditional music of the Celtic lands, you feel a palpable sense of the past, as if the collective emotions of every previous generation from time immemorial are contained in the music. Those who have gone before and those who are living now come together to create a breathing, vibrant tradition. The geographical isolation of the Celts, living as they did— and do—on the edges of Europe, almost guaranteed that the old ways would survive. And survive they did.

Early Celtic Music and Culture

Various prehistoric Bronze Age instruments existed in the Celtic world as early as 800 B.C., although music scholars believe these primitive attempts at musical expression were used more for rituals rather than musical accompaniment. Cautioned Irish music historian Charles Acton, "there is no direct connection other than a romantic and imaginative one between those bronze instruments and the rest of our musical lineage."

The Celts were an Indo-European group, ancestors of the modern Irish, Scots, Welsh, Cornish, Bretons, and Manx. This enigmatic people arrived in the British Isles from the European continent as early as 2000 B.C. The third and fourth centuries A.D. witnessed a significant migration of Celts from Ireland, the Gaels—called Scotti—to what is now Scotland where they settled along the western coasts of Argyll. By the fifth century, this new kingdom, called Dalriada, had become an independent kingdom of Gaelic-speaking Scots with their capital situated at Dunadd.

Additional bands of Irish Celts settled in southwestern Wales and Cornwall. From there they would eventually move to the Armorican peninsula in northwestern France in sufficient enough numbers that by the late sixth century, the land became known as Brittany, or Little Britain.

The earliest written references to music and musicians in Ireland appear under the fifth-century Brehon Laws (Brehon from the Irish *brithem,* meaning "judge"), a codified and complex system of jurisprudence. Musicians also appear in the early prose sagas or cycles (collections). The bards and minstrels were part of a cast of larger-than-life characters, which included Cuchulain, the form-shifting mythic hero of the Ulster Cycle. The centerpiece of the Ulster tales is undoubtedly the "Tain Bo Cuailnge" ("Cattle Raid of Cooley"), which centers around the possession of a coveted prize bull.

Ancient sacred landmarks, such as the Celtic high crosses dotted throughout the Irish and Scottish landscapes, acknowledge the special talents and skills of musicians. In Scotland images of pipers and harpers appear on ninth- and tenth-century Pictish stone carvings.

It is more than likely that the early Celts sang psalms and other religious songs. Although evidence is sparse, there are indications that the early Irish church, for example, had its own form of Latin chant with strong links to the Coptic chant of Egypt. The noted music scholar John Purser pointed out that Scots Gaelic psalm singing resembles Middle Eastern chanting not only in the pace of delivery and type of decorations but also by employing the same pentatonic scale. Chants were apparently of ecclesiastical origin. Meters used by the bards were derived originally from the Latin hymns of the early church. In addition, communal singing by monks was an important part of liturgical affairs in the early Irish church; this singing probably included both Latin and Irish hymns, some biblical and some written in honor of a saint.

 ## STRANGE CONNECTIONS

Much of traditional Celtic music is pentatonic. Pentatonic refers to a scale that has five tones to the octave. On the piano the pentatonic scale can be reproduced by playing only the black keys. And yet the total pentatonic scale occurs in the music of nearly all ancient cultures—China, Polynesia, Africa—as well as that of the Native Americans and the Celtic peoples. Gregorian melodies and plainsong melodies are also pentatonic.

Irish music in particular does not use the same scale as European or Western music and, in fact, is closer to some forms of Eastern music. Irish music is primarily modal, in contrast to the more harmonic characteristics of Western music; notes appear in clusters, as in chords or in harmony singing. Traditional Celtic music largely depends on a single melody line.

Scottish-music scholar John Purser has noted the similarity between Gaelic psalm-singing (for a description of psalm-singing, see chapter 5) and Middle Eastern chanting; in particular, he compared the music of a Christian community in Ethiopia and a Christian community in the western Highlands and arrived at some rather startling conclusions. Despite having no direct or indirect contact with one another for hundreds of years, "if at all," the two solo chants use the same pentatonic scale, in exactly the same manner; the decorations of the main notes are "almost identical and the pace of delivery is the same."

His explanation? "The best that can be suggested is that the Gaelic-speaking people, whether the church wanted it or not, retained a style of singing with roots in very ancient chant."

Regarding interrelatedness, musical historians remind us that the Indian sitar has a keynote "drone" built in, just like the Scottish bagpipe. As further proof of the link between East and West, remember that the pentatonic scale is also the basis of Chinese music. And so we find this same "Chinese" scale surfacing in Scottish folk songs from "Coming Through the Rye" to "Over the Sea to Skye." Said English historian Dr. Charles Burney back in 1789: "The Chinese scale, take it which way we will, is certainly very Scottish." Hence, the traditional music of the Celtic lands share much common ground with the folk music of Eastern Europe, Asia, Africa, and the Middle East.

Apart from church music, there's very little evidence of Irish music being performed or produced before the late sixteenth century. Irish music, like Irish literature, was primarily an oral tradition. Constant warfare and the subjugation of native culture to an occupying force were hardly conducive to the preservation of manuscripts, and they took their toll over the centuries. Despite these formidable obstacles, scholars know from both literary and visual evidence that music played an important role in the social life of medieval Ireland. We also know that harp players enjoyed a high status in the Irish social hierarchy.

During Ireland's days under English domination, two musical cultures existed: the music of the native Irish-speaking community and the music of the colonial ruling class—essentially the music of western Europe. The Gaelic heritage found expression in its folk songs and tunes, the Anglo heritage in European music, perhaps best epitomized by the performance of Handel's *Messiah* in Dublin in 1742.

Despite its constant struggle to survive over the centuries, traditional Irish culture did not disappear, nor did it atrophy to any noticeable degree. Rather it adopted a low profile, but always maintaining its deep-rooted ties to the hearth.

Early Irish society consisted of a number of small kingdoms, called *tuathas*. By the late eleventh century these kingdoms were replaced by a handful of powerful provincial kings vying for control over the length of the land. The arrival of the Normans in the twelfth century brought a cultural renaissance of sorts to the country and quelled a rather chaotic political situation. Among the new bureaucrats and politicians to arrive on the scene included Giraldus Cambrensis from Wales. A well-educated and opinionated man, he studied law, philosophy, and theology in Paris. Compliments did not come easy to him. Although he found little to admire in the Irish themselves, whom he labeled "barbarians" (he was somewhat more generous toward the Scots), he was quite smitten with their musical abilities: "I find among these people commendable diligence only on musical instruments, on which they are incomparably more skilled than any other nation I have seen. Their style is quick and lively."

Anglo-Norman control was confined to the Pale, referring to the twenty-mile radius around Dublin. Yet despite this limited area, the Normans left an indelible stamp on Irish culture. Courtly love songs, influenced by the French and Spanish troubadours, were assimilated into native Irish verse. Within a generation they began to adopt Irish customs—becoming, as the saying goes, "more Irish than the Irish themselves." They learned the language and used the Irish forms of their names. Norman knights intermarried with the native population.

Attitudes slowly changed, though. By the fourteenth century official policy toward this cultural intermingling had taken a turn for the worse. In 1366 the Crown passed the Statutes of Kilkenny, which tried, unsuccessfully, to restrict Irish laws, language, and customs.

The reigns of Henry VIII and subsequent Tudor monarchs, including Queen Elizabeth I, the last of the Tudors, had a profound impact on the cultural and political life of Ireland. Fearing that Spain, England's erstwhile enemy, might ally with Ireland, and driven by a zeal to exploit the resources of her island neighbor, England embarked on an ambitious and long-standing plan to bring

Ireland to its knees. A large part of that plan was to strip the Catholics, the vast majority of the native population, of their basic rights—in effect, to make Ireland a Protestant country by law, if not in actuality. The artistic life was not spared, either. Between 1563 and 1603 Irish musicians were persecuted by six statutes. Henry knew the powerful sway that the musician had in medieval Ireland, and knew how important a role music played in Ireland's social life. The existence of the island's cultural life was threatened by the suppression of the activities of its pipers, harpers, and bards. By attacking the music and poetry that the Irish loved so dearly, the English slowly chipped away the essence of the Celtic soul. Elizabeth's proclamation of 1603 went even further by decreeing that bards and harpers be executed "wherever found" and that their instruments be destroyed.

Stripped of their patronage, the once-privileged bards wondered the countryside, homeless and virtually penniless, relying on the occasional patron to eke out a living. As we shall soon see, conditions worsened under Cromwell. Harpers and pipers—indeed, all wandering musicians—were forced to obtain letters from local authorities before being allowed to travel through their own country.

 ## THE BRIAN BORU HARP

The Brian Boru harp is the oldest surviving Irish harp in the world. Named after the Irish high king who died on Good Friday 1014 at the Battle of Clontarf, it is located at Trinity College in Dublin. It actually dates from the fourteenth century and thus could not have been played at the battle scene. Originally strung with thirty brass strings and having a range of four octaves, it was played in the traditional way—with long fingernails. Unlike the modern gut-strung harp, it has a clear, bell-like quality.

Yet not everyone in Ireland meekly acquiesced. Ulster in the 1590s was a veritable hotbed of rebellion. From this area emerged two great legendary figures and Irish patriots, Hugh

O'Neill and "Red" Hugh O'Donnell. O'Neill launched a successful military challenge to the Earl of Essex, who failed miserably in his task to subdue his Irish enemy. But the Irish victory dance was short lived.

On Christmas Day 1601, Essex's successor, Lord Mountjoy, defeated O'Neill and O'Donnell at the Battle of Kinsale, a watershed event in both Irish musical and literary history, more for what it symbolized—the beginning of the end for the old Gaelic order and its traditional system of patronage—than for its actual results. Several years later, in 1607, Rory O'Donnell, brother of "Red" Hugh, and ninety other Ulster chiefs went into voluntary exile and fled to the safety of the European continent. Referred to as the Flight of the Earls, it marked another major turning point in Irish history, again having dire consequences for the country's culture.

Within a century more than half of the land in Ulster would be transferred to the new English and Scottish colonists who were settling in the North. Thousands of native Irish were cleared from lands in Tyrone, Derry, Amtrim, and Armagh and replaced by Lowland Scots as well as Gaelic-speaking Presbyterians from Galloway and Argyll—indeed, the roots of the present "Troubles" in Northern Ireland date from this time period. These new arrivals brought with them the jigs and songs of their native land and, in the process, transformed the cultural face of Ireland.

Cromwell arrived in Ireland in 1649 at the head of a Puritan army and hastened the demise of the old order. Determined to crush the royalist cause in Ireland, Cromwell forced the leaders of the various Irish rebellions to forfeit their land and property rights to his Commonwealth. Many were relocated to the counties of Clare and Connacht. What's more, in an affront to the Catholic faith, Catholic priests were effectively outlawed and the Mass was forbidden.

The accession of the Catholic James II to the throne in 1685 was but a blip in time, for three years later he was brushed aside by the bloodless Glorious Revolution, which brought the Protestant William of Orange and his wife, Mary, to power. The following year, 1689, in a determined attempt to regain control, James and his army arrived in Cork before making their way to Ulster. In July 1690, at the famous Battle of the Boyne, William defeated James's lesser forces. William's victory—James fled the battlefield to ever-lasting infamy—assured that the Protestant ascendancy would flourish in Ulster. To this day the Battle of the Boyne, the final defeat of Catholic Gaelic Ireland, looms large in the imagination of Ulster Protestants, and such popular and enduring Protestant marching tunes as "The Boyne Water" date from this turbulent era. The ultimate death knell occurred after the signing of the Treaty of Limerick in late 1691 with the departure of the last of the Irish nobility—the so-called Flight of the Wild Geese—who left Ireland to join French and Spanish armies on the Continent.

The notorious anti-Catholic Penal Laws began during William's reign and continued under George II. The laws, which took effect in 1695, were designed to force Irish Catholics to abandon their religion or, if they refused, to surrender property and any chance for a decent education. According to these laws both Protestant dissenters and Catholics were compelled to pay tithes to the established church. Catholics, in particular, were harshly punished. They were forbidden from serving in parliament, the navy, the legal profession; indeed, could not freely participate in any government services. Nor could they teach or even buy land. For all intents and purposes, they were removed from the most basic infrastructure of Irish society. What Cromwell had wrought several decades earlier was now complete.

 ## WERE YOU AT THE ROCK?

During the height of Catholic suppression, not only were Catholic priests outlawed but the Mass was also forbidden. The Irish were forced to rely on surreptitious open-air services at a mass rock—a large stone typically set in a remote part of the country that functioned as an altar. The traditional song "Were You at the Rock?" recounts these terrible times.

> *Did they go then to the grey rocks,*
> *and behind a wind-swept crevice there,*
> *did you find our Mary gently waiting,*
> *our lady, sweet and fair?*

Did the sun shine brightly 'round her
making gold darts through her hair?
and will you stay silent as the day
when the wind has left the air?

THE IRISH HARPERS

The harp has always held a special place in the musical history of Ireland. Indeed, from early medieval times to the late eighteenth century the harp was considered *the* instrument of the Irish, and the music of the Irish harpers the true art music of the Irish. Harpers were accorded professional status; and from at least the eleventh century they had acquired an exalted position in the Irish social strata. They were trained court musicians who were attached to the retinues of kings and chiefs. The music of the harpers formed the third division of Irish music, wedged as it was between the art music composed by professionals and folk music performed by the ordinary folk. Essentially, harp music was the art music of Ireland's Gaelic culture.

The golden age of the Irish harp took place roughly from the eleventh to the sixteenth centuries. A solo instrument, the harp was used to accompany the recitation of epic poetry. The harping tradition was largely an oral one passed by ear from player to player, not written down until fairly recently.

Indeed, the harp was the preferred instrument of the upper classes in Ireland until the end of the eighteenth century. The breakup of the Irish courts under English rule led to the unraveling of the traditional system of Irish harp patronage. Harpers were the only Gaelic musicians with any formal training. The old Irish harpers had extremely long fingernails and played on brass strings. (Modern players tend to play nylon strings.)

According to singer and harpist Robin Williamson, the word *harp* derives from the Anglo-Saxon *harpe* or *hearpa* (the old Irish word was *crwyth*, the Welsh, *telyn*). During the Middle Ages traveling harpers would go from town to town, market to market, performing at weddings and feasts and recounting tales of heroism and treachery.

From the seventeenth century onward, the harp in Ireland declined at a fairly rapid and steady pace. The turmoil of the political climate adversely affected the island's always fragile cultural life. With the changing of the guard from Gaelic to Anglo-Irish, harpers in particular paid dearly. While a few were able to secure positions as harpers to the new landed gentry—the aforementioned Anglo-Irish, who largely replaced the old Gaelic chiefs—many, if not most, lost their social status and their livelihood and were reduced to impoverishment or, at the least, such a lower standard of living that they had to turn to other occupations to survive. Many became small farmers.

Those who were willing and able had no choice but to learn how to adapt to the new situation. Whereas before they performed Gaelic music for their fellow Gaels, now they had to accommodate entirely different and usually more sophisticated musical tastes—the musical needs and desires of London and the Continent.

Other harpers, unable to secure positions, became traveling musicians, going from house to house and creating music for anyone who would grant them hospitality, a place to rest, or a meal to carry them through the day. This situation had its good points: For one, it led to a cross-fertilization in musical styles. Before, the harpers had been associated with formal, highly stylized music; now they were exposed to the more casual music of the folk musician. It freed them up tremendously.

But by the late eighteenth century the harp tradition in Ireland had virtually died out. Since the tradition of the harpers was an oral one, scholars now know little of their music—with one exception, and it's a major one: the Belfast Harp Festival.

The Belfast Harp Festival

In 1792 a nineteen-year-old folk-music collector and organist from Armagh named Edward Bunting transcribed the music of ten of the finest harpers in Ireland during a festival in Belfast. They represented the best—and the last—of the great Irish harpers. He walked among them, talked to them, and took down their tunes.

The Belfast Harp Festival was the last time that the great Irish harpers would play together. Yet this festival is an important milestone in Irish musical history for another reason as well—it was the first and last time that the music of the harpers would be written down. It truly marked the end of an era and an ancient tradition that had continued unbroken for generations.

The festival took place in Belfast's Exchange Rooms on July 11–13, 1792, and was organized by several prominent Belfast citizens, including Thomas Russell, Henry Joy McCracken, and Dr. James MacDonnell. Both Russell and McCracken were also members of the Society of United Irishmen. As an enticement, the organizers offered a number of monetary prizes: "A considerable sum will be distributed in premiums in proportion to their merits." Despite this carrot, only ten Irish and one Welsh, Damere Williams, came. According to musician and noted harp scholar Gráinne Yeats, "they were dressed plainly in grey homespun material, though," she added, "some had silver buttons." For three days these musicians played their repertoire of Irish music.

 ## BELFAST HARP FESTIVAL HARPERS

The Irish harpers were:

Denis Hempson, 97, blind	*Patrick Quin, 47, blind*
Arthur O'Neill, 58, blind	*Charles Fanning, 56*
Rose Mooney, 52, blind	*Charles Byrne, 80*
Daniel Black, 75, blind	*James Duncan, 45*
Hugh Higgins, 55, blind	*William Carr, 15*

Hempson had been born in 1695 in County Derry and would die there some 112 years later. Blind since the age of three, he trained as a harper and traveled for many years through both Ireland and Scotland. It's even been said that he played for Bonnie Prince Charlie in Edinburgh in 1745. He was the only harper at the Belfast festival to play in the old traditional style—long fingernails on brass strings—and he refused to play anything but Irish music.

According to the Irish patriot Wolfe Tone, who attended the festival, Fanning was the most skilled player at the festival.

Edward Bunting was born in Armagh in 1773 to an Irish mother and an English father. He published his life's work, the *General Collection of the Ancient Music of Ireland,* in 1796.

After the festival ended, Bunting visited some of the harpers in their homes, taking down more music and learning from them details of their playing techniques. He also collected music from many folk musicians and published his findings in three sets over a period of fifty or so years. The Bunting Collection is considered the first extensive publication of Irish traditional music. It included simple folk tunes, music for dancing to the pipes or the fiddle, as well as sophisticated melodies that were clearly written by trained musicians. A few are attributed to particular harpers, such as Turlough O Carolan.

Turlough O Carolan, Last of the Irish Harpers

Turlough O Carolan, the last of the wandering minstrels, embodied the image of the old bards. Chieftain harpist Derek Bell remarks that "Carolan's music is evocative of a school of harp playing so ancient that we cannot put a date on it."

Carolan (1670–1738), probably the greatest of the Irish harpers, was a transitional figure in Irish musical history. He lived during a tumultuous time in Ireland, when the odious Penal Laws, which attempted to eradicate Catholicism in Ireland and assure a Protestant supremacy were at their height and less than thirty years after Oliver Cromwell's systematic and methodical destruction of the old Gaelic order. Carolan bridged the gap between art and folk music but, more than this, he also went back and forth between the two types. Wisely, he tailored his music to appeal to the tastes of his new audience, containing both Irish and non-Irish selections from baroque and vernacular dance music to the Italian baroque music inspired by the great composer Corelli.

Carolan was born in 1670 in Nobber, County Meath, the son of John Carolan, a small subsistence farmer. At age fourteen, young Carolan moved with his family to Roscommon, where the elder Carolan worked for the McDermott Roe family of Ballyfarnon. When he was eighteen Carolan contracted smallpox, which left him permanently blind. Since one of the few occupations open to a blind person at that time was music, Carolan picked up the harp.

Mary McDermott Roe, a friend and patron of the family, played a crucial role in his musical education. She placed him under the apprenticeship of a local harper, and when she felt he was ready to pursue the harping profession on his own—after three years of study—she provided him with a harp, a horse, and a helper. The helper acted as his guide and actually carried the harp. For the next four decades or so Carolan made his way around Ireland, particularly in Connacht, and found patrons among members of the Gaelic, Anglo-Norman, and Ascendancy families.

 ## CAROLAN AND THE CHIEFTAINS

Without the intervention of the Chieftains—and particularly their harpist, Derek Bell—it is very likely that the music of Carolan would still fall under the obscure category. It is no exaggeration to say that the Chieftains singlehandedly revived his music.

The Chieftains recall the lost era of the Belfast Harp Festival in their recording *The Celtic Harp: A Tribute to Edward Bunting*, a remarkable piece of work, part of which was recorded on May 12, 1992, with the Belfast Harp Orchestra at a gala concert in Ulster Hall. "Tribute to Bunting," arranged in a classical setting, consists of several of the best harp tunes that Bunting collected, including "Deirdre's Lament for the Sons of Usneach," often called the oldest piece of Irish music in existence.

Carolan's repertoire consisted of arrangements of popular songs and airs, traditional dance tunes set to the harp, marches and laments, as well as his own compositions. He would usually compose a piece while traveling and have it ready before arriving at his destination. His original work consisted primarily of three main types: The bulk of his tunes are *planxties*, tunes written in honor of his patrons. The others are arrangements of traditional airs attributed to him and laments.

"In writing his songs, Carolan composed the music first," remarked Gráinne Yeats on her CD *Belfast Harp Festival*, "and then thought up the words to go with the tune." As she noted, this "marked a fundamental reversal of a centuries old tradition."

Even in death, Carolan did things with style and panache. When he felt the end of his life was approaching he returned to the house of his old friend, Mrs. McDermott Roe, where he reportedly composed his last piece of music, titled, appropriately enough, "Carolan's Farewell to Music." When Roe greeted him at the door, the old, fragile composer reportedly confessed, "I came after all I've gone through, to die at home at last, in the place where I got my first learning and my first horse." With that, she invited him inside, where he downed a drink of his beloved whiskey and played his piece for her. When he died at the age of sixty-eight in 1738, his wake lasted four days, and people throughout Ireland came to pay their last respects.

THE SCOTTISH HARP

As with the case of Ireland, of Scotland's three national instruments—the harp, the pipes, and the fiddle—the harp or *clarsach* is by far the oldest instrument. In the Highlands the harper was an important member of the Highland chief's household retinue.

Two of the older harps still survive: the Caledonian or Lamont Harp and the Queen Mary harp, both in the new Museum of Scotland in Edinburgh. The Lamont harp is said to date from at least 1464, when it was brought from Argyll by a daughter of the Lamont family of Argyll to Lude in Perthshire. The Lude family also came into possession of the Queen Mary harp, which is said to resemble the harp of Brian Boru (now in Trinity College, Dublin), slain at the Battle of Clontarf in 1014. Scholars tell us there was little difference between the Scottish and Irish harps at that time.

Harp music existed in the Scottish Lowlands prior to the Reformation, although the ancient Scottish harp had fallen into disuse by the eighteenth century; indeed, until recently much Scottish harp music has not been heard for hundreds of years. Some aristocratic families, however, had retained the use of a harper as late as the seventeenth century. Highland harpers seem to have played mainly a wire-strung *clarsach*, whose strings were made of brass wire.

The Last of the Highland Harpers

Most of the early Scottish harpers remain unknown to us today. But there are a few exceptions, most notably one Roderick Morison (circa 1660–1713), otherwise known as Rory Dall (Blind Rory) or An Clarsair Dall (The Blind Harper) and considered the last of the great Highland harpers. He was both bard and harper; some of his poetry has come down to us. Unfortunately, none of his harp music has survived, just his reputation.

Morison was born in the Isle of Lewis circa 1660. The son of a well-to-do tacksman (the Gaelic equivalent of real-estate agent), he contracted smallpox while attending school in Inverness and subsequently lost his sight. His aspirations of becoming a cleric had to be put aside. Instead, like others in his situation, he turned to music. Fortunately, he was a gifted musician. It is believed he studied with a Scottish harper, an arduous and time-consuming task and then traveled to Ireland for further training. Upon his return to Edinburgh in 1681, at the age of twenty-one, he met Iain Breac, Chief of Clan Macleod, who promptly offered him the position of harper to the clan. Morison accepted. He was harper to Macleod at Dunvegan Castle in Skye until the chief's death in 1693.

The Clarsach Revival

The sweet sounds of the small harp, or *clarsach*, remained silent in Scotland until the *clarsach* revival of the late nineteenth century. In the early 1890s Lord Archibald Campbell asked an Edinburgh bagpipe-making firm to make three *clarsachs;* he later asked a Glasgow piano maker to create an additional six. Campbell was the first president of An Comunn Gaidhealach (The Highland Organization), and introduced competition for the playing of the *clarsach* at the first Gaelic *mod*, or competition, in 1892 in the western Scottish town of Oban.

But it was probably Patuffa Kennedy-Fraser, daughter of the controversial collector Marjory Kennedy-Fraser, who really got the revival going. In 1914 the younger Fraser played the *clarsach* as accompaniment to her mother's songs. The mother-daughter duo performed concert tours in the United Kingdom; the United States; and throughout Europe after World War I. Her enthusiasm and genuine interest in the instrument and its music inspired others to take up the cause. In 1931 the Clarsach Society (Comunn na Clarsaich) was formed.

The Celtic harp revival of the late nineteenth and twentieth centuries did much to bring to light the music and heritage of Scotland's harpers. In our own day several musicians have been in the forefront of the late-twentieth-century revival, including Alison Kinnaird, Robin Williamson, and the harp duo, Síleas (pronounced "Shee-las").

THE WELSH HARP

Wales's leading exponent of the uniquely Welsh triple harp is Robin Huw Bowen. Born in Liverpool to Welsh-speaking parents, Bowen considers it his national duty to help retrieve Wales's "lost" dance music.

Karen Mueller, an expert in all things Welsh, has written extensively on the Welsh harp. "From simple, diatonically tuned instruments, traditionally strung with horsehair, gut, or even leather, to the chromatic, triple-strung wonder of the sixteenth century, and later, the pedal harp, the harp has remained a cornerstone of the Welsh musical tradition," she emphatically declared.

Indeed, Wales has an unbroken harp tradition spanning some fourteen centuries. The triple harp in particular is said to have originated in Italy around 1580; it was brought to the British Isles about 1629. In 1660 Charles Evans, considered the first of the Welsh triple harpists, was appointed harper to Charles II.

Strung with three rows of strings rather than one, to allow for accompaniment, the triple harp has a distinctive steep-curved, high-headed shape. Unlike the pedal harp it is fully chromatic.

 ## PENNILLION

Pennillion is an ancient form of Welsh music typically performed by a harper and a singer. The harper plays a well-known harp air and the singer extemporizes words to a somewhat different melody (similar in theory perhaps to the Breton *kan ha diskan* with its vocal and musical interplay and, in other ways, to the Scots Gaelic highly satirical *flytings*). Although the harper can change the tune as often as desired, the singer must keep up with the music. Scholars think *pennillion* belongs to a time when heroes fought with their wits rather than weapons.

THE REVIVAL OF THE BRETON HARP

During the Middle Ages a great deal of musical exchange existed among the harpers of Brittany, Wales, Scotland, and Ireland. Yet economic, social, political, and cultural shifts in attitude separated them by the late eighteenth century.

It took the work and passion of Alan Stivell, a one-man Breton revivalist, to turn things around. The son of a harp maker from Brittany by the name of Jord Cochevelou, he began to learn the piano at age five and the harp a few years later. His father had been preoccupied with reviving the Breton harp for some time when, after many years of work and contemplation, he unveiled his harp "prototype" for the first time before the public on November 28, 1953.

Stivell carried the idea further, turning his obsession with Breton and pan-Celtic culture to new lengths and combining classical with traditional and popular culture. Today, years later, he remains the greatest practitioner of the Breton harp in the world.

CLASSICAL CELTS

On April 13, 1742, George Frideric Handel's *Messiah* premiered in Mr. Neal's New Musick Hall in Fishamble Street in Dublin. Fifty years later, in 1792, at the age of nine John Field (1782–1837) made his solo debut. Born in Dublin, Field is credited with inventing the nocturne, short lyrical piano pieces, and for several decades he was considered the greatest living pianist in Europe.

Classical composers have often looked to folk and traditional music for inspiration. Consider the work of Ralph Vaughan Williams in England, Anton Dvořák in Czechoslovakia, or Edvard Greig in Norway.

Today this musical mingling of classical and traditional is taking place at increasingly frequent intervals from the traditional Irish band Altan being backed by a string quartet or Robert Matheson's minuet for Highland pipes to Cherish the Ladies teaming up with the Boston Pops Orchestra and the numerous Celtic suites that have surfaced in recent years.

Classical Meets Traditional

In the sixteenth century the Scottish court encouraged the appreciation of the so-called *music fyne*, a sophisticated type of music that primarily consisted of church polyphony, courtly love songs, and instrumental music. The French influence was considerable. The marriages of James V to French women brought French music and dance—including the stately pavan and livelier galliard—to the court, creating a vibrant cultural scene in the Scottish capital.

The Scottish Reformation of 1560 put a momentary end to the institutional patronage of Latin church music and encouraged the use of simple psalm-singing in the vernacular. But with the succession of James VI to the Scottish throne following the execution of his mother, Mary, Queen of Scots, in 1587, cultural conditions noticeably improved.

James was a music lover and employed many musicians and poets in his court. He did his best to repair the damage that the Reformation had wrought by gathering around him a coterie of poets—led by Alexander Montgomerie—and musicians. When he moved south to England to succeed the childless Queen Elizabeth as the new King of England, court patronage in Edinburgh virtually vanished.

In the early seventeenth century the English took a particular liking to "northern tunes." The Restoration of 1660 helped make Scottish music popular south of the border. Music collections such as the Playfords' *The English Dancing Master* (1651) or *A Collection of Original Scotch-Tunes (Full of the Highland Humours) for the Violin* (1700) included musical selections from Scotland. And by end of the century such major composers as Henry Purcell were arranging Scots melodies.

In the eighteenth century numerous Scottish composers or composers who wrote in the Scottish style, such as Alexander Munro, Charles MacLean, and William McGibbon, published or performed their work to willing audiences. But the most significant, and certainly the most prolific, Scottish composer during this period was James Oswald, whom music historian John Purser called "one of the most remarkable and unsung heroes of Scottish music."

James Oswald (1710–1769) was a dancing master, singer, and composer in Dunfermline before he moved to London in 1741 to begin working for publisher John Simpson in St. Martin's Lane. When Simpson died, Oswald took over the firm. A staunch Scots patriot, Oswald thought Scottish music could stand on its own alongside the music of the Continent, especially Italian music which was so popular in his day.

Oswald was the best representative of the *style galant*, a melodic and gentle type of music popular in the mid-eighteenth century. He composed in both the Scottish and classical idioms and, during his long career, collected and published many volumes of Scottish music. Appointed chamber composer to King George III in 1761, he founded the Temple of Apollo, a composer's society in London that consisted of mostly Scottish composers working in the capital city.

A good part of the music of several major nineteenth-century Scottish classical composers is imbued with a Scottish spirit and a much honored love of melody. Scottish themes, too, are often present.

Sir Alexander Campbell Mackenzie (1847–1935) wrote the *Pibroch Suite* for violin, which takes its name, if not its musical inspiration, from the classical music of the Highland bagpipes. Most of the major works of Hamish MacCunn (1868–1916) are based on Scottish themes. *The Land of the Mountain and the Flood*, for example, evokes pastoral images of the Scottish countryside—"In the Glen" was written for solo piano—while "The Dowie Dens o' Yarrow" is based on the darkly murderous Border ballad of the same name. MacCunn also mined literary sources. His opera *Jeanie Deans* takes as its inspiration Sir Walter Scott's novel *Heart of Midlothian*. Still another composer, John Blackwood McEwen (1868–1948), a native of the Scottish Borders, composed *Under Northern Skies* for a wind quintet and *Grey Galloway*, a "border ballad," for full orchestra.

Contemporary classical composers have continued to find a rich source of material in the traditional music of the Celtic lands. Peter Maxwell Davies is probably the best modern example—certainly one of the most prolific—of someone who is able to combine the two traditions, classical and traditional, successfully and effortlessly. Although born in England, he lived in Orkney for many years and became intimately involved in the cultural goings-on of the local community—he founded the highly respected St. Magnus Festival in 1977. A large proportion of his work in the past few decades has been infused with a strong Orcadian flavor.

An ominous chamber opera, *The Lighthouse*, was based on a real-life story that took place on December 26, 1900, at the Flannan Islands lighthouse when three lighthouse keepers mysteriously vanished. In such works as *Hymn to Saint Magnus* and the chamber opera *The Martyrdom of Saint Magnus* he has turned to the Orcadian past to create contemporary music.

In 1985 he composed perhaps his best-known work, *An Orkney Wedding, With Sunrise*, which musically evokes a wedding on the

Orcadian island of Hoy, where he lived for many years. He sets the scene: The wedding party arrives, followed by a processional; the band tunes up for a wedding dance; and at the big climax, the by-this-time inebriated guests leave the hall, walking home as the sun, personified by the Highland bagpipes, rises over Caithness, the northernmost county on the Scottish mainland and a short but choppy ferry ride away.

A recent work, *The Jacobite Rising*, is Davies's first major choral work for the Scottish Chamber Orchestra. Texts range from contemporary Jacobite lyrics such as "Johnnie Cope" to modern reflections on war and violence inspired by the poetry of Wilfred Owen and Sorley Maclean.

MUSICAL SAINTS

Many composers have written music honoring the Celtic saints and sacred Celtic sites:

- Cappella Nova's *Scottish Medieval Plainchant: The Miracles of St. Kentigern* (Gaudeamus). In this recording dedicated to Glasgow's patron saint; Cappella Nova, Scotland's only professional a cappella ensemble, performs a dramatic selection of scenes from his life. The same ensemble recorded *Columba, Most Holy of Saints* (Gaudemaus), a musical celebration of the life of this most famous of Celtic saints.
- William Jackson, harpist and a founding member of the traditional Scots group Ossian, has made several records with sacred themes. *Inchcolm* (Linn Records) is a gorgeous collection of mostly original compositions. "The Pure Land" begins with a Gaelic prayer from *Carmina Gadelica*, an anthology compiled by Alexander Carmichael (1832–1912), with vocals by Mairi MacInnes; the chant "Salve Splendor" is from the thirteenth-century *Inchcolm Antiphoner* from the Scottish island of the same name; "Columcille" features Jackson on the harp and whistles, Fred Morrison on pipes, David Tulloch on percussion, and the accompaniment of the Scottish Chamber Orchestra strings. Equally beautiful is Jackson's *St. Mungo: A Celtic Suite for Glasgow*

(Greentrax), recorded live in Glasgow in 1990 and performed by the Scottish Orchestra of New Music. With roots firmly embedded in the tradition, Jackson and friends perform contemporary orchestral music. Dividing the piece into the four symbols contained within Glasgow's coat of arms—the bird, the tree, the bell, and the fish—Jackson is accompanied by numerous traditional musicians, including fellow Ossian members Tony Cuffe on guitar, Iain MacDonald on flute and whistle, John Martin on fiddle as well as Mae McKenna on vocals and keyboard.

- Nóirín Ní Riain's *Soundings* (Sounds True Audio) features spiritual songs from many traditions, with a strong emphasis on the Irish and Scottish traditions, including an adaptation of a folk prayer from Alexander Carmichael's *Carmina Gadelica* and a haunting Christmas carol from the Irish tradition.
- Savourna Stevenson's *Calman the Dove* (Cooking Vinyl) is another recent work that celebrates the spirit of St. Columba while the text of Scott Macmillan's *Celtic Mass for the Sea* (Marquis) is based on early Celtic writings. Traditional Celtic musical themes—rowing songs, funeral chants, sea-songs, pipe and fiddle tunes, work songs—are interwoven with conductor and guitarist Macmillan's original compositions. The Halifax-born Macmillan has created a score that features uilleann pipes, flute, guitars, mandolin, fiddle, string orchestra, and full choir.
- James MacMillan's *Ninian*, a concerto for clarinet and orchestra that draws on elements of the pibroch as well as hymnody, is based on the life of the Celtic saint St. Ninian, who helped bring Christianity to southwest Scotland circa 400 A.D. In early 1997 "í (A Meditation on Iona)" was first performed as a collaborative work with sculptor Sue Jane Taylor at Glasgow's City Chambers.

Composer and conductor John McLeod, born in Aberdeen, wrote the film soundtrack for Mike Radford's *Another Time, Another Place.* A major work, *Visions from the North,* includes "The Gokstad Ship," composed for the National Youth Orchestra of Scotland's tour of Orkney and Scandinavia; this work explores Scotland's Nordic connections.

One of the youngest of Scotland's classical composers is the prolific James MacMillan (born 1959). A devout Catholic, many of his themes revolve around Scottish identity. His music is infused with folk elements and strong religious imagery. *The Tryst* by Scots poet William Soutar (1898–1943) is set in the style of an old Scots ballad. In *The Confession of Isobel Gowdie*, about witch-burning during the Reformation, MacMillan interweaves elements of Scottish folk music as well as Gregorian chant, the Scottish ballad "The Cruel Mother," choral tunes, and references to Gaelic psalmody. *As others see us*, a suite for mixed ensemble, takes its title from the poetry of Robert Burns.

Thomas Wilson's *St. Kentigern Suite* uses plainsong melody to honor Glasgow's patron saint. He has also adapted James Hogg's masterpiece *The Confessions of a Justified Sinner* into opera. Ronald Stevenson's *In Memoriam Robert Carver* is a musical tribute to one of Scotland's finest, and most overlooked, Renaissance composers.

Another contemporary composer, Edward McGuire, a flautist and long-time member of the Whistlebinkies folk group—Scotland's equivalent of the Chieftains—blends traditional Scottish music with the classical. The climax of "Calgacus," a major work for orchestra, culminates with the flourish of the bagpipes. Calgacus, the Pictish leader who was defeated at Mons Graupius in northeastern Scotland by the Romans, recited his famous "desert" speech ("You make a desert and call it peace") before battle. The Roman historian Tacitus overheard the comment and recorded it for posterity.

Another contemporary Scottish composer who incorporated the folk idiom into his music is William Sweeney. His *Sunset Song* title derives from the novel of the same name by Lewis Grassic Gibbon; *Psalm of the Land* was the first major piece by a classical composer to use the Gaelic language.

DISTANT VOYAGES

Patrick Cassidy from County Clare is a rather adventuresome sort and one of the most prolific of the current batch of Irish composers. Like fellow composers Charlie Lennon and Shaun Davey, he is utterly steeped in the history and lore of his native land. Paying his musical dues in various garage bands may not be the usual training ground for a classical composer, but then, Cassidy is hardly your typical classicist. The fact that the island nation has a rather limited classical tradition works to his advantage.

"For two centuries we were a peasant nation," he once said, "and so there was no classical music here. For me, as an Irish composer now, that's almost an advantage, because there is so much unexplored territory. I think it made it a lot easier for me to find a voice than if I had been born a German composer, or an Italian composer, with the weight of all that tradition bearing down on me!"

"Most people will have heard *Riverdance*, or Enya, or what I call New Age Irish music. And that's lovely, but to me, the music of the Irish bardic harpers is so much more interesting. It was the closest thing we had to a baroque music in Ireland."

Cassidy's oratorio *The Children of Lir* is inspired by the story of Lir, an Irish king. On the death of his wife Aobh, Lir marries his sister-in-law Aoife. All goes well for a while until Aobh, consumed by jealousy over her new husband's love for the children of her dead sister, plots her revenge. One day as they bathe in an Irish lake, she transforms them into four swans and gives them an interminable sentence—to drift on the lake for nine hundred years. The spell is broken with the arrival of St. Patrick and the birth of Christianity in Ireland. Once again, Liam O'Flynn contributes some fine work on uilleann pipes.

Another Cassidy piece, *Deirdre of the Sorrows*, is taken from the story of Deirdre in the twelfth-century *Book of Leinster* and belongs to the Ulster Cycle of grand Irish tales.

Shaun Davey has mined the mythical lore of his native Ireland for much musical inspiration. He composed *The Brendan Voyage*, an orchestral suite for uilleann pipes, after reading explorer Tim Severin's account of the sixth-century voyage to America of the Irish monk and his crew, with the orchestra representing the natural elements and the pipes symbolizing the explorers' small leather boat. The suite, which is accompanied by the fluid piping of Liam O'Flynn, musically interprets aspects of Brendan the Navigator's voyage to the New World from setting sail for the first time ("The Brendan Theme") to his arrival ("Newfoundland").

Building on the notion of a traditional soloist performing with an orchestra—Liam O'Flynn once again at the helm—Davey wrote an even more expansive and all-encompassing Celtic suite, *The Pilgrim*, as a sacred pilgrimage through the Celtic lands, including a musical exploration of the cult of St. James. The saint's bones are said to be buried at Santiago de Compostela in Galicia, one of the great Christian pilgrimage destinations since the tenth century. Other major Celtic pilgrimage sites form part of Davey's journey from Derry to Iona, while the composer features the poetry of St. Columba, St. Patrick, and other Celtic saints.

Davey's other Celtic suites include *Granuaile*, which is based on the legend surrounding the life of the pirate queen, Grace O'Malley, and *The Relief of the Siege of Derry*, a piece of music commissioned by Derry City Council to celebrate the tercentenary of the Siege of Derry in 1689.

Another important Irish composer is Mícheál Ó Súilleabháin, who holds the prestigious chair of music at the University of Limerick, Ireland's newest university and home to the country's largest music department. In 1994 he established the Irish World Music Centre at Limerick, having moved from the music department at the University of Cork.

Ó Súilleabháin fuses classical music with traditional music, although jazzy overtones also are a part of his larger sound. *Becoming* (Virgin) is a work for piano and orchestra; *Oilean/Island* a three-movement suite for traditional flute and chamber orchestra. Like Davey, he uses the services of traditional musicians: fiddler Eileen Ivers (among many others) in the former and the Chieftain flute player Matt Molloy in the latter.

Several moving pieces of music have been composed in honor of the Great Irish Famine. Patrick Cassidy's *Famine Remembrance*, probably his most heartfelt work—moody, grand, poignant, and pensive—was composed for orchestra, choir, and uilleann pipes. Cassidy selected texts from Irish prayers and Latin Mass excerpts and set them to music. Paddy Keenan offers his services on the pipes.

Equally moving is Charlie Lennon's *Flight from the Hungry Land,* a suite written to commemorate the famine and performed by the RTE Concert Orchestra and an ensemble of traditional musicians. The suite is presented in three parts: the period immediately prior to the famine of 1845, the period from 1845 to 1849 when many were forced to emigrate to survive, and life in the New World. The suite's finale, "Merging Cultures," begins as a sedate dance which soon turns into a country dance before transforming itself into a spirited Irish reel.

Lennon's first suite, *Deora and Deoiri: The Emigrant Suite,* was written for pipes and strings. It was followed by *Island Wedding,* which consists of sixteen movements for traditional instruments and orchestra.

 ## OPERAS

Traditional music and opera have proven to be successful bedfellows. Based on three short folk tales collected by nineteenth-century travelers, Judith Weir's opera *The Vanishing Bridegroom,* which received its American premiere in St. Louis in 1992, weaves into the story various folk elements, including the chant-like psalms of a Gaelic congregation and the traditional Gaelic work songs of women. In Weir's wonderfully titled *Sketches from a Bagpiper's Album,* the clarinet represents the chanter of a bagpipe.

Numerous operas and major concert works have used Celtic themes over the centuries. *Mary Stuart* was set to music by Gaetano Donizetti with text by Giuseppe Bardari after the play *Maria Stuarda* by Friedrich Schiller. Many of Sir Walter Scott's novels have been adapted into operas, including *Rob Roy, The Heart of Midlothian, The Bride of Lammermoor, Ivanhoe, Kenilworth,* and *The Fair Maid of Perth.*

Robert Burns's poem, "Tam o' Shanter," has inspired several classical composers. including Alexander Mackenzie's Scottish Rhapsody No. 3, Op. 74. The first German translations of his poems inspired such varied composers as Schumann and Brahms and, in more recent years, Shostakovich, Tippet, and Britten. In 1996, the bicentennial of his death, the Glasgow-based composer Michael Norris wrote an opera based on "Tam o'Shanter," while John Maxwell Geddes set a number of Burns's songs for two hundred children's voices, called *Bardsangs*.

The contemporary combination of art and traditional music reaches its liveliest fruition in the work of the Canadian-based ensemble Puirt a Baroque ("poorsht-a-ba-roke"). The ensemble, which consists of David Greenberg on baroque and modern violins, Scott Macmillan on classical and steel-string guitars (Macmillan was replaced by Terry McKenna on guitar on the trio's second recording), and David Sandall on harpsichord, performs Scottish/Cape Breton traditional music with music from the baroque era. This unusual juxtaposition actually has its roots in Scots drawing room music. Founded in 1994, the trio's name is a tongue-in-cheek play on the Scots Gaelic *puirt-a-beul*, or "mouth music."

The end of the baroque era coincided with the so-called golden age of Scottish fiddling—"a time," according to the trio, "when rural fiddler and trained concert musician alike participated in the bloom of national music." The ensemble's repertoire consists of major art-music composers, Scottish art music, and traditional-style composers as well as twentieth-century Cape Breton composers. Employing bagpipe or folk-style ornaments, the Cape Breton treatment of baroque-period tunes is a lovely thing to behold. In a *Bach Meets Cape Breton* selection, movements from Partita No. 3 for Solo Violin in E Major by J. S. Bach somehow find a natural musical partnership with traditional Cape Breton reels.

RECOMMENDED LISTENING

The Baltimore Consort. *On the Banks of the Helicon: Early Music of Scotland* (Dorian). A collection of *music fyne*: traditional native airs and English imitations. Instruments used on the CD are similar to those that would have been heard at the Scottish court: lute, *cittern, bandora*, and viols. The members have also added a flute and a single-droned bagpipe.

Sir Arnold Bax. *Tintagel* (Chandos). A tone-poem to Cornwall's wild Atlantic coast. Written in 1917, Bax's surging score evokes the area's rich historical and legendary associations from King Arthur and King Mark to Tristram and Iseulto.

Derek Bell. *Carolan's Receipt* (Shanachie). The music of Carolan by the Chieftain harpist and Carolan devotee extraordinaire.

Elinor Bennett. *Darluno's Delyn/Portait of the Harp* (Sain). Music from the golden age of the Welsh harp, circa 1730 to 1830 performed by one of the finest practitioners of the esteemed instrument.

The work of Patrick Cassidy comes highly recommended, including *The Children of Lir* (Celtic Heartbeat), *Deirdre of the Sorrows* (Windham Hill), and, especially, the poignant *Famine Remembrance* (Windham Hill).

The Chieftains. *The Celtic Harp* (RCA Victor). The Belfast Harp Festival comes alive in this marvelous recording.

Shaun Davey's Celtic suites explore Irish myth, legend, and history in wondrous musical terms—*The Brendan Voyage* (Tara), *Granuaile* (Tara), and *The Relief of Derry Symphony* (Tara). With *The Pilgrim* (Tara), he expands his musical plate to encompass the rest of the Celtic world.

Alison Kinnaird. *The Harp Key* (Temple). Kinnaird is the leading exponent of Scottish harp music; this recording features music of Rory Dall (Blind Rory), the great Highland harper, as well as music of the court, and dance tunes of Scotland. In *The Harper's Gallery* (Temple), she sings and plays music for the Scottish harp, including a Border ballad, two Gaelic songs, and a Latin prayer said to have been written by Mary, Queen of Scots, on the eve of her execution. With the American Ann Heymann, Kinnaird recorded *The Harper's Land* (Temple), a musical exploration of two different, but related, small harps.

Charlie Lennon. *Flight from the Hungry Land* (Worldmusic). At turns lively and somber, an always tasteful examination of the Great Irish Famine and its legacy.

Séamus McGuire. *The Wishing Tree* (Green Linnet). Taking its name from Seamus Heaney's poem, McGuire offers a deft mixture of traditional and classical influences as well as music from distant sources (Finland, Shetland, the Basque provinces, Lebanon, and the South Pacific). Most of the selections are slow pieces and airs, producing an exquisite recording of much gentleness and tranquility.

Robert MacKillop and William Taylor. *Graysteil: Music from the Middle Ages and Renaissance Scotland* (Dorian). Lute and wire-strung harp music, from the thirteenth-century "Ex te lux oritur" (written to celebrate the weddings of Margaret and Eric II of Norway) to the sixteenth-century Mass for Three Voices, by Robert Carver. Concludes with a rendition of the old ballad "Greysteil" sung by Andy Hunter.

The Music of O Carolan (Shanachie, 1992) Arranged for fingerpicked guitar, concertina, Northumberland pipes, cello, flute and hammered dulcimer and performed by Steve Tilston, Duck Baker, Alistair Anderson, Madeline MacNeil, Maggie Boyle, among others. Liner notes provided by John Renbourn.

James Oswald. *Airs for the Seasons* (Altamira Records). The music of one of Scotland's most underestimated composers, this recording consists of twenty-four short sonata movements, each named after a different flower or shrub.

Puirt a Baroque. *Bach Meets Cape Breton* and *Kinloch's Fantasy: A Curious Collection of Scottish Sonatas and Reels* (both Marquis Classic). Part traditional music, part art music, the two CDs feature the music of Scots fiddlers William Marshall and Niel Gow, Cape Breton fiddlers Dan Hughie MacEachern and Donald Angus Beaton, as well as traditional Cape Breton reels, theater pieces by Henry Purcell, and more. Dares to leap between cultures and across centuries. But it works. A third release, *Return of the Wanderer* (Marquis Classics), features Gaelic and Scots songs.

The Rowallan Consort. *Notes of Noy, Notes of Joy* (Temple). Songs and music performed on the lute and *clarsach* from circa 1400 to 1700. Recordings gleaned from various Scottish lute manuscripts, including Skene, Rowallan, Straloch, and Wemyss, as well as newly reconstructed lute songs from the courts of James V and James VI and popular songs of the early seventeenth century.

Síleas. *Beating Harps* and *Delighted with Harps* (both Green Linnet). Scottish harp duo of Patsy Seddon and Mary MacMaster perform on both metal- and gut-strung clarsachs.

Scotland's Music: Selected Works from the History of Scotland's Music (Linn Records). A two-CD set devoted almost exclusively to the Scottish classical music tradition, from pre-Christian laments and ninth-century bells to medieval songs and contemporary pieces.

Alan Stivell. *Renaissance of the Celtic Harp* (Rounder). A pan-Celtic approach to harp music by the undisputed leader of the modern Breton Celtic harp revival.

Bill Whelan. *The Seville Suite* (Celtic Heartbeat) Eight movements that tell the story of the flight to Spain of Red Hugh O'Donnell and his comrades after the defeat at Kinsale in 1601 and their subsequent flight to Galicia under the protection of the court of Prince Philip. Features Davy Spillane on uilleann pipes and low whistle, accordionist Mairtin O'Connor, members of Milladoiro, and the RTE Concert Orchestra.

Robin Williamson. *Legacy of the Scottish Harpers*. Vols. 1 and 2 (Flying Fish). A contemporary Scots harper performs the traditional music of the early Scottish harpers.

Gráinne Yeats. *The Belfast Harp Festival 1792/1992* (Gael-Linn). This two-CD set consists of twenty-two examples culled from the repertoire of the traditional harpers and twenty harp solos and songs from Carolan. Extensive liner notes.

3

Dancing at the Crossroads

From Riverdance *to the Devil's Box*

Traditional fiddling in America has its repertorial and stylistic roots in the British Isles of the 18th century, where, insofar as the written record may be trusted, elements of the particular cultural milieu conspired to generate a new class of instrumental tunes out of the ancient stock of British folk melodies and the new leaven of the Baroque violin.

–ALAN JABBOUR, NOTES TO THE LIBRARY OF CONGRESS'S *AMERICAN FIDDLE TUNES* COMPILATION

You've seen the images over and over again. Faded photographs of couples, dressed in their best finery, dancing under an open sky. They seem to be swaying back and forth to the melodies of a roadside fiddler, the lightest of breezes disturbing the stillness of a summer night. In the days before commercial dance halls, dancing was a social pastime conducted on domestic ground, whether in the great outdoors or, during inclement weather, in the smallest of kitchens or in the back of barns.

Dancing at the crossroads.

A timeless image, torn from the pages of a family photo album, indelibly etched in the collective memory. What could be more quintessentially Celtic? more quintessentially traditional?

The Irish journalist Fintan O'Toole captured the essence of Irish dance music when he stated:

> The basic form is circular, repetitive and predictable. It expresses a sense of life as being fixed and stable, of a community containing within itself all that needs to be known or experienced. It is, in other words, traditional. But the pleasure of the music lies in the play of improvisation and ornamentation against this basic form. Trills and grace-notes, careful disorderings of the tune, swoops and soarings, are the ornamentations that reflect the unpredictability of events.

Ah yes, the unpredictable pleasures that lurk among the mundane. What a delicious thought and how aptly it describes the cyclical nature of Irish dance—indeed, of all the Celtic arts, from the repetitive litany of ancient Celtic prayers and the intricate knotwork of medieval illuminated manuscripts to the rhythmic thumping of a Hebridean *waulking* song to the dense patterns of the *pibroch*. Celtic music is circular. What a comforting thought. Think about it: Whatever we do, wherever we go, we will always arrive back home. We will never truly get lost. Everything is related; everything—past and present—is connected; the end leads to the beginning. Given such a mind-set, the world doesn't seem like such a frightening place after all.

DANCING FEET

The types and styles of traditional Celtic dances vary. The bulk of traditional Irish and Scottish music consists of dance tunes—jigs, reels, and hornpipes for the most part, although in recent years, polkas, mazurkas, and others of "foreign" origin have entered the tradition. Reels and hornpipes arrived in Ireland in the late eighteenth century; most historians contend that the reel probably came from Scotland, the hornpipe from England. The *strathspey*, a slow reel of sorts, is also indigenous to Scotland and developed in the eighteenth and nineteenth centuries using an intricate and complex bowing technique.

The Irish word for dance, *damhsa*, first appeared in 1520 and is derived from the French *danse*, but credit the Normans for introducing the round dance, or *carol*—that is, dancing in a circle—to the country.

But of course the height of Celtic dance is the step dance, which usually refers to the jig, the reel, the slip jig, and the hornpipe. Indications suggests that step dancing first surfaced in Scotland in the fourteenth century, although there is little in the way of actual documentation until as late as the seventeenth century. After the Act of Proscription of 1746, fiddling and dancing went hand in hand, since the bagpipe, for all intents and purposes, was officially silenced. The step dance developed in Ireland during the eighteenth century.

 ## SOME COMMON DANCE TERMS

Half sets   Two couples dancing.

Highlands   The Donegal version of a Highland fling.

Hornpipe   Of English origin, traditional tune in 2/4 or 4/4 time; that is, the number of beats per measure. It is similar to a reel but slower and more heavily accented.

Jig   Traditional dance tune in 6/8 or 9/8 time; the oldest dance tunes in Ireland, they come in three forms: single jigs, double jigs, and slip jigs (see below).

Polka   Traditional dance tune in 2/4 time; a set dance.

Quadrille   Dance in which couples face each other in the form of a square; popular during Napoleonic era.

Reel   From the Anglo-Saxon *rulla*, meaning "to whirl"; traditional dance tune in 4/4 time; a favorite for sets and step dancing.

Slide   Traditional tune in 6/8 time; associated with parts of Clare, Cork, Limerick, and Kerry.

Slip jig   Traditional dance tune in 9/8 time; steps consist of hopping, slipping, and sliding; considered the most graceful of the step dances.

Solo or *step dance*   A type of Irish dancing that first emerged in the eighteenth century; step dancing usually takes the form of reels, jigs, and hornpipes. Considered the most accomplished style of Irish dance.

Strathspey   A kind of slow reel indigenous to Scotland and distinguished by its pronounced staccato effect.

THE DANCING MASTER

Some professions seem hopelessly outdated and ridiculously romantic—which, of course, accounts for a large part of their charm, especially from an early-twenty-first-century vantage point. Consider the role of the dancing master, an antiquated notion if there ever was one. Sure, there are dancing instructors today, but it isn't quite the same.

Dancing masters appeared on the Irish and Scottish scene in the eighteenth century. Although peripatetic, the dancing master was no ordinary teacher or musician. He prided himself on being a cut above the traveling piper or fiddler; a gentleman of the countryside. Consequently, he dressed to the nines—dapper hat, knee-breeches, and cane—and affected a bit of, shall we say, an attitude. He expected to be treated with respect. Most sessions were conducted in groups, but to those few students whom he deemed worthy of special treatment he would offer the highest compliment: solo dance lessons.

In truth, the dancing master taught dancing to all social classes. The community welcomed him and indeed, looked forward to his arrival—he usually stayed six weeks at any given time. Typically, he would arrange to stay in a farmer's kitchen or barn in exchange for dancing and music lessons. Dancing classes were held in local houses or outdoors at the crossroads. And given his elevated status as a gentleman, it was only natural for him to also teach deportment and etiquette pointers.

Arthur Young, an eighteenth century traveler in Ireland, observed that "Dancing is almost universal in every cabin and dancing masters travel through the country from cabin to cabin with a fiddler or blind piper."

Rivalry between dancing masters was quite common, especially in rural Ireland. Each master had his own territory, which usually amounted to about ten square miles. When a rival instructor encroached upon another's territory, a dancing contest would take place. Custom then dictated that the two rivals would compete against each other, often in a well-trafficked place, such as the village square. The victor—that is, the one deemed the best dancer— earned the right to teach anywhere in the district, whereas the loser was ostracized to another territory.

In the seventeenth century Irish dancing tended to be of a communal nature—the group dancing or country dancing of the countryside. In the eighteenth century, though, emerged an altogether different type of dancing—the solo or step dance—which changed the face of the Irish dancing tradition and became, in the words of journalist Sam Smyth, "the single most important development in the history of Irish dance . . . "

It was this fundamental change in attitude toward dance that made possible the existence of the professional dancing master. After all, the specialty of the dancing master was these very step dances. It was here where all his expertise could come into play. Several qualities in the dancer were revered—control and restraint coupled with vigor and speed. Thus keeping the body rigid, with movement restricted to the hips down and the back ramrod straight, was the dancing-master ideal. Or, as Breandán Breathnach explains, "the good dancer . . . could dance on eggs without breaking them and hold a pan of water on his head without spilling a drop."

LORDS AND LADIES OF THE DANCE

This step dancing ideal—that of minimal body movement combined with fancy footwork—remained the model of traditional

Irish dance until *Riverdance* erased all preconceived notions of what constituted proper Irish-dance technique when it premiered on April 30, 1994, in Dublin. Irish dance would never be the same. With *Riverdance*, traditional step dancing had now jumped from its domestic roots to the professional milieu of the stage and television studio. Such a major shift inevitably led to changes, but the soul of the tradition remained intact.

Unlike traditional Irish music, which has experimented with various forms during the past thirty years, traditional Irish dance has remained relatively unchanged, adhering to strict rules and customs and rarely veering from tradition. *Riverdance* changed all that. By daring to experiment, by borrowing freely from other traditions, *Riverdance* totally reinvented traditional Irish dance. Sure, some of it was hokey, and, occasionally, unintentionally funny. But when it worked—and it worked most of the time—it was sublimely beautiful, a successful juxtaposition of cultures and traditions, folk roots and pop culture, Ireland and America, step dancing and tap dancing.

 ## DANCING IN BRITTANY

Each region of Brittany has its own distinctive music, dance, native costume, and subtleties of language. There are three major categories of dance in Brittany:

- The oldest dances: Often performed as a three-part suite, most commonly in lines or circles, they include the *gavotte, an dro, laride*, and *dans plinn*.
- More recent dances: These are influenced by the English dances of the seventeenth-century or French dances of the eighteenth.
- Modern dances: Polkas, mazurkas, or scottishes have appeared in recent years.

Released from the artistic straitjacket of traditional Irish dance, the members of *Riverdance* took advantage of their newfound freedom—exploring, tweaking, and flaunting it to the utmost. Off came the heavy wool skirts and ornate embroidered Celtic-designed dresses, to be replaced with shorter, lightweight dresses and tights. The end result was an altogether freer, more spontaneous, and certainly more sensuous performance. It created instant stars—Jean Butler and Michael Flatley, who found success through individual expression or, in the case of Flatley, unabashed star turns—and it revived a tradition that heretofore had paid little heed to the fickle attitudes of pop culture.

Riverdance began as a seven-minute interlude on the popular *Eurovision Song Contest*. It later expanded to a full two-hour-plus production. The first half is spent in Ireland while the second half traces the impact of the Irish diaspora in the New World, drawing connections between not only traditional Irish dance and African-American tap dance but also—admittedly, here is where the global links become a bit stretched—Spanish flamenco and Russian folk dance. After devoting the first half of the production exploring indigenous Irish roots, it is significant that the opening of the second act, aptly entitled "American Wake," is set at a crossroads and culminates with the departure of a young couple for the New World.

One of the highlights of *Riverdance* is the exciting give-and-take between the apprehensive Irish dancers and the cocky African-American tap dancers. In a manner of minutes and amid a flurry of dancing feet, the often overlooked connection between the two surprisingly similar dancing styles comes into sharp focus. The Irish writer and record producer P. J. Curtis for one has gone so far as to describe African-American tap dancing as an "descendant of the Irish jig or hornpipe." Give even a cursory glance to popular dance in America and it will become clear that Irish traditional dance left its mark on everything from Southern tobacco plantations to minstrel shows, the American music hall, and vaudeville.

By blending—and bending—the music and dance of different cultures, *Riverdance* composer Bill Whelan was able to make connections that most people never even considered. And isn't that a large part of the show's universal appeal?—its ability to locate the finest of threads that connect me to you, that connect a person to a place, a place to a country, a country to the world. *Riverdance* played on our innate human need to relate to someone other than ourselves—playing up the emotions of the emigration experience was certainly one method—and it did it in an enormously entertaining way.

In short *Riverdance* had it all: great music, dancing feet, the sorrow of displacement and loss, the joy and exhilaration of starting over, all forged in the Irish spirit but reinvented by American—or, more accurately, Irish-American—ingenuity and imagination. As Fintan O'Toole pointed out, its choreographer and principal dancers were children of Irish immigrants. Ireland and America—the ebb and flow, the push and pull of emigration—both played their respective parts not only in its phenomenal success but also in its execution. With *Riverdance*, Irish dancing became an integral part of American pop culture.

By intermingling pop culture with tradition, Whelan succeeded in creating a hybrid product with one foot firmly planted in the deep roots of the earthy Irish soil and the other scattered about the broad vista of the American landscape.

THE WANING OF THE DANCE

Yet traditional dancing was not always greeted with such goodwill. In fact, Irish dance music has been under on-and-off attack by the church and other watchdogs of the public trust from the seventeenth century and up to the early decades of the twentieth.

House dances and crossroad dances kept the dance-music tradition alive. The music of the people survived the famine, but it could not withstand the pressure of the church.

Over the centuries official sanctioning of dancing has ebbed and flowed, depending on which direction the social and political winds were blowing. In mid-nineteenth century Ireland, for example, an especially virulent type of repression set in, with the local church playing its part. Indeed, dancing came under attack from the Catholic Church, when the clergy, backed by the state, waged a vigorous campaign to rid the countryside of wayward dancers and musicians. The members of the cloth maintained that dancing could not only lead to bad thoughts but also—and this applied even to the purest of parishioners—bad behavior. Stories of priests prowling the country roads at night and disrupting crossroad dances, breaking up house parties, and condemning the inhabitants to eternal damnation or excommunication were widely reported. Priests were known to physically attack the musicians and even destroy their instruments.

Similar circumstances occurred across the Irish Sea in Scotland with the Disruption of the Church of Scotland in 1843. Ministers did their utmost to ban both music and dancing. "At Kilmuir in Skye pipes, harps and fiddles were piled in a great heap and burned," noted author and piper, Ian L. McKay.

The next century was no different. During the antidancing hysteria of the 1930s in Ireland, the Gaelic League banned set dancing because of its so-called foreign influences—during the 1920s waltzes and quick steps and fox trots were all the rage—and instead, in an attempt to project the cleanest of images, encouraged solo competition, led by young girls in elaborately designed costumes. Sam Smyth has called it "a diversion from Irish dancing's traditional spontaneity and sensuality."

Soon the police and national government joined forces in what proved to be a formidable partnership. Their joint cooperation resulted in the Public Dance Halls Act of 1936. From there on in, dancing became not only sinful but also illegal. The act required that all dances be licensed and operated under strict supervision. House dances, the breeding group of authentic Irish music, were outlawed in most areas of rural Ireland. Thus the only legitimate venue for dancing was in the church hall. Packed church halls meant more money pouring into church coffers, but the clergy controlled dance revues did irrefutable damage to the traditional-music cause in general and to Irish step dancing in particular, which had already been on an inexorable decline since the turn of the century. Faced with such dire conditions, many traditional musicians chose to emigrate to England or, more often, start all over again in America.

Another consequence of the Dance Halls Act and the clergy-controlled dance halls was the founding of the *ceilidh* (or *ceili*) bands, a sort of compromise between church-sanctioned oppression and the people's love for a good time. Such outfits as the Kilfenora Ceili Band or the Tulla Ceili Band were more than happy to entertain dance-hungry audiences in parish halls throughout rural Ireland. Hence began a new era of Irish dance music—not without serious repercussions on the viability of traditional music.

A typical Irish *ceilidh* band consisted of fiddles, flute, accordion, concertina, banjo, and later, perhaps drums. The musicians played for hours on end. Composer Séan Ó Riada despised the *ceilidh* band and all that it represented—he felt it belittled traditional music—but, in all fairness, it did have its good points. Not only did it keep countless Irish musicians gainfully employed—many if not most of whom came from a traditional background anyway—but it also inspired a number of musicians, including Chieftain uilleann piper Paddy Moloney, to explore the roots of the music.

The dancing that took place at these revues was the more uniform *ceilidh* dancing. For the most part, step dancing had no place on the crowded dance floors. In the late 1950s and early 1960s, show bands replaced the *ceilidh* bands. Show bands played the popular songs of the day—from covers of rock and roll hits to skiffle, country-western, Irish and *ceilidh* tunes. Young Irish men and women thronged to dance halls that accommodated up to two or three thousand people. A typical show band of the era consisted of a lineup of seven to eight musicians playing guitars, bass, drums, and a brass section, accompanied by an outgoing singer who knew how to work the crowd.

IRISH DANCE IN AMERICA

Irish dance and American pop culture are not the strange bedfellows that they appear to be at first glance. Early emigrants to American shores, the Protestant Scots-Irish, brought with them to the New World their own jigs, ballads, and, of course, dance steps.

DANIEL EMMETT

One of the most famous figures to emerge from the minstrel scene was Daniel Emmett (1815–1904), the composer of "Dixie," a favorite minstrel song that was popularized by Bryant's Minstrels. Emmett and his comrade George Christy assembled entire shows drawn from African-Irish dances, songs, and skits. Among his most popular tunes are "The Blue-Tailed Fly" (probably better known as "Jimmy Crack Corn") and "Turkey in the Straw." Both compositions were inspired by Irish hornpipes.

Traveling Minstrel Shows

From its earliest days the Irish dominated minstrelsy, which employed thousands of Irish performers, from the plethora of Irish tenors to Irish comics and dancers. Minstrel shows featured Irish and Scottish music and dances, jigs, reels, songs, and ballads as well as African-American sermons, parodies, and satires. Hundreds of black-faced minstrel groups were populated by Irishmen.

The minstrel show, essentially a caricature of African-American music and culture, consisted of a series of tunes, jokes, and skits performed by white men in blackface. Indeed, blackface minstrelsy—its songs and dances—was the most popular form of entertainment in nineteenth-century America. Folklorist Richard Crawford has described it as being "[b]ased upon theatrical whites' observation of the musical practices of plantation and city blacks . . . " Musician and folklorist Mick Moloney called minstrelsy "a caricature of African-American plantation culture."

Indeed, it was not unusual, given their proximity to one another, for African and Irish cultures to come together. Stephen Foster, the composer of "Oh Susanna" and other American standards, has his roots in minstrelsy. His great-grandfather Alexander Foster emigrated from Derry in the late 1720s and reportedly started his songwriting career in the South by writing for the traveling minstrel shows.

Irish emigrants dressing up in black face dates back to at least 1750. Around that time an itinerant group of Irish actors and musicians, who had just arrived in Kentucky, tried their hand at making a living by strumming banjos and, according to P. J. Curtis, "adopting a step-dance that was a hybrid of an African foot-stomp and an Irish jig."

THE STAGE IRISHMAN

The stage Irishman first emerged on the theatrical scene in seventeenth-century English drama and then made its way across the Atlantic to America. Nothing less than a buffoon, this strange creature was described by the historian Carl Wittke as a "bizarre individual, preposterously dressed in a red-flannel fireman's shirt affecting a swagger, and with a shillelagh in hand."

The Irish stereotype had its roots in British colonial rule. Yet the heyday of the stage Irishman was roughly from 1830 to 1860 when, observed Mick Moloney, he "found a ready home in nineteenth-century America where the establishment was British and Protestant and the immigrant Irish were the first major urban underclass of unskilled, uneducated wage earners."

The first minstrel troupe was formed in New York in 1843. Called the Virginia Minstrels, the lineup included the presence of the ubiquitous Dan Emmett. But minstrelsy's first star was yet another Irish-American named T. D. (Thomas Dartmouth) Rice (1808–1860). Rice, Emmett, George Christy, and other Irish Americans would become successful tap dancers in their own right. Rice invented a dance routine called the "Jim Crow" that was lifted from an old Irish fiddle tune. "From this dance," wrote Curtis, "came the 'Buck and Wing' and the 'soft shoe shuffle' much favoured by the famous 'hoofers' of the early twentieth century." According to Curtis, Rice got the idea for the dance after seeing a young African-American slave dancing his version of an Irish jig in a back alley. And there are many stories of white minstrels modeling their dance steps not only on the movement of black dancers but also on authentic Scots and Irish dance steps.

Ceilidhs and Chorus Lines

In the 1860s more than one hundred minstrel companies spanned the country. Yet within two decades their numbers had declined, as changing times and attitudes in post–Civil War America dictated the need for a gentler, or at least a less aggressive, form of popular entertainment. The rise in popularity of first variety theater and then vaudeville fit the bill.

Variety theater, the forerunner of vaudeville and the successor to minstrelsy, catered to a family audience with its cleaned-up combination of acrobats, magicians, singers, dancers, comics, and animal acts. By the 1840s the comic figure of Paddy, the stage Irishman, was already familiar in American popular theater. Paddy had even appeared in blackface in the minstrel shows.

Like its predecessor minstrelsy, vaudeville employed scores of Irish musicians as well. Galway-born comedian and uilleann piper Patsy Touhey, for example, worked the vaudeville circuit along with that other great Irishman George M. Cohan for a number of years. The Irish were both on stage and off, since a significant portion of the audiences were Irish immigrants.

And wherever the Irish gathered, the dance was not terribly far behind. "In vaudeville, to be Irish was to dance," declared William H.A. Williams. "Irish immigrants brought traditional step dancing to America, where it became a part of theatrical dancing." Before teaming up with Nathan Birnbaum, who would later adopt the rather Scottish-sounding name of George Burns, Gracie Allen appeared, when still a teenager, with her sisters as one of the "Four Colleens." She had learned Irish step dancing from her father. Dancing and dance routines were an inseparable part of most Irish vaudevillian acts.

More than most, George M. Cohan came to epitomize the quintessential song-and-dance man, the hoofer who bridged high art with low art. Although many people are surprised to learn that Cohan was an Irishman, his Irish roots run quite deep; his heritage a natural part of his art. Cohan's grandfather was one Michael Keohane from County Cork, and his father, Jerry, the son of famine immigrants, was a traditional Irish dancer in minstrel shows. According to Fintan O'Toole, Jerry "developed new versions of jigs and reels for the traveling variety show in which his son first appeared on stage, dancing to Irish tunes played by the great uilleann piper Patsy Touhey."

Although Cohan's popular songs, such as "Give My Regards to Broadway," "She's a Grand Old Flag," "Over There," among countless others, had little or no Irish subject matter, at least one of his songs, "Harrigan" did use an identifiably Irish name. And of course when someone like James Cagney plays the title role in "Yankee Doodle Dandy" we can't help but make the Irish connection, as well as acknowledge the subtle link between the *ceilidh* tradition and the Broadway chorus line.

Several decades later, traditional Irish music found a home in the various dance halls scattered across urban centers throughout the land. New York's Irish scene during the 1950s and 1960s was particularly strong. Foreshadowing the musical hybrid of *Riverdance*, Brendan Ward and his twelve-piece All Star Orchestra, a fixture at the City Center Ballroom, played popular American standards, Americanized versions of Irish songs, as well as Strauss-like waltzes, rumbas, cha-chas, tangos, and—to appease the old-timers in the crowd—old-time Irish waltzes and popular Irish songs.

In retrospect the leap from Brendan Ward's All Star Orchestra to *Riverdance* doesn't seem that drastic after all.

THE DEVIL'S BOX

In order to dance, most people prefer the services of a musician. And the instrument of choice in both the Old and New Worlds during the eighteenth and nineteenth centuries was the fiddle. In fact, as early as the latter decades of the seventeenth century, the fiddle had replaced other stringed and bowed instruments as the people's favorite.

Whether you call it a violin or a fiddle it doesn't really matter. It's still the same instrument. The fiddle has been called the "devil's box"—and other less than flattering nicknames—for many generations by countless fire-and-brimstone preachers.

Yet the fiddle has a fine pedigree. In the United States alone Thomas Jefferson's father, Peter, an early fiddler and mapmaker, handed down to his son, the future third president of the U.S., a love of the instrument. Indeed, it's been said that young Thomas practiced three hours each day. Another noted Virginian, Patrick Henry, himself the son of an Aberdeen merchant, was said to be an avid fiddler.

Emigrants brought the fiddle to the New World in the late seventeenth century and early eighteenth century and, with them, the fiddle tunes of Scotland and Ireland. The names may have changed in the crossing—"Lord McDonald's Reel" in Scotland became "Leather Breeches" in America—but the general feeling of spirited community and celebration remained the same.

The fiddle soon became a popular instrument at country dances so that by the late nineteenth century fiddle music emerged as the dominant instrumental music in the southern mountains and rural America. Fiddlers were always in demand, whether it be for log raisings, husking or quilting bees, weddings, or wakes. The American Civil War helped to expand the fiddler's repertoire, and in the American South fiddling contests were held starting as far back as the 1730s—the first fiddling contest was reportedly held in Hanover County, Virginia, on 30 November 1736, to celebrate St. Andrew's Day—and remained popular in the South and much of the Midwest until as late as the mid-1930s, when vocalists began to predominate. Country-music historian Bill C. Malone has commented on the "universal passion for dance found among rural Southerners."

The roots of American and contra dances lie in the dances brought over by English, Irish, and Scots immigrants. Indeed, many of the dance steps of American, Irish, and British country dances have a lot in common. The differences lie primarily in style and terminology.

Before the potato famine immigrations to America, Irish emigrants took their Irish dance up and down the East Coast and into Appalachia. There it mixed with other folk dances to produce such indigenous American music as clog and square dancing. Irish historian and author Gearóid Ó hAllmhuráin found similarities between clogging and "the *sean-nós* steps of Connemara and the Highland step dancing of Cape Breton."

In the old frontier tradition, house parties—community dances held in private homes—were held on Saturday nights. You can imagine the bonhomie that must have reigned, with fiddlers wailing, guitars strumming, and dancers dancing long into the wee hours of the morning. Many of the country string bands, such as Gid Tanner and His Skillet Lickers, emerged from the house parties of the South.

Distinct regional fiddling styles developed in southern Appalachia, the Ozarks, northern Georgia, and the Southwest. Yet particular tunes remained consistently popular, such as "Sally Goodin'," which featured the use of a drone string that some feel recalls the sound of the bagpipe.

Irish Fiddling Styles

The sound of the fiddle is usually determined by the way a player holds the instrument and, in particular, the manner in which he or she holds the bow. Other factors that come into play include how it is made and the movement and pressure placed on the fingers. The fiddle, being well suited for dance music, was popular throughout Ireland by the eighteenth century. Indeed, much of Irish dance music was composed by fiddlers. Scots fiddle music also had a great influence on the Irish fiddling tradition, as we'll soon see.

There is no right or wrong way to hold the fiddle in traditional music, and there are just as many different approaches to playing technique. Some fiddlers tuck the instrument under their chin; others rest it against their chest, shoulder, or upper arm. The method of holding the bow and amount of movement of bow while playing also vary tremendously. In fact, it is the bowing techniques that help determine a particular style. In a sense, you can say that fiddle playing all comes down to fingering and bowing. How your fingers play the notes or how you bow determines the sound quality, the volume, and the tone. The fiddler also a number of musical tricks, or decorations, at his or her disposal—rolls and slides, for example—that help create a unique sound.

It's been said that some Irish musicians, with their sensitivity to sound, can tell what county a fiddler hailed from and even which village depending on his or her playing style. Types and styles of dances also vary according to region. Donegal, for instance, has its highlands (a variation of the Highland fling), Kerry its slides and polkas, Clare and Galway their set dances. Many of the latter have military origins, introduced, as they were, in the mid-nineteenth century by soldiers returning home from the Napoleonic wars.

The style of Donegal fiddling, for example, is marked by strong bowing and double stopping and is often compared to Cape Breton fiddling. Because of the historical connection with Scotland—seasonal migrations were common to southeastern Scotland—there is also a strong Scots influence such as single-stroke bowing, a strong staccato that indicates the influence of the bagpipe, and an overall forceful and driving attack.

Donegal tends to use less ornamentation and employ a loud, driving technique. Unlike most traditional Irish music, the Donegal style is designed more for playing and listening than for dancing. In Donegal, *strathspey* tunes are referred to as "highlands" with an emphasis placed on rhythm and swing. Think of Altan or the playing of Tommy Peoples and you'll have a good idea of the sound.

The Clare style is similar to the Sligo but with more rhythm and a more staccato sound. The Sligo style is softer and more ornate with occasional flamboyant and flashy decorations. Michael Coleman, who we will discuss further in chapter 8, is considered the consummate Sligo fiddler.

One of Dublin's most revered musical families was the Potts family, who originally hailed from County Wexford. John Potts was an expert uilleann piper and his sons, Tommy and Eddie, played fiddle and pipes. Tommy, in particular, went on to become a truly great and innovative fiddler whose unusual style and experimentation with what can only be called improvisational techniques transcended the traditional dance music of his day. Among his pupils was an equally daring musician named Tommy Reck.

As a general characteristic the Scots tend to use the bow more than the Irish. Says Shetland fiddler Aly Bain:

Our reels are pretty much an individual bow for an individual note, which is kind of like some bluegrass playing. When you hear someone like [Texas fiddler] Mark O'Connor playing bluegrass music, it's much nearer Scots music than anything else.

In Scots music, it's the rhythm that matters, not the amount of notes. Irish music is full of triplets and grace notes. In Scots music, there's less fancy stuff with the fingers but much more urgency with the bow. There's more dynamic range. It's much more dignified and precise. It's very staccato, and you get that lovely cleanness in the music.

Among the best of the contemporary Irish fiddler music is the sweet sound created by Kevin Burke. Burke grew up in London listening to traditional players from Clare, Cork, and Kerry. He has been involved with most of the major Irish supergroups during the last few decades, including a stint as fiddler with the Bothy Band, one with Ireland's first traditional supergroup, Planxty, and a third with its current, Patrick Street. Recently, he has experimented with various musical cultures as a member of Open House and, along with John Cunningham and Christian Lemaitre, forms the third part of the Celtic Fiddle Festival trio.

Irish fiddling at its most expressive and most eloquent is the specialty of Martin Hayes whose uniquely regional style from the mountains of eastern Clare. Recently, he has been teaming up with Chicago-born guitarist Dennis Cahill—by all accounts a match made in musical heaven.

Scots Fiddle Styles

The fiddle is one of the national instruments of Scotland.

The *fedyl* or *fethill*, and the *rebec*, ancestors of the modern violin, were played by a bow rather than plucked with the fingers or with a plectrum. However, it was the viol, the precursor of the violin, that was the instrument of choice in the Scottish court and among polite society. Around the time of the Restoration in 1660 the viol was replaced by the fiddle.

Fiddles were bought by members of all economic classes in eighteenth-century Scotland, for they were relatively cheap—local fiddle makers copied the better-known Italian models. The most famous of Scottish fiddle makers were the Hardie family. The fiddle arrived at a perfect time in Scottish music history, for the eighteenth century saw a tremendous increase in the popularity of a favorite native pastime, dancing.

Around 1770 Scottish dance music began to be dedicated to patrons. Up until that time, most fiddlers were considered amateurs and earned their living through other, nonmusical jobs. During the latter half of the eighteenth century, though, some fiddlers were actually able to earn their living by giving dancing and violin lessons and from the occasional performance. And, as we have seen. The eighteenth century saw the arrival of the dancing master on the scene. In his classes dancing and instrumentation worked nicely together.

The eighteenth century also witnessed a plethora of fiddle collections. The first publication devoted to fiddle music belongs to Robert Bremner's *Scots Reels or Country Dances* in 1757. Other collections were published by Daniel Dow of Edinburgh (1776), Alexander McGlashan of Edinburgh (1780), Angus Grant of Grantown (1780), among many others. The greatest of the collections, though, appeared in 1815: Captain Simon Fraser's *The Airs and Melodies Peculiar to the Highlands of Scotland*, still a wonderful resource.

LIKE IRELAND, SCOTLAND too has its various fiddle styles.

The open lower strings of the West Highland fiddle imitate the drone of a bagpipe. It's a slower and very emotional style with frequent ornamentation, in contrast to the Perthshire style whose distinctive feature is the up-bow stroke. A jerk of the wrist on the upstroke of the bow gives a peculiar sound called the Scots snap. This technique is usually heard in the playing of the *strathspey*, a slow, traditional Scottish dance whose name derives from the *strath* (valley) of the River Spey.

In the nineteenth century the heart of the traditional fiddle tradition shifted from Perthshire to the northeast. There it reached its peak of popularity in the late nineteenth century. Much of this popularity was due to the playing of J. Scott Skinner, the "Strathspey King."

James Scott Skinner was probably the most prolific of all Scots fiddle composers, combining both classical and traditional musical elements. Born in 1843 in the Deeside town of Banchory, he died in Aberdeen in 1927 and along the way composed somewhere along the line of about six hundred tunes. This feat, remarkable in itself, earned him quite rightly the nickname of the Strathspey King, given by an Aberdeen newspaper editor.

Skinner was a master of the traditional *strathspey* style of bowing, which he augmented with classical flourishes. His early training was spent under fiddler and composer Peter Milne (1824–1908), where Skinner learned the art of the *strathspey*, followed by a six-year apprenticeship in England with Dr. Mark's "Little Men" Orchestra, a celebrated adolescent orchestra of its day. Returning to Scotland, he was able to make a comfortable living as a teacher and dancing master in the north of Scotland—Skinner's father, William, had also been a dancing master and fiddler. Born James Skinner, he added Scott to his name as a tribute to his dancing teacher, William Scott. Skinner toured extensively and performed as far away as America on two occasions, in 1893 and 1926.

Skinner's repertoire consisted of his own compositions as well as the work of such classical composers as Paganini and Mozart. Although he published many collections during his long life and career, his masterpiece is *The Harp and Claymore Collection* (1904), which contains 233 airs and was edited by the scholar and musician Gavin Greig.

The granite memorial stone over his gravesite in Aberdeen's Allenvale Cemetery honors THE GREATEST VIOLIN EXPONENT & COMPOSER OF SCOTTISH NATIONAL MUSIC and is accompanied by the opening bars of "The Bonnie Lass o' Bon Accord," probably his best-known tune. His home town of Banchory is also graced with a Skinner memorial.

A RALLY OF FIDDLERS

One of the earliest Scots tunes associated with a particular fiddler is "The Auld Man's Mare's Deid" by Patrick (Patie) Birnie (circa 1635–1721) from Kinghorn in Fife. Birnie also wrote the words to the song.

Another and more notorious early example is "MacPherson's Rant," composed by the fiddler and freebooter James MacPherson in the final hours before his execution at the market cross in Banff on November 16, 1700. Although the leader of a band of thieves, MacPherson fancied himself a latter-day Robin Hood who "never committed any cruel or atrocious deed."

According to the story, MacPherson, for his last request, was allowed to play the composition on the scaffold. Afterward, he offered the fiddle to anyone in the crowd who wanted it. When no one dared to take up his offer, MacPherson broke the instrument over his knee and tossed the pieces aside. The remains of MacPherson's famous fiddle now rest safely in the MacPherson Clan Museum in Newtonmore, Inverness-shire.

The title of the greatest of all Scottish fiddlers must go to Niel Gow (1727–1807). Born in the tiny hamlet of Inver, near Dunkeld, in Perthshire, Gow started playing the fiddle at the age of nine. He was largely self-taught—although he did receive some instruction from a John Cameron of Grandtully—and became known throughout Scotland as one of the country's finest fiddlers, playing at all the important balls and great parties in the major cities. Gow composed many tunes as well, including reels, jigs, hornpipes, and *strathspeys*, especially slow strathspeys—tunes played in a typical *strathspey* rhythm but at a slower pace and in a more pronounced staccato fashion. His son, Nathaniel Gow, was also a well known fiddler and composer.

Another talented and prolific Scots fiddler was William Marshall (1748–1833), born at Fochabers in Morayshire. He published *A Collection of Strathspey Reels* in 1781 and wrote more than 250 tunes. He was also something of a renaissance man, with strong interests in astronomy, architecture, and clock making. In addition, he was a fine athlete and dancer. Robert Burns considered him "the first composer of *strathspeys* of the age."

A native of Aberdeen, Hector MacAndrew can trace his fiddling lineage directly back to Niel Gow. His grandfather was taught by Niel's last pupil, James MacIntosh of Dunkeld. MacAndrew arrived on the Scottish fiddling scene in the 1930s and became an influential figure of his generation.

Of the current crop of Scots fiddlers, you can't do wrong with any of the recordings of Aly Bain, Alasdair Fraser, John Cunningham, and, the youngest of the bunch, John McCusker.

As a long-standing member of the Boys of the Lough, Aly Bain is the best-known and, indeed, probably the most important fiddler playing today in the Celtic tradition. A Shetlander, he is a consummate fiddle player, and his music is as much influenced by Scandinavian sources as Scottish. Born in Lerwick, Shetland, in 1946, Bain learned to play the fiddle at the age of eleven. His mentor was the late Tom Anderson, considered the epitome of the Shetland fiddling style.

Bain has always been interested in exploring the various connections between seemingly diverse fiddle styles. He has produced or been involved with various television programs exploring the roots of Celtic music. In 1986 *Down Home with Aly Bain in North America*, a British television documentary, traced Celtic music's ancestry from Scotland and Ireland to Appalachia and featured the playing of Cape Bretoner Buddy MacMaster, Texas fiddler Mark O'Connor, the late bluegrass king Bill Monroe, and ballad singer Jean Ritchie.

Scots-born, but California-based fiddler Alasdair Fraser explores the Scottish roots of Cape Breton music in *The Driven Bow* (Cul-

burnie) and plays examples of an older style of fiddling that survived in an isolated island environment.

John Cunningham has been a major figure on the fiddling scene
since his days as a member of Silly Wizard. He has since played
with the band Relativity and has toured as a member of Celtic Fiddle Festival. He can play tremendously fast reels, he can play heart-
breakingly slow airs. Fiddling, it seems, comes as naturally to him
as breathing.

Cape Breton Fiddlers

An older and more traditional style of Scottish fiddling can be
found in Cape Breton, among players of Highland ancestry. Highland settlers first came to Cape Breton during the first half of the
nineteenth century. Here the reels are played slower than in Scotland but a little faster than the *strathspeys*. The distinctive bowing
of *strathspeys* is emphasized and it is this technique, the way the
bow is "driven," that gives the Cape Breton style its distinctive
quality. Equal force is given to the up-bow and the down-bow.
This method differs greatly from the classically-influenced bowing
styles found in the northeast of Scotland.

Some thirty thousand emigrants from Scotland, mostly Highlanders, settled in Cape Breton between 1800 and 1850, and they
brought with them a particular way of playing the fiddle, a
Scottish-based style that has been preserved by subsequent generations of Cape Breton fiddlers. The so-called golden age of folk violin dates from this era. Some of these Cape Breton fiddlers later left
their island home to settle in Boston, including such acknowledged
masters as Angus Chisholm and Winston "Scotty" Fitzgerald. Joe
Cormier, from the French-speaking area of Cape Breton, lived in
Boston during the 1960s and organized the Cape Breton Symphony, a group of six Cape Breton fiddlers with accompanying piano and string bass.

The typical Cape Breton style consists of solo fiddle with piano
accompaniment, sometimes with guitar. Like the Irish tradition,
Cape Breton fiddling is primarily dance music. A *strathspey*-reel

combination of some sort is quite common. Yet the core of the repertoire consists of largely eighteenth-century Scottish fiddle music by the likes of the Gows and Marshall, as well as tunes from the Simon Fraser Collection. The first published collection of indigenous Cape Breton tunes, *The Cape Breton Collection of Scottish Melodies for the Violin,* did not appear until 1940. This seminal anthology contains compositions by all the big names—Dan Hughie MacEachern, Ronald MacLellan, and Sandy MacLean. In recent years other composers have added to the tradition, including Donald Angus Beaton, Jerry Holland, the late John Morris Rankin, and Brenda Stubbert. The late Donald R. MacDonald (1911–1976), though, probably holds the title of most prolific Cape Breton composer, with more than two thousand tunes under his belt.

Two of the finest young Celtic fiddlers playing today, Ashley MacIsaac and Natalie MacMaster, hail from Cape Breton. MacIsaac's recording, *Hi, How Are You Today?* brought him a lot of attention, as much for his unusual stage persona as his fiddling.

MacIsaac's older cousin, MacMaster began playing fiddle at age nine. She takes to the instrument quite naturally. She was encouraged by her father and influenced by her famous uncle, Buddy MacMaster.

The Gaelic language adds another important element to the Cape Breton fiddle style. The ornamentation of the melodies try to emulate as accurately as possible the nuances and inflections of the Gaelic tongue in the form of grace notes or accents of the bow. When someone says a fiddler has "got the Gaelic"—inflections of the language in fiddle style—that is quite a compliment indeed. Noted Kate Dunlay, who has done much research on the island, "Cape Breton is the only place in which a continuous tradition of *Highland* Scottish fiddling has been maintained to any degree."

CHARACTERISTICS OF CAPE BRETON FIDDLING

Cape Breton fiddling is primarily dance music, and it is a solo tradition (one fiddler with one piano accompanist). The repertoire and aspects of bowing have much in common with Scottish fiddling, although the traditions are distinct and can stand on their own. There is also much ornamentation on individual notes, something shared with the Irish tradition.

Cape Breton fiddling enjoys a close connection with step dancing—a strong accent on the beat brings out the "flavor" of a tune; it adds some umph to it.

"Because Cape Breton fiddling is descended from the Highland tradition," Dunlay added, "it is stylistically different from the Northeast type of fiddling prominent in Scotland today, although the traditions share much of the repertoire. The Northeast style tends to be more formal, partly because it has a closer relationship with art music than does Highland fiddling, and partly because it is the music of the Lowland ballroom."

According to piper Hamish Moore, who has spent much time and energy researching the music of Cape Breton, the key to understanding Cape Breton music is step dancing, which he maintains offers the rhythm that he says is missing from modern Scottish music and that has been a crucial influence on the fiddlers' repertoire and style. Many of the older fiddling tunes have Gaelic titles.

"Because step dancing is such a large part of Cape Breton culture," he explained, "it is that that has kept the strathspeys and reels the same. The reels are very specific when you play for step dancing. And when you hear the old-style fiddlers play absolutely spot on for step dancing, that is when the music starts to make sense. When I started to hear the rhythms of the music and the intricacies and subtleties, it was like opening a veil that had been down."

If Scottish country dancing was brought over from France via England, Cape Breton fiddling and step dancing infuse the spirit of pre-Culloden Scotland, for Cape Bretoners also have a vibrant step-dancing tradition. More flexible than their Irish counterparts, Cape Breton step-dancing evolved from the *lancer* and quadrille sets of France. The set dancing of Cape Breton is vastly different from the country dances so dominant in Scotland today, many of which are of military origin. The contemporary and immensely popular Cape Breton band Leahy incorporates step dancing into their routines, much to the delight of their usually vocal audiences.

Cape Breton step dancing involves dancing from the knees down. "The dancer's main objective," wrote Sheldon MacInnes, Cape Breton educator and author, "is to gain equal co-ordination of both legs and feet, a basic requirement of a good Cape Breton stepdancer." Individual style and regional variations also add immeasureably to the Cape Breton step-dancing tradition.

 ## THE HARDANGER FIDDLE

The Hardanger fiddle originated in the Hardanger area of western Norway. The earliest reference to it dates back to 1650. Traditionally, it is played as a solo instrument. Like Celtic music, the repertoire is known for its "non-Westernness." According to Loretta Kelley, the premier American player of the *hardingfele*:

The music is polyphonic in a style that might be called "movable drone," where the melody is played against a drone that shifts to create different harmonies. This shifting of drone against melody is so seamless that it is difficult for even a trained violinist's ear to believe that is really only one person producing the music. The music is also thickly textured, with a myriad of extremely rapid, delicate ornaments that serve to create expression and rhythm.

The Hardanger fiddle is usually tuned between 1/2 and 1 1/2 steps higher than the ordinary fiddle.

Shetland

Shetland was part of Norway until it was annexed to Scotland in 1612. Before the arrival of the violin the stringed instrument preferred in this northern land was the *gue*. Its Norse counterpart is the eight-string Hardanger fiddle, Norway's national folk instrument, which is indigenous to western and southern Norway. A characteristic of the Shetland fiddle style are its distinctive "ringing strings" above and below the melody line.

SCANDINAVIAN FIDDLE MUSIC

Fans of Celtic and bluegrass music have found much to admire in Scandinavian traditional and folk music. A number of Scandinavian acts, such as JPP and the Finnish accordion player Maria Kalaniemi, record for Celtic music labels. Green Linnet in particular has several Finnish artists on its roster, such as Varttina.

The following recordings share a common spirit with the Celtic world. Many of the tunes project a moody, haunting, and timeless quality.

Knut Buen. *As Quick as Fire: The Art of the Norwegian Hardanger Fiddle* (Henry Street Records). For those who have even the slightest interest in the music of Scotland's Northern Isles and its connection with Norway, this CD is a must. Buen is a master of the art of the *hardingfele*.

JPP. *Devil's Polska: New Finnish Folk Fiddling* (Green Linnet). A seven-member band from rural Finland.

Maria Kalaniemi (Green Linnet). Rousing and melancholy. Kalanmiemi plays the five-row accordion and includes everything from seventeenth-century Finnish and Swedish folk tunes to Argentine and gypsy music.

Nordisk Sang (Albion) The vocal quality of some of the Norwegian songs are remarkably similar in tone and mood to those of Gaelic song. This CD contains a sampling of recordings, mostly made between 1977 and 1988. Starkly beautiful, sublimely haunting Norwegian songs, lullabies, and tunes.

Sven Nyhus. *Traditional Norwegian Fiddle Music* (Shanachie). Nyhus is considered the best-known exponent of eastern Norwegian folk music today and is the son and grandson of noted country fiddlers. Includes examples of numerous *hallings* and bridal marches.

Ottopasuuna (Green Linnet). An all-instrumental melange of traditional Finnish folk melodies and dance tunes with a Celtic flavor from a wonderful Finnish quartet.

Varttina. *Seleniko* (Green Linnet). Music of the group's native Karelia in eastern Finland, featuring four-part female harmonies accompanied by accordion, double bass, mandola, flute, fiddle, and percussion. At times they swing like a Celtic band, at others they offer the Finnish equivalent of a German oompah band.

The music of the finest Shetland fiddlers—Aly Bain, Tom Anderson, Willie Hunter, Davy Tulloch—possess strong melody lines and rhythms. The energy is derived from the unusual bowing style that ranges from single bowing to droning effects to double stopping—techniques that imitate the Hardanger fiddle. It's a very complex and appealing sound.

The Hardanger fiddle was popularized in the United States by the nineteenth-century Norwegian violinist Ole Bull (1810–1880). Modeled after the European violin, it has four main strings and four to five "sympathetic" strings that vibrate when the main strings are played. Classical composer Edvard Greig, himself of Scottish ancestry, found much inspiration in the folk instrument.

Bull had learned Norwegian folk music directly from the Hardanger fiddlers themselves. Their modal or pentatonic folk melodies have an affinity with the minor-keyed melodies that resemble aspects of Appalachian and gypsy music. One can hear in this music Slavic, Balkan, and Hungarian influences and, dare I say, even a touch of the Appalachian string band.

The fiddler was an important figure at any Shetland wedding. Bridal marches are an especially popular part of the tradition. The fiddler would accompany the groom's party to the bride's home. Typically, a march was played during the walk to the site where the minister would preside over the ceremony. Another march was played on the way back from the ceremony, and a tune was played as a welcome of the return of the bridal party to the bride's home.

The tunes and their titles reflect Shetland customs and rituals. "Day Dawn," for example, is played only on the morning of Yule Day, that is, Christmas Day. The "Muckle Reel" or "Auld Reel" has a strong connection with the Norwegian *halling*, while the faster Shetland reels show a pronounced Irish influence. *Hallings* belong to the oldest repertory of dance tunes in the Hardanger fiddle tradition of western Norway. Shetland reels have the same overall structure as Scottish or Irish reels; for that matter, many are actually Scottish tunes with Shetland names.

The fiddle is used primarily for dance music in Shetland. What makes Shetland fiddling different from Scottish and Irish is its particular *lilt*, a term that refers to the variety of note lengths. The Shetland fiddle repertoire consists of *muckle* or auld reels, traditional Shetland reels, marches, polkas, waltzes, *strathspeys*, and wedding tunes. Many Shetland tunes known as *trowie* tunes refer to fairies or trolls.

All kinds of influences have made an impact on Shetland fiddle music. According to Aly Bain, hoedowns were particularly popular in Shetland. "American music was a familiar sound. . . . It wasn't a foreign sound. Virtually every good American record that featured fiddle music would find its way to Shetland." Of course, Scandinavian influences and the call of the sea were always omnipresent. Growing up in Shetland's capital of Lerwick, Bain has recalled playing not cowboys and Indians, "but Vikings and Picts. . . . To the east lay the sea, only a short distance from the house, where we played among the rocks and small cliffs from dawn until dusk."

Shetland's southern neighbor, Orkney, also has its own fiddling style although not quite as distinctive—the Orcadian fiddle-playing tradition tends to be a mixture of Scottish and Norse styles.

Two of the finest, and youngest, musicians to emerge from the area are the Wrigley sisters, Jennifer and Hazel, who hail from Deerness in Orkney. They have written some fine original compositions with typically Orcadian titles or themes, including "Eynhallow Sound"; "Horse of Copinsay"; "Stoned Giants" about the Ring of Brodgar, Orkney's Stonehenge; and "Huldreland." The word *huldre* is said to derive from the Norse *hilda*, which translates as "mirage." Hazel plays guitar and piano; Jennifer various fiddles, including the Hardanger fiddle.

OTHER TRADITIONAL INSTRUMENTS

Other instruments that form an important part of the Celtic music tradition include the melodeon, concertina, accordion, and tin whistle.

The melodeon, or box, as it is commonly known, grew in popularity as a dance instrument during the last decades of the nineteenth century. The growth in popularity of the melodeon coincided with the decline of the pipes in that time, and went hand in hand with the popularity of Irish dancing. It was simpler to play than the pipes and more versatile.

The concertina comes from England and is hexagonal in shape. Although popular throughout Ireland at one time, it is now restricted to County Clare and the surrounding area. Chicago-born John Williams is probably the finest example of a modern concertina player and one of the few Americans to choose it as his chief instrument.

Similar to the melodeon, the accordion has a second row of keys, which gives it a fuller, more complicated sound. It began to be adapted by traditional players by the late 1920s and in a short time almost completely replaced the melodeon. In the hands of masters like Phil Cunningham, formerly of Silly Wizard, it remains a remarkably expressive instrument. Jackie Daly is equally at home on the accordion and concertina. One of the youngest accordion players on the scene today, Sharon Shannon has turned many heads with her energetic and cheeky displays of musical virtuosity.

The flute has been popular in Ireland no earlier than the eighteenth century. The traditional instrument is wooden and thus has a warm tone. It remains the preferred instrument of the traditional flute player today, since the possibilities for ornamenting the melodies are greater with a wooden flute than a metal flute. One of the best flute players around today is Matt Molloy of the Chieftains.

The tin whistle is older and more firmly established in the Irish tradition than the flute. The earliest whistles date back to the thirteenth century. Most whistles today are made of metal with plastic mouthpieces. They are inexpensive, portable, and easy to play—all qualities that account for the instrument's longevity. In many ways the tin whistle is the most democratic instrument in the tradition and one that expresses various moods from joy to sorrow with great subtlety. Wonderful practitioners of the art of tin whistling include Mary Bergin from Dublin and the American-born Joanie Madden.

RECOMMENDED LISTENING

Aly Bain. *Lonely Bird* (Green Linnet). A mixed bag. Features compositions by J. Scott Skinner, traditional Shetland reels, a tune from the American fiddler Junior Daugherty, and, from Finland, the melancholy title cut. On the other hand, Bain and the BT Scottish Ensemble *Follow the Moonstone* (Whirlie) is thoroughly Scandinavian in theme and mood, with its focus on the fiddle music of Scotland, Shetland, and Norway and Sweden. Divided into three sections (Scandinavian Suite, Shetland Suite, and Scottish Suite), it is a lovely musical journey through Scotland's Scandinavian roots from Norwegian psalms and carols to Shetland sword dances.

Aly Bain and Phil Cunningham. *The Pearl* (Green Linnet). Bain on fiddle, Cunningham on piano accordion, keyboards, cittern, and tin whistle prove to be a formidable duo.

Mary Bergin. *Feadoga Stain 2* (Shanachie). A large portion of the selections features the music of the late Kerry fiddler Padraig O'Keeffe. The considerable influence of the uilleann pipes is evident in much of the music.

Joe Burke. *Traditional Music of Ireland* (Green Linnet). Burke's classic accordion is joined by Charlie Lennon on piano. *The Tailor's Choice* (Green Linnet) showcases his talents on flute, tin whistle, and accordion.

Kevin Burke. *If the Cap Fits* and *Up Close* (both Green Linnet). Two amazing recordings; Burke is joined on the first by Paul Brady, Dónal Lunny, and Jackie Daly and on the second by Matt Molloy, Joe Burke, and Gerry O'Beirne.

Pete Clark. *Even Now: The Music of Niel Gow* (Smiddymade). Highlights include such popular Gow tunes as "Farewell to Whisky," "Niel Gow's Lament for the Death of his Second Wife," and his last tune "Dunkeld Bridge."

John Cunningham. *Fair Warning* (Green Linnet). From the elegiac air "Archibald McDonald of Keppoch" to the sprightly "Celtic Society's Quickstep/42nd Highlanders Farewell," Cunningham's debut solo recording is a lovely listen from beginning to end.

Jackie Daly. *Music from Sliabh Luachra* (Green Linnet). Music on the accordion and concertina, from slow airs to slides and polkas.

Down Home: Fiddle Music and Song. The Historic Journey from Scotland to North America (Lismor). Based on the British television documentary, the recording features music from Cape Bretoners Buddy MacMaster and Jerry Holland, French-Canadian Jean Carignan, Americans Junior Daugherty, Mark O'Connor, and Bill Monroe, and Shetlanders Aly Bain, Tom Anderson, and Willie Hunter.

Alastair Hardie's Compliments to "The King": A 150th Anniversary Tribute to James Scott Skinner (The Hardie Press). Includes some of the best Skinner compositions, such as "Bovaglie's Plaid" and "The Bonnie Lass o' Bon Accord." Features airs, strathspeys, reels, and the "patriotic pastorals" of "Sir William Wallace" and "King, Robert the Bruce."

Martin Hayes (Green Linnet). Debut recording from the County Clare wonder, lately of Seattle, Washington.

Noel Hill and Tony MacMahon. *In Knocknagree* (Shanachie). The first recording to feature a concertina and accordion playing together; recorded in Dan O'Connell's pub in Knocknagree on the Cork and Kerry border on a chilly night in October 1985. Includes reels, hornpipes, and airs.

Jerry Holland. *The Fiddlesticks Collection* (Green Linnet). Cape Bretoner Jerry Holland features the fiddling traditions of three traditions—Canada, Scotland, and Ireland—with a few American touches thrown in, including Jay Ungar's wistful "Ashokan Farewell."

Joe MacLean. *Old Time Scottish Fiddle Music from Cape Breton Island* (Rounder). Joe MacLean's people came from the Isle of Barra, and the warmth of that far-away Hebridean island is felt in this recording. Extensive liner notes.

Joanie Madden. *A Whistle on the Wind* (Green Linnet). A tin whistle and flute player and member of Cherish the Ladies, Madden is the only American-born Irish musician to have won the Senior All-Ireland tin whistle title. Listen to this CD and you'll learn why.

Matt Molloy. *Stony Steps* (Green Linnet). Reels, jigs, and slow airs from the irrepressible Chieftain's flute player. He is joined by Arty McGlynn on guitar and Dónal Lunny on *bouzouki, bodhran*, and synthesizer.

Moving Cloud (Green Linnet). This County Clare quintet, including Paul Brock on accordion and melodeon, plays some of the finest traditional *ceilidh*-band style music currently being performed.

Micho, Pakie, and Gussie Russell. *The Russell Family of Doolin, County Clare* (Green Linnet). The music of brothers Micho, Pakie, and Gussie Russell on flute, whistle, and concertina. Oh yes, the pride and joy of Doolin also sing.

Brendan Power. *New Irish Harmonica* (Green Linnet). All-Ireland harmonica champion and native New Zealander of Irish ancestry, Power takes the underrated Irish harmonica to new heights with his artistry and breathtaking improvisation. Includes reels, slow airs, jigs, hornpipes, and two Carolan tunes.

Sharon Shannon. *Out the Gap* (Green Linnet). Joyful music from a young and rising Irish musician who is equally adept on the melodeon, button accordion, and fiddle. Already considered one of the greats.

Shetland Sessions. 2 vols. (Lismore). A compilation of great music from Shetlanders and non-Shetlanders alike, including Aly Bain, the Poozies, Hom Bru, Simon Thoumire, Willie Hunter, the Easy Club, Barely Works, Phil Cunningham, and Rock, Salt, and Nails.

The Silver Bow: The Fiddle Music of Shetland (Topic). An important collection of traditional Shetland fiddle music from reels and bridal marches to slow *strathspeys* and airs. The Norse connection has never seemed stronger. Features the great Aly Bain and his mentor Tom Anderson as well as Dave Tulloch, Violet Tulloch, and Willie Johnson. A must.

Bill Whelan. *Riverdance* (Celtic Heartbeat). Music from the smash theatrical show featuring a stellar lineup of traditional Irish musicians: Maire Breatnach and Eileen Ivers on fiddles, Davy Spillane on whistle and uilleann pipes, Mairtin O'Connor on accordion, Tommy Hayes on *bodhran* and spoons, Ronan Browne on uilleann pipes, and the choral group Anuna.

John Williams (Green Linnet). Virtuoso accordion and concertina playing from a young American-born master. Features the final recording session of County Clare tin whistle legend Micho Russell.

Jennifer and Hazel Wrigley. *Huldreland* (Greentrax). A wonderful selection of tunes, most of them original and most of them with Orcadian connections, played on the fiddle, Hardanger fiddle, and guitar.

4

The Splendorous Drone

The Music of the Pipes

The greatest melodic art everywhere is unmeasured, and the best examples I have found in Europe are in Gregorian chant and the piobaireachd *of the Gael.*

–COMPOSER FRANCIS GEORGE SCOTT

O that I had three hands, two for the bagpipe and one for the sword.

–"THE CAVE OF GOLD," OLD GAELIC SONG

It's all in the details. That's the secret to understanding the mystery of the Highland bagpipes.

Of all the traditional instruments in the Celtic world, the Highland bagpipes elicit the most emotional response. You either love them or hate them. There's no in-between. A large part of the sometimes negative reaction amounts to their enigmatic quality: Even those who confess to liking them can't quite explain their appeal. Most people probably associate the pipes—and here I'm referring to the Highland war pipes—with funerals and parades, that is, the instrument's public functions. To understand the secrets of a great *pibroch*—the classical music of the Highland bagpipes—is to better appreciate the inner workings of the Gael.

 ## MILITARY PIPE BANDS

After the collapse of the traditional Highland way of life, there were few avenues of employment open to the piper. Many thus joined the numerous Highland regiments of the British army, the Black Watch being the most famous. Highland regiments helped preserve the music of the pipes at a time when it appeared the instrument was in danger of becoming extinct. Pipe bands first formed in the 1850s; prior to this, army pipers played solo, and they usually played *pibrochs*. Today the majority of the tunes in a piper's repertoire consists of marches.

THE HIGHLAND BAGPIPES

Many countries throughout the world have a bagpipe tradition, but only in the Scottish Highlands did the instrument develop its own serious music.

It is generally believed that the bagpipe originated not in Scotland but in the Near East, and was spread across Europe by wandering musicians during the twelfth and thirteenth centuries. By the late fourteenth century itinerant pipers were a common fixture in rural communities from Greece to Ireland, from Italy to Sweden. Although there is no record as to when pipe music first arrived in Scotland, most agree that the pipes were well established in Scotland by the fifteenth century.

According to music scholar John Purser, the earliest reference to the bagpipe in Scotland is in Dunbar's *Testament of Mr. Andrew Kennedy,* which was published in 1508. By the sixteenth century they were established as military band instruments.

Until the pipes came, popular music in the Highlands was confined to song, drum, and a single pipe. The harp was the traditional instrument of the great halls, but it was not suitable for the outdoors. The two-drone bagpipes, on the other hand, could be heard for at least a mile, perhaps two or more, down the glen— some say that, given the proper weather conditions, and if played loud enough, the pipes can be heard as far as ten miles away. They can even be played in the rain—an all-purpose, all-weather instrument! Perfect for Scotland. Eventually, regimental pipers teamed with the traditional drummers of the British army, and thus the military pipe band was formed.

The Highland bagpipes consist of a chanter (the pipe of a bagpipe on which the melody is played) and three drones (the part of the bagpipe that sounds a continuous tone) attached to a bag that is filled with air by the player's mouth through a blow pipe. The bag inflates either by air blown through a blow pipe or by a set of bellows. The player plays the chanter which has a scale of nine notes, to produce the melody. Each of the drones produces a continuous tone. Rhythm and expression are achieved through a very precise sense of timing and the use of grace notes, which can range from very short notes to complicated strings.

THE PIBROCH

The Gaelic word *piobaireachd*, Anglicized as *pibroch*, means "piping" or "pipe music." The simplest way of describing the *pibroch* is "a long tune with variations," but this in no way conveys its complexity. More specifically, *pibroch* refers to a particular type of pipe music—the classical music of the Highland bagpipe, considered the highest form of bagpipe music and Highland Scotland's unique contribution to world culture.

Although the earliest written description of Highland pipe music was Joseph MacDonald's *A Compleat Theory of the Scots' Highland Bagpipe* in 1760, the origins of the *pibroch* are rather obscure. Some believe that it evolved from the repertoire of the *clarsach* or Celtic harp, others that it was vocal in origin. To gather a clan the piper played a clan's signature tune, but he also faced the challenge of having to master ways to extend the tune without repeating it endlessly—that is, to invent variations of a tune.

Highland pipe music falls into two broad categories: *ceol beg* (small music) and *ceol mor* (big music). *Ceol beg* consists of dance tunes, especially reels, *strathspeys,* jigs, quicksteps, marches, and slow airs; in other words, the typical repertoire of pipe-band music.

Ceol mor, or *pibroch*, was composed on an altogether grander and more complex scale. It is serious music for serious occasions. *Ceol* is the Gaelic word for "music" but, as John Purser reminds us, it really means something more along the lines of "to pipe like birds." The most common types of *pibrochs* are laments, salutes, or clan gatherings—ceremonial pipe music. *Pibroch* composers were usually the personal pipers retained by the clan chieftains. They were considered an elite group, operating like a medieval craft guild.

Pibroch is built on the same principle as Highland dancing or, for that matter, most any type of traditional Celtic dance. Like step dancing, a basic pattern is established, which is then embellished in fine detail and increasing in complexity as the particular tune develops. Hence, a *pibroch* starts from a few notes, then grows to a slow theme, called *urlar* in Gaelic or "ground" in English; this is followed by a sequence of increasingly complex musical variations before ending with a repetition of the main theme. The theme may be longer than an ordinary tune, and the variations follow its melody. The final variation(s) culminate in the *crunluath*, in which the principal notes of the melody is played in a steady rhythm and then embellished with grace notes.

BEST-KNOWN PIBROCHS

It is remarkable that from such a restricted art form—the Highland pipes cannot play harmony and are confined to nine notes—emerged such a rich body of material. "The bagpipe," Francis Collinson has pointed out, "is a *solo*, or at least a *unison, melodic* instrument which is only required to harmonize to the sound of its own drones."

The following are examples of some of the best-known *pibrochs*:

"Lord Lovat's Lament." Commemorates Simon Fraser, Lord Lovat and chief of Clan Fraser during the Jacobite Risings of 1715 and 1745, who was beheaded on April 9, 1747.

"The Munro's Salute." Composed by Iain Dall Mackay (1656–1754), piper to Mackenzie of Gairloch; Mackay was a pupil of Patrick Og MacCrimmon and composer of some twenty *pibrochs*, including "The Lament for Patrick Og Mac-Crimmon." He was also a true friend to Clan Munro and wrote this *pibroch* in honor of them.

"MacLeod of Raasay's Salute." Composed by Angus Mackay of Gairloch to celebrate the birth of James MacLeod of Raasay in 1761.

"The Desperate Battle of the Birds." Attributed by Angus Mackay of Gairloch after reportedly witnessing a fight between black birds.

"My King Has Landed in Moidart." Composed by John Mac-intyre, piper to Menzies of Menzies, on the landing of Bonnie Prince Charlie on the Scottish mainland in 1745.

"The MacGregor's Salute." In honor of the famous clan. Be-cause of the MacGregors's nefarious activities, which included cattle rustling, over the centuries, the government in 1603 enacted a piece of legislation that required them to change their name, un-der penalty of death; it remained in force off and on until 1775.

MacCrimmon
Pibrochs

About twenty or thirty *pibrochs* have been attributed to various members of the MacCrimmon family.

Donald Mór's *pibrochs* include:

> "Lament for the Earl of Antrim"
> "MacLeod of MacLeod's Lament"
> "The MacLeod's Controversy"
> "MacDonald's Salute"
> "MacLeod's Salute"

Patrick Mór's *pibrochs* include:

> "I Got a Kiss of the King's Hand"
> "Lament for Mary MacLeod"
> "Lament for the Children"

The performance of a typical *pibroch* is slow, hypnotic, graceful, and dignified; it usually lasts from ten to fifteen minutes. *Pibroch* composition reached its artistic height during the seventeenth and eighteenth centuries.

The Highland bagpipes are, quite simply, perfect for the *pibroch*. Because of the instrument's continuity of sound—no breaks or pauses between notes are allowed—there is no means of varying the volume of a particular note; in other words, no way to make it sound softer or louder. Artistic expression depends on other methods, such as the length of the notes and the embellishment or ornamentation of the grace notes.

Pibrochs were originally composed and taught entirely by ear. As with *clarsach* players, the method of teaching was mostly oral, although there was a unique method of notation, called *canntaireachd*, used by the pipers that was vocalized as well as written down. Using this system, pipers learned to sing the melody of the tune from the singing of their teacher. Different vowel sounds indicated the pitch of the note; consonants, the finger movements that ornament the note. When sung, the vowel sounds approximate the tune's principal notes and the consonants the grace notes. Hence, no written score is required. *Canntaireachd* is unique to Scotland and resembles, in its musical inflections and intonations, the Gaelic language itself.

PIPING COLLEGES

The first reference to piping colleges dates back to around 1700. Numerous chiefs sent their pipers to study under a special master. Some of these teachers, or families, kept up the tradition and became famous, including the Rankins of Mull, the MacArthurs of Skye, the Mackays of Gairloch, and—especially—the MacCrimmons, pipers to the MacLeods of Dunvegan in Skye.

Types of Pibrochs

The term *pibroch* not only applies to pipe music; there are also fiddle *pibrochs* and *pibroch* songs.

Fiddlers who successfully imitate the pipes on their instrument do so by creating a drone effect. By experimenting with double stopping—playing more than one note at a time—and employing various bowing techniques, the skilled fiddler can approximate the sound of the pipes.

The term *pibroch* can also apply to songs. Not surprisingly, *pibroch* songs are similar in structure to *pibroch* tunes. To cite but two examples; "Moladh Ben Dorain" by the Gaelic poet Duncan Bán Macintyre was written in the 1750s and consists of more than five hundred lines of poetry. It was intended to be sung as a *pibroch* with variations. First the poet praises the mountain; he then celebrates a small bird before returning to the main theme of the mountain. And "MacCrimmon's Lament" is probably better known as a song than as a *pibroch*, but essentially the words are set to the main melody.

PIPING FAMILIES

Like the bards and the *clarsach* players, the piper held a very important place in Gaelic society. They held hereditary lands, and the skill of various pipers was passed down through families from generation to generation. The honor of being the earliest and most famous piping family belongs to the MacCrimmons of Skye, hereditary pipers to the MacLeods of Skye for some three hundred years.

 ## THE PIPING
HERITAGE CENTRE AT BORERAIG

According to tradition, the MacCrimmon Piping Heritage Centre, at Boreraig on Loch Dunvegan, on the Isle of Skye, is located on ancestral holdings of the MacCrimmons, hereditary pipers to the chiefs of MacLeod and the first composers, players, and teachers of the *pibroch*. The center, a modern museum depicting the story of the great Highland bagpipes and their music, faces the MacCrimmon memorial cairn and the ruins of the piping college.

The MacCrimmons of Skye

MacCrimmon is a name associated with the Highland pipes and the Isle of Skye. The most renowned of the early piping families, the MacCrimmons are credited with creating the *pibroch;* they formed an unbroken line of composers, players, and teachers of the *pibroch* from the sixteenth to the nineteenth century.

Sometime in the sixteenth century a MacCrimmon became personal piper to the Chief of Clan MacLeod at Dunvegan Castle. This MacCrimmon passed his piping skills on to his sons. As hereditary pipers to the clan chief, the MacCrimmons were awarded, rent free, the valuable and strategically important farm of Boreraig, at the head of Loch Dunvegan. Until 1773 the MacCrimmon College of Piping at Boreraig on Skye was a mecca for Scottish pipers.

Despite the family's fame, its origins are vague. All MacCrimmons around the world, according to Gaelic scholar Derick Thomson, are related to these MacCrimmons, who appeared suddenly in the parish of Glendale in Skye in the sixteenth century. Some say they came from the Isle of Harris, others believe they hailed from Ireland, and still others attest to the rather fanciful claim that they originated in Cremona, Italy. Whatever their origin, the MacCrimmons are thought to be responsible for developing the *pibroch* into an art form comparable to and worthy of the classical music of any country. Before their arrival on the scene, the bagpipes were a rather primitive and simple instrument.

The earliest-known MacCrimmons were named Finlay, Iain Odhar, and Padraig Donn. The next famous MacCrimmon was Donald Mór, born in 1570, who succeeded to the title of hereditary piper in 1620. Earlier, in 1603, he was commissioned to compose a special tune following the end of hostilities between the MacLeods and the MacDonalds. He composed not one, but three: "MacLeod's Controversy," "The MacLeods' Salute," and "The MacDonalds' Salute." They are considered three of the most finest and important tunes in the entire *pibroch* repertoire.

In 1610 or so, Donald Mór's brother, Patrick Caogach, was murdered and Donald Mór retaliated, by burning numerous houses in Kintail. He then fled to Sutherland, where he lived for several years before returning to Skye. He died in 1640. He was succeeded by his son, Patrick Mór (1595–1670), who was considered the greatest composer of all the MacCrimmons. He in turn was succeeded by his son Patrick Og (born in 1645), whose fame surpassed even that of his father, for Patrick Og was considered the best player, the best teacher, and the most famous of a very famous line. Patrick Og's successor was Malcolm (1690–1760), who continued the piping school at Boreraig until his death.

That the MacCrimmons held a unique position on the Gaelic social scale is made clear by the story of yet another son of Patrick Og, one Donald Ban. During the Jacobite Rising of 1745, Donald Ban joined the government forces against Bonnie Prince Charlie and was taken prisoner at the battle of Inverurie. The next morning an eerie silence fell upon the Jacobite camp. The familiar sound of the pipes was absent, for none of the pipers would play while a MacCrimmon—even a MacCrimmon in the enemy camp—was held prisoner. Donald Ban was thereupon released. Unfortunately, he was killed in battle at the Rout of Moy the following year.

Donald Ban is commemorated in the haunting lament "Cha till Mac Cruimen" ("MacCrimmon Will Never Return" or, more simply, "MacCrimmon's Lament"). He composed it before leaving Skye. The chorus of the song, in a premonition of his own death, chillingly predicts that he would never return—he was, in fact, the only casualty on that fateful day in 1745. Traditionally, "MacCrimmon's Lament" was sung or the pipe tune played as the emigrant ships pulled away from the harbor or quayside, making their way to the New World.

The tale of the MacCrimmons ends with Malcolm's sons, Iain Dubh (1730–1822) and Donald Ruadh (1740–1825). They held the post of hereditary piper at various times. Iain waged a dispute with MacLeod over terms regarding the Boreraig estate. Because of the dispute he planned to emigrate to America but changed his mind at the last minute and returned to Skye, where he died. His brother, Donald Ruadh, however, did go to America and became an officer with a regiment of Scots Loyalists, fighting, as many Highlanders did, on the side of the Crown during the American War of Independence. He later returned to Scotland and died in

London at the age of eighty-two in 1825. The long line of hereditary MacCrimmon pipers died with him.

Other important piping families included:

- The MacArthurs, hereditary pipers to the MacDonalds of Sleat. They moved their piping school from the island of Ulva to lands granted them at Hunglatter on Skye (Charles MacArthur, founder of the MacArthur School, was a pupil of Patrick Og).
- The MacDougalls, hereditary pipers to their own clan chief; for many years they ran a piping school near Glasgow.
- The MacKays of Gairloch. John Roy, the last of the clan's hereditary pipers, emigrated to America in 1805.
- The MacKays of Raasay. John MacKay also studied with Patrick Og.
- The MacPhersons. Angus MacPherson was piper to the Scottish-American industrialist and philanthropist Andrew Carnegie at Skibo Castle in the far north of Scotland between 1898 and 1905. He composed "The Cairn at Boreraig" to commemorate its unveiling by MacLeod of MacLeod in 1933.

In recent years Scotland has witnessed a new generation of pipers, both Highland and Lowland. Gordon Mooney is a master of the Lowland pipes; Gordon Duncan's fiery spirit and unconventional style has angered some and delighted others; and Allan MacDonald, one of the three piping brothers from the western Highlands, has spent considerable time researching the relationship between the *pibroch* and Gaelic song. He believes that the *pibroch* performance style of two hundred years ago was not the slow style we hear today but rather consisted of livelier tunes.

THE LOWLAND OR BORDER PIPES

The Highland bagpipes are not the only pipes indigenous to Scotland. Much less known but currently enjoying a revival of sorts are the Lowland pipes, or Border pipes (also known as *cauld*, or cold, wind pipes). Unlike their Highland counterpart, they are bellows blown rather than mouth blown. This makes them comparable to the Irish uilleann pipes and the English Northumbrian pipes. Several types of Lowland pipes exist: the Scottish small pipes, the Lowland or Border pipes, and the pastoral pipes.

 ## MODERN PIPING SCHOOLS AND CENTERS

In 1990 Carnegie-Mellon University in Pittsburgh became the first institution of higher learning in the United States to offer a bachelor of arts degree in music performance with a major in bagpipe, the only program of its kind. The university takes its Scottish connections seriously. Bagpipes have been a presence on the campus for years—on the football field when they lead the school's kiltie band, as well as at commencement exercises during graduation ceremonies.

Andrew Carnegie founded the Carnegie Technical Schools, which later became the Carnegie Institute of Technology. The student union of the university is named Skibo, after Carnegie's luxurious castle of the same name in Scotland's far north. The "prof," James McIntosh, teaches students bagpipe maintenance and history as well as various aspects of music theory.

Meanwhile the College of Piping and Celtic Performing Arts in Summerside, Prince Edward Island, in the Canadian Maritimes, founded in 1990, is reportedly the only year-round institution of its kind in North America. The school offers summer classes in stepdancing and piping and presents a summer concert series featuring pipers, stepdancers, and fiddlers.

The Piping Centre in Glasgow houses a school along with rehearsal rooms and a performance hall, a museum and interpretive center, and reference library.

Bellows-blown pipes have existed in Scotland since at least the eighteenth century. They enjoyed their highest level of popularity at various dances and festivals in the Borders but also in Perthshire and Aberdeenshire in the eighteenth and nineteenth centuries. By the late nineteenth century, though, they had died out.

Border pipes were a particular favorite of the *toun* (town) pipers. The Border piper was a popular figure at local fairs and weddings and especially around harvest time, when, during breaks in the workday, ring dances were performed to the music of the Border pipes. Like the Highlands, the Borders also had their share of famous piping families, including the Allans of Yetholm; the Andersons, for generations the *toun* pipers of Kelso; and the Hasties of Jedburgh.

All the Scottish small pipes are bellows blown. Their most distinctive feature is the open chanter, which distinguishes them different from their English and Irish pipes counterparts. The chief difference between the Scottish and Northumbrian small pipes is that the chanter of the Northumbrian pipes is stopped up at the end so that when all holes are covered by the fingers, there is no sound. This makes it possible to repeat a note.

With the Northumbrian pipes the chanter is permanently stopped, while the uilleann piper usually plays with the chanter stopped on the knee. The Scottish small pipes are similar in sound to the Northumbrian small pipes, and yet the latter have a higher pitch and more of a staccato sound. Pastoral pipes are similar to uilleann, although the tones of the chanters are a bit different.

HAMISH MOORE'S
FINE OBSESSION

In 1985 Hamish Moore, a veterinarian by profession, made the first complete recording of the Lowland or small pipes (also called the *cauld* wind, or cold wind, pipes) of Scotland. *Cauld* wind was the traditional name for the bellows-blown pipes, refers to the "cold" temperature of the air in the bellows as compared to the warm breath of the mouth-blown Highland pipes.

Moore taught at the Gaelic College in Cape Breton and became an advocate of the old Gaelic style of piping that had been preserved in Nova Scotia but unfortunately lost in Scotland. The old style of piping in Scotland changed for many reasons: the Battle of

Culloden in 1746, which changed forever the traditional way and customs of Highland life (see chapter 5, pages 129–30, and chapter 6, pages 169–70); the subsequent Act of Proscription that so negatively affected Gaelic self-esteem; the devastating consequences of the Highland Clearances that resulted in much forced emigration, including the loss of many traditional musicians; additional emigration because of poverty, overpopulation, and high rents; the often oppressive tactics of the church; the popularity of fiddler J. Scott Skinner and his predilection for classical techniques; the crossover from step dancing to country dancing.

As I noted in chapter 3, step dancing was brought to Cape Breton by waves of early Scottish settlers. In Cape Breton dancing and music are inseparable. Cape Breton's unique piano style developed from the rhythm of the step dancing. Before the piano was introduced, all Cape Bretoners had was feet! Playing the pipes for step dancing required a different style of piping in order for the dancers to keep time. The ornamentations brought out the natural rhythms of a tune.

 ## OTHER CELTIC PIPES

In the northeast of England, just south of the Scottish border, lies the county of Northumberland (in an earlier life it had the more poetic-sounding name of Northumbria). Not quite English and certainly not Scottish, Northumberland stands on its own, a northern land with its own tunes, its own traditions, its own distinctive body of music. The Northumbrian small pipes belongs to this ongoing tradition.

Like the uilleann pipes, the Northumbrian pipes are a small, sweet-toned instrument that is bellows blown. The end of the chanter (that is, the melody pipe) is permanently closed and is played with a closed fingering system unique to this instrument—only one hole is open at a time. The movement of only one finger creates a staccato effect.

Probably the greatest practitioner of the Northumbrian small pipes working today is Kathryn Tickell. Despite her youth—she turned professional in 1986 at the tender age of eighteen—she has reworked the music of her native Northumberland with usually grand results. "My style is a mixture between very traditional Northumbrian, Shetland, and maybe a little tinge of Irish," she once said.

A major influence on most Northumbrian pipers, including Tickell, was the enigmatic Billy Pigg, who died in 1968. "His playing was really wild," Tickell once told an Irish journalist. "His timing was all over the place sometimes and the excitement in his playing was phenomenal.

"He was open to so many musical influences—yodeling, Hawaiian guitar, brass band. He listened to it all with an open mind, and here and there you can hear bits of it creeping into his playing, along with Highland piping ornamentation—that came from his father, who played the Highland pipes."

Alistair Anderson, the concertina and Northumbrian small pipes player, also learned part of his repertoire from Billy Pigg. As a member of the High Level Ranters, he introduced the sound of Northumbria to the outside world.

Other bagpipe traditions in the Celtic world include the Breton *biniou* and the Galician *gaita*. The Breton bagpipes, which date from the nineteenth century, are mouth blown, but unlike the Highland pipes have only one drone and emit a higher pitch—an octave higher.

The Galician *gaita*, on the other hand, is high pitched and bellows blown and like its Irish and Northumbrian cousins, projects a mellower tone. In the hands of someone like a Carlos Nuñez, who plays the *gaita*, recorder, whistle, and *bombarde* on The Chieftains' *Santiago* (RCA Victor), or members of the Galician band Milladoiro, it sounds downright joyous.

The early settlers to Cape Breton brought with them too the old piping styles of their native land, which was, maintained Hamish Moore, "very different from the modern 'traditional' style, which has developed since the beginning of the nineteenth century" and are based on the standardized and very rigid army style of piping, the confines of the solo competitive piper. Old style, said Moore, is based on rhythm, not technique. Since many pipers also played the fiddle, the old piping style carried over in the fiddling of contemporary Cape Bretoners. Concluded Moore, "The style of playing the reel, the jig and in particular the strathspey in Cape Breton today, is basically the same as it was in Scotland in the eighteenth century and before."

"[T]he standard way of piping, which everyone in the world is taught, is not the only way," noted Moore. "There are older exciting styles using what modern pipers would call non-standard techniques. This piping is based entirely on rhythm because it was used for dancing . . . you don't need to dress it up, you don't need to do anything to it, you just need to play it. It is rock and roll. It's eighteenth century rock and roll."

THE IRISH PIPES

The earliest representation of pipes in Ireland occurred in the ninth century—a wood carving of a piper appears in County Kilkenny—although it wasn't until the fifteenth or sixteenth century that an actual written reference appears, to war pipes. The emergence of the distinctively Irish uilleann pipes did not occur until the eighteenth century (William Shakespeare in *The Merchant of Venice* referred to them as "woollen pipes"). By the end of the nineteenth century, the original mouth-blown pipes (*an Piob mhor*) had all but died out in Ireland.

Uilleann is Gaelic for "elbow," yet some historians theorize that the name is derived from the Act of Union of 1800 between Ireland and Britain. And indeed the first important collection of traditional Irish music, O'Farrell's *Collection of National Irish Music for the Union Pipes*, was published the same year as the historic act of parliament.

The chanter on the uilleann pipes is fully chromatic and has a broader range than the Highland war pipes—two octaves. The uilleann pipes are basically set in the keys of D and G, the preference of most traditional musicians. Bellows, not a blow pipe, inflate the bag. Traditionally, the bag is made from a soft dry-cured sheepskin.

The uilleann pipes are an immensely sophisticated instrument and one that takes years to master. The Irish piper generally uses two styles of playing: loose or open fingering and tight or close fingering. These styles were once regional; the open fingering style is traditionally associated with Leinster and the eastern parts of Munster, the close style with Connacht and areas along the western coast. Regional differences now tend to get lost.

The bellows are strapped to the right arm, which blows air into a reservoir bag controlled by the left arm. The bellows are then "pumped" with the right elbow. The pipes consist of three drones, while the regulators have thirteen keys that produce harmony, allowing the musician to play chords along with the tune. Unlike Highland pipes, which are single reed, uilleann pipes are softer and more pliable double reeds, and so produce a mellower, softer tone. For this reason the pipes are best heard indoors, where subtleties of sound and texture can be appreciated.

The pipes are played sitting, with the drones lying across the player's knee. The pipes themselves consist of an eight-hole chanter (on which the melody is played), three drones (a bass, baritone, and tenor), and three regulators (pipes stopped at the end). Fingering is similar to that of a tin whistle.

"A Kind of Rapture"

Because of their complexity, not to mention their scarcity and expense, the general populace lost interest in the uilleann pipes around the turn of the century. Yet during the early decades of the twentieth century there were more than a few individuals who found in the sound of the pipes something of the spirit of the old Ireland, of a long-ago place in a long-ago past that they not only tried to recapture but to preserve.

He must have looked like quite a sight—a swarthy man with exceedingly high cheekbones playing the uilleann pipes instrument on a village street in County Clare. For by the 1930s, the heyday of the pipes had been long gone. Yet piping was in Johnny Doran's blood. The so-called last of the traveling pipers, Doran crisscrossed the Irish countryside during the 1930s and 1940s, playing for crossroad dances, wakes and weddings, soirees, functions, and village fairs.

Born in 1907 into a family of professional traveling musicians and a descendant of the great nineteenth-century Wicklow piper, John Cash, Johnny Doran carried on the uilleann-playing family tradition. He preferred to play outdoors in a legato or open-pipe style in order to attract more folk.

Writer P. J. Curtis describes his piping style "as wild and exciting as it was technically brilliant . . . all who have heard Johnny Doran in the flesh speak of falling into a kind of rapture on hearing his headlong rush of bewitching music."

It was this "kind of rapture" that attracted so many people to the man and his music, to his seemingly endless repertoire of airs and dance tunes and to his very persona with its otherworldly air. He had a tremendous influence on several generations of uilleann pipers, too. Among the modern players who owe him a great debt are Paddy Keenan, Finbar Furey, and Davy Spillane. A tragic accident contributed to his untimely death in 1950 at the age of forty-two.

Another giant among Irish pipers was the late Willie Clancy, who was also an excellent flute and tin whistle player as well as possessing a fine voice. He hailed from Miltown Malbay, a bastion of traditional music in County Clare.

Willie's father, Gilbert, was a flute player and singer who learned most everything he learned from the blind traveling piper Garrett Barry. In turn Willie learned from that other traveling piper, the great Johnny Doran. It was said that Clancy followed Doran around Clare to fairs and dances, absorbing the tunes and Doran's piping style so thoroughly into his bones that they became his own. He also was influenced by various West Clare styles.

Willie emigrated to London where he earned his livelihood as a carpenter. Previously, he had settled for a short spell in Dublin, where he met some of Ireland's greatest pipers, including John Potts, Seamus Ennis, and Tommy Reck. He returned home in the late 1950s. A later generation of pipers, including Liam O'Flynn, has been greatly influenced by Clancy.

After Clancy's death in 1973, friends went about establishing the Willie Clancy Summer School as a living tribute to him. It started modestly enough, but now the annual summer school in Clancy's hometown of Miltown Malbay has since grown as *the* place for traditional Irish music. In early July of each year the old market town celebrates the memory of Willie Clancy in the only way possible—by hosting a veritable musical feast of fiddles, flutes, concertinas, singers, dancers, and of course uilleann pipes.

Leo Rowsome (1907–1970), a major figure in traditional Irish music, also helped to change people's attitudes toward the pipes. He in fact devoted his entire life to piping, not only as a performer but also as a teacher and pipe maker.

Rowsome came by his piping skills naturally through strong family ties. His grandfather, Samuel Rowsome, a farmer from County Wexford, was also a piper. He influenced younger generations of pipers, including Liam O'Flynn's smooth, closed style and Paddy Keenan's fast, open style.

A much more delicate and less flashy style belonged to Seamus Ennis, although he probably is best remembered today as a collector and broadcaster of Irish traditional music. In 1942 the Irish Folklore Commission hired Ennis, age twenty-three, to collect songs and tunes on the Aran Islands and in Connemara. He also collected in Cork, Kerry, Donegal and as far afield as the Hebrides. Many of these recordings were broadcast in the 1940s on the BBC radio program *As I Roved Out*. Ennis remains an important figure in the folk revival both in Ireland and in Britain.

Both as piper for the Bothy Band and on his own, Paddy Keenan has proved an inventive piper, with an exciting, driving style modeled after Johnny Doran's. The third generation of pipers in his family, he began playing the pipes at the age of twelve.

As I noted in chapter 2, Liam O'Flynn has extended the range of the uilleann pipes and opened up their sound through his ongoing association with classical composer Shaun Davey on such recordings as *The Relief of Derry* and especially on *The Pilgrim*. The ex-Planxty piper has also contributed much to the tradition with his own solo work. While Davy Spillane, one of the pipers with Moving Hearts, has gone beyond the bounds of traditional music with his collaborations with Van Morrison and Elvis Costello, the spirit of the pipes infuses the best of his work.

Paddy Moloney, uilleann piper with the Chieftains, has probably done more than anybody playing the instrument today to bring it to international attention. Wherever the Chieftains roam, the soulful sounds of Moloney's pipe follow—from the Great Wall of China to the inside of a Nashville studio.

In the early twentieth century the uilleann pipes seemed on their way to extinction. Now it's hard to believe that this most Irish of instruments could ever have faced the threat of oblivion. Credit must go to the work of Moloney, O'Flynn, Keenan, Spillane, and others. All have taken to their hearts an instrument that for many people captures the true soul of Irish music.

RECOMMENDED LISTENING

Alistair Anderson. *Steel Skies* (Flying Fish). Concertina player and Northumbrian small piper Anderson has crafted a musical suite, weaving old and new, to his native Northumbria.

John Burgess. *King of the Highland Pipers* (Topic). *Pibrochs*, marches, slow airs, jigs, hornpipes, strathspeys, and reels—it's all covered by the master, Burgess.

Willie Clancy. *The Minstrel from Clare* (Green Linnet). An excellent selection of music and song that illustrates Clancy's remarkable versatility as a warm singer and a great piper. This recording captures the expansive spirit of the man himself.

A Controversy of Pipers (Temple). Covers most pipe styles, including marches, slow airs, hornpipes, *strathspeys*, reels, and *pibrochs* by some of Scotland's finest solo pipers.

Johnny Doran. *The Bunch of Keys* (CBE-Gael Linn). Classic 1940s recording of a piping giant.

The Drones and the Chanters: An Anthology of Irish Pipering (Claddagh). An important source for modern pipers that features solo tunes in a number of styles.

Seamus Ennis. *The Wandering Minstrel* (Green Linnet) and *Forty Years of Irish Piping* (Green Linnet; cassette only). Two piping classics that belong in the collection of any serious Irish-traditional-music lover.

Dr. Angus MacDonald. *A' Sireadh Spors: Music Played on the Great Highland Bagpipe* (Temple). One of the three musical MacDonald brothers; most of the tunes are traditional, along with some original compositions.

Gordon Mooney. *O'er the Border: Music of the Scottish Borders Played on the Cauld Wind Pipes* (Temple). Mooney is at the forefront of the recent *cauld* wind revival. He plays Border pipes, Scottish smallpipes, and Northumbrian smallpipes.

Hamish Moore. *Cauld Wind Pipes* (Dunkeld). Originally released in 1985, it was the first complete recording of the Lowland, pastoral, and small pipes of Scotland after an eighty-year gap. And in *On Dannsa' Air An Drochaid/Stepping on the Bridge* (Greentrax), Moore explores the Cape Breton/Scottish piping connection. He plays Highland pipes, Border pipes, and Scottish small pipes with a freestyle approach favored by Cape Breton pipers and fiddlers. An important recording.

Liam O'Flynn. *Out to Another Side* (Tara). The ex-Planxty piper has created a marvelous combination of classical and traditional, with his spirited playing of the uilleann pipes soaring ever higher. And in a masterwork O'Flynn showcases the distinctive harmonies of the Voice Squad on "After Aughrim's Great Disaster."

Rare Air. *Space Piper* (Green Linnet). For something completely different, try this Celtic pop rock funk jazz with a bagpipe sound.

Tommy Reck. *The Stone in the Field* (Green Linnet; cassette only). With the exceptions of Johnny Doran and Willie Clancy, Reck was considered the best piper ever to emerge from Ireland and a major influence on later generations. Features hornpipes, reels, jigs, polkas, a mazurka, and a slow air. Essential.

Leo Rowsome. *The King of the Pipers* (Shanachie). A twentieth-century master uilleann piper and mentor of many of today's finest pipers. Includes reels, jigs, and hornpipes.

Shotts & Dykehead Caledonia Pipe Band. *Another Quiet Sunday* (Temple). One of the finer pipe and drum bands around.

Kathryn Tickell. *Borderlands* (Black Crow). Old Northumbrian tunes rub shoulders with Scottish laments. Tickell plays Northumbrian small pipes and fiddle and is joined by fellow Northumbrian Alistair Anderson on concertina, Rod Clements (of Lindisfarne fame) on bass and slide guitar, and a very young Martyn Bennett on Scottish small pipes. Her latest recording, *Debateable Lands* (Park Records), is a lovely thing to behold. It contains many pleasures, from the dignified "The Return," a musical celebration to bring the Lindisfarne Gospels back to Northumberland, to the circular effect of "Rothbury Road."

The breathtaking title suite is Tickell's musical distillation of Border history from the chaos and random violence of the Border *reivers* (cattle raiders) to the (much quieter) present day. Both pensive and wild, it is a perfect summing up of England's northern lands.

Robert Wallace. *Chance Was a Fine Thing* (Claddagh). One of Scotland's major contemporary pipers.

The Whistlebinkies. *A Wanton Fling* (Greentrax) and *Anniversary* (Claddagh). Scotland's answer to the Chieftains; features Rab Wallace on Lowland pipes and Scottish small pipes.

5

The Language of Angels

Songs of the Gael

*Without Gaelic the entire world, the whole of humanity,
would be impoverished.*

–JAMES HUNTER, HISTORIAN

There is no word in Gaelic for goodbye, only for farewell.

–ALISTAIR MACLEOD, CANADIAN WRITER

Gaelic is one of the oldest and richest languages in Europe. The songs of the Gael are breathtakingly beautiful, with a haunting quality that is both delicate and robust. These songs emanate from the soul of a people who have witnessed much suffering over the centuries at the hands of various authorities, including their own kind, yet, in their sorrow, have exhibited a remarkable resilience and emerged from the darkness of their past to the bright day of a full-fledged, late-twentieth-century Gaelic revival. Like the Gaels themselves, the land that they inhabit remains majestic, wild, and stern. Yet beneath the Gaels' thorny exterior lies an unexpected gentleness, a sense of innate dignity and grace that masks the emotional tempest of a tormented soul. To be a Gael is to be both trapped and rejuvenated by the past.

The music of the Gael expresses this inner turmoil. You can hear it in the profoundly sad laments and in the mournful strains of melancholy airs. But there's also a lightness, a randy quality even, that dares to celebrate the mixed emotions that come with living. It is a music of great sorrow and exquisite tragedy but also of remarkable joy and tremendous spirit. Like the enigmatic Gaels themselves, it is a music of paradox. Perhaps because of this paradoxical quality, the music seems to echo the very essence of what it means to be human. No matter what your native tongue, the songs of the Gael connect on a deeply emotional level. True emotions never need any translation.

THE BARDIC TRADITION

The rhythms of Irish and Scottish music are closely intertwined with the rhythms and meters of Gaelic poetry. Much of traditional Gaelic poetry was oral and meant to be sung. The *filidhs*, or trained poets, composed in a literary language—that is, a formal language reportedly derived from early Christian Latin hymns that was common to the educated classes of both Scotland and Ireland—Irish and Scots Gaelic having the same linguistic ancestor.

The highest category on the Celtic social ladder belonged to the *filidhs,* who traveled around the countryside in a manner befitting a king. They would utter panegyrics, or praises, wherever they went, surrounded by a retinue of about two dozen men. Households were expected to extend hospitality to them or face the threat of punishment.

The *filidhs* committed to memory the traditions and genealogies of the people as well as writing original verses. They sang of great Celtic heroes like Cuchulainn and Fionn. The skills that they mastered so thoroughly were taught in bardic schools, which were well established in Scotland by the thirteenth century and flourished in Ireland as late as the seventeenth century. Students in the bardic schools studied heroic literature and often served a twelve-year apprenticeship.

"By the thirteenth century," remarked Gaelic scholar Meg Bateman, "the professional poets had evolved and standardized a literary form of Irish which was used as a lingua franca in both Ireland and Scotland, a form which was to remain unchanged for the next four hundred and fifty years."

KEENING

The Celtic peoples lived in a harsh environment. Death was taken seriously and accorded the proper respect. If a death occurred in a traditional Gaelic-speaking community, for example, the dead person would be watched over for days by close friends and neighbors. Sometimes a plate of salt was laid on his or her chest. The men carried the coffin on their shoulders, often for miles, to its final resting place in the family burial plot. In the Hebrides, every township had a mourning woman who would walk behind the coffin performing a lament called keening (or *caoning* in Gaelic) in the Irish tradition, which is probably the oldest type of Irish song. For a dead chieftain it functioned as an elegy and was composed in syllabic meter by the bard.

Around the turn of the century the Irish playwright John Millington Synge visited the Aran Islands, where he witnessed a keening:

> *While the grave was being opened the women sat down among the flat tombstones, bordered with a pale fringe of early bracken, and began the wild keen, or crying for the dead. Each old woman, as she took her turn in the leading recitative, seemed possessed for the moment with a profound ecstasy of grief, swaying to and fro, and bending her forehead to the stone before her, while she called out to the dead with a perpetually recurring chant of sobs.*

In Wales mourning women were sometimes referred to as "sin-eaters" because they assumed the sins of the dead person—in effect, taking on the role of the local pariah. It was the women who stayed on to comfort the loved ones and prepare food for the men on their return from the burial ground. A death in such close-knit communities was looked upon as a personal loss for everyone. After a funeral on the tiny and now virtually uninhabited island of St. Kilda, the entire population went into mourning for a week.

The bards were employed by clan chiefs. They had to undergo strenuous training, which could involve the memorization of up to 350 poems and stories. The more they could retain, the higher they rose on the bardic social ladder. Some accounts have them memorizing the stories in complete darkness with a blanket wrapped around their heads. This was done, it was said, to aid concentration.

The gift for poetry was not confined to Ireland and Scotland. Much of the best Welsh poetry was written during the twelfth century. Some sources attribute this Celtic renaissance to the patronage of the Welsh king Gruffudd ap Cynan, who spent his youth in Ireland before returning to his native Gwynedd. Others say he brought back to Wales a battery of Irish poets and musicians.

In any event there began a stricter, more rigorous form of composition that was carefully preserved by the families of the hereditary bards. Irish bards, for example, composed many songs that subsequently became part of the repertoire of medieval troubadours.

Irish bards and musicians had been important members of the great households of the Irish aristocracy for many centuries. With the defeat of the last of the Gaelic kings, Hugh O'Neill, at the Battle of Kinsale in 1601, though, the old order fell into an irrevocable decline. Now the once-proud bards wandered the countryside, reduced to a state of virtual poverty. Up until that time the poet had been the principal figure in the musical retinue of an aristocratic household, composing poems that were performed to the accompaniment of the harp. The two roles eventually merged and the later poets were also harpers.

Gaelic songs tend to be very straightforward and realistic, rarely employing narrative; instead they share the thoughts and feelings of the protagonists. The emotions are genuine and, often, surprisingly candid, almost blunt. Said Derick Thomson: "Qualities of passion, tenderness, vividness of imagery, a personal tone and so on are, in fact, the criteria which have determined whether a song is favored or rejected in the general folk tradition of the Gaels."

The well-turned phrase met with much admiration within the Gaelic world. Traditional Gaelic poetry employed an elaborate and complex system of internal rhymes, assonances, and alliteration. The values of Gaelic song stem from an essentially conservative society, one that, according to poet and critic Roderick Watson, was "isolated, clan-based and bound by strong family ties and an enduring sense of place." From the earliest times poetry played a vital role in the perpetuation and preservation of Gaelic society. The poet was amply rewarded for his wordsmithing skill with land, cattle, and gold.

Gaelic poetry tends to be objective, detailed, and descriptive, from the bardic praise poems to the vernacular poems of the eighteenth century. The bardic poems were impersonal in nature, and their verse elaborate. The traditional praise poem could honor a horse, a chief's ancestry, a musical instrument, the land, or the beauty of a young woman. Other poems were laments to a fallen leader or even something as traumatic as the passing of an era. Typically, bardic verses were based on the *rann*, a self-contained four-line stanza that consisted of two couplets and a variety of rhetorical devices, such as internal rhyme and alliteration.

An early and particularly virulent form of Scots Gaelic poetry was the *brosnachadh* poem, which essentially functioned as an incitement to war. A large part of this power comes from the Gaelic bardic system. The poet could either eulogize or satirize the chief; it was a wise leader who knew how to manipulate the special talents and skills of his court poet.

By the sixteenth century Gaelic songs flourished in a sturdy, more vernacular style. Some two centuries later Scots Gaelic vernacular poetry reached its artistic zenith with the work of Alexander MacDonald, Robert Mackay (Rob Donn), and Duncan Bán Macintyre.

GAELIC BARDS AND STORYTELLERS

Probably the most celebrated of the Highland bards was Alexander MacDonald (Alasdair Mac Mhaighstir Alasdair; circa 1695?–1770), who was also the first cousin of the legendary Flora MacDonald. Almost half of his poems were written to further the Jacobite cause and to promote, as Roderick Watson so cogently said, "a vision of resurgent Gaeldom, free at last from the taunt of Lowland manners and values." MacDonald supported Bonnie Prince Charlie during his ill-fated 1745 campaign to restore the Stuart monarchy to the British throne and in the grand *brosnachadh* tradition wrote scathing attacks against King George and Clan Campbell, the ancient enemies of the MacDonalds. He also wrote a poem praising Gaelic as the language spoken by Adam and Eve in the Garden of Eden:

> *She it was that Adam spoke*
> *In Paradise itself*
> *And Gaelic flowed*
> *From Eve's lovely mouth*

Other important Scots Gaelic poets include William Ross (Uilleam Ros, 1762–1790), one of the leading Gaelic love poets of the eighteenth century. His poems are unusual for their passionate first-person accounts, many involving loves lost. Rob Donn (Robert Mackay, 1714–1778) chronicled rural society as well as writing a number of powerful elegies, while Duncan Bán Macintyre (1724–1812) composed songs about the remote hills and running deer of his native Highland glen. Like many Highland poets of his time, he had no formal education. In fact, he was illiterate, yet he managed to create a specific literary vision—he dictated to others who wrote down his words. His most famous work, "Praise of Ben Dorain" was based on a pipe tune, its animated rhythms imitating the *pibroch* changes of theme and variation. He died in Edinburgh in 1812 and is buried within the somber gray walls of Greyfriars kirkyard.

CELTIC WOMEN

Like their Lowland counterparts, women played a vital role in Gaelic Scotland. Although no women were allowed in the bardic schools, they did compose in the folk-song tradition. These were largely work songs—milking, spinning, weaving, and, especially, *waulking* songs, which I will discuss shortly.

Women have also played an important role in the composition of Gaelic songs and poems over the centuries. Although occupational songs, such as *waulking* songs, were primarily written by women and thus expressed women's experiences, women also composed songs of a political nature.

Mary MacLeod (Mairi Nighean Alasdair Ruaidh) (circa 1615–1707) was an important figure in the musical history of Gaelic Scotland, living as she did in a period of transition from the classic to the modern style of Gaelic poetry. She not only wrote laments or eulogies for distinguished members of the great Highland houses but was also the first person to write court poetry in the popular style. Her songs were meant to be sung.

MacLeod was born in Rodel, on the island of Harris, the daughter of Alexander MacLeod, a descendant of the clan chief, and worked as a nurse in the chief's household. While still relatively young, she began to compose poetry. Not all of her work met with approval—she apparently composed a song while in Skye that offended her patron so much that he banished her to the Isle of Mull. MacLeod was allowed to return to Skye with the understanding that she would write no more. She agreed and returned to Dunvegan Castle. But write again she did, which of course incurred the chief's wrath. Scholars dispute why she was forbidden to write but theorize that she may have overstepped her duties as a woman or as a poet, or that her songs may have been too bawdy for contemporary tastes.

Mary MacLeod died at the grand old age of 105. She received an ignominious funeral, buried face down under a pile of stones—a custom, according to Meg Bateman, "introduced by the Norse for the burial of witches." Perhaps her youthful transgression had something to do with it.

Probably the most important Scots Gaelic woman poet of the nineteenth century was Mary MacPherson (Màiri Mhór nan Óran, aka "Big Mary of the Songs," 1821–1898) of Skye. She became one of Gaeldom's great heroes as much for her determined support of Gaelic causes as for her larger-than-life personality and even-larger girth. A nurse by training, she was imprisoned in Inverness for shoplifting, a charge she vehemently denied. Insisting she was framed, she began to protest this and other injustices in song. In "Brosnachadh nan Gaidheal" ("Incitement of the Gaels"), she championed the struggle of the crofters (farmers) to achieve justice during the turbulent land-reform wars on Skye during the 1880s.

> *In the country granted us by the Father*
> *we may not wander the moor or strand,*
> *everything of any worth or value*
> *they deprived us of by the law of the land.*

Contemporary Gaelic singer Catherine-Ann MacPhee offers sensitive interpretations of MacPherson's songs in *Catherine-Ann MacPhee Sings Màiri Mhór* (Greentrax). MacPhee is an emotional singer and her sweet and powerful voice is a glorious instrument that expresses the anger, pride, hope, and ineluctable sadness that infuses MacPherson's songs. It's an elegiac musical portrait of a lost way of life and belongs in the collection of anyone who has even the slightest interest in Gaelic song.

TYPES OF GAELIC SONG

There are many categories of Gaelic song—some unique to Ireland, some to Scotland, and some common to both countries.

CHARACTERISTICS OF SEAN-NÓS

Sung in Irish
A cappella
Unaccompanied

No vibrato
No fluctuation between loud and soft
Emotion expressed through vocal ornamentation, not through
　loudness or softness
Nasal quality
Use of glottal stop or dramatic pause
Melody varies from one verse to the next

Sean-Nós

A distinctive type of traditional Irish song and the oldest surviving form of traditional Irish music, *sean-nós* is a highly ornamented style that owes much to the ancient bardic tradition when poems were transmitted orally from generation to generation. It also draws some of its characteristics from medieval bardic poetry. Some of the songs date back to the pre-Christian era, although most are two or three centuries old. Each dialect of Irish has its own *sean-nós*.

Sean-nós, or old-style singing, as it is called, is sung a cappella and tends to stress the lyrical over the narrative, involving an elaborate system of ornamentation consisting of rolls, melismatic decoration (the addition of several tones to a syllable), and grace notes. In *sean-nós*, important notes are lengthened and the glottal stop—the abrupt ending of a note—is a frequent device. The *sean-nós* singer does not use vibrato; he or she allows the song to speak for itself. Observed Irish musician and writer Tomas O Canainn: "The normal Irish artistic restraint combined with a minute attention to intricate patterns is exhibited in the dance just as surely as in the sean-nós style of singing."

Sean-nós singers don't convey emotion through how loud or soft they sing but rather through ornamentation—how they shape and mold the words and sounds or how much they stress the melody and rhythm.

The *sean-nós* singer sings according to individual taste, which alone determines the pace of the song. The song takes on a life all its own with its own archaic rituals. The singer, appearing as if in a trance, lives very much in the moment, allowing the momentum of the song—its heartfelt presence—to carry the day.

 ## The Blasket and Aran Islands

For centuries a robust Gaelic culture thrived on the Blasket and Aran Islands off the western coast of Ireland.

The Blasket Islands, off the coast of southwest Kerry, consists of six islands and a series of smaller islets. An Blascaod Mor, the largest of the islands, was inhabited until 1953, when the last of the islanders requested to be settled on the mainland. Island pastimes were singing, dancing, storytelling, and conversation. Music functioned not merely as a form of entertainment but also, and most importantly, as a cohesive social force, a common bond within the isolated community. House dances were an integral part of island life, and the common tongue was the Irish language.

Another Irish-language stronghold, the Aran Islands, are situated at the mouth of Galway Bay. John Millington Synge's play *Riders to the Sea* was set on the middle island, Inishmaan, while American filmmaker Robert Flaherty shot his classic documentary *Man of Aran* on Inishmore, the largest island. The indigenous Irish songs are not narrative in the general sense, like the old Scottish and English ballads, but rather are poetic expressions—bits of reflection here, bits of commentary there. Another characteristic of the area and a long-established folk style in the west of Ireland is the use of melisma (the addition of several tones to a syllable).

In many ways *sean-nós* epitomized the inherently cyclical nature of Gaelic art. Traditional Irish singing, like Irish storytelling, is full of ornamentation and elaboration. Joe Heaney, probably the finest *sean-nós* singer of this century, has noted that some of the old tales "would take three months to tell . . . without the story, the song is lost." A good *sean-nós* singer will never sing the same song twice, but will find new meaning, new nuances, a fresh perspective each time. Said Heaney: "When you're telling a story, when you're before an audience telling a story, you've got to elaborate on that story, you can't just tell the story the way you heard it. Add a bit on to it."

More than one critic has observed that the decoration of *sean-nós* bears a striking resemblance to Arabic music. Charles Acton went so far as to compare the warfare and politics of medieval Ireland to the lifestyle and customs of the Beduoins up to the early 1940s.

Sean-nós singers usually have a very nasal quality, giving the impression that the voice may be pitched too high. The closest American analogy would be the singing of the great Appalachian balladeer Jean Ritchie or some bluegrass singers. Irish writer John Millington Synge describes the otherworldly—and not entirely positive—effect the music had on him during his extended stay in the Aran Islands during the early years of the twentieth century:

> The music was much like what I have heard before on the islands—a monotonous chant with pauses on the high and low notes to mark the rhythm; but the harsh nasal tone in which he sang was almost intolerable. His performance reminded me in general effect of a chant I once heard from a party of Orientals I was traveling with in a third-class carriage from Paris to Dieppe, but the islander ran his voice over a much wider range.

When the old Gaelic order collapsed in the seventeenth century as the English assumed power over most of Ireland, there was very little need for songs performed in an ancient and, presumably, archaic language. Gradually, the tradition of *sean-nós* diminished. It did not, however, disappear.

In recent years there has been a resurgence of interest in this most ancient of singing. Another important *sean-nós* singer and a contemporary of Joe Heaney, Paddy Tunney was born in Glasgow in 1921 but raised in Ireland. The love of music ran through his veins—his mother, Brigid, was a singer. Not as traditional sounding as Heaney, perhaps—and hence a bit more accessible to modern ears—Tunney's rich lilting voice recalls the intricate notes of pipe and fiddle music.

The Connemara Gaeltacht is one of the few places left in Ireland where _sean-nós_ is still very much a living tradition. And in recent decades the Munster tradition of _sean-nós_ in western Cork has undergone a latter-day renaissance.

Some traces of _sean-nós_ can even be found in Celtic pop culture. Liam Ó Maonlaí, lead singer of the Irish rock band Hothouse Flowers, has credited the ancient _sean-nós_ tradition in developing his own style while Sinéad O'Connor's taut vocals in "I Am Stretched on Your Grave" owe much to _sean-nós_. The voice of Afro-Celt Sound System's Iarla Ó Lionáird is a magical instrument all its own, a voice rooted in the past yet very much in tune with the present and as close to Celtic soul music as you're likely to get within the tradition.

WAULKING THE WOOL

The act of _waulking_ is actually that of beating wool into shape. Fulling or _waulking_ of homemade cloth was carried out by pounding the material against a board or trampling it with the feet. The way the wool was _waulked_ varied from place to place but generally a wet cloth was beaten on a wooden board, which could vary in length and width. Tweed, up to seventy yards long, was soaked in a solution of stale urine and water in order to camouflage the oils that had been used for dressing the wool. Then the cloth was placed on a board and, typically, a team of six to twelve women either beat or rubbed it with their feet or their hands.

Ossianic Ballads and Fenian Lays

Ossianic ballads (sometimes known as Fenian ballads) were sung in court and celebrated the feats and adventures of Fionn and his band of warriors known as the Fianna Eireann (the soldiers of Ireland), army of the High King, Cormac Mac Airt.

The adventures of Fionn and his son Ossian (or Oisin), the legendary poet of Irish and Scottish tradition, were retold in lays. In some versions, Ossian comes back from the Land of Youth (Tir na nOg) to accompany Patrick on his mission to Christianize Ireland.

Ossianic ballads, considered the highest type of song in a Gaelic singer's repertoire, were usually set in stanzas or four-line verses, each line consisting of seven syllables. Lays were sung by all classes in Gaelic society. Themes tend to be of the romantic or other-worldly variety. "Over the centuries the lays were tremendously popular with all classes of Gaelic society, from the most southerly tip of Ireland to the most northerly point of Gaelic Scotland," wrote the noted Irish music scholar Breandan Breathnach. Believed to have arisen in medieval times—some were composed in the twelfth century or later—they were sung to chants thought to be ecclesiastical in origin. Indeed, some find them slightly reminiscent of Latin plainchant. Until fairly recently, they were still sung in Gaelic-speaking areas, especially in the Hebrides and, in particular, the islands of North and South Uist.

Waulking Songs

"One [woman] sings the song, while all take up the chorus, weird and plaintive, and as they toss and tumble the cloth, passing the folds from hand to hand, a stranger, who saw them at the work of the first time, might be pardoned for thinking them mad." So said Mrs. Morrison, in *Transactions of the Gaelic Society of Inverness* (1887).

While the Highland bards were keeping their bosses happy, the ordinary folk had their own songs to entertain them, such as these Gaelic labor songs or *waulking* songs. Mostly anonymous in origin, some songs can be traced as far back as the sixteenth century. *Waulking* (pronounced "walking" and known as *luadh* in Gaelic) is often described as one of the central institutions of female society in Gaelic Scotland.

Waulking sessions (called milling frolics in Cape Breton) were social gatherings. A night was chosen, women gathered, and food was prepared. In the cold Hebridean winter, it was a good way to pass the time, get some work done, and have some fun in the process. It wasn't all just singing, either. *Waulking* was also a time to hear the latest island gossip, to share tales and jokes, to catch up on old news.

Waulking songs are usually very rhythmic and fast. They had to be, to keep up with the pace of the work. The songs were often sung in a call-and-response pattern. A typical *waulking* song consists of lines or couplets interspersed with refrains of words or what are called vocables or sometimes both, often having little if any meaning in the conventional sense. The work was made easier, of course, by the rhythmic singing. To help stretch out the song a bit—and prolong the night's pleasure—the chorus was sung after every line, and in many cases each line itself was repeated.

Thematically, the songs were often lighthearted and trivial, but they also spoke directly to matters that concerned women. A good number of them are laments—men lost at sea is a common theme. Others are matchmaking songs, and it may surprise some listeners to learn just how bawdy some of them can be.

Waulking songs flourished the longest in the Hebridean communities of Barra, South Uist, and Benbecula. Although the songs are still an important arsenal of any traditional Gaelic singer worth his or her salt, the actual *waulking* of cloth has apparently not been done—except perhaps in an artificial way—since World War II, when industrialization made it obsolete. The last domestic *waulkings* in the Hebrides are said to have taken place in the 1950s.

Mouth Music:
Celtic Rap?

Mouth music or *puirt a beul* (pronounced "poarst-a-beeal") is a style of Scots Gaelic vocal music intended for dancing. In Ireland it's called diddling, or lilting. Whatever the name, it literally means "tune-from-mouth." Sometimes it's described as employing "nonsense" words, but more than a few singers would take issue with this. And indeed, although the words many not mean anything in the usual sense, it is the *sound* of the words that takes precedence. In fact, some performers of mouth music go so far as to insist that *puirt-a-beul* are more tunes than songs. Still, many do have lyrics, even if they tend to be of a rudimentary nature. In an increasingly mechanized world, it's somehow reassuring to know that the sound of the human voice still can work its own magic.

Mouth music conjures up the sound of the bagpipes. There are three main types of mouth music: dance music (*ceol beg*); vocalization (*ceol mor*) that evokes the *pibroch*; and a combination of the two. Similarly, there are two primary styles: the ornamental use of vocables, which are rhythmic but with no particular meaning, and the performance of actual songs. Sometimes the Gaelic phrases imitate the calls of birds.

"Scottish Gaelic is unusual in that vowels can be of different lengths," noted Michael Newton in the Cape Breton newspaper *Am Briaghe*, "and the language itself has naturally within it rhythms and cadences which can encode very complex musical phrases." It is this very complexity that makes Gaelic and *puirt-a-beul* the perfect musical match.

In the late nineteenth century, a particularly virulent form of religious fervor swept the Highlands and people were once again—it seems to occur in cycles—encouraged to put down their fiddles and pipes. Some ministers even insisted that burning them to be the only true solution to the "problem." Music, insisted the clergy, could lead to dancing and other "sinful" practices, which is not to say that the musical impulse disappeared. Although instruments may have been hard to come by or played at the risk of raising a minister's considerable wrath, that most noble of instruments—the human voice—remained. *Puirt-a-beul* (mouth music) kept the musical spirit alive during these dark days.

> The good men and the good ministers . . . did away with the songs and stories, the music and the dancing, the sports and the games that were perverting the minds and ruining the souls of the people . . .
>
> They made the people break and burn their pipes and fiddles. If there was a foolish man here and there who demurred, the good ministers and the good elders themselves broke and burnt their instruments.
>
> —WOMAN, ISLE OF LEWIS (1928), FROM ALEXANDER
> CARMICHAEL'S *CARMINA GADELICA*

Today, mouth music is featured prominently in the repertoire of most traditional Gaelic singers.

Gaelic Psalm Singing

Another major category of Scots Gaelic song is psalm songs—the unison singing of psalms in Gaelic that is indigenous to the western Highlands and Islands. Gaelic psalm singing is almost exclusively confined to Gaelic services in Presbyterian churches in Scotland, the most ornamental styles in the islands of Lewis and Harris— with the exception of the American South and some areas of the Gaidhealtachd, where, said Morag MacLeod, distinguished Gaelic music authority, "The Gaels have held on to it stubbornly and have made it their own."

"Nothing like it is to be heard anywhere else in western Europe," declared John Purser, while the distinguished American folk collector Alan Lomax has referred to the pre-Christian choral songs of the Hebrides as "among the noblest folk tunes of western Europe."

During the Reformation and post-Reformation a desire for simplicity in church services as well as in the presentation of church music developed in Scotland and England. In 1643 the Westminster Assembly suggested that, since many members of congregations could not read, the minister "or some other fit person appointed by him" should recite the psalm, line by line, before being sung by the rest of the congregation. This person, whether minister or the minister's proxy, is called the precentor and the actual process of introducing each line to the congregation is called lining out. The overall effect is one of emotion freely expressed, with everyone using their own grace notes yet somehow the whole congregation coming together.

Scottish psalm tunes written during the Reformation were published in English in Edinburgh in the mid-sixteenth century. Eventually these tunes made their way north, where they were given a Highland feel. By decorating each note heavily, the original melody became virtually unrecognizable. Some music scholars have described psalm songs, known as long tunes, as the vocal equivalent of *pibrochs*.

The sum total of the Gaelic psalm-singing repertoire consists of only seventeen to twenty tunes—such songs as "Dundee," "Martyrs," and "Elgin" form the heart of the tradition—yet it is a formidable heritage that shows no signs of dying out or of losing its ability to move or capture the attention of the casual listener. Indeed, for the visitor, linking the printed tune with the sung Gaelic version is an effort in frustration. Noted Morag MacLeod:

> There is no clear break between the precentor's chant and the beginning or end of the original musical text; the singing is very slow, possibly to convey the solemnity of the occasion even if a psalm is a joyful one; and passing notes and grace notes are introduced to decorate the basic melody . . .

A parallel of sorts can be drawn with the early American shape-note songs. The southern singing master taught countless of country people—many illiterate—to sight-read choral music using the simple "shape-note" method where particular shapes indicated the musical scale. The songs contained three- and four-part arrangements for unaccompanied voices. Recalling their Hebridean counterparts, the songs smack strongly of the most severe kind of Calvinism. What's more, quite a few of them were set to Scottish tunes, such as "The Blue Bells of Scotland" or "The Braes o' Balquhidder" or, in some way, either through melody or rhythmic pattern, suggest a Celtic background.

By the nineteenth century the long tunes were no longer a part of ordinary worship in the Hebrides—perhaps their length and complexity had something to do with it—but a similar process was applied to newer tunes and still survives to this day, again on the islands of Lewis and Harris in particular.

The American music historian Robert Cantwell hears a connection between Gaelic music, especially the psalm songs, and bluegrass. Indeed, others have also said that the high lonesome sound of bluegrass may be rooted in traditional psalm singing, which uses a tense, high-pitched style that often turns into a falsetto. Songs are frequently shouted and ornamented with rising and falling notes.

Some detect less obvious parallels with other parts of the world. John Purser, for example, describes a similarity between Gaelic psalm singing and Middle Eastern chanting. In his book *Scotland's Music*, he compared the singing of two Christian communities, one in Ethiopia and one in the western Highlands, and found the same scale and pitch, and the identical manner of decorations.

Purser explained the Gaels retained a style of singing with roots in a very ancient Christian chant tradition. Ethiopian church services had existed in isolation for centuries and are said to have retained the oldest Christian music in the world. Somehow these two separate yet strangely similar worlds are closer than either community realizes.

Other Types of Gaelic Song

Many Gaelic songs are associated with solitary activities, such as milking, spinning, and churning songs. Lullabies are quite prominent in the Gaelic tradition, although most modern listeners would cringe at the violent subject matter. One of the most famous, and most graphic, is "Griogal Chridhe" ("Beloved Gregor"), in which the wife laments the killing of her husband. It seems to date as far back as 1570 and includes a reference to the ancient practice of drinking the blood of a dead sweetheart.

Flyting was a type of Gaelic song especially popular in fifteenth- and sixteenth-century Scotland that survived well into the eighteenth. Involving a complex pattern of internal rhymes and alliterations, *flytings* were essentially satirical jabs full of venom and bite.

Romanticism and the Celtic Twilight

It's hard to believe now, but a few centuries ago a young Highlander and schoolmaster from the Inverness area named James Macpherson (not to be confused with the fiddler James MacPherson discussed in chapter 3) set the civilized world afire with the darkly evocative tales of an ancient Celt named Ossian. So widespread was the impact that everyone from Lord Byron to Thomas Jefferson was affected. Indeed, Jefferson went so far as to proclaim Ossian "the greatest poet that has ever existed."

In 1759, when still in his twenties, Macpherson confided to the playwright John Home about his forays into the Highlands, where he had collected a number of Gaelic tales said to be third-century manuscripts written by the ancient Celtic hero Ossian. Intrigued, Home asked Macpherson for a translation. The young Scot was more than willing to oblige, and Home dutifully brought a copy to an Edinburgh publisher. In doing so, he set in motion one of the most remarkable publishing success stories of the eighteenth or, indeed, any century.

At the height of its popularity, *Ossian* was translated into numerous languages: Italian in 1763, German in 1764, and French in 1774. Even today a certain stubborn interest persists—a Japanese translation appeared in 1971, a Russian translation as recently as 1983. Macpherson's *Ossian* influenced many writers and composers, including Friedrich von Schiller, Victor Hugo, William Blake, William Butler Yeats, and, in the music world, Brahms and, most especially, Mendelssohn, whose *Hebrides Overture (Fingal's Cave)* was composed in 1830.

Some of Macpherson's "poems" were based on the Fenian cycle of heroic tales. "But," wrote Roderick Watson, "he could never produce the manuscripts he claimed he had seen and the poems remain essentially his own work, a vision of a lost age of gentle and valiant warriors."

Other critics are more forgiving of his lapses. "He was not a sham—no more than [Robert] Burns," says John Purser. "Like Burns he mixed his own ideas with traditional material and it's not always easy to say where one stops and the other begins."

How to explain its inexplicable appeal? Some feel *Ossian* represented the Gael as the ultimate Romantic, epitomizing Rousseau's "noble savage," and offered a welcome opium from the deadly reason and intellect of the Enlightenment. Here was writing ruled by passion and exemplifying larger-than-life heroic virtues. The modern city dweller could thus vicariously identify with this most noble of earth's creatures, a hero worthy of Homer and Dante and what's more, a homegrown Celtic hero, a Celtic warrior who had lived in a misty, fog-shrouded past, safely removed from the political machinations of the modern world.

Macpherson may have set the scene for a Celtic explosion, but it was Sir Walter Scott who carried the torch forward and took it to new heights of popularity with works like *The Lady of the Lake* in 1810 and the *Waverley* novels of later years. In its first year alone, *Lady* sold some twenty thousand copies, an enormous number for its day.

Scott drew on Scottish history and literature to create a romantic image of his homeland—a Paradise Lost landscape of mountains and lochs and lone pipers in a remote glen, a Celtic Twilight fabricated by non-Gaels for the enjoyment of non-Gaels. Writers and visitors "discovered" the Highlands, too, and, since then, have never stopped coming. Queen Victoria made it a fashionable place to visit.

The Ossianic fad was certainly fueled by the Celtic Twilight movement, part and parcel of a broader romantic movement and a rage for things Celtic that swept across much of Europe as a direct reaction against the Enlightenment. Among the romantics were the Lake District poets of Wordsworth, Coleridge, and Southey, as well as Keats, Byron, Shelley, and the mystical visions of William Blake and the bucolic earthiness of Robert Burns.

TARTAN AND GAELIC IDENTITY

According to historian Hugh Cheape, the word *tartan* probably derives from the French *tiretaine* and was in circulation by the early sixteenth century, when Scotland enjoyed close links with France.

Generally speaking the use of checks and stripes in patterned cloth has existed throughout history and in different cultures. Yet the story of tartan is a bit more complex—it is a distinctive woolen cloth woven in a regular pattern called a *sett* (a term now usually associated with a family or clan name).

Originally tartan was not intended to express identity, noted Cheape. Rather, more often than not, a plant or flower worn on the side of a hat indicated where one's loyalties lay. But through the work of writers and the illustrations of artists as well as the influence of politicians and members of the monarchy not to mention the growth of the commercial fashion and manufacturing industries, tartan came to be connected to specific clans. The clan *(clann* is Gaelic for "family") refers to a grouping of individuals or families who claim descent from a common ancestor or are connected in other significant ways, such as through military service, geography, or shared interests.

Prior to the sixteenth century, said Cheape, "there is no evidence in Scotland for tartan" as we know it today, although, he added, it is likely that various fabrics with checks and stripes did exist. For the most part though a typical Highland male of the period would have donned a shirt "and a plaid or mantle worn over it," with his legs exposed. It was not until the late seventeenth or early eighteenth century, he noted, that any attempt at uniformity "was adopted by family, clan or district." By the 1880s clan societies had mushroomed across Scotland, fostering in their wake an even deeper sense of clan identity.

Conventional Gaelic praise poetry often mentioned tartan and its connotations of dignity and nobility. According to Cheape, "the Gaelic word most commonly used to describe tartan is *breacan*," which refers to the plaid "gathered at the waist by a belt" or "pinned on the shoulder by a brooch," again with the legs exposed since fashion of the time dictated that the plaid be "kilted above the knee," as the expression went. Short hose or stockings were also worn, noted Cheape. The leg covering was a sort of close-fitting trousers known as *trews*.

It was not until the Act of Union of 1707—that is, the union of the parliaments of England and Scotland—that tartan began to be widely associated with Scottish nationalism. In 1745 Prince Charles Edward Stuart adopted the Highland dress as the uniform for his tattered Highland army; thus tartan became a potent symbol of Jacobitism—in other words, a blatant advertisement for Scottish nationhood. Essentially, the Westminster government felt threatened by the tartan and all that it represented. The following year the Act of Proscription outlawed the wearing of Highland dress. For those who transgressed, the punishment could be harsh—including imprisonment and, in severe cases, transportation to the colonies. In 1748, for example, Cheape cites the experience of a man named Mackay who was arrested in Inverness and charged with wearing the ancient costume. He protested to the authorities that he had no other clothes and, anyway, was "unaware" of the law. Nevertheless, the hapless Highlander was sentenced to six months' imprisonment. In 1782 the act was finally repealed.

The legislation outlawing Highland dress did not affect those who served in the Highland regiments, however. The military success of the troops helped popularize—and indeed legitimize—the wearing of tartan. The Highland soldier, swathed in tartan and evoking the image of a heroic Gaelic past, represented all that was good and just and noble about Scotland.

The interest continued into the next century. In the 1860s English critic Matthew Arnold referred to the Celtic spirit as a "bromide" for raging materialism, while a few decades later, in the 1890s, another type of Celtic revival occurred. This latter-day Celtic Twilight was a literary movement that took its name from a collection of short stories by William Butler Yeats. These purveyors of the Celtic Twilight attributed to Gaelic poetry and Gaelic society in general qualities that it never really possessed. Meanwhile, William Morris and John Ruskin were advocating a new type of art and a particular brand of utopian socialism, respectively. In the publishing sphere Glasgow professor James G. Fraser (1854–1941) began work on his seminal *The Golden Bough*.

A new outburst of interest in "Ossianism" influenced craft and design and art-nouveau styles that incorporated Celtic-inspired decorations of the sort being produced in Glasgow by the Macdonald sisters, Herbert MacNair, and the young architect and designer Charles Rennie Mackintosh. Today, Mackintosh is enjoying a well-deserved acceptance that he never received during his own lifetime.

In Ireland, the Aran Islands were to become a popular Celtic pilgrimage site. In search of an elusive Celtic soul, a new generation of Irish scholars and writers—many of them members of the largely Protestant Anglo-Irish Ascendancy—looked to the islands as the repository of the country's ancient Celtic language and culture, in much in the same way that Americans looked to the South as "authentic" culture or the Scots to the Highlands. Hence, the Arans and their Irish-speaking inhabitants were transformed into a powerful symbol of the Irish cultural revival. Seminal figures of the revival included William Butler Yeats, John Millington Synge, and Lady Gregory. This literary renaissance was accompanied by a revival of interest in traditional Irish music and folklore, especially in the native Celtic languages.

Ironically, as the tradition declined, interest among collectors increased. Forde, Hudson, Piggott, Goodman, Petrie, and others like them scoured the countryside searching for authentic Irish songs and tunes. At the same time, the Young Ireland movement introduced popular patriotic songs in English.

Political activities and the movement for the restoration or, at least, the appreciation of the Irish language toward the end of the century helped stress the importance of traditional Irish music. In 1888 P. W. Joyce published *Irish Music and Songs*, the first collection to contain words in the Irish language that were connected to the tunes.

Of Mods and Festivals

In 1891 An Comunn Gaidhealach (the Highland Society) was founded. The following year the first National Mod, an annual competitive festival of Gaelic song and literature, took place in the western Highland town of Oban. The *mod* was very much a product of its time and perpetuated numerous late-nineteenth-century ideals of what constituted Gaelic song. Essentially, it introduced alien elements into the Gaelic tradition, such as group singing, the use of harmony, and the addition of piano as an accompanying instrument. Quite often, performers were judged by non-Gaels based on Western musical standards.

One long-standing legacy of the mod is the existence of choral groups. Today Aberdeen, Dingwall, Edinburgh, Glasgow, Inverness, the Isle of Mull, Stornoway, among other Scottish cities and towns and rural communities, boast their own Gaelic choirs.

The *mod* continues to be an annual event on the Scottish musical calendar. Each October the week-long National Mod is held in a different Scottish location. There are also local *mods*.

GAELIC
SONG COLLECTORS

A controversial figure in the Gaelic song collecting tradition, Marjorie Kennedy-Fraser was born in Perth in 1857 and came from a large musical family. She used to accompany her famous father on his many singing tours.

Kennedy-Fraser first began to study Gaelic music in 1882. Years later, in 1908 she met Kenneth MacLeod, who collaborated with her on *Songs of the Hebrides* (1909). The first volume was published in 1909, followed by subsequent volumes in 1917 and 1921 and finally in 1925. In recent years numerous musicologists have argued that they did more harm than good. Kennedy-Fraser may have been a folk song collector and a musician, but she was looking for melodies to perform in a concert hall setting. Thus she changed and "improved" the songs to fit her audience of mostly middle- or upper-class tastes, altering the rhythms and tempo to conform to a more typically classical mode.

Compare Kennedy-Fraser's dubious work with the achievements of John Francis Campbell (1822–1885), John Lorne Campbell, Margaret Fay Shaw, or, earlier, the collections of Frances Tolmie, a native of Skye. Campbell is best remembered today for his studies of the Gaelic oral tradition. Inspired by the Brothers Grimm in Germany and by Scandinavian scholars, he set out to gather the popular tales of the West Highlands. His aim was to capture, as accurately as possible, the words of the storytellers and to translate them literally, a far cry from the methods of a Kennedy-Fraser. Tolmie collected Gaelic songs in the 1850s. And, a century later, in 1950, the Library of Congress commissioned the American folklorist Alan Lomax, with the assistance of Calum Maclean and Hamish Henderson, to collect Gaelic songs in the Highlands and Islands.

One suspects that Christine Primrose, one of the finest of the current crop of contemporary Gaelic singers, was referring to the *mod*, when she commented that "there has been a tendency to undervalue traditional Gaelic singing. Certain sectors of the Scottish musical establishment have tried to mold it into a kind of stylized, drawing room entertainment."

Fortunately, in recent decades attitudes have shifted away from competitive festivals to a more relaxed and authentically Gaelic atmosphere in which music and song develop from the natural environment. In the early 1980s there emerged an alternative to the highly structured *mod* in the form of the modern *feis* (festival) movement. The first *feis* took place on the island of Barra in 1981 and has since been joined by at least two dozen others. Unlike the *mods*, these festivals are strictly noncompetitive and cater specifically, but not exclusively, to children, offering residential tutoring in Gaelic song and music.

Another welcome addition to the Gaelic music scene is Ceolas, a week-long music and dance summer school of Gaelic step dancing, music, and song held in South Uist and organized by Proiseact nan Ealan (The National Gaelic Arts Project). This school explores the connections among traditional Scottish music, song, and dance. It's the brainchild of piper Hamish Moore, and what sets it apart from other summer schools is a sincere and thus far successful attempt to place the music within its natural environment. Students learn, for example, how Gaelic song and fiddle and pipes are interrelated and how they play off one another.

OTHER TYPES OF CELTIC SONG

Brittany

Breton-language song is called *kan ha diskan*, a type of responsive singing found in central western Brittany. Traditionally, it is sung by two singers, a *kaner* (meaning "singer" in Breton) and a *diskaner* or "counter-singer." The *kaner* begins and the *diskaner* repeats each phrase.

Gwerz consists of a repertoire of ballads of a historical, legendary, or dramatic nature while *son* refers to the remainder of Breton-language songs, including love songs, drinking songs, and lighter songs for dancing.

Wales

The Welsh developed an elaborate system of classical poetry and an impressive body of medieval literature. Yet the reign of the Tudors and their attempts to anglicize the native population placed tremendous strains on indigenous Welsh culture. One unfortunate result was the almost complete loss of the Welsh musical tradition. Still, although the music of the court may have been irrevocably damaged, the music of the folk, or *gwerin*, lived on in taverns or indeed most anywhere that ordinary people gathered. During the eighteenth century, however, the Welsh received another major body blow to their language and culture with the conservative Methodist revival.

A distinctively Welsh musical feature is *pennillion*—the singing of improvised verses or set poems to an original counterpoint that, in turn, is built around a well-known harp melody. A national *pennillion* festival is held annually. Another traditional fixture of mid-Wales is the three- and four-part harmony of *plygain* carol-singing, which is performed from midnight to dawn on Christmas morning. Welsh male choirs remain a regular feature of Welsh rural life.

The Isle of Man and Cornwall

An independent island, the Isle of Man is part of the British Commonwealth. The island enacts its own laws and has its own parliament, called the Tynwald, which is located in the capital of Douglas. The island is named after the Irish sea god Manannán or, in Manx, Ellan Vannin.

In 1896 A. W. Moore published *Manx Ballads and Songs*, which contains probably the largest collection of songs in the Manx language. In recent years there has been a revival of interest in Manx songs. A few new songs as well as several hymns have been composed in the old Gaelic tongue.

Two of the best known and loveliest Manx songs must be "Tra Va Ruggit Creest," an old Manx carol whose title means "When Christ Was Born," and the traditional Manx lament "Ny Kiree fo

Niaghtey" ("The Sheep Under the Snow") about the loss of more than two thousand sheep during a devastating winter storm. Both melodies appear in Charles Guard's Celtic harp recording *Avenging and Bright* (Shanachie).

Although Cornish as a living language died out in the late eighteenth century, some old Cornish literature has been preserved, including five mystery plays, the fifteenth-century *Ordinalia*, and the saint's play *Bewnans Meryasek* of the early sixteenth century. Our own day has seen a revival of interest in the Cornish language and Cornish-language song. The Cornish revival band Bucca has probably done more than anybody in recent memory to promote the indigenous culture of Cornwall.

THE GAELIC REVIVAL TODAY

The modern Gaelic-music revival in Scotland started in the early 1980s. Bands like Runrig and more recently Capercaillie have brought Gaelic to the forefront, in the process introducing it to new generations of Gaels and non-Gaels alike. Indeed, several years back, Capercaillie entered the British top forty with a Gaelic *waulking* song.

In the early 1980s Barry Ronan, a native of the Aran Islands, recorded original compositions, all in the Irish language, one of the earlier attempts to sing rock songs in Irish. Significantly, several of the biggest names on the Irish music scene today are Irish speakers, including members of Altan and Hothouse Flowers. Considered the best traditional Irish group around, Altan is led by the singing and fiddling of Mairéad Ní Mhaonaigh, who hails from Donegal.

The younger generation of singers in Irish includes Tríona Ní Dhomhnaill, formerly of the Bothy Band, the short-lived Skara Brae, and Relativity; and the Brennan family from the Donegal Gaeltacht, who make up the membership of the versatile and durable Clannad. In the early years of their career, they sang almost exclusively in Irish. Truth be told, lead vocalist Maire Brennan has enjoyed a fairly successful solo career, although it pales in comparison to the overwhelming success of the family's youngest sibling, Enya (born Eithne Ni Bhraonain), whose otherworldly vocals—and influence—seem to be everywhere from automobile commercials to best-selling motion picture soundtracks and Christmas recordings.

Traditional Gaelic singers Flora MacNeill, Anne Lorne Gillies, and the late Kitty MacLeod have been bringing the songs of the Gael to mainstream audiences for decades. In recent years they have been joined by a younger generation of Gaelic singers, including Christine Primrose from Lewis, Mairi MacInnes from Arran, Catherine-Ann MacPhee from Barra, and Arthur Cormack from Skye.

Mac-talla (meaning "echo") is a Scots Gaelic supergroup that consists of Primrose, Eilidh MacKenzie, Alison Kinnaird, Blair Douglas, and Cormack. Primrose, one of the foremost Gaelic singers of today, is a bit ahead of her time. Her first record of Gaelic songs, *Alte Mo Ghaoil* (Temple), released in 1982, was refreshingly free of the overly referential treatment that many singers previously had brought to the music. On the contrary, Primrose was not afraid to explore her own style, allowing later Gaelic singers to express themselves freely and openly.

Eilidh MacKenzie, also from Lewis, is one of the youngest of the traditional Gaelic singers and a respected Gaelic scholar in her own right. She earned her degree in Celtic studies and music at the University of Glasgow and has spent some time in Nova Scotia and Prince Edward Island. Recently, Eilidh joined her sisters Fiona and Gillian to form a new band called, appropriately enough, MacKenzie. And, in what must be one of the most encouraging developments in the Gaelic-speaking world, she has written a number of original songs in the language, both on her solo recording *Eideadh Na Sgeulachd (The Raiment of the Tale)* (Temple) and with her sisters, Fiona and Gillian, on their debut CD, *Camhanach*.

The Edinburgh-born Kinnaird is probably the foremost player of the Scottish harp and wire-strung *clarsach* and has led the way in the contemporary revival of the harp in Scotland. In 1978 she recorded *The Harp Key*, the first record of Scottish harp music, after conducting much original research into old manuscripts and collections.

Accordionist and keyboard player Blair Douglas was an early member of Runrig and hails from Skye, as does Arthur Cormack. At seventeen Cormack was the youngest singer to receive a gold medal at the Mod, the annual festival of Gaelic song. Today he is an active figure on the burgeoning Gaelic-music scene as a performer, activist, record producer, and indefatigable promoter of all things Gaelic.

In a category by herself is Talitha MacKenzie. A native New Yorker (real name: Nancy Claypoole), MacKenzie learned Gaelic from a teach-yourself manual and Gaelic singing from a book on Hebridean folk songs. A Russian major at Connecticut College, she graduated from the New England Conservatory of Music with a degree in music history and ethnomusicology. Arriving in Scotland for the first time in 1979, she returned in 1984 and three years later enrolled at the School of Scottish Studies in Edinburgh. By that time she had committed herself to a new country and a new career.

MacKenzie is probably best known as being one-half of the world-music duo Mouth Music, whose debut recording in the early 1990s topped the *Billboard* charts. After her musical partner Martin Swan left, she continued the original Mouth Music project under her own name and released a second solo album *Solas (Solace)* in 1993.

Mouth Music's patented blend of African rhythms with Gaelic-language vocals raised more than a few eyebrows at the time of the duo's initial release. MacKenzie has insisted, though, it was never her intention to start a fire amid the smoking embers of traditional music. But start a fire she did—intentional or not—and other artists ranging from Afro-Celt Sound System to Paul Mounsey have experimented with various musical minglings.

"I never set out to be controversial," said MacKenzie. "I never set out to be avant-garde. I like to go under the umbrella of world music because that gives me carte blanche.

"For the most part the people I met who were very knowledgeable about this music were quite content to sing in a house concert . . . or maybe in a village hall. But nobody in my group had the aspiration of taking it and bringing it to a wide amount of people. As a matter of fact, the mindset at the time was that if you went commercial with the music you were destroying it, or destroying the soul of it."

MacKenzie thought otherwise and ventured forward on her personal quest to see where the mingling of cultures would lead. In a recent CD, *Spiorad* (Spirit), she showcases Serbian, Breton, and Bulgarian selections accompanied by a various instruments including marimba, saxophone, conga, African drum, bowed sitar, and even a recording of crackling fire.

MUSIC FROM THE WEST

The most important rockers to emerge from the Scottish Gaidhealtachd is Runrig, a six-man band from the Isle of Skye in the Western Isles. The best Gaelic poetry is simple and direct, and Runrig follow in this tradition. Its common reference points are to Gaelic place-names and people such as Neil Gunn and Sorley Maclean—although they can just as easily mention readily identifiable names from Western culture, from Elvis to the Beatles. More than any Gaelic band before or since, Runrig have raised the profile of Gaelic in the broader mainstream culture.

In 1978 the members released their first record, *Play Gaelic*, which, as its name indicates, consisted of all-Gaelic material. Some may have considered it a rather foolhardy and wasteful choice. But, said former lead singer Donnie Munro, "That was a statement for the time.

"There's always been this confusion amongst people about the band's development. I think there was a feeling of relief for some people to know that there was actually a new Gaelic album for young people committed to doing new writing. There also was the old guard, who saw it as a threat in some way to the actual tradition, and didn't like the type of presentation. But generally speaking, there was a very favorable, supportive reaction."

Like most young people of their generation, they had grown up listening to rock music, and saw no reason why they couldn't perform the music they loved, but from a Celtic perspective. Where was it written that rock could be sung only in the English language? Although Munro is reluctant to accept credit, Runrig almost singlehandedly created a new genre: Gaelic rock.

"We never saw writing in Gaelic as a political statement," Rory Macdonald once said. "People tell us we've done so much for Gaelic, but we never ever set out to write in Gaelic in order to broaden the acceptance of the language."

 ## ALISTAIR MACLEOD: HAUNTED BY ANCESTORS

And what is the significance of ancestral islands long left and never seen?

—Alistair MacLeod

A strong sense of place suffuses the work of the Scots-Canadian writer Alistair MacLeod. In his excellent short story "The Closing Down of Summer," a group of Cape Breton miners gather around the grave of a comrade who died a violent death, shouting a few farewell words in Gaelic. Just as these miners are aware of their own imminent mortality, the narrator is aware of the precarious nature of the Gaelic language, teetering, as it does, between life and a museum piece. He and his co-workers speak "in an old archaic language private words that reach no one," preferring to sing the old Gaelic songs rather than modern hits because they belong to the world of the "privately familiar."

In his first novel, *No Great Mischief*, MacLeod tells the story of a particular branch of the MacDonalds, Red Calum, or Calum Ruadh's, clan. Like virtually all of MacLeod's work, it revolves around two familiar themes: family obligation and loyalty. In MacLeod's rather insular world, the past is never far from the present; indeed, it often comes back to haunt you.

MacLeod doesn't write in a vacuum, though. There are others like him, such as fellow Cape Bretoners D.R. MacDonald and Tess Gillis, who are inspired by the old songs, by the aching melodies, and who are indeed haunted by ancestors. The music—the mournful ballads, the timeless airs—link the living with the dead, the past with the present.

MacLeod is a late-twentieth-century embodiment of the voice of the oral tradition, in this case, a Celtic tradition that has survived many centuries and many miles. He writes of an ancestral past that affects—no, permeates—the present. In a world characterized by raging capitalism and anonymity, that in itself is a remarkable achievement.

Macdonald's comments notwithstanding, the music of Runrig is revolutionary in the sense that they are considered the first fully-fledged rock band to emerge from the Gaidhealtachd and, most important for the perpetuation of Gaelic culture, they are one of the few bands to create contemporary compositions in the Gaelic tongue. Indeed, many of Runrig's songs have already entered the repertoires of traditional Gaelic singers, such as Catherine-Ann MacPhee from Barra and Mairi MacInnes from Arran. For the first time in modern pop culture, young Gaels could hear rock songs sung in their own language. By writing songs in a rock vein, Runrig, in essence, reclaimed Gaelic for the young. They made the language—which until fairly recently was considerable a barbarous and backward tongue—something that young people could embrace with pride and dignity. Gaelic culture was not only worth saving, they told us, it was worth promoting.

Munro, who left the band in 1997 in rather acrimonious conditions to pursue a career in politics, is, according to journalist Tom Morton, the descendant of a blind nineteenth-century Skye fiddler also named Donald Munro (An Dall Munrotha). Converted by evangelical preachers who were touring the Hebrides, this older Munro then proceeded to destroy his fiddle, and his music was gone forever. It's ironic that his descendant, Donnie Munro, would sound the clarion call for a new generation of Gaels.

Gaelic in the New World

Cape Breton island is the last and only bastion of a living Gaelic culture in North America.

Highland Scots first arrived in Cape Breton during the eighteenth century. Approximately twenty thousand alone came between 1763 and 1775, largely as a result of gross overpopulation, rising rents, and dire poverty. Later, the tragedy of the Highland Clearances, where Lowlanders and English landowners evicted people to make room for the more profitable sheep, led thousands more to emigrate to the New World.

The Gaelic tongue is experiencing its own revival on the other side of the Atlantic. Although estimates indicate that there are fewer than a thousand Gaelic speakers in Cape Breton today, there is lively interest in Gaelic culture throughout the Maritimes. The Ceilidh Trail School of Celtic Music, located in Broad Cove, for example, offers fiddle, guitar, stepdancing and other music-related classes and workshops in what was once an empty schoolhouse. Meanwhile, the tiny community of Mabou forms the center of Gaelic culture on the island. During the summer the village sponsors three *ceilidhs* a week.

Storytellers Joe Neil MacNeil and Dan Angus Beaton, and the great Gaelic poets Malcolm Gillis and John Maclean, have added immeasurably to the island's Gaelic tradition, while the distinctive and long-standing fiddle tradition remains as strong as ever, as evidenced by the international success of Ashley MacIsaac and Natalie MacMaster.

One of the most active of the younger generation of Gaelic singers in Cape Breton today is Mary Jane Lamond. Her father's people originally came from North Uist, her mother's people from Halifax. Like many Maritimers, her parents left Nova Scotia for Ontario and so each summer the family would make the long journey back "home." Her fine record *Bho Thir Nan Craobh* ("From the Land of the Trees") consists of songs written or sung by the Scottish Gaels who emigrated to Canada since the second half of the eighteenth century. A more recent release, *Suasel*, explores Cape Breton's Gaelic song tradition.

In 1997 Lamond became president of Comhairle na Ghaidhlig, Alba Nuadh (The Gaelic Council of Nova Scotia), a grassroots organization consisting of individuals, institutions, Gaelic societies, and community groups that supports the use of Gaelic in area schools and communities.

If the future of North American Gaelic resides anywhere, it is here with Lamond and others like her who have grown increasingly determined to preserve—and, if necessary, revive—the ancient tongue of their ancestors.

RECOMMENDED LISTENING

Irish Gaelic

Beauty an Oileáin. Music and Song of the Blasket Islands (Claddagh). Archival selection of music and song from the Blasket Islands; the earliest selection dates back to 1957.

Joe Heaney. *The Best of Joe Heaney: From My Tradition* (Shanachie). One of the great *sean-nós* singers; a compilation of several previous recordings.

Sarah and Rita Keane. *Once I Loved* (Claddagh; cassette only). Songs in Irish and English performed in unison duets.

Vail O Flatharta. *Blath Na Nairni* (Claddagh; cassette only). *Sean-nós* singer from Connemara.

Darach Ó Cáthain. *Traditional Irish Unaccompanied Singing* (Shanachie). Considered one of the finest singers in the Irish language; consists largely of eighteenth-century love songs.

Iarla Ó Lionáird. *The Seven Steps to Mercy* (RealWorld). Mesmerizing vocals by a fine young Irish Gaelic singer. A good introduction to Irish language song for the uninitiated.

Songs of Aran: Gaelic Singing from the West of Ireland (Ossian; cassette only). Irish songs as sung in the homes and pubs of Aran circa 1955. Includes superb songs, playful lilting (Irish mouth music), and an absolutely riveting example of keening, the Irish cry of the dead.

Scots Gaelic

Capercaillie. *Delirium* (Green Linnet). Uniformly excellent songs in Scots Gaelic and English, most with a Highland theme. Includes "Coisich, a Ruin," the band's breakaway British chart topper.

Arthur Cormack. *Nuair Bha Mi Og/When I Was Young* (Temple). Blessed with a warm voice and clear delivery, Cormack is one of the finest of the younger Gaelic singers.

Alison Kinnaird and Christine Primrose. *The Quiet Tradition: Music of the Scottish Harp, Songs of the Scottish Gael* (Temple). Harpist Kinnaird and singer Primrose combine forces to produce a lovely and important recording.

Mackenzie. *Camhanach* (Macmeanmna). By dint of the gorgeous harmonies and haunting arrangements, the three MacKenzie sisters have created one of the most satisfying Gaelic recordings in recent years.

Talitha MacKenzie. *Solas* and *Spiorad/Spirit* (both Shanachie). Both recordings contain MacKenzie's irresistible combination of traditional and modern. Sparks of genius surface throughout.

Flora MacNeill. *Craobh Nan Ubhal: Traditional Gaelic Songs from the Western Isles* (Temple). One of the truly great Scots Gaelic singers. Features many of the best-loved Gaelic classics, including the lament "Mo run geal og" ("My Fair Young Love") and perhaps the quintessential Gaelic song of unrequited love, "Iain Ghlinn Cuaich" ("John of Glen Cuaich").

Catherine-Ann MacPhee. *The Language of the Gael, I See Winter,* and *Catherine-Ann MacPhee Sings Màiri Mhór* (all on Greentrax). A truly magnificent Gaelic singer from Barra. The latter recording features the songs of Màiri Mhór, a fiery nineteenth-century Gaelic poet from Skye.

Mac-talla. *Mairidh Gaol Is Ceol/The Gaelic Song Tradition in Scotland* (Temple). Features the best of the current generation of Gaelic and non-Gaelic singers and musicians—Christine Primrose, Eilidh MacKenzie, Alison Kinnaird, Blair Douglas, and Arthur Cormack.

Anne Martin. *Co.?: Gaelic Song from the Isle of Skye* (Whitewave). Gaelic songs from a young Gaelic singer from Skye. On several selections the connection between Gaelic song and *pibroch* is clearly evident.

Runrig. *Runrig Play Gaelic: The First Legendary Recordings* (Lismore). Debut recording from the band that put Gaelic rock on the musical map. Runrig's most traditional effort; it is an often lyrical and poignant portrait of Hebridean life full of elegiac images: old photographs, early morning light, village hall *ceilidhs*, the end of summer, lost romances.

Anthologies

The following Greentrax recordings are culled from the tape archives of the School of Scottish Studies at the University of Edinburgh.

Scottish Tradition 2. *Music from the Western Isles*. Includes choral works songs, mouth music, a Fenian lay, a *pibroch* song, and an evangelical hymn.

Scottish Tradition 3. *Waulking Songs from Barra*. Features the work songs of the Western Isles.

Scottish Tradition 6. *Gaelic Psalms from Lewis*. Otherworldly music from the fringes of the Celtic fringe. Stunning in its simplicity, devastating in its bald-faced emotion.

Scottish Tradition 16. William Matheson. *Gaelic Bards & Minstrels* (double cassette only). The Reverend Matheson was for many years on the staff of the Department of Celtic at the University of Edinburgh. Includes seventeen Gaelic songs from the finest of the Gaelic bards (Mary MacLeod, Iain Lom, John MacCodrum, Alexander MacDonald, Roderick Morison, William Ross); an accompanying booklet contains Gaelic texts and translations.

Cape Breton

Mary Jane Lamond. *Bho Thir Nan Craobh/From the Land of the Trees* (B&R Heritage). A Cape Breton Gael with a fine, strong voice, Lamond explores the musical links between the Gaels who settled Cape Breton and their descendants. *Suasel* (Turtlemusik/A&M Records) brings tradition and modernity together with often surprising and inventive results.

Other

Carolau Plygain (Sain; cassette only). Christmas carols from Wales.

Dafydd Iwan. *Caneuon Gwerin/Traditional Welsh Folk Songs* (Sain).The incomparable Welsh singer/songwriter sings his favorite Welsh folk songs.

Sian James. *Gweini Tymor/Serving Season* (Sain). Wales's singer-composer-harpist performs her own singular arrangements of traditional Welsh folk songs.

Les Soeurs Goadeg. *Moueziou Brudez a Vreiz* (Keltia Musique). Traditional Breton singing of *gwerziou* (ballads) and *kan ha diskan* singing.

Plethyn. *Seidir Ddoe/Yesterday's Cider* (Sain). Popular trio from Powys performs Welsh plygains, the beautifully stylized, three-part harmonies indigenous to Wales.

6

Fundamental Passions

Ballads, Songs, and the Folk Revival

Ballad Scots merges into ballad-English, for the simple reason that England and Scots-speaking Scotland—and indeed English-speaking Ireland—really form one single great ballad-zone. . . . What makes much of the Scottish balladry so very different in feel from the English is that our ballad composers really do seem to have had what has been called a "fiercer imagination" than their English counterparts, and also that so many of the tunes they used were ultimately of Celtic origin.

–HAMISH HENDERSON, SONGWRITER, POET, AND
PIONEER IN SCOTTISH FOLK STUDIES

What could be more down-to-earth than a ballad? Doesn't the ballad, better than most types of music, represent the essence of simplicity?

For all its so-called simple style, though, the ballad has a complex history, a rich, multilayered story all its own to tell.

The ballad's roots date back as far as the twelfth century, if not farther. Although not Celtic in the literal sense, for our purposes the ballad earns a prominent place in this book simply because it looms so large in the popular consciousness and in the deep-rooted traditions of the Celtic lands, particularly Scotland and Ireland. Its considerable influence and popularity transcend both time and distance. It resurfaces in modern guise in the work of such latter-day troubadours as Bob Dylan, Bruce Springsteen, Steve Earle, John Wesley Harding, and Billy Bragg.

But let us pause for a moment to consider the ballad's storied past. The ballad tradition in the English-speaking world culminated with the popular ballads of Scotland and England. It is there that our ballad hunting begins.

WHAT IS A BALLAD?

Let's begin with a quick definition. A *ballad* is a narrative poem usually intended to be sung or, to put it in even simpler terms, it is a song that tells a story. Ballad making has been called storytelling at its finest and most dramatic.

Historian Albert Friedman's definition of the ballad is as succinct and thorough as we could want: "A short, traditional, impersonal narrative told in song, transmitted orally from generation to generation, marked by its own peculiar structure and rhetoric, and uninfluenced by literary conventions."

The word *ballad* derives from the French *ballade* which, in turn, comes from the Latin word *ballare,* meaning "to dance." Traditional ballads were preserved in the memory of the folk and were transmitted orally from generation to generation. The ballads changed with every singer; the more popular the ballad the more the versions and variants.

The ballad is a distinct literary form found throughout Europe. Popular or traditional ballads are among the most universal types. The Scottish ballad in particular derives from an oral tradition in narrative songs that flourished during the sixteenth and seventeenth centuries. Folk ballads were sung by ordinary people, around the fireside, in the pub—wherever folk would gather in good spirit and friendship. Although music was an important part of ballads, not all ballads were sung. It seems, though, that the most popular ones were indeed set to music. Of course, it was the words that came first, the words that took precedence.

The popular ballad was popular for a good reason—it was entertaining! Even a cursory look at the subject matter of balladry would evoke nods of recognition from contemporary consumers. It's all there—tragic love, murder, betrayal, unrequited love, adultery, even supernatural comings and goings. In a way the ballad was the ultimate crowd pleaser. It relied on elemental and larger-than-life themes that had universal appeal.

The oldest ballad in the British Isles, "Judas," one of the famous Child ballads—more about them later in this chapter—is said to date from the late thirteenth century, yet some scholars maintain that the earliest ballad fragments are as old as circa 1100, indicating that the metrical and musical influences of balladry borrowed heavily from medieval hymnody.

TRAITS OF THE TRADITIONAL BALLAD

The traditional ballad typically featured:

- Straightforward narrative
- Simple rhymes
- Incremental repetition
- Common phrases
- Dialogue that advances the story
- Inevitability of outcome
- Hyperbole

MINSTRELS AND BROADSIDES

Medieval minstrels were professional entertainers who performed for the aristocracy, but they also spun tales for the lower classes. The minstrel ballads differ from the popular ballads in several crucial ways. While the popular ballads are impersonal, the minstrel ballads employ a narrator who exhorts his listeners to "sit up and listen." Where the popular ballads are intentionally vague about location, the minstrel ballads describe geographical details. Where the popular ballads waste no time in telling a story, the minstrel ballads are more leisurely. Friedman believes that the minstrel ballad was "almost certainly" recited rather than sung.

Another type of ballad was the broadside. After the printing press was invented, vendors of broadside ballads sold their wares on the streets of London and in provincial towns throughout Britain. The ballads were sold for a penny or a half penny apiece, printed on one side of paper about the size of a handbill, and usually decorated with a woodcut of some sort. Below the title appeared a notation saying it was to be sung "to the tune of . . . ," a popular melody that almost everyone of the time would have known. Broadsides functioned as the urban equivalent of a folk ballad. They were even more detailed than the minstrel ballads, though, containing specific names, dates, and places, and often describing lurid tales of murders and scandal. Think of the medieval equivalent of the *National Enquirer* in America or *News of the World* in Britain. Many of these broadsides became part of the oral tradition.

BALLAD CHARACTERISTICS

A ballad usually concentrates on one theme, perhaps even on a single episode. We can find ourselves in the thick of things as a song begins and the story unfolds. Background information is given to us as we go along—or sometimes not at all. The plot develops rapidly and naturally by action or dialogue. The story usually advances impersonally; that is, the author is never identified.

There's also a peculiar rhythm at work, often of a repetitive nature.

> *Lie still, lie still, my own dear son,*
> *Lie still and take a sleep . . .*

Ballad language is formal and highly structured; there's also a distinctive vocabulary used. A horse just isn't white, it's milk white. When music is involved, many of the tunes are modal—they don't fit into the major and minor scales of most Western music.

Another characteristic is the use of incremental repetition, a literary device that moves the story forward by variations of a repeated pattern. So a stanza thus repeats the previous stanza while adding a new bit of information. An example is "The Maid Freed from the Gallows":

> *O good Lord Judge, and sweet Lord Judge,*
> *Peace for a little while!*
> *Methinks I see my own father,*
> *Come riding by the stile.*
> *Oh father, oh father, a little of your gold,*
> *And likewise of your fee!*
> *To keep my body from your yonder grave,*
> *And my neck from the gallows-tree.*
> *None of my gold now you shall have,*
> *Nor likewise of my fee;*
> *For I am come to see you hanged,*
> *And hanged you shall be.*

The fourth and fifth stanzas are then identical to the first and second except for the words *mother* and *father*, and so on. In the thirteenth and fourteenth stanzas we have the happy ending:

> *Some of my gold now you shall have,*
> *And likewise of my fee;*
> *For I am come to see you saved,*
> *And saved you shall be.*

The ballad is also very straightforward. There is no holding back of emotion. In "The Cruel Brother," when the heroine is stabbed by her brother John (who was angry that he was not consulted about her choice of future husband), the dying girl announces what she will leave behind in her will: a "silver-shod steed" to her father, a "silken scarf" to her sister, and to her brother? "The gallows-tree to hang him on."

Thus the ballad conformed to a specific format, style, and pattern. But it was also very flexible. A story could, for example, remain fairly constant yet assume local color and characteristics wherever it traveled. In fact, the ballads were transmitted much the same way that a joke passes into popular circulation in our own day.

The ballad employs a series of *mnemonic* devices—techniques that assist or intend to assist memory. The most common ballad pattern consists of *abcb,* such as in "The Wife of Usher's Well":

> *There lived a wife at Usher's Well,*
> *And a wealthy wife was she;*
> *She had three stout and stalwart sons,*
> *And sent them oer the sea.*

The rhyming scheme of the ballads are very predictable—not too surprising when you consider that these songs had to be memorable enough to be passed along. So we find something like:

> *Lady Margaret died on the over night,*
> *Sweet William died on the morrow;*
> *Lady Margaret died for pure, pure love,*
> *Sweet William died for sorrow.*

Ballads deal in hyperbole. Actions are exaggerated. Characters become larger than life, their emotions worn openly on their sleeves. This more-is-best penchant was carried over to the American tradition of tall tales. The early-twentieth-century ballad and children's favorite "The Big Rock Candy Mountain" by Harry McClintock combines visions of a glorious utopia and a topsy turvy world where virtually every human need is not only met but satiated.

BALLAD COLLECTORS

The man credited with starting the interest in the ballad tradition—with stoking its antiquarian appeal—is the English clergyman Thomas Percy (1721–1811), a young poet and later Bishop of

Dromore. The first edition of Percy's *Reliques of Ancient English Poetry* was published in 1765 and contained 176 items. Yet this seminal work, although important in its own right, contained but a fraction of the original unpublished manuscript that Percy had stumbled across by sheer luck.

This large folio-size manuscript, which many consider the most important single document in ballad history, consisted of nearly 200 texts, including 17 romances, 24 histories, 45 Child ballads, and more than 100 miscellaneous songs. The manuscript was compiled around 1650 from various sources.

Percy wrote the following note describing the circumstances of his remarkable discovery:

> This very curious Old Manuscript in its present mutilated state, but unbound and sadly torn . . . , I rescued from destruction, and begged at the hands of my worthy friend Humphrey Pitt Esq., then living at Shiffnal in Shropshire, afterwards of Priorslee, near that town; . . . I saw it lying dirty on the floor under a Bureau in ye Parlour: being used by the Maids to light the fire.

The publication of Percy's *Reliques*—that is, the abridged version of the original manuscript—touched off a wave of ballad hysteria that had reverberations well into the Celtic Twilight period of the late nineteenth century.

Unfortunately, Percy, like many other scholars both before and since, altered many of the lyrics in an attempt to make the collection more palatable to his eighteenth-century audience.

 ## A SAMPLING OF IMPORTANT BALLAD HUNTERS

Allan Ramsay (circa 1685–1758). One of the earliest collectors of Scottish ballads. It's been said that he started the antiquarian rage that was so popular in the eighteenth century.

MAJOR WORKS: *The Evergreen* (1724);
Tea-Table Miscellany (1724–1737)

Thomas Percy (1729–1811). Another early collector, Bishop Percy was known to take editorial liberties with ballad texts. Yet his influence on future generations of writers and poets was considerable.

MAJOR WORK: *Reliques of Ancient English Poetry* (1765)

David Herd (1732–1810). Herd published the earliest collection of strictly Scottish balladry, which included ballads and songs from Ramsay and Percy as well as popular pieces collected for the first time from broadsheets and countryfolk.

MAJOR WORK:
Ancient and Modern Scottish Songs (1776)

Robert Burns (1759–1796). Scotland's national poet was also a great collector and composer of songs. Among his best-known songs and ballads are "Auld Lang Syne," "Green Grow the Rashes O," "Flow Gently, Sweet Afton," "Corn Rigs," "John Anderson, My Jo," "Scots Wha Hae," "Logan Water," "The Banks o' Doon," "My Heart's in the Highlands," and "Parcel of Rogues."

MAJOR WORK: *The Scots Musical Museum* (with James Johnson) (1787–1803)

Joseph Ritson (1752–1803). Unlike Bishop Percy, Ritson demanded editorial integrity—the texts had to be presented untampered with. And unlike most collectors of his day, Ritson printed, whenever possible, the music for his selections.

MAJOR WORK: *Scotish Song* (1794)

Sir Walter Scott (1771–1832). Scott imitated Bishop Percy, "improving" texts when he deemed it necessary and frequently creating original compositions. Scott's work is arguably the most influential of the many Scots balladry collections.

MAJOR WORK: *Minstrelsy of the Scottish Border* (1802–1803)

Robert Jamieson (1780–1844). Another important Scottish collector.

MAJOR WORK: *Popular Ballads and Songs* (1806)

William Motherwell (1797–1835). Motherwell adopted a scholarly approach. He influenced the Danish collector Sven

Grundtvig, who, in turn, influenced the American collector Francis James Child.

MAJOR WORK: *Minstrelsy: Ancient and Modern* (1827)

Francis James Child (1825–1896). American-born editor of the most prestigious ballad collection within the Anglo-Scottish tradition.

MAJOR WORK: *The English and Scottish Popular Ballads* (1882–1898)

Gavin Greig (1856–1914). Aberdeenshire schoolmaster who collected ballads in the Northeast of Scotland and proved that the tradition remained strong years after Child's death.

MAJOR WORK: *Last Leaves of Traditional Ballads and Ballad Airs* (1925)

THE BARD AND THE STORYTELLER: ROBERT BURNS AND SIR WALTER SCOTT

Robert Burns, Scotland's national bard, was more than just a poet. He was also a fine storyteller, songwriter, and erstwhile collector of songs.

Burns (1759–1796) was born in a two-room cottage in Alloway in Ayrshire, Scotland's southwestern corner, the eldest of seven children of poor working-class parents. From his mother he committed to memory the old Scottish ballads and tales. Although he had an insatiable desire to learn, his formal schooling was minimal at best, much of it on his own time. He especially had a strong interest in Scottish and English literature.

Eventually, Burns composed stories in the Scottish dialect of his native Ayrshire. His first volume of poetry, *Poems, Chiefly in the Scottish Dialect,* was published in 1786, which turned him into somewhat of a literary sensation in Edinburgh.

Long a student of Scottish song, Burns, who had a phenomenal memory, would note down airs from people and saved old songs from extinction. He also wrote new songs—classic love songs,

songs of joy and sorrow, songs of great friendship (and parting), and songs of war.

By the 1780s Burns had made the acquaintance of James Johnson, an Edinburgh publisher, who had started work on what was to supposed to be a compilation of music from throughout Britain. When Johnson lost interest in the project Burns took over and, with the help of organist Stephen Clarke, assembled *The Scots Musical Museum*. This impressive collection consisted of six volumes of a hundred songs each. Burns wrote or is associated with at least 350 of the songs.

 ## JAMES HOGG, THE ETTRICK SHEPHERD

Born in 1770 at Ettrick Hall and nicknamed the "Ettrick Shepherd," James Hogg was the second of four sons of a poor farmer. From his mother he learned the great ballads and folklore of the Borders. In his midteens he taught himself to read and write and play the fiddle. In the early years of the eighteenth century he was working as a shepherd on a farm in Yarrow for the Laidlaw family. Around this time Walter Scott was wandering the Border valleys searching for ballads. Hogg became a great resource.

Inspired by the success of Robert Burns, Hogg began his own publishing career by writing songs. In 1819–1821 he published the collection *The Jacobite Relics of Scotland*, which contained more than three hundred songs and tunes. Several years later, in 1824, he wrote his masterpiece and what is now considered a classic of nineteenth-century Scottish literature, *The Private Memoirs and Confessions of a Justified Sinner*.

Hogg, who never matched the achievements of his mentor, Burns, was buried in the kirkyard at Ettrick within a mile of his birthplace.

Many, if not most, of the texts of the first volume were taken from Allan Ramsay's *Tea-Table Miscellany*, but the second volume in March 1788 contained thirty-six songs, either Burns's originals or reworked fragments. In the third, fourth, and fifth volumes, about half of the texts in each were written by Burns. The sixth and last volume—published after Burns's death—contained twenty-six songs by the bard. All in all, it was a remarkable achievement.

Another figure forever linked with Scottish balladry is Sir Walter Scott (1771–1832). His childhood in the Scottish Border country brought him into contact with singers and storytellers who knew the characters of the old ballads as intimately as their own family members. Scott himself was descended from rich Border-country stock.

When Scott was thirteen, he read a copy of Percy's *Reliques*, which had a profound effect on him. He would often recite the ballads to his schoolmates.

As a young man, Scott attended the University of Edinburgh until illness forced him to leave. Always someone with a fierce practical streak, he took up the study of law while devoting much of his free time to collecting the old ballads. And when he was made sheriff of Selkirkshire, conveniently located in the heart of Border country, his many tours of the area gave him yet another chance to learn the songs and tales of the region.

In late 1799 Scott wrote to James Ballantyne, a printer in the Border town of Kelso, and mentioned almost matter-of-factly that he had been collecting Border ballads for years. Encouraged by Ballantyne's interest, Scott felt that he could put together "a neat little volume."

As part of his ongoing research, Scott had written to Bishop Percy. And, several years later, in 1802, Scott had the good fortune to meet William Laidlaw, a farmer in the Border village of Yarrow, who, in turn, introduced him to James Hogg, then a struggling shepherd. Hogg and Laidlaw were Scott's chief sources for his famous balladry collection.

The Romantic Age and especially the popularity of German poetry motivated Scott to do something about the native traditions of his own land. Percy's *Reliques* had already been enthusiastically received on the continent. Hence in January 1802 Scott published the first two volumes of *Minstrelsy of the Scottish Border,* and in April 1803 the third volume appeared. It was a great and unqualified success.

Scott had no qualms about "improving" the ballads. Unlike Percy and others, though, he openly admitted that he made additions and changes. If he came across several versions of the same ballad or if the ballad appeared fragmentary in nature—if words or entire sentences were missing, for example—he would write new material, but in the traditional idiom. When he did so, he always made it clear to the reader. In this way, Scott created what has come to be known as the "standard" text of a ballad.

Traditional balladry also had an effect on his own writing. Much of his best-known romantic poetry was inspired by the ballads, such as "Marmion," "The Lady of the Lake," and "Lochinvar."

"I DREAMED A DREAM THE OTHER NIGHT"

> *The Borders is not a line but an area, in many respects historically and traditionally almost an independent region, certainly so in the eyes of the inhabitants who gave us the Ballads.*
>
> —JAMES REED, HISTORIAN

The Border country between Scotland and England stretches from Berwick on the River Tweed to the Solway Firth. For almost three hundred years, from the late thirteenth century to the middle of the sixteenth, the people who dwelled on either side of the border lived in an essentially lawless state of perpetual violence and bloodshed. The great Border tribes, both Scottish and English, feuded continuously among themselves. Robbery and blackmail were everyday occurrences. This violence had nothing to do with war between the two countries; most of the time they were officially at peace with each other. Rather, they waged war upon themselves. Some families often belonged to both sides.

Yet from this precarious and chaotic Anglo-Scottish frontier emerged a rich ballad tradition—from the classic Riding ballads

("The Raid of the Reidswire," "The Rookhope Ryde"), to tales of great tragedy and woe ("The Dowie Dens of Yarrow") to grand narrative ballads ("Kinmont Willie"). The tales were populated with *reivers* (cattle raiders), thieves, and outlaws, larger-than-life characters—many if not most drawn from history—with wonderfully descriptive names like Jamie Telfer, Hughie the Graeme, Little Jock Elliot, Hobbie Noble, or Dick o' the Cow. But probably the most notorious of all Border outlaws was Johnnie Armstrong.

 ## Ballad Outlaws: From Johnnie Armstrong to Jesse James

Outlaw ballads hold an important place in the history of Scottish and Irish music. Indeed, such American antiheroes as Jesse James and Bonnie and Clyde have much in common with Border ballad heroes. "Jesse James" in particular is cut from the same cloth as are those of the great Border ballads.

Perhaps the ballad of the Missouri train robber can be linked, metaphorically at least, to the story of one Johnnie Armstrong, who played much the same role in the Border tradition that Robin Hood did in England or Ned Kelly in Australia. Although he earned a reputation as a fearless rogue among the nobility, Armstrong was a folk hero in Scotland and was held in high esteem by the common people.

The Armstrongs earned a well-deserved reputation for their lawless ways. Johnnie was considered the most notorious of the Border bandits. Of course, he is the subject of a popular Border ballad, "Johnnie Armstrong."

In 1530 James V gathered an army of about twelve thousand men to pacify the Borders. According to legend, Johnnie was lured to his final resting place, unarmed, by the king. They met at Carlanrigg in an area of the Borders known as Teviotdale in the heart of Armstrong country. Armstrong reportedly pleaded for his life, swore his loyalty, and insisted, hoping to appeal to the Scottish king's patriotic side, that because he'd never robbed anyone in Scotland, he should be set free (he supposedly raided only south of the border). But James would not listen. Like Jesse

James and Bonnie and Clyde, Johnnie was also betrayed by someone whom he thought he could trust. Armstrong and his followers were hung without trial, from trees in the Carlanrigg churchyard. Today a memorial marks the spot.

The story of Jesse James bears remarkable similarities to the story of Johnnie Armstrong. Like their Scottish counterpart, Jesse and Frank James grew up in turbulent conditions in an area, Missouri, marked by border warfare, civil strife, and seemingly interminable blood feuds. The earliest-known version of the "Jesse James" ballad dates from the 1880s.

Although the Border ballads make up only a small part of the Child collection, they do offer many exciting tales. Scott's *Minstrelsy of the Scottish Border* is perhaps the most famous Border ballad collection of all.

One of the greatest causes of conflict in the Borders was the blood feud. When a man was killed, his family didn't just quarrel with the slayer but rather railed against the entire clan. Hence, the feud could last for generations. Some feuds, such as the Maxwells and the Johnstones, amounted to civil war; others were resolved in one single combat. It wasn't always along national lines, either: Scot fought against Scot, English against English. In the Border country, your surname was more important than your nationality.

"DEAR HARP OF MY COUNTRY"

Meanwhile, in Ireland, an Irishman in Dublin named Thomas Moore (1779–1852) was busy on his own projects. Moore's *Irish Melodies* was quite different from the ballad collections of his Scottish neighbors, however.

Published in 1808, *Irish Melodies* contained lyrics to popular airs. More than half of the melodies in the collection were taken from Edward Bunting's seminal 1796 anthology of tunes. Additional volumes followed, some containing Moore's own compositions, others derived from the tradition. All together, Moore published ten volumes between 1808 and 1834. Songs like "Believe Me, If All Those Endearing Young Charms"; "The Harp That Once Through Tara's Halls"; and "Dear Harp of My Country" found their greatest support, ironically, within English drawing-room society. Years later, Moore's lyrics still managed to have their effect on Ireland's literary imagination. According to the Irish-American tenor James W. Flannery, who has studied Moore's life and times, a Moore song, "Oh, Ye Dead!" reportedly served as a partial inspiration for James Joyce's classic short story "The Dead."

The songs in Moore's *Irish Melodies* were not folk songs or ballads but rather art songs modeled after the *amhran mór*, or classical "high songs" of ancient Ireland. Flannery offers some provocative insights into Moore's work:

> Moore has often been accused of diluting or falsifying his Gaelic sources. Yet, as a lyricist, he introduced into English certain oracular, incantatory and dream-like sound patterns taken directly from the Gaelic tradition . . . . Thus he carried over into English the aristocratic heritage of Gaelic song and poetry.

Indeed, Flannery points out that Moore used techniques common in Gaelic poetry—such as alliteration and assonance or the repetition of similar vowels—in his songs. In other words, Moore echoed the old bardic influences of ancient Ireland.

WOMEN AND BALLADRY

Women played a big part in the perpetuation of the ballad. Notes Catherine Kerrigan in her introduction to *An Anthology of Scottish Women Poets*: "women played such a significant role as tradition bearers and transmitters that it can be claimed that the ballad tradition is one of the most readily identifiable areas of literary performance by women." Sir Walter Scott gained much of his knowledge of balladry from the mother of James Hogg, the Scottish poet.

Women were the most prominent carriers of the oral tradition. The ballads were not only orally transmitted they were orally "transmuted" as well; thus, the best singers could change things, add variations without changing the crux of the story. Just as the teller of jokes or master storyteller never tells the same joke or the same story twice in the exact same way, so ballads were passed along. The details varied according to the ballad maker's mood, environment, or audience.

The ballads of Anna Gordon, otherwise known as Mrs. Brown of Falkland, are considered the oldest existing body of traditional ballads in the Anglo-Scottish tradition. For this reason, the now obscure Mrs. Brown has been given the unofficial title of the most famous single figure in Scots ballad-history.

Anna Gordon was no back country peasant: She was a member of the Scottish aristocracy. Born in Aberdeen in 1747, she was the daughter of Thomas Gordon, chairman of the Humanities Department at the city's most respected institution of higher learning, King's College. In 1788 she married the Reverend Andrew Brown.

Brown learned the ballads at a very young age—by the age of ten, according to one source, twelve, according to another—mostly from her maternal side. Her mother, Lillian Forbes, came from a singing family in the Braemar district of Scotland's northeast. Her main source, though, was her aunt, who was married to the proprietor of a small estate near the mouth of the River Dee.

Like many people of her day, Brown had a wonderful memory and learned all the songs that she heard while growing up from the nurses and older women who sang in the area. Years later, as an adult, she wrote them down entirely from recollection for, as she admitted, "I never saw one of them in print or manuscript."

Brown re-created the ballads, that is, she didn't just memorize the text, but sang the songs from the heart. Hence, she was an active participant in the perpetuation of the ballad tradition, singing different versions of the same story. And indeed, Anna Gordon Brown's collection is very much from a woman's perspective

Anna Gordon Brown died in Aberdeen on July 11, 1810. As part of her legacy, she left behind three Brown ballad manuscripts: the

Jamieson Brown manuscript, the Tytler Brown manuscript, and the Fraser Tytler Brown manuscript. Sir Walter Scott used the latter two sources while compiling his *Minstrelsy of the Scottish Border*.

Like many ballad makers, Brown separated the oral ballad tradition from the printed manuscript version. Scholars equate this tendency with the general dichotomy that manifested itself in eighteenth-century Scotland; indeed, to some extent, this "national schizophrenia" still continues. The Union of the Crowns of England and Scotland in 1707 and the loss of an independent Scottish parliament had a devastating effect on Scottish culture and Scottish identity. In particular, they quickened the decline of the Scots language. Thus Scots who wanted to "get on in the world" were encouraged to speak "politely," that is, to speak standard English. From the eighteenth century on and to this very day, the Lowland Scots essentially speak two languages—Scots at home and English at the workplace. Or as the poet Edwin Muir wryly observed: Scots *felt* in Scots and *thought* in English.

Scholars believe this is the reason why the Lowland Scottish tradition includes such a rich body of folk song and folk culture. The Scottish ballads expressed a distinctive Scottish outlook on life, a particular Scottish spirit that was increasingly not allowed expression in the everyday world. In short, the ballads helped maintain a strong sense of national identity.

The Brown Collection illustrates some of the classic characteristics of the ballad world. The plot of the ballads take place in a distant time. Their characters more often than not are noble—queens and ladies, kings and knights. The traditional ballad maker enjoyed telling the tales of the mighty and well born. After all, in pre-eighteenth-century Scotland the bulk of both performers and audience for these ballads were the rural folk. The worlds they sang about—the glamorous settings of court and castle—were far removed from the harsh and mundane worlds of their own day-to-day lives.

Similar conditions existed in the American South. The "big ballads" that are such a part of the rich heritage of Appalachia—many of which, of course, originated in Scotland and England—

spoke of events and people from another time and place, larger-than-life themes that expressed the sentiments of the ordinary man and woman.

RAGGLE-TAGGLE GYPSIES AND NUT-BROWN MAIDS: MUSIC OF THE NORTHEAST

The northeastern corner of Scotland was known for its rich traditional folk heritage—being, as it was, the province of the Scots *muckle sangs*, or "big songs." The noted scholar David Buchan has described the balladry of the northeast as "unmatched in quality and quantity by any other regional culture in Britain." Songs like "The Gypsy Laddies," "The False Knight upon the Road," "The Twa Sisters," "Lord Thomas and Fair Ellen," and many more speak to a time when the hearth, a roaring fire, and the reassurance of the human voice were all you needed to get through the long winter evenings.

An important collector of ballads from this ballad-rich area was Gavin Greig. He was born at Parkhill in the parish of Newmachar, Aberdeenshire, on February 10, 1856. He was fortunate to have inherited a formidable musical pedigree—he seems to have been related to Edvard Grieg, the great Norwegian composer, on his father's side and Robert Burns on his mother's. In the 1760s an Alexander Greig (the family changed the spelling of the name), the grandfather of Edvard Grieg and a native of the Fraserburgh area, emigrated to Bergen.

Greig was educated at Dyce Parish School, at the Old Aberdeen Grammar School, and at Aberdeen University, where he graduated with a master of arts in 1876. In 1879 he was appointed schoolmaster at Whitehall, in the parish of New Deer, Aberdeenshire. He remained there until his death on August 31, 1914.

Greig was a man of many talents. He was an organist in the parish church. But he was also familiar figure in the area and warmly welcomed at homes throughout Aberdeenshire, from the wealthiest to the most humble. He wrote four novels, a dramatic sketch, an operetta, and two comedies of rural life and manners. He also lectured and wrote a series of newspaper articles on the poetry of Aberdeenshire, as well as editing a folk-song column in the *Buchan Observer*. These latter articles were privately published as *Folk-Song of the North-East*.

In 1904 Greig was asked to put together a volume of traditional music. He had already accumulated a fair amount of material from his years of roaming the Aberdeenshire countryside. The Reverend J. B. Duncan assisted him in his search. Ultimately, their work amounted to 3,050 texts (2,500 collected by Greig) and 3,100 tunes (2,300 of them by Greig).

Greig collected the tunes and texts in various ways. He recorded some of them personally either from recitation or from singing; others were taken down by his assistants. Some were even written by the sources directly. Still others were dictated to them, quite often by grandchildren.

Greig's most important source was Bell Robertson, who reportedly provided him with almost four hundred ballads. She learned most of them from her mother and others from her aunt, a girlfriend, a gypsy boy, and a blacksmith. Unlike Anna Gordon Brown, however, Bell Robertson learned the ballads through rote memorization. As a result, only a third of the eighty-four ballads that she gave Greig are complete. Another important difference is that Robertson did not *sing* her ballads—she recited them, which may go a long way to explaining the rather fragmentary nature of her collection.

David Buchan has claimed that literacy changed the method of ballad transmittal. A nonliterate person learned many versions of a ballad and so through constant repeatings came to "own" the song, while a literate ballad singer merely memorized the text. It was a matter of creative composition versus memorization. The memorized texts do change over the years, he pointed out, but usually with negative results—lines are dropped or simply forgotten.

Greig found that ballads were, for the most part, handed down within families, through the generations. The same ballads were often sung to different airs, the same airs sung with different ballads. For example, *Last Leaves* contains 250 airs but only 100 distinctive tunes. Only a few of these tunes in Greig's collection were actually indigenous to Aberdeenshire. The most popular of ballads were found equally in the Lowlands as well as across the Irish Sea in Ireland. Most were essentially Lowland in character.

BOTHY BALLADS

One of the richest category of songs from the northeast is the bothy ballads, or narrative songs sung by mostly unmarried farm workers in late Victorian and Edwardian times. The bothy was a stone-built farm cottage used by the laborers.

Rural Scottish society was divided into small group of wealthy farmers and farm workers, who vastly outnumbered the former. The majority of the farm laborers were single men. They lived in the bothy (those who were married usually stayed in cottages near the farm), which typically consisted of two rooms: one where the men had their meals and the other where they had their wooden beds. A bothy could house as many as eight men.

The men spent a great deal of whatever leisure time they had making their own music. The instruments of choice were usually the fiddle and the melodeon. Although they were called "ballads," the bothy repertoire also included what are commonly deemed folk songs. There were harvest songs, songs of love and marriage ("The Rigs o' Rye," "Bogie's Bonny Belle"), and songs relating to farm life and work ("Drumdelgie," "The Barnyards o' Delgaty"). Even various nonsense rhymes made their way into the collections.

 ## "THE GREAT SELKIE OF SULE SKERRY": A CLASSIC CHILD BALLAD

> *I am a man upon the land,*
> *I am a selchie in the sea,*
> *an' whin I'm far from every strand,*
> *my dwelling is in Sule Skerry.*

So begins one of the most haunting of the traditional Child ballads, a favorite of balladeers throughout the English-speaking world from Jean Redpath and Joan Baez to Ivan Drever of Wolfstone and singer/songwriter Gordon Bok from Maine.

In this timeless classic the selkie, or seal, changes into human form and fathers a child with a nurse. The nurse lullabies the child. The child becomes a seal and joins his father in the sea, where both are shot by a gunner. The nurse recognizes her selkie-son by the gold chain that he wears around his neck.

Many ancient peoples believed that animals could transform themselves into human shape and assume their characteristics. In Orkney and Shetland the seal-people are called selkies. Unions between mortals and immortals are destined to be short-lived and usually tragic.

Commonly, there were two types of seals. The common seal or tang fish and the larger great or grey seal. The selkie-folk belong to the latter category. According to folklore, their natural form is human, they live in an underwater world on lonely rocks, or skerries, and don their seal skins. Some say the selkie were fallen angels who were condemned to their present state. Others say that they were human beings who, for some grave transgression, were condemned to assume the seal's shape and live in the sea, but were allowed to take human form on dry land.

Sometimes male selkies became the lovers of married women, as in the case of Lady Odivere, a story which by some accounts dates as far back as 800 A.D., although the actual legend may be even older.

In 1989 Gordon Bok produced *The Play of the Lady Odivere*, a musical setting based on the legends of the seal-folk and using as its foundation the classic Scots ballad "The Great Selkie of Sule Skerry." (Sule Skerry is a tiny islet about twenty-five miles west of Hoy Head in the Orkney Islands, off the northern coast of Scotland.) Bok's interest in the seal legend dates back many years. In 1972 he composed another tale of the sea called *Seal Djiril's Hymn*; even earlier, in *Peter Kagan and the Wind*, a sailor is caught in a storm at sea when his wife, one of the seal-folk, saves him.

The selkie legend has proved a durable and extremely flexible; it's popular with writers and artists on both sides of the Atlantic. Other variations of the seal legend in popular culture include:

- The late Orcadian author George Mackay Brown worked the traditional Orkney ballad "The Lady Odivere" into his nonfiction piece *An Orkney Tapestry*, and also used it as the basis for his short story "The Seal King." "The Great Selkie of Sule Skerry" is incorporated into another short story by

Mackay Brown, "Sealskin." In this story Magnus Olafson, the son of a seal-woman, is a rich and famous composer who returns to his native land only to be treated like a foreigner and rejected.

- In Eric Linklater's short story "Sealskin Trousers," a man is driven mad by the sight of his lover, who joins the seal-folk.
- *The Secret of Roan Inish* is John Sayles' lyrical cinematic adaptation of the selkie legend transported from its original Orcadian setting to western Ireland.

The breakdown of the old class system led to gross inequities of the bothy way of life. The farm workers' existence was close to slavery. They would hire (or fee) themselves to farmers for the next season's work, usually for six-months or yearly terms. James Allan, an Aberdeenshire man, recalled the bothy life:

Feeing markets always remind me of the old days when slaves were bought and sold by their general physical appearance. . . . I myself have had my wrists examined by farmers, to see what appearance of strength there was about them.

He continued:

We worked ten hours a day . . . from six to eleven and from one to six with no half holiday on Saturday. In addition, we got up at five or earlier to feed and clean our horses before breakfast at five-thirty; and the horses required attention in the evening. In harvest we worked an eleven hours' day from six to ten, from eleven to two, and from three to seven. All our food was brought to us in the field.

The term *bothy ballads* can refer either to all the songs actually sung in the bothies or to songs that described bothy life and the everyday events of the community. The ballads resemble in structure, style, attitude, and content—a smidgen of insouciance here, a dash of devil-may-care humor there—the cowboy, lumberjack, and miner ballads of other traditions.

THE MAN FROM HARVARD

Ironically, the greatest ballad collector of them all was not even from the British Isles. Instead, the honor must go to a stubbornly persistent American scholar named Francis James Child. By the time he died in Boston at the age of seventy-one in 1896, he had edited the seminal five-volume *English and Scottish Popular Ballads*, considered the definitive traditional-ballad collection.

Born in Boston on February 1, 1825, the third in a family of eight children, Child graduated from Harvard University in 1846 and tutored for three years in English, mathematics, history, and political economy. After studying for four years in Germany, he returned to Harvard as Boylston Professor of Rhetoric, Oratory, and Elocution. In 1876 he became a professor of English, a position that he held until his death in 1896. He edited an anthology of British poets, a five-volume tome on Spenser, and, if all that wasn't enough, he was considered an expert on Chaucer.

Child's years in Germany led to the work of the Brothers Grimm, which inspired him, on his return to America, to study the origin of the ballad. Yet his first ballad collection grew out of his work on the British poets collection. In the mid-1850s he prepared an eight-volume collection called *English and Scottish Ballads*. He devoted two years to this project, which only whetted his appetite for further study. He became determined to find out everything he could about balladry, to go to the original sources rather than relying on previously printed material. Whenever possible, he sifted through the popular literature of other lands to look for potential parallels. In short, his goal was to obtain every possible version of every existing English and Scottish ballad, a monumental task. If necessary, he would devote the rest of his life to it. He did just that.

It took twenty years for Child to compile the collection. He had to face many obstacles during his course of study, one of which was the rather obscure nature of the work itself. Because he did most of his research from America, he had to explain in minute detail to his sources just what he was looking for. This involved massive letter writing over the years. For this he had to enlist the help of many assistants in Scotland and England. One, in particular, a William MacMath, copied down thousands of lines for him. Sometimes though he was met with indifference. He once made the following astute observation:

> A very large and wearisome part of my "preparation" has been the endeavor to stir up Scotsmen to an interest sufficient to induce them to exert themselves to save the things that may still be left. It is in vain. The Scot loves his ballads but is incurious about them.

Child used many sources for his collection. Among them were the original unpublished manuscript by Thomas Percy titled "Bishop Percy's Folio Manuscript" and the "Abbotsford Papers," the latter a collection of songs that would later appear in its edited form as Scott's *Minstrelsy of the Scottish Border.* But these were the original sources—before the pen of Percy and Scott cleaned them up for public consumption.

 ## SOME WELL-KNOWN JACOBITE SONGS

"The Skye Boat Song" tells the famous story of Bonnie Prince Charlie's escape to freedom with the help of Flora MacDonald. The song though was actually written by an Englishman, Sir Harold Boulton, in 1884.

"Will Ye No Come Back Again?" The most popular Jacobite ballad sung in Scotland today has been transformed into a wistful song of parting.

"Such a Parcel of Rogues in a Nation" is Robert Burns's passionate attack on the Union of Parliaments of 1707.

"Charlie Is My Darling" is an old Jacobite rallying cry that years later and an ocean apart transformed itself into "Johnny Is My Darling" during the American Civil War.

"Johnnie Cope" refers to the Battle of Prestonpans in which the Jacobite army, led by Bonnie Prince Charlie, routed a numerically superior English force led by General John Cope.

"Scots Wha Hae," Scotland's unofficial national anthem, was written by Burns and inspired by the Jacobite Risings.

"Loch Lomond" commemorates the return of the Jacobite army from Derby via Carlisle. The Jacobite soldier who awaits execution says he will reach Scotland before his companion, because his spirit will travel by the "low road."

In June 1896 Child was ready to begin work on the final volume, which was to contain a glossary, various indexes, a bibliography, and an elaborate introduction. Unfortunately, he died before he could put the proper finishing touches to his life's work.

Yet his legacy lives on, becoming an important aspect of the 1960s folk revival when Child ballads were favorites of numerous pop/folk singers, from Joan Baez ("Mary Hamilton") to Simon and Garfunkel ("Scarborough Fair").

RUNNING THROUGH THE HEATHER

The ill-fated attempt by Charles Edward Stuart ("Bonnie" Prince Charlie of folk legend) to regain the throne of his ancestors created a body of Scottish balladry and song that was second in popularity only to the ubiquitous love song.

The term *Jacobite* refers to the supporters of King James VII of the Stuart dynasty (1633–1701) after he was deposed by William III (1650–1702) and his wife, Queen Mary, during the Glorious Revolution of 1688. The name itself is derived from *Jacobus*, Latin for James.

The Jacobite Risings of 1715 and 1745 produced the greatest number of Jacobite songs. Two major categories exist: songs written during the time of the Jacobite rebellions, and songs written later, especially by people not even remotely connected with the Risings.

The Battle of Culloden of April 16, 1746—the last battle fought on British soil—marked the end of an era and the extinction of an ancient social order. Determined to break the Highlander and the clan system once and for all, the government confiscated the estates of leading Jacobites and clan chiefs and prohibited the wearing of the tartan. More important, the once-omnipotent clan chiefs were abolished.

For more than a century after Culloden, Jacobitism was a forbidden subject. It wasn't until 1814 and the publication of Sir Walter Scott's *Waverley* that it became fashionable. The attitude toward the prince changed as his fortunes changed. When the prince was at his most dangerous—that is, when there seemed to be a real chance they he would actually regain the British throne—songwriters (mostly in England, it seems) condemned him and his Highland army as rogues and thieves.

The 1760s and 1770s produced very little new Jacobite material—only a handful of new songs. You could argue that this lack of material reflected the death of the Jacobite cause—the Highlands were disarmed, the clans dispersed, and it was unlawful to wear the tartan. In other words, the traditional Highland way of life was well on its way to an inevitable end.

And yet, around this time the seeds of a future for the Jacobite song were already being sown. The movement began its journey toward accommodation. Before long songwriters would wax nostalgic about the vision of a heroic past that could become the cultural heritage of all Scots. An early example of this was David Herd's anthologies of 1769 and 1776, which dared to refer to a handful of older Jacobite songs as "heroic ballads."

Another important change was the recognition of the Highlander within the realm of a larger Scottish identity and the acceptance by the previously reluctant Lowland Scot of traditionally Highland symbols—kilts and tartans and the like—as national emblems. Scotland came to be considered as essentially a Highland country—a remarkable turnaround in attitude.

Indeed, during the first half of the eighteenth century an altogether new and improved image of the Highlander in the broadsides and popular songs began to emerge—that of the noble Highland hero and warrior, or as historian William Donaldson called him, the "bonny Highland laddie" (for an exploration of the links between the myth of the Highland warrior and the myth of the cowboy, see chapter 7).

No one's influence on Jacobite song was greater than Robert Burns's. In *The Scots Musical Museum*, which he helped collect, he printed nearly thirty Jacobite songs, two-thirds of which were written by the poet himself.

THE LITERARY BALLAD

The influence of the ballad on literature is considerable. Nineteenth century poets were especially influenced by both traditional and broadside ballads. Many poems even deliberately imitated the ballad either in form, manner, or subject. The ballads of John Gay, Jonathan Swift, and Alexander Pope, for example, were modeled on broadsides. Gay's *Beggar's Opera* in 1727 contained more than sixty songs, virtually all well-known street songs and folk airs set to new lyrics.

Later generations of British poets admired the simplicity of the popular ballads. Wordsworth, for example, looked to the ballads for inspiration and created poems of literary quality with ballad roots. Although you won't find much in the way of familiar ballad traits— such as incremental repetition and the like—in his poems, what does emerge is balladry refined to suit his own special purposes. Wordsworth's lyrical ballads are more interested in emotions and feelings than narrative and plot, often employing a first-person narrator rather than the impersonal nature of the traditional ballad.

 A LITERARY COMPENDIUM

For centuries there has been give and take between literary and folk poetry in the ballad tradition. Some of the better-known poets and writers who were influenced by the traditional ballad include Thomas Hardy, Rudyard Kipling, William Butler Yeats, Robert Frost, and especially A. E. Housman. Here are some examples:

Samuel Taylor Coleridge's "The Rime of the Ancient Mariner," with its repetition and third-person narrator, is modeled after the minstrel ballads.

John Keats's "La Belle Dame sans Merci," considered the greatest of literary ballads, uses a modified ballad style. The abrupt opening is a common ballad device, as is the use of moving the narration forward through dialogue. But it is still very much a romance with medieval roots, a romantic poem in the high Gothic style.

Rudyard Kipling's "The Last Rhyme of True Thomas" was inspired by the traditional Scottish ballad "Thomas the Rhymer" and even uses many ballad phrases ("milk white thorn," "earls three by three"). Kipling's first barrack-room ballad, "Danny Deever," also owes a major debt to the ballad tradition.

Alfred Lord Tennyson's "Charge of the Light Brigade" is reminiscent of a broadside ballad, while the balladlike construction of "The Lady of Shalott" employs a medieval setting with an Arthurian theme.

The refrain of Lord Byron's "So, We'll Go No More A-Roving" comes from the Scottish song "The Jolly Beggar" ("And we'll gang nae mair a roving/Sae late into the nicht").

William Wordsworth's "Lucy Gray," based on a local incident, employs ballad motifs.

The supernatural ballad "The Elfin Knight" (Child 2), about a young woman's sexual awakening, reportedly inspired Joyce Carol Oates's short story "Where Are You Going, Where Have You Been?"

Other literary ballads include Oscar Wilde's "Ballad of Reading Gaol"; A. E. Housman's "The Culprit"; Ezra Pound's Christ-like hero in "Ballad of the Goodly Fere"; Dante Gabriel Rossetti's "Sister Helen," whose refrain and use of repetition is inspired by the traditional ballad "Edward"; Stephen Vincent Benet's "John Brown's Body" is reminiscent of "Johnnie Armstrong," while his "Jack of the Feather" has the urgency and atmosphere of the old ballads. Even the title has the ring of an authentic Border ballad.

THE IRISH BALLAD TRADITION

Unlike Scotland and England, the ballad form is not indigenous to Ireland. However, over the centuries the Irish have made it their own, fashioning it to suit their own character. The Irish tradition does contain several aspects that are unique to the Emerald Isle. One is the *aisling*, or vision poetry, the other the *reverdie*.

 ## SOME CLASSIC IRISH BALLADS—NEW AND OLD

"The Salley Gardens." Written by William Butler Yeats, who supposedly heard an old gentleman singing a tune that inspired the poet. *Salley* is from the Irish *saileach*, or "willow."

"My Lagan Love." Traditional love song; one of the *amhrain* or "high songs" of Ireland.

"Danny Boy." At Limavady, just northeast of Derry, Jane Ross heard and recorded an old air, which was published as a tune with no title in 1855. The most popular of the lyrics that have been attached to it—and there have been several—was written by an English barrister named Fred Weatherly who also happened to be a fine opera librettist.

"The Town I Loved So Well." A contemporary classic by Phil Coulter, who sings of his native Derry with great heart.

"There Were Roses." A touching ballad by Tommy Sands about the human cost of the "Troubles" in Northern Ireland.

"Song for Ireland." Probably the most frequently performed contemporary Irish song on either side of the Atlantic—everyone from Mary Black to Dick Gaughan has recorded it—Phil Colclough's modern classic is a wish in musical form for peace to come to Ireland's troubled north.

In the eighteenth-century *aislings* the wandering poet sees, in a dream or vision, the image of a grieving woman who is supposed to represent an oppressed Ireland. These vision songs were usually set to tunes that were already known and in this way became available to the entire community. In the *reverdie*, the songwriter believes the woman in the song is a supernatural visitor but discovers she is mortal.

Much of the content of Irish love songs, both in Irish and in English, is said to have derived from the songs of the French troubadours. The French influence, scholars agree, is due to the Norman invasion of the twelfth century. Thus, many songs that had their origin in the folk poetry of southern France became incorporated into the Irish folk-song repertoire.

The concept of love as an incurable illness is one that was passed along by the Normans and one that is very common in European folk songs. One ballad, for example, tells of a young man who is happily married but falls in love with another woman. He cannot sleep at night nor function during the day. Finally he asks a fairy woman if he can be cured. She answers, "When love enters the heart it will never be driven from it."

 ## IRISH REBEL SONGS

"Brennan on the Moor" is about an Irish highwayman, William Brennan, who stole from the rich landowners and merchants. He was caught and hanged in 1804.

"The Croppy Boy." *Croppy* is said to be the nickname given to natives of County Wexford, reportedly because of their close-cropped hair; has become synonymous with *rebel*.

"Erin Go Bragh" (which means "Ireland Forever"). An eighteenth-century street ballad.

"Kevin Barry." One of the best-known Irish rebel songs. Barry was an eighteen-year-old student when he was hanged as a rebel in November 1921.

"The Rising of the Moon." Written by John Keegan Casey, a young poet who died in prison at the age of twenty-three but wrote the song when he was only fourteen, inspired by the 1798 Rising. According to the Clancy Brothers, the air is known as "The Wearing of the Green" (wearing green was a capital offense in Ireland in 1798). Arguably the most popular of the Irish rebel songs.

"The Wind That Shakes the Barley" functions both as love song and rebel song. Once again, it was inspired by the 1798 Rising. The lament was written by Robert Dwyer Joyce, a professor of English literature at Catholic University in Dublin in the nineteenth century. A rebel himself, he fled to America because of his Fenian activities and established a career publishing Irish songs and ballads. He eventually returned to Dublin, where he died in 1883.

Allegorical songs were usually associated with politics or sensitive national issues and were quite common to Ireland, especially during the nineteenth and early twentieth centuries.

The Industrial Revolution greatly diminished the importance of Gaelic in Irish daily life. Gradually, the national language lost its significance. These changes were reflected in music. Many of the new songs and ballads were written in English so they could be sold to English-speaking customers.

The change from Irish to English created a type of song where both languages were used. Known as macaronic, these songs were composed with phrases, lines, or couplets that alternated between the two tongues. Folk songs in English tended to fall into two groups: English and Scots songs and Anglo-Irish songs, the latter being songs composed by the Irish in English. The English and Scots songs were introduced into Ireland by the English and Scots settlers of the seventeenth century. Many also came from the imported ballad sheets that were printed in England and circulated in Dublin and other good-size towns.

REBEL SONGS

"The use of balladeers for rabble-rousing has had a long history in Ireland," stated Turlough Faolain in *Blood on the Harp*. The rebel song emerged in Ireland as early as the twelfth century in the form of *rosg catha*, the retelling of bardic tales on the eve of a big battle. By the late eighteenth century the tradition had become a permanent part of the Irish vocal heritage.

Although sung all over Ireland and throughout the Irish diaspora today, there was a time not too long ago—in the early 1920s—to sing or even whistle a tune was a punishable offense. Most of the classic rebel songs date from the Risings of 1798. Seven years earlier, the great Irish patriot Wolfe Tone had founded the Society of United Irishmen. Under his leadership, Irish, Anglo-Irish, and even Catholic and Protestant came together to fight for independence from the Crown. Later, in the 1840s and 1850s, came the Young Ireland movement and, later still, the subversive activity of the underground Fenian Brotherhood.

In the 1960s the Clancy Brothers and Tommy Makem made a career out of singing the rebel songs of their native land to American audiences, who were so smitten by their enthusiasm that the lads became superstars on both sides of the Atlantic.

THE BALLAD AND THE FOLK REVIVAL

In the late 1950s a new kind of music was being performed throughout Britain. Called *skiffle*, it combined elements of folk and jazz and was based on and inspired by American music, especially African-American music, though you could also hear the sounds of Uncle Dave Macon and Woody Guthrie. Glasgow-born Lonnie Donegan recorded a skiffle rendition of Leadbelly's "Rock Island Line" in 1954, which became the first British record to dent the American top ten. After a short time, skiffle splintered into folk on the one hand and rock on the other. Yet interest in traditional music continued to grow.

By this time folk clubs began to form. The performers would sing just about anything, from Leadbelly's blues to Jeannie Robertson ballads to Gaelic songs. In the early postskiffle era, the influence was still largely American—in addition to Leadbelly, I would have to include Muddy Waters, Woody Guthrie, the Weavers, and Pete Seeger. Eventually, though, and thanks to the influence of Ewan MacColl, Robertson, and others, more and more singers began to develop an interest in their own music and culture. Which is not to say that the American influence disappeared, because it didn't. In the 1960s, for example, there were scores of Bob Dylan imitators. And there were also Irish and English influences, such as the Clancy Brothers and the Watersons and Martin Carthy. Ballad groups such as the Dubliners, the Wolfe Tones, and the Fureys appealed to enthusiastic crowds in Ireland while, across the water in Scotland, the folk harmonies and nationalistic pride of the McCalmans and the Corries met with similar success.

The roots of the modern folk revival in Scotland date back to the founding of the International Festival of the Arts in Edinburgh in 1947 and the First People's Festival in 1951, where for the first time traditional musicians and ballad singers from rural Scotland performed in front of an urban audience. It was at these *ceilidhs* that city folk, many for the first time, heard the singing of Jeannie Robertson and Jimmy MacBeath.

Along with the late Calum Maclean, Hamish Henderson was one of the founders of the School of Scottish Studies in Edinburgh. Henderson also wrote some of the revival's more popular songs, including "Freedom Come All Ye."

Radio and television also played an important role in the early revival. Peter Kennedy's *As I Roved Out* radio programs showcased traditional singers, as did other important programs, such as *A Ballad Hunter Looks at Britain* and *Ballad and Blues*.

While earlier folk revivals, such as the nineteenth-century revival, were primarily academic, the 1950s revival in Scotland was largely grassroots and people driven. Much of it, too, had a political charge to it. Industrial decline, appalling social conditions, and a powerful socialist movement virtually guaranteed that.

 ## THE TRAVELERS

The term *travelers* refers to a group of nomadic families, hawkers and traders, who roamed throughout Scotland and Ireland in highly organized clans and tribes. They probably have their origins in a medieval Celtic tinsmithing group, hence, their nickname tinkers, which is considered pejorative. In ancient times they were better known for their iron-making skills, and traveled from clan to clan making weapons. They often did seasonal work, such as harvesting crops or fruit. In some ways they are considered the Scottish equivalent of the eastern and southern European gypsies, although they claim no kinship with them. Common traveler surnames in Scotland include Robertson, Stewart, Macgregor, Whyte, and Williamson. Their secret language is known as *cant*.

One of the seminal figures of the folk revival on both sides of the border was the late Ewan MacColl (1915–1989). The son of Scottish parents, MacColl grew up in the north of England and began writing songs when still a boy. His talent was bred in the bone—his mother was a traditional singer. (MacColl is probably best known in America as the composer of "The First Time Ever I Saw Your Face," which was a big hit for Roberta Flack in the 1970s.)

MacColl played a key role in starting and promoting the folk revival. He was one of the founders of the Ballads and Blues Club, which became the leading folk club in England. It was there that he started a controversial policy—singers who wished to perform in his club must perform the music of their native land.

In the late 1950s MacColl was commissioned by BBC Radio to write a documentary called *The Ballad of John Axon*, an English railroad man who had been killed attempting to avoid an accident. It combined speech, sound effects, and music and was the first of the "radio ballads," a series of eight documentaries about different segments of the British population that featured narrative and interviews in addition to bringing traditional music to the attention of a wider audience. Some of the best songs of the Scottish revival, including MacColl's "Freeborn Man" and "Shoals of Herring," emerged from these seminal programs. The radio ballads broke new ground in their presentation of both traditional and contemporary song. Vernacular and local speech and dialect were broadcast to a national audience, often for the first time, as well.

 ## FATE ON WHEELS: TRAIN WRECKS, WRECKS ON THE HIGHWAY, AND OTHER ODES TO THE GRIM REAPER

The American folk heritage is shot through with imagery of twisted train (and, more recently, car wrecks). It's almost an American pedigree, a New World rite of macabre passage. From the mythical "Wabash Cannonball" to the ghostly "Mystery Train," train lore looms large in American balladry, evoking the spirit of its Celtic inspirations. Particularly potent imagery can be culled from the words of popular songs, such as "The Wreck of the Old 97" to J. Frank Wilson's "Last Kiss" to Bruce Springsteen's poignant "Wreck on the Highway."

The nation's rails and highways seem to be littered with the deadly aftermath of outings gone terribly wrong. Throughout it all, heroes emerge, some reckless like the engineer Casey Jones while others, like the African-American laborer John Henry, fit the more classically noble mold. The historical John Henry, a steel driver on the railroad, died in the early 1870s during the construction of the Big Bend Tunnel in West Virginia. The song "John Henry," which folklorists Alan and John Lomax called America's greatest ballad, is said to recall the text of the Scottish ballad "Mary Hamilton" (others see resemblances to the English ballad "The Cherry Tree Carol.") A reputable source, the Lomaxes have claimed that the tune is derived from a Scottish melody.

In our own day, the 1960s witnessed a slew of "sickie" songs, morbid ballads such as Ray Peterson's "Tell Laura I Love Her" and Dickie Lee's "Patches"—car accidents and mysterious illnesses are featured prominently—that wallow in self-pity but whose historical antecedents can be traced back to the old Scottish and English ballads.

Another key figure of the revival, and considered by many to be the greatest of all Scots traditional singers, was Jeannie Robertson (1908–1975). She acquired her repertoire from her mother and grandmother. Her ancestors belonged to the traveling clans (Stewarts and Robertsons) who roamed the Scottish northeast. She possessed what can only be called a voice full of conviction. She was absolutely committed to and immersed in her material, able to find the truth of a song and to make it her own. She was "discovered" in 1953 by Hamish Henderson while he was collecting and recording songs of the Scots tradition for the School of Scottish Studies.

The best traditional Scottish singer working today must be Jean Redpath, Jeannie Robertson's natural successor. After Hamish Henderson introduced Redpath to Robertson's singing, she became active in the Folk Song Society in Edinburgh. Before long she got caught up in the middle of the booming folk scene in Greenwich Village.

But her heart and soul have always rested with traditional Scottish songs, and as an interpreter of the rich ballad tradition, she has few peers. Redpath's repertoire includes traditional Scottish ballads, the songs of Robert Burns, the Scottish songs of Haydn, and contemporary songs in the traditional idiom. She possesses a rich, warm contralto voice, which she controls with exquisite ease.

In recent years she has spent much of her time recording the songs of Robert Burns. Burns's poems, as you will recall, were in many instances song lyrics that over the years became separated from their melodies.

Other important traditional singers include the Stewarts of Blairgowrie, which consisted of the great Belle Stewart, her husband, Alex, and daughters Sheila and Cathie. Belle was born in 1906 but not "discovered" until the mid-1950s when Hamish Henderson became aware of her songs. A natural performer, she had a wonderful rapport with whomever she came into contact, whether in Scotland or in America. Employing subtle use of ornamentation, she had a clear, pure voice that communicated to modern, sophisticated audiences the old ballads of long ago.

Born in 1894, MacBeath was one of the last men to work under the brutal bothy system; in fact, much of his repertoire consisted of bothy ballads. Although he died in the early 1970s, he is still considered one of Scotland's finest traditional singers and as much admired for his genial personality—he was "a character"—as for his encyclopedic knowledge of the ballad tradition.

Glasgow-born Archie Fisher, who didn't become familiar with folk songs until he was in his teens, is a versatile singer, equally at home performing an ancient ballad and a contemporary song. He remains one of the major influences on the Scottish revival as performer, songwriter, and broadcaster.

Another important figure, Dick Gaughan, hails from Leith, Edinburgh's seaport, and is of mixed Irish and Scots heritage. He comes from a musical family. He first developed an interest in folk song as a purely intellectual exercise; only later did he begin performing the songs. He has been a member of the Boys of the Lough, Five Hand Reel, and, more recently, Alba. He employs a highly syncopated and uniquely distinctive guitar playing and boasts one of the most powerful singing voices on the current scene. He is also an avowed socialist, and many of his songs have strong political overtones.

Probably the most frequently sung ballads composed in recent years must be Eric Bogle's "No Man's Land" and "And the Band Played Waltzing Matilda." A former accountant from the Border town of Peebles, Bogle has lived in Australia for many years although he performs frequently on both sides of the Atlantic.

LINKS ON THE CHAIN

The human link that connects rural with urban America is Woody Guthrie. He began writing his own songs in the 1930s. In 1937 Guthrie, like other refugees from the Dust Bowl, traveled to California, where he found regular radio work. He soon began writing protest songs. During the Great Depression, he wrote a column for a West Coast communist paper. The turning point in his life came when he met Alan Lomax at a benefit for migrant workers in 1940. Lomax took over Guthrie's career and recorded him for the Library of Congress.

Guthrie, sometimes called the American Robert Burns, wrote almost a thousand songs, although it must be said that he borrowed traditional melodies and set his own lyrics to them. Some of his best known are "This Land Is Your Land," Reuben James," "Tom Joad," and "Roll On, Columbia." His influence was enormous and can be heard in everyone from folk (Pete Seeger) to country (Willie Nelson) and rock (Dylan, Springsteen). Indeed, Guthrie influenced an entire generation of roots singers from Tom Paxton and Phil Ochs to Donovan and Ry Cooder.

From Guthrie, the American folk boom is only a short jaunt away.

The early days of the American folk boom can be said to have begun in the 1950s with the release of the Kingston Trio's recording of the traditional American ballad "Tom Dooley," about the gruesome murder of a young love. The purists cringed, of course, but the public ate it up—"Tom Dooley" reportedly sold some three and a half million copies. Although the ballad had its origins in North Carolina, the performers who popularized it were a trio of West Coast college students. Its popularity proved, in the words of music writer Norm Cohen, "that one need not be a political leftist or a counterculture rebel to sing folk songs." In short, by polishing and refining it, the Kingston Trio turned a tragic American ballad into a pop hit.

In the 1960s there emerged a new generation of singer-songwriters—from Phil Ochs and Tom Paxton to Joan Baez and Bob Dylan—who, although initially influenced and inspired by traditional balladry, soon followed their own path by composing their own songs. The early repertoire of Baez, who is of mixed Mexican and Scots ancestry, consisted of American and Anglo-Celtic traditional balladry.

Dylan began singing in New York City folk clubs in early 1961. At first he emulated his hero and role model, Woody Guthrie. His early recordings contained traditional blues material; then he began writing his own material in the folk protest vein that would become increasingly common in the turbulent 1960s, including such instant classics as "A Hard Rain's A-Gonna Fall," "Blowin' in the Wind," and "Masters of War." Later albums would introduce harder-edged songs with their openly political lyrics ("The Lonesome Death of Hattie Carroll," "Only a Pawn in their Game"). In the mid-1960s *John Wesley Harding* continued Dylan's exploration of roots music, with the Minnesota-born singer creating a sound that resembled Appalachian mountain music more than Greenwich Village folk.

Although Guthrie-esque in both style and content, Dylan quickly found his own voice and, of course, became one of the most influential performers of the American folk revival. And when in 1965 at the Newport Folk Festival, he changed from acoustic to electric guitar, the days of the folk boom were numbered. A new hybrid was born: folk-rock, which had rock's beat with folk's thoughtful lyrics. It soon found avid converts, from Dylan and the Byrds to Simon and Garfunkel. The wild success of the Beatles ensured that the folk boom was indeed over.

Around the same time a Colorado-born singer named Judy Collins recorded her debut album, *A Maid of Constant Sorrow*, which was primarily traditional material. In the early 1970s she had an international hit with her arrangement of the traditional hymn "Amazing Grace." The same recording, *Whales and Nightingales*, contained another traditional gem, the old Scottish whaling song "Farewell to Tarwathie." Clearly, the influence of the old ballads remained.

The folk boom ended in the mid-1960s with the merging of folk with rock. For a short time, though, it was the dominant youth music of its day, an appealing alternative to frivolous pop songs and obscure jazz.

CONTEMPORARY BALLAD MASTERS

Such contemporary Irish singers as Mary Black, Maura O'Connell, Eleanor Shanley, and Eleanor McEvoy have given the ballad new life.

But no one is finer than Dolores Keane.

Born in Caherlistrane, County Galway, from a traditional singing family, Keane made her public debut at the age of five on Irish radio. She has also appeared on numerous television programs with her aunts Rita and Sarah Keane, who are themselves justly famous for their *sean-nós* singing. Dolores learned many of her songs from them.

Few singers in Celtic music have a voice as appealing and as expressive as that of Andy M. Stewart, the most romantic of contemporary Celtic musicians. He has a sweet and expressive voice, an emotional voice that also happens to be sincere. If it lacks the sheer power of a Dick Gaughan or the urban sophistication of an Archie Fisher, it still remains an effective instrument in its own right.

Stewart, was for many years the lead singer of the popular Scots folk band Silly Wizard. His traditional pedigree is a good one—he is a member of the well-known Stewart family of Blairgowrie, in the Central Highlands. Like many musicians of his generation, though, Stewart was weaned on rock music. Despite his contemporary-musical upbringing, he has chosen to build his career on the folk and traditional material of his native land.

Whether singing his own songs or interpreting someone else's, in both style and substance Stewart harks back to the popular music of an earlier era. He is a direct descendant and inheritor of Allan Ramsay, Robert Burns, James Hogg, Sir Walter Scott, and even the genteel Victorian parlor music of Lady Nairne and Sir Harold Boulton, two popular nineteenth-century songwriters.

Stewart manages to combine the best of two worlds—the traditional and the folk. He effortlessly performs material learned from the oral tradition as well as songs from printed and recorded sources. He has also employed both traditional and modern instrumentation without diluting the essence of the material. Scots balladry, Gaelic song, Victorian parlor music, the lonesome quality of a country ballad, contemporary pop, and even hilariously funny stories that poke good-natured fun at everything from the natural wear and tear of aging to hapless lovers unlucky in love—Stewart incorporates all of these disparate elements into a seamless and oftentimes very moving body of work.

A Deep River of Song

In the late twentieth century cultural diversity is in, yet today's artists have proved that some sort of common ground can be shared; that bothy ballads and cowboy songs, outlaw ballads and Border ballads, Jacobite songs and Civil War songs, labor songs and Dust Bowl ballads, Woody Guthrie and Bob Dylan, Bill Monroe and Willie Nelson, Jean Ritchie and Jean Redpath are connected and that somehow performers as diverse as Suzanne Vega and the Indigo Girls or Bruce Springsteen and John Mellencamp can trace their musical roots back to an earlier time—as far back as Francis James Child and, before that, Sir Walter Scott, Robert Burns, and the countless anonymous voices of ballad singers who have been heard through the ages.

Recommended Listening

Joan Baez. *Joan Baez 5* (Vanguard). The early Baez of traditional American and Child ballads. Includes "The Death of Queen Jane," "The Unquiet Grave," and "So We'll Go No More A-Roving," the latter written by American folksinger Richard Dyer-Bennett based on a Lord Byron lyric. In many ways it is a product of its time and place—the glory days of the American folk boom of the early- to mid-1960s when the golden-voiced Baez was the darling of the coffeehouse set.

Bothy Ballads: Music from the North-East (Greentrax). Classic working songs and music from the Scottish northeast, including some fine examples of diddling. Offers a window to a lost world.

Eric Bogle. *Scraps of Paper* (Flying Fish). Eric Bogle's music veers from sublimely silly to supremely sad. At his best, he has written among the most compassionate and deeply moving social and topical songs of the modern folk era. *Scraps of Paper* features some of his finest efforts—the anti-war anthems, "No Man's Land," "And the Band Played Waltzing Matilda," the touching "Now I'm Easy," and, especially, "A Reason For It All," which dares to find hope amid the cruelty of the human condition.

The Clancy Brothers & Tommy Makem. *The Rising of the Moon: Irish Songs of Rebellion* (Tradition). There's no denying the passion that these famous Irish folk figures bring to this fine collection of rebel songs, which includes such classics as "The Rising of the Moon," "The Croppy Boy," "The Wind That Shakes the Barley," and "Kevin Barry."

Bob Dylan (Columbia). There's nothing pretty about this recording. Rather what you have is a young singer/songwriter with many influences and interests from raw country blues and traditional Southern mountain folk song to old spirituals and traditional Scottish ballads searching for his own voice. Listening to this early Dylan you can hear Guthrie, Presley, Jack Elliott, Sonny Terry, Leadbelly, and other ghosts of American music past. Dylan gives the Scottish ballad "Pretty Peggy-O" a decidedly southern American flavor—all nasal twang and New World energy. Includes Dylan's paean to his mentor Woody Guthrie, "Song to Woody." Produced by John Hammond, who also produced Springsteen's first recording *Greetings from Asbury Park, N.J.* in the days when the Jersey rocker was being lauded as the new Bob Dylan.

English and Scottish Folk Ballads (Topic). Features such classic ballads and performers as "The Demon Lover" by A. L. Lloyd, "Reynardine" by Anne Briggs, "The Bramble Briar" by Louis Killen, "The Cruel Ship's Carpenter" by Mike Waterson, and "Lord Randal" by Ewan MacColl.

Archie Fisher. *The Man With a Rhyme* (Folk Legacy). Traditional ballads and traditional-sounding ballads from a modern balladeer; simple, tasteful arrangements. Much more lush is *Will Ye Gang Love* (Green

Linnet), which features some of the best songs in the Scottish tradition ("Broom o' the Cowdenknowes," "Men of Worth") sung by one of the best singers around.

Folk Song America: A 20th Century Revival (Smithsonian). A crash course in American folk music from the history of the folk song revival to the urban folk music of the singer-songwriter era during the 1970s. Most everyone who had anything to do with folk music in the twentieth century is represented, including Guthrie, Jean Ritchie, New Lost City Ramblers, Dylan, Tom Paxton, Richard and Mimi Farina, the Byrds, Simon and Garfunkel, Judy Collins, Steve Goodman, and Peter, Paul, and Mary. Full of surprises, it features several Child ballads (such as "The Maid Freed From the Gallows" by John Jacob Niles) and closes with two klezmer reels performed by De Dannan. A remarkable achievement. Accompanied by a 106-page booklet by music historian Norm Cohen.

Folkways: A Vision Shared, A Tribute to Woody Guthrie and Leadbelly (Columbia). Includes inspired interpretations of Guthrie songs by Bob Dylan ("Pretty Boy Floyd"), Bruce Springsteen ("Vigilante Man"), and Emmylou Harris ("Hobo's Lullaby").

Dick Gaughan. *Handful of Earth* (Topic). The definitive Gaughan recording—full of typical Gaughan fire and brimstone as well as gentle touches. Worth the price alone for his masterful and definitive version of "Song for Ireland" and his own "Both Sides the Tweed," a musical plea for respect between two ancient enemies, Scotland and England.

Woody Guthrie. *This Land Is Your Land*. The Asch Recordings. Vol. 1 (Smithsonian Folkways). Plain-spoken songs with simple melodies mask a remarkably complex number of themes from migrant workers to outlaw ballads by the master of American folk song. Guthrie's influences are widespread and his influences well-documented. Some of the most prominent figures in contemporary music have sung his praises from Dylan to Springsteen in the New World but you can also detect his indelible stamp in the music of Dick Gaughan, a Scot, and Christy Moore, an Irishman. Includes such Guthrie classics as "This Land Is Your Land," "Hobo's Lullaby," "Pastures of Plenty," "Grand Coulee Dam," "Jesse James," and an interpretation of the great Scots ballad "Gypsy Davy."

Dolores Keane. *The Best of Dolores Keane* (Dara). Contains such great songs as "Caledonia" by Dougie Maclean, "Never Be the Sun," and the classic emigration ballad "Teddy O'Neill."

Ewan MacColl. *Black and White: The Definitive Collection* (Green Linnet). The best of MacColl; includes such classics as "Dirty Old Town," "The Shoals of Herring," "The Moving On Song," and, his best-known composition, "The First Time Ever I Saw Your Face."

Ewan MacColl with Peggy Seeger. *The Jacobite Rebellions* (Ossian). Classic Jacobite songs performed by a towering figure of the ballad revival. Includes spirited renditions of "Parcel of Rogues," "The Bonnie Moorhen," "Johnnie Cope," and "Will Ye No Come Back Again?"

Dougie Maclean. *Real Estate* (Dunkeld). All of Maclean's recordings are eminently listenable, full of intelligence and compassion. *Real Estate* is classic Maclean.

The Muckle Sangs: Classic Scots Ballads (Greentrax). The best of Scotland's great ballad singers are here—Jeannie Robertson, Sheila MacGregor, Lizzie Higgins, Betsy Whyte, Jimmy MacBeath, and Willie Scott—singing Child ballads ("The False Knight Upon the Road," "The Twa Brothers," "Tam Lin," "Lord Thomas and Fair Ellen," "Sir Hugh and the Jew's Daughter"), Border ballads ("Jamie Telfer o' the Fair Dodhead"), and others.

Jean Redpath. *Leaving the Land* (Rounder). A combination of traditional ("Scarborough Settler's Lament") and modern (Ron Hyne's wistful "Sonny's Dream") songs that proves just how versatile Redpath can be. For those who prefer her traditional recordings, try *Father Adam*, which contains "Sir Patrick Spens," "Bonnie Susie Cleland," "The Twa Brothers," and "The Shearin's No for You" or *Song of the Seals* and *Lowlands* (all Philo).

Jeannie Robertson. *The Great Scots Traditional Ballad Singer* (Ossian). Timeless emotions come shining through in this wonderful collection of ballads by a seminal figure in the folk revival.

Bruce Springsteen. *The Ghost of Tom Joad* (Columbia). Springsteen continues the minimalist bent that he mined so effectively in *Nebraska* in the 1980s, treading the well-worn terrain of deserted highways and sterile factory plants populated with his familiar cast of losers, outcasts, and societal misfits. With its lonesome harmonica, literate lyrics, and subdued mood, *Ghost* evokes not only the spirit of Guthrie and early Dylan but also recreates the simple emotions of traditional balladry. Sparse and lean, these concise vignettes of ordinary people caught in the crossfire of daily living are examples of urban folk at its most primordial, while clearly filtered through a rock perspective.

Andy M. Stewart. *By the Hush* (Green Linnet). Stewart's solo debut features modern songs and traditional songs with modern arrangements. Poignant lyrics, impeccable instrumentation, and Stewart's expressive voice add up to one of the best recordings of the contemporary folk era. Includes the touching "I'd Cross the Wild Atlantic." A recent solo recording, *Man in the Moon* (Green Linnet), contains arguably his best performance on record, "Land o' the Leal," a poignant ballad of irrecoverable loss. All of his recordings with Silly Wizard are a pleasure: *Kiss the Tears Away* (Shanachie) contains his adaptation of the traditional "If I Was a Blackbird" and a modern gem, "The Fisherman's Song"; *So Many Partings* (Shanachie), the wistful "Valley of Strathmore"; and *Dublin Lady* (Green Linnet), the classic bothy ballad "Bogie's Bonnie Belle." With Phil Cunningham and Manus Lunny he recorded *Fire in the Glen* (Shanachie), which includes new versions of traditional songs ("I Mourn for the Highlands," "Brighidin Ban Mo Store") and originals (the title cut and "Young Jimmy in Flanders").

The Stewarts of Blair (Ossian). Great songs ("Queen Amang the Heather," "Dowie Dens o' Yarrow," "Young Jamie Foyers") performed by one of Scotland's leading families of folk.

The Songs of Robert Burns. Vol. 7 (Greentrax). Part of a series of Burns's songs researched and arranged by American composer Serge Hovey and sung by Jean Redpath. Six were recorded in the United States.

Watersons. *For Peace and Spicey Ale* (Topic). A cappella singing at its best. The Watersons have influenced everyone from Traffic to Christy Moore.

7

Country Hearts, Celtic Ways

Religion, Bluegrass, and That Long Lonesome Highway

If Heaven ain't a lot like Dixie then I don't want to go.

–HANK WILLIAMS, JR., COUNTRY SINGER

I know as many country and western songs as I do Gaelic songs.

–CATHERINE-ANN MACPHEE, GAELIC SINGER

Country music is largely the product of a white, Protestant, Anglo-Celtic tradition, a deceptively simple music form whose beginnings go back hundreds of years and thousands of miles to Scotland, Ireland, and England. And since it fermented in the South, it includes not only traditional Anglo-Celtic ballads and tunes but also sacred hymns and African-American spirituals, all blended into today's "country" by contemporary, mostly Southern singers and songwriters.

Country music looks to the past while simultaneously embracing the present. It is at once a nostalgic and sad but also optimistic music. Country celebrates stability and continuity, but at the same time laments the passing of familiar things. Still, it has a natural, good-natured resiliency about it that defies its stereotypical cry-in-your-beer image. Country music developed from the balladry and tunes brought to the United States by Anglo-Celtic immigrants. Much of the traditional Southern instrumental music, for example, originated in Scotland and Ireland, especially the old-time fiddle music. Irish dance music in particular has had a major influence on Appalachian music.

Gradually, country music absorbed other influences, until it was able to create a distinctively indigenous sound with its own ballads and its own traditions. Hillbilly music it came to be called, a term that essentially referred to the social music of the rural South, especially the Appalachian South (according to folk-music historian Archie Green, the term *hillbilly* first appeared in print in April 1900 in the *New York Journal*). It consisted primarily of Americanized interpretations of English, Irish, Scots, and Scots-Irish traditional music, shaped by African-American rhythms, and containing vestiges of nineteenth-century popular songs, especially those of the minstrel tradition.

"Hillbilly music," wrote Neil Rosenberg in *Bluegrass: A History*, "was a form of theater, and just as comedians dressed in costume, the musicians dressed for their role."

Despite its multicultural background, a claim can be justifiably made that country music is quintessentially American music. After all, just to cite one obvious example, who could be more typically American than Elvis Presley? Presley, the poor white Mississippi farm boy who hit pay dirt in the big city, helped transform hillbilly culture into a grander and wealthier version of American pop culture. Jimmie Rodgers may have been the first genuine country music star, but Elvis (himself of Irish—or is it Scottish?—ancestry) was the first southerner to transcend his country roots and appeal to a much broader—and younger—audience. Yet he never forgot his roots. Significantly, one of his early recordings was the Bill Monroe bluegrass standard "Blue Moon of Kentucky."

Like many young people growing up in the rural South, Presley was a regular churchgoer; he attended the Pentecostal First Assembly of God Church. His Calvinistic upbringing was a contemporary remnant of the Great Revival that had swept across the South in the nineteenth century. The church where he worshiped was both a sanctuary and a warning about the profane world that beckoned beyond the church doors. Like the camp meetings of earlier generations, the church was a place where saints and sinners, the saved and the unsaved, could all come and sing together under one roof. Elvis, the white man who brought country music and African-American music together, is perhaps the best example of the essentially free-spiritedness that lies at the heart of country music.

The history of country music, then, is a paradox: It is a profoundly conservative music—conservative in theme, style, and substance—that, in order to survive and protect itself, has been forced to adopt an outsider mentality. Long looked down upon by the so-called sophisticated elite, the country-music artist has spent many years trying to be accepted by mainstream America. For most of country's life, it has been the music of an insular community—the kind of music performed on a front porch on a warm summer evening, or in the privacy of the living room surrounded by family and friends. It was music made especially for the hearthside; for this reason it did not travel well outside the rural South. Taken out of its natural environment, removed from its particular context, it was often misunderstood or misinterpreted. Indeed, for most of its existence country music has been treated with disdain and an overall lack of respect. The country performer was never taken quite seriously enough, never received the type of support—emotional, financial, or otherwise—that other musicians took for granted.

John Shelton Reed, author, professor, and sage observer of southern life and mores, once wrote that the most notable country singers came from a particular region of the South: "Most," he said, "are from a fertile crescent that reaches from southwest Virginia through Kentucky and the eastern two-thirds of Tennessee, over into northern Arkansas, southeast Missouri, Oklahoma, and Texas."

Country music is a product of the fringe, of the margins of the Appalachian and Ozark regions. Much of this outsider mentality, of course, is due to the unique and complicated history of the South, a region that in a sense has always been on the outside looking in. Historian Henry Shapiro refers to "the otherness of Appalachia" and goes on to say that "[i]t was simply a fact, like Scottish otherness." The South is different from the rest of the country in several important ways: by virtue of its pronounced accent, its tumultuous and controversial past, its rural heritage, and its basic ethnic homogeneity.

Strife, Feuds, and the Ties that Bind

More than 60 percent of the settlers in the southern backcountry in the eighteenth century were immigrants—or children of immigrants—who originally had come from five counties in Northern Ireland, six counties in the north of England, and five counties in southern Scotland, according to historian David Hackett Fischer. Thus the culture of the Border country was brought across the Atlantic to America. The backcountry that I'm referring to includes southwestern Pennsylvania; most of West Virginia; western portions of Maryland and Virginia; North and South Carolina; and adjacent parts of Georgia, Kentucky, and Tennessee.

Southern culture closely resembles traditional Celtic culture in habits, customs, and values. Indeed, the strong kinship ties that are found throughout the South are quite similar to the clan system of the Highland Scots and to the tight familial ties of the Border country. Seven centuries of almost continual warfare along the border between England and Scotland had produced a people who were fiercely individualistic, wary of authority, and accustomed to doing things their own way. They were also stubborn, determined, and proud.

From Newcastle to Edinburgh the countryside was ravaged by fighting between warlords on both sides, especially in the area described as "the debatable land" (land that was claimed by both sides). Powerful and dangerous clans with names like Scott, Kerr, Nixon, Bell, Graham—and, most notorious of all, Armstrong—engaged in rustling, murder, and a Border custom known as reiving, or stealing from one's neighbors. The reivers would wait until nightfall and then attack with fire and sword, sweeping down on their "enemy," ransacking property, and stealing livestock.

Acute poverty and random violence had a long-term effect on the collective psyche and the culture that it produced. Loyalty to family and clan became of the utmost importance, and a deep suspicion of strangers became internalized. To humiliate one member of a family was to violate the honor and dignity of the entire clan—and nothing could be a more grievous sin. As a result, blood feuds among Border families were constant and seemingly endless. The same attitude spread to the southern backcountry when Border emigrants had made the dangerous Atlantic crossing: Sectarian conflicts or feuds became almost as common in the South as they had been in the Borders. One of the most famous feuds, that between the Hatfields and McCoys, reportedly arose over a dispute involving hogs and claimed a dozen lives, and perhaps as many injuries, over a period of twelve years.

Although settlers of pre-Revolutionary America were roughly of similar ethnic and social backgrounds, the South developed along a different path than the rest of the nation. This was especially so when religion was involved. Southerners took their religion seriously. Many of them, for example, were strongly Calvinistic. They were in awe of death, and both respected and feared the profound power it had over their lives. Like many cultures where endemic violence was a fact of life, the backcountry folk tended to be fatalistic, and felt an overwhelming need to be saved. On the frontier, where anarchy percolated close to the surface and life was precarious at best, rituals took on added significance. Wakes and funerals meant more under such circumstances; everyone was expected to pay proper respect.

It was in the South, too, where the camp meeting, a fervent example of religious celebration, was transplanted from the Border country to the frontier. Thousands were known to attend these outdoor services, which frequently lasted for several days. These meetings commonly began with much preaching and praying and then climaxed with shouting and wild displays of emotion.

Thus, not surprisingly, religion has played a crucial role in the growth of southern music. "A Jesus-haunted country," Walker Percy has called the South. Revivalist and fundamentalist sects as well as mainstream Protestant denominations—such as Methodism, Presbyterianism, Baptism—made inroads in the South shortly after the Revolutionary War. Preachers traveled the back roads and footpaths of the rural South into the remote mountains, carrying the word of God with them. Their brand of religion was decidedly democratic, a populist style that strongly appealed to the individualistic tendencies of the backcountry. And the popularity of these evangelical groups was due, in no small measure, to congregational singing.

In addition to the church, the frontier camp meetings also were popular places to sing. The songs portrayed a black-and-white world of good and evil, where God was ever present and omniscient, kind and generous to the faithful but stern and unforgiving to sinners.

Harmony singing evolved from New England church singing-schools, to which shape-note or sacred harp singing had been brought over by English immigrants. The itinerant singing-school master traveled across the country, and in this way brought the tradition to the South. The tradition eventually traveled as far west as Arkansas and into Texas.

Group singing in the South first developed in the early nineteenth century. The concept of shape notes was introduced in 1801 by William Smith and William Little in *The Easy Instructor: A New Method of Teaching Harmony* in Philadelphia. This method of singing was said to be so simple that even the most illiterate backwoodsman could grasp it. In it the pitch of the musical note was essentially indicated by its shape rather than by musical notation. Folklorists Alan and John Lomax sometimes referred to shape-note singing as "surge songs," and noted that they "followed the psalm singing style of New England colonial congregations. Puritan ecclesiastics believed in long sermons, heavy praying and doleful music." In both sound and manner, it is highly reminiscent of Gaelic psalm singing, which we discussed in chapter 5.

During the Great Awakening of the eighteenth century, which generally is said to have occurred between 1739 and 1742, many dissenters broke away from the established Protestant church, disturbed, as they were, by its rigidity and strict adherence to a formal liturgy.

Following the Revolutionary War, the Baptist denomination gained widespread popularity in the South, especially in the frontier state of Kentucky. The songs these congregations sang reflected their growing isolation, and almost by necessity they searched for new songs that would match the soaring intensity of their emotions. Thus the old psalms were not quite enough; rather, folk tunes in the form of balladry, as well as jigs and secular love songs, soon entered the hymnbooks, although camouflaged in appropriately somber texts. In this way hymnbook makers compiled these new songs into shape-note hymnals. Shape-note books were published in South Carolina in 1835 and in Georgia in 1844.

THE IMPACT OF THE GREAT REVIVAL

In the early nineteenth century another religious phenomenon—the Great Revival—swept across the South, through Virginia, Kentucky, Tennessee, and much of the rural South.

The followers of this religious movement were the descendants of the early Scots and Scots-Irish pioneers, and the songs they sang were based on both African-American and white spirituals. As I've noted, such a strict religious upbringing had had its effects on the southern psyche. The southerner, especially the southerner on the frontier, adopted a fatalistic and somber outlook, looking to life beyond the grave as the ultimate salvation. This melancholy streak found expression in the Anglo-Scot American ballad tradition: A large proportion of the repertoire consisted of sad songs about unrequited, lost, or betrayed love; murder tragedies also were quite common.

Scholars have spent many years studying why the musical paths of the country's two main regions—North and South—differ so drastically. The reasons, of course, are varied, and range from geography and climate to history and tradition. The southern region developed in a far different manner from that of its northern neighbor. Southerners nurtured an agricultural economy and became committed very early to a rural way of life. Philosophically and socially, they were conservative. As their "peculiar institution"—slavery—came increasingly under fire from outside sources, they retreated into their hollows and mountain foothills, and became even more insular and defensive. Thus, as noted country-music historian Bill C. Malone has pointed out, traditions that once had been shared in common throughout the United States survived in the South long after they had been abandoned or forgotten in the North.

Country music, then, developed out of this sturdy folk tradition. Singing the old ballads from the mother country alleviated the loneliness and isolation of frontier life. In the hollows and back-country of the Old South the music gained its most dedicated followers; the cultural isolation that persisted from the Virginia Tidewater to the East Texas scrub virtually guaranteed its perpetuation. It was these ballads and tunes that formed the foundation of what would eventually be called country music. Thus, the country singers were singing melodies of ancient origin, or at least were following a pattern that already was centuries old, as I noted in chapter 6. The modal scale so evident in the earlier country music eventually gave way to harmony singing and the use of musical instruments.

As in the Celtic countries, oral tradition in the South was valued and nurtured. Long tales were handed down from generation to generation, with each new version embellishing and expanding a bit on the original story. From the Jack tales to the tall yarns of Br'er Rabbit and the saga of Harry McClintock's "Big Rock Candy Mountain," the South boasts an abundant oral culture in ballads, folk legends, and folklore. Southern speech is peppered with colorful idiomatic expressions, proverbs, and hyperbole. And of course it is the South that has produced such immensely talented and strikingly individualistic writers as William Faulkner, Tennessee Williams, Flannery O'Connor, Carson McCullers, Jesse Stuart, and, in our own day, Cormac McCarthy, Ellen Gilchrist, and Dorothy Allison. In Bobbie Gentry's 1960s classic story ballad "Ode to Billie Joe," Bill C. Malone finds the "perfect musical distillation of the kind of southern storytelling that has brought fame to such authors as Eudora Welty, William Faulkner, and Flannery O'Connor."

In this rich, fertile soil of oral culture there grew a natural affinity for stories both detailed and complex—"big ballads," the Southerners called them and, indeed, they are the descendants of the Scottish *muckle sangs* that we met in chapter 6. They were "big" because they dealt with big, almost primordial subjects, such as love and death, murder and betrayal. For many years these big ballads formed the very bedrock of southern oral traditions.

 ## Sharyn McCrumb

"I come from a race of storytellers," best-selling author Sharyn McCrumb declares in the introduction to her first-ever collection of short fiction, *Foggy Mountain Breakdown*. And that she has. Her great-great-great-grandfather Malcolm McCoury, a Scot, was kidnapped as a lad from his native Islay in 1750. After a lifetime of grand adventures, including a brief stint as a cabin boy on a sailing ship, he finally settled in western North Carolina in 1794.

With that as a family pedigree, how could she not be a storyteller?

In addition to her work as a consummate crime writer, McCrumb is also the author of the popular Ballad Novel series: *If Ever I Return, Pretty Peggy-O; The Hangman's Beautiful Daughter; She Walks These Hills*; and *The Rosewood Casket*. Throughout these haunting tales, populated by quirky and colorful characters and set amid the brooding Appalachian hill country, the dark narratives of the ballad tradition remain marvelously alive.

BLACK AND WHITE

Two musical styles tended to dominate in the South: the African-American tradition and the rural white tradition. Each had a profound effect on the other; the two borrowed and shared arrangements and material. The resulting style usually consisted of unaccompanied solo vocals sung in a high-pitched nasal voice, the lyrics set to simple melodies. To compensate for the lack of instruments, singers would often develop an elaborate singing style or ornamentation, to embellish the melody.

The Celtic equivalent may be that of the *sean-nós* or old-style singing in the Irish tradition, which I discussed at length in chapter 5. As already mentioned, *sean-nós* is a distinctive and highly ornamented style of singing that owes much to the Gaelic bardic tradition, in which poems were transmitted orally from generation to generation. Like the bluegrass singer, *sean-nós* artists don't convey emotion through how loudly or softly they sing but rather through the use of ornamentation—that is, how they sing and mold the words, or how much they stress melody and rhythm.

"The Gaelic singer," wrote music historian Robert Cantwell, "dresses his song—which preceded him in the world and which will endure long after he is gone—with a decorative tracery that is as intricate and fragile as the song is hard and unyielding." This style, called melismatic, was often heard in the southern mountains. Long before Hank Williams composed his heartbreaking paean to loneliness, "I'm So Lonesome I Could Cry," the earliest country singers had a soft spot in their hearts for melancholy laments or lonesome dirges. Yet the introduction of musical instruments into the country tradition necessitated some changes. As Bill C. Malone described it, "The old songs, with their minor keys and modal structure, were flattened in order to allow easier accompaniment." Thus the high wail of the traditional country singer adapted itself to the lush, full sound of harmony singing, as typified in the singing of the late Bill Monroe or the Stanley Brothers.

There was nothing very fancy about the typical country song. Lyrics tended to address conservative themes, steeped as they were in such traditional values as family, country, and religion. These mountain ballads were sung without rhythm and were usually performed without accompaniment, a capella, in a high, mournful voice.

Country lyrics still revolve around simple and universal themes of love (usually of the sad, unrequited, or tragic variety), happiness, religion, home, country, and death. Country songwriters tend to be practical sorts who derive practical solutions to mundane problems. Indeed, the country lyricist has always confronted the realities of life head-on, whether it be alcohol abuse or a cheating spouse.

For a stubborn morality lies at the heart of traditional country music. The old values—home, hearth, purity—are upheld. Live a good, pure life, the songs tell us, and we will be rewarded with a better world beyond the boundaries of this corrupt and polluted earth. Moreover, if we look closely at the social origins of the backcountry folk, we discover that those early pioneers had an abiding interest in all things magical. In a word, they were superstitious. This attitude carried over into their daily habits; rather than making the most of their time, like their Yankee cousins, they chose to resign themselves to passing time by simply letting events take care of themselves. This attitude was reflected in their mountain ballads, songs that told of stability and continuity but also warned of betrayal and treachery. Nothing, it seemed, was ever guaranteed.

The old songs from Scotland and England survived longest in the Southeast, especially in the more remote mountain regions, but the lyrics didn't always remain intact. Over the decades, the indigenous population made changes, softened the content a bit, or adapted the lyrics to American soil. Thus the supernatural elements were diminished in favor of good old-fashioned religion. Often the words were changed even when the original melodies remained; in this way, American ballads came to be sung alongside the ancient Anglo-Celtic ones.

Examples of ballads that were altered during the Atlantic crossing or transformed in the new homes were numerous. "The House

Carpenter" (sometimes called "The Demon Lover" and occasionally "James Harris") underwent a drastic transformation. In the original, a man leaves his sweetheart to go to sea and drowns. His ghost returns years later and persuades his former lover—who has since married a house carpenter—to leave her husband and young child and elope with him. This she does, but at sea she begins to weep for her abandoned husband and child. The ghost, angry and revengeful, destroys the ship.

In the American version, though, the supernatural elements have vanished completely. The plot follows much the same line, except not only is there no ghost but also the ship sinks during a natural disaster.

Various changes occur during the transmission of songs, of course: lines are lost, names are altered, and some details invariably omitted. "Pretty Polly" (also known as "The Lass of Roch Royal") is another good example of what can happen when a song crosses the Atlantic. The changes transformed a traditional ballad with clearly supernatural themes into a straightforward American murder mystery. In the original, the murderer tries to escape while aboard a ship. The ship, however, will not move, and the captain is thus convinced there is a violent criminal on board. All the sailors, including the murderer, deny any wrongdoing—until the ghost of Pretty Polly appears with the murderer's baby in her arms. In Appalachia, however, the mountain singers transformed it into a simple murder ballad, with a common-enough theme: The young man chooses to kill his lover instead of marrying her when she becomes pregnant. It is a theme that has been the subject of countless novels, short stories, and films.

Many of the best-known indigenous American ballads have Celtic connections. "John Henry," considered one of America's greatest ballads, is about an African-American railroad worker who was killed in an accident in West Virginia around 1873. With its Scottish-inspired melody and almost apocryphal story of an African-American hero forging a new life in a new country, it is perhaps one of the finer examples of the cross-fertilization of white and African-American traditions.

Civil War balladry, too, looked to the Celtic lands for many of their themes and melodies. Indeed, a fair amount of these songs borrowed freely from English, Scots, and Irish melodies, stitching them onto new lyrics. "Johnny Has Gone for a Soldier," for example, was based on an old Irish folk song, the doleful "Shule Aroon" (from the Gaelic *shule agrah* or "come with me, love"), which laments the flight of Ireland's finest soldiers—the "Wild Geese"— who fought for France during the seventeenth-century Continental wars; and "Johnny Is My Darling" was based on an old Jacobite rallying cry, "Charlie Is My Darling." One of the most stirring Civil War anthems, "When Johnny Comes Marching Home," is believed to have been written in 1863 by Patrick Sarsfield Gilmore. Some historians, however, insist that the Irish-born Gilmore filched the melody from the Irish antiwar ballad, "Johnny, I Hardly Knew Ye."

The popular cowboy lament "The Streets of Laredo" apparently traces its origins, according to John and Alan Lomax, to late-eighteenth-century Cork, where our young hero is a soldier who has contracted a deadly case of syphilis. On the journey to his final resting place, the coffin is accompanied by the full flourish of fife and drums and a weeping contingent of adoring suitors ("for we all loved our comrade, so brave, young and handsome/we all loved our comrade although he done wrong"). The soundtrack of the television documentary *The Long Journey Home* contains both versions of the classic, including the Irish, titled "The Bard of Armagh" (sometimes "The Cowboy's Lament") and sung with masculine authority by country singer Vince Gill.

 ## DROVERS AND COWBOYS

I was much more of a cowboy than a ploughboy . . .
there's more in common between a Celt and a cowboy
than between a Celt and an Englishman.

—Josh MacRae, Scots singer

David Wilkie and his band Cowboy Celtic hail from Alberta on the Canadian plains. By performing the music of the American and Canadian West, they have taken cowboy songs back to their Scottish and Irish roots. Their CD *Cowboy Ceilidh* features adaptations of songs and tunes brought over by Scots and Irish emigrants as well as original compositions. It illustrates the link between the Highland droving traditions that flourished until the 1880s and the cattle business in Texas, Wyoming, and Montana, where Scots were heavily involved as ranchers and cattle barons.

Recorded partly in Ireland and Scotland, *Cowboy Ceilidh* features Scots musician Phil Cunningham on accordion and whistles on several tracks, while Arthur Cormack sings the plaintive vocal on "Farewell to Coigach (Mo Shoraidh Leis A'Coigach)," apparently the only surviving cowboy song in North America written in Gaelic. Composed in Montana before World War I by Murdo Maclean, one of the many Highland Gaels who worked the American West as cattlemen, shepherds, and cowboys, "Farewell to Coigach" is a poignant paean to the land and sweetheart he left behind.

"The Celtic cowboy link is . . . no myth," says Rob Gibson, a musician and authority on Scots music and history. "Scots by birth and descent carried on the cattle trade on the great plains of Western Canada and America." Gibson organized Cowboy Ceilidh's successful tour of the Highlands and Islands during the summer of 1998.

The droving industry held an important place in the Scottish economy for nearly four centuries. The term *drovers* refers to the men who brought the cattle from the Highlands to the Lowland markets or *trysts*. According to the historian A. B. Haldane, they ranged from great landowners, nobles and chieftains "who bred the cattle on their wide estates" to others like the legendary Rob Roy who "provided the capital needed for cattle dealing enterprises."

The great cattle *trysts* at places like Crieff, Doune, and Falkirk attracted drovers from all over Scotland. "At the beginning of the nineteenth century, it was not uncommon to find 100,000 sheep and 60,000 cattle at the Falkirk tryst," noted Gibson. Brian McNeill, ex-Battlefield Band fiddler and singer, even wrote a song about the the Falkirk *tryst*, called "The Lads of the Fair." The Falkirk tryst was held three times a year—in August, September, and October—and it attracted a lively bunch of gamblers, ballad singers, fiddlers, beggars, and other assorted types.

The drovers endured long journeys from Kintail to Crieff, from Caithness to Falkirk, and even from the Highlands to Norfolk in southern England. A typical drove might consist of one, two, or even three hundred animals, with each drover responsible for some fifty to sixty of the creatures. Cattle would usually travel about ten to twelve miles in one day. The droving season in the Highlands lasted from May or early June to late October. The arrival of the railways ended the droving life in Scotland. Old drovers' inns are still found throughout Scotland, though. Some of Scotland's major roads started as drove roads.

Who are cowboys but the North American equivalent of the Scottish drovers? Many of the original cowboys came from the Celtic lands. Some were displaced immigrants, victims of the Great Famine in Ireland or the Highland Clearances in Scotland. Others were entrepreneurs who chose, like emigrants before and since, to start over in the New World. The cowboy-song repertoire largely consisted of Scots, Irish, English, and Welsh ballads. Indeed, Wilkie considers these songs the "real folk music" of the North American West. It's no surprise then that Robert Burns and Sir Walter Scott were particular favorites among American cowboys.

The Matador Ranch in Texas was founded by men from Dundee in the 1880s and stayed in business until the 1950s, while the Prairie Land & Cattle Company was based in Edinburgh. Major roads in the Canadian city of Calgary are named after the old cattle routes, such as the Glenmore Trail or the McLeod Trail. John Clay, originally from Berwickshire in southeastern Scotland, was a leading cattle baron, as was the half-Scots, half-Cherokee Jesse Chisholm, for whom the Chisholm Trail (where cattle were driven from Texas to Abilene, Kansas) is named.

"The Drover's Song" ("Oran na Drubhairean") was a tune popular in Wester Ross in the eighteenth century. Set to words by the Gairloch poet William Ross, it was collected in Sutherland, Scotland's northernmost county, in 1943. The popular "Streets of Laredo" started life as an Irish ballad called "The Bard of Armagh," while the Aberdeenshire whaling ballad "Farewell to Tarwathie" became transformed into "The Railroad Corral."

JEAN RITCHIE

In chapter 6 I discussed the Child ballads. Yet the Child ballads traveled well beyond Scotland and England: They found great popularity in America, especially among the mountaineers of Appalachia. Perhaps the most influential traditional singer in America, and certainly one of the greatest American interpreters of the Child collection, is Jean Ritchie. Music critic Norm Cohen credits Ritchie with introducing urban audiences to "the 'high lonesome style' of the Appalachians: a slow, metrically irregular, highly melismatic old hymn style, probably traceable to Scots church singing." Ritchie used an ornate and embellished style of singing, sung in a slow and methodical manner.

The youngest in a family of fourteen, Ritchie was raised in Kentucky and learned the ballads her ancestors had brought with them from Britain. It has been said that she possesses the vocal equivalent of what has come to be known in bluegrass music as the "high lonesome" sound. Ritchie has explained it in this way:

These old songs and their music were in our heads, or hearts, or some part of us, and we never needed to write them down. They were there, like games and rhymes and riddles . . . to be employed and enjoyed when the time came for them.

We sang and listened to them for themselves, for the excitement of the tale, or for the beauty and strength of the language or for the graceful tunes, for the romantic tingle we got from a glimpse of life in the long-ago past . . . .

As I remember, it took a special time for us to appreciate these "big" ballads . . . . We hummed them about the housework and when walking along the roads, and in the fields, but that wasn't really "singing them out." It had to be a quiet time for that, as when the family gathered on the front porch, evenings.

CECIL SHARP

Another important figure was the English folk-song collector, Cecil Sharp. A composer and music teacher, Sharp spent the period between 1903 and 1914 collecting songs and tunes in the English countryside. His reputation for impeccable scholarship traveled across the Atlantic, and he was invited to New York in 1914 to assist in a production of *A Midsummer Night's Dream*. The following year, while teaching at a summer music school in Maine, he received a visit from Dame Olive Campbell, whose husband, John, was a director of the Southern Highland Division of the Russell Sage Foundation. She encouraged Sharp to visit Appalachia, to hear for himself those mountain ballads that so enchanted her with their beauty and timelessness.

Sharp agreed, and between 1916 and 1918 spent forty-six weeks in the mountains of North Carolina, Kentucky, Virginia, Tennessee, and West Virginia, during which time he collected almost seventeen hundred songs and tunes. In 1919 he published his *English Folk Songs from the Southern Appalachians*, which contained the music and lyrics of 122 songs and ballads and 323 melodies. Due partly to his work and partly to the romanticization of a nostalgic rural past, Appalachian southerners were soon being touted in some academic circles as a "pure" race of people who lived life much as their seventeenth-century ancestors had done.

 ## THE BONNY HIGHLAND LADDIE AND THE SINGING COWBOY

The Scottish Highlands and the American South share a similar mythology.

Popular literature's image of the Highlander circa late seventeenth century was that of a gallant, romantic figure. The earliest song of this type appears in Ramsay's *Tea-Table Miscellany*. This new and improved Highlander owes his existence to the cultural sea change in attitude toward the Jacobite cause. Defying all odds, he came to symbolize Scottish nationalism and cultural distinctiveness.

Generations later and miles apart the American cowboy came to epitomize freedom and independence. Yet the ancestors of both the hillbilly and cowboy, wrote cultural historian Richard Peterson "were created in the philosophy of Locke, Wordsworth, and Thoreau, were seen in the politics of Andrew Jackson, and were given life in the novels of James Fenimore Cooper and Herman Melville."

Like the case of the clansmen and the Highlands, the legend of the cowboy had little to do with the authentic Old West. The mythic cowboy emerged in the 1880s, just as the real cowboys began to fade. The first cowboy novel, *The Hermit of the Colorado Hills* by William Bushnell, was published in 1864. And in 1902 Owen Wister's *The Virginian* became the first "literary" western novel. Eight years later, in 1910, John A. Lomax published his *Cowboy Songs and Other Frontier Ballads*. Dime novels, pulp fiction, and Hollywood movies all added to the allure. And as Robert Cantwell pointed out in his book *When We Were Good*, to cement the generally positive image that the cowboy enjoyed in American society, in 1912 no less than Teddy Roosevelt—the epitome of rugged American individualism—wrote a preface to Lomax's book, making the perceptive observation that in their "sympathy for the outlaw," the cowboy songs emulated English and Scottish ballads.

And yet cowboy music and song date back to the early days of western settlement. The occupational cowboy songs, though, did not appear until the post–Civil War. Initially the songs they sang were, understandably, the songs they were already familiar with—the popular songs of the East or the ballads of England, Scotland, and Ireland but also traditional hymns and camp-meeting songs.

The heyday of cowboy music took place in the 1930s. Cowboy songs were heard on the radio, while the cowboy mystique became a favorite theme of Tin Pan Alley songwriters—look at "The Last Roundup" (1933)—all of this culminating in the Broadway musical *Oklahoma*. Singing cowboys graced the Hollywood screen, from Gene Autry and Ken Maynard to Tex Ritter and Roy Rogers. Indeed, according to writer J. R. Young, "The singing cowboy represented the first popular commercialization of country music on a grand and sweeping scale."

Many parallels could be drawn between the mythical South, beloved of American popular song and the Tin Pan Alley tradition, and mythical Scotland. In much the same way that Yankee songwriters created the palatable and rosy-colored portrait of a romantic South, English or Lowland Scots songwriters portrayed a wild and verdant Highlands populated by kilted noble-savage types. When Bill Malone wrote, "Southern folk culture and music had been alternately scorned, viewed with condescension, exploited for their humor, romanticized, or, most often, merely ignored," it sounded remarkably similar to the patronizing attitude directed at Gaelic folk culture and music.

Of course, many country singers adopt a cowboy or western image, donning cowboy shirts, string tie, and Stetson hats. In recent years the so-called neotraditionalists George Strait, Garth Brooks, Alan Jackson, and Clint Black, to name a few, have become part of the cowboy mystique.

"The cowboy will retain his appeal," wrote Malone, "as long as Americans identify with the kind of freedom that he supposedly represents, or as long as they cling to the illusion of their country's preindustrial virtue and innocence."

THE INSTRUMENTAL TRADITION

The instrumental tradition in the South also owes a great deal to the Celtic lands. The fiddle, for example, was brought to America by Celtic emigrants in the late seventeenth and early eighteenth centuries; some say, in fact, that rural whites had started playing the fiddle in the South even earlier, in the seventeenth century. Whatever the year or decade, there is no denying that many of the tunes they were playing came from Scotland and Ireland. Most fiddlers were amateur musicians. They were especially popular at social gatherings, such as barn raisings or quilting bees, hoedowns and corn-shuckings, as well at wakes and weddings. Not everyone, however, appreciated the fiddle. Religious fundamentalists in particular did not take kindly to the musicians nor to their rowdy contraption, which soon earned the nickname of "the devil's box" (as it had in Scotland and Ireland too).

Fiddling contests, which reportedly peaked about 1865 but which had existed at least since the 1730s, were especially popular in the late nineteenth and early twentieth centuries. The first well-publicized fiddlers' convention, sponsored by the Georgia Old Time Fiddlers' Association, took place in Atlanta in 1913, according to folk-music historian Norm Cohen. The convention was held annually until 1935.

The banjo was another popular instrument in the South. Originating in Africa, it was introduced to America about the middle of the eighteenth century, when it came over with the slaves. It soon became an indelible part of plantation life. The clawhammer style of banjo playing entered the southern music scene during the middle of the nineteenth century through the medium of the minstrel show. Indeed, it has been said that white musicians in these shows brought the banjo to the attention of the general public.

The five-string banjo was apparently popularized by a young Virginian named Joe Sweeney. Its importance was that it could be picked; this would eventually would make it such an essential element of country music. In the clawhammer style, made popular by the minstrel or mountain banjoist, the player uses the force of the wrist—and sometimes of the forearm—and brings the back of his fingernail down upon the string then, with a snap, brings it back. The fifth or thumb string has been traced to the drone of the Highland bagpipe, although many scholars, such as Robert Cantwell, author of *Bluegrass Breakdown*, find it more likely that the thumb string originated on the plantation, "if not in Africa."

Around the beginning of the twentieth century, another stringed instrument—the guitar—began gaining popularity among the southern working class, and with the arrival of this instrument the old-time string band was born. Typically, the line-up consisted of a fiddle, guitar, and banjo. Other popular instruments included the dulcimer, the harmonica, and the mandolin.

These shows reflected the influence of non-Anglo-Celtic roots too; they consisted of a fast-talking pseudodoctor and a wagonload of "patients" and entertainers who helped warm up the crowd. Many of these traveling shows—along with circuses and tent shows—became a fixture of southern life in the years before World War I, providing work for many early country musicians, among them Uncle Dave Macon, Jimmie Rodgers, Roy Acuff, and Hank Williams. Folk-music historian Norm Cohen said, "The older Anglo-American fiddle tunes and dances gave way to ragtime and jazzy numbers. Reels and hornpipes carried across the Atlantic by Scots and Scots-Irish fiddlers . . . "

Other influences on southern music included traveling preachers, salesmen, railroad workers, vaudeville shows, and Tin Pan Alley songsmiths as well as parlor songs, church music, and blues ballads. Indeed, music scholars point out that bluesmen and country singers have shared a common background of songs and motifs since the mid-seventeenth century.

THE BIRTH OF HILLBILLY MUSIC

A direct descendant of the traveling tent show was the early hillbilly string band. The musical groups that fell into this category were destined to give the 1920s and 1930s the nickname "The Golden Age of Hillbilly Music." Among the most important of the early country musicians were Uncle Dave Macon, Bradley Kincaid, Dick Boggs, and Charlie Poole, all of whom acquired their considerable repertoires mostly from traditional sources, although some would later write original compositions in the style of the older pieces. They were considered the first white folk musicians to be commercially recorded in the United States.

Hillbilly records catered specifically to rural southern whites of Appalachia and the Ozarks during the first few decades of the twentieth century. Early hillbilly music consisted of two traditions: that of the semi-professional string bands and minstrel singers, and that of the music created strictly in the home. It was this latter influence that helped to preserve many of the traditional Scottish and English ballads. The guitar, five-string banjo, and fiddle were the most commonly used instruments in the early recordings, although mandolin, autoharp, and Hawaiian steel guitar were also occasionally employed.

Two forms of hillbilly music evolved during the formative years of the recording industry—country and mountain. Country stressed individual singing, used more nontraditional instruments, and was influenced by both popular and African-American music. Its chief practitioner was Jimmie Rodgers. The mountain strain relied more on traditional songs and tunes for its repertoire, and the material tended to be performed in the customary high-nasal harmony style. Its sound was best characterized by the music of the Carter Family, whose repertoire included traditional Elizabethan ballads, hymns, gospel songs, cowboy ballads, railroad songs, hobo songs, topical songs, and sentimental parlor songs—in short, a virtual compendium of southern rural music.

During the early 1920s the recording industry was in its infancy. Southern record stations, aware of the strong musical tradition of the rural South, encouraged local musicians to perform live, but it didn't take long for the record companies to realize that a profit could be made by catering to specialized markets. The OKeh Phonograph Corporation was especially aggressive, closely followed by such labels as Columbia, Victor, and Gennett.

The first traditional rural whites to record probably were Alexander "Eck" Campbell Robertson, a Texas fiddler, and Henry C. Gilliland, an Oklahoma fiddler. But the records that are considered the turning point in hillbilly music were those of Fiddlin' John Carson, on the OKeh label. In 1923 Ralph Peer, on a field trip through the South, recorded two songs by Carson, a local musician, who thus became one of the first—if not *the* first—traditional southern musician to be captured on vinyl.

Peer also is credited with bringing to the attention of the general public several other seminal figures of the Southern music scene, including the Carter Family, one of country music's best-known groups, and Jimmie Rodgers, country's first bona fide superstar. Although his recording career was short—1927 through 1933—Rodgers dominated the industry like no other and is credited with stirring up interest in country music on a national scale for the first time.

Rodgers populated his repertoire with images of the wandering hobos and the cowboy on the range. He also sang Tin Pan Alley numbers, railroad ballads, and blues; indeed, he popularized the white country blues. The success of performers such as Rodgers and the Carters made the singing of such music more popular and "respectable."

The 1930s were considered the glory years for country music, years when the hobo and railroad music of a Jimmie Rodgers struck a familiar chord for countless people. With his everyman voice and down-to-earth persona, Rodgers found a ready audience in rural and small-town homes across the country, especially in his native South. Yet his influence extended far beyond the Mason-Dixon Line, and was echoed in later generations of entertainers from Gene Autry to Hank Snow; many of his songs have actually entered the nation's oral tradition.

The Carters also reached their peak of popularity during the depression years; in keeping with the country's mood, their material was somber and serious. Their mountain songs seemed to address the personal worries and concerns of the common folk of the country. Significantly, they contributed greatly to the perpetuation of the traditional Anglo-Celtic balladry.

Around this time, too, country music began to adopt a more contemporary attitude, so that by the early 1930s the ancient ballads and tunes had begun to lessen their influence on the typical country performer in favor of original compositions and modern arrangements. Even so, many of the new songs still demonstrated their derivation from the folk tradition. Slowly, though, the regional music began to be replaced by a more national style, ultimately epitomized by today's commercial Nashville sound.

During the 1930s and 1940s some elements of American culture—including reformers, radicals, and intellectuals—began to glorify hillbilly music, strengthening the impression that the rural singers and musicians of the South were the carriers of "authentic" American music.

One of the best examples of a southerner with strong traditional roots who was able to appeal to all segments of American life was Woody Guthrie. Born in Oklahoma, he was weaned on traditional balladry, which he had learned on his mother's knee. Despite his rural background, Guthrie ironically became the epitome of the urban folksinger and writer. Countless city folk—from Bob Dylan to Bruce Springsteen—would later use him as their role model.

In 1998 English folk singer Billy Bragg, no stranger to protest music himself, carried the message of Woody Guthrie to a new generation of music lovers. With the encouragement of Guthrie's daughter no less, Bragg, along with members of the band Wilco, set new melodies to Guthrie's lyrics on the CD *Mermaid Avenue* (Elektra/Asylum).

THE HIGH LONESOME SOUND

Probably no type of country music is as close to its Celtic roots as bluegrass. Originally confined to the mountain areas of Tennessee, North Carolina, Virginia, and Kentucky, bluegrass has now reached every corner of the United States with bluegrass festivals attracting some of the most loyal and devoted fans anywhere. Bluegrass echoes the old mountain themes of death, tragic love, family, and religion, yet its roots range from Elizabethan balladry to minstrel shows. It enjoyed its peak of popularity in the 1950s, but then in the 1960s urban professionals and political activists embraced it as the perfect example of authentic American music.

Alan Lomax was one of the first American folklorists to recognize bluegrass as a reputable music in its own right, a music worthy of study and reflection. He called bluegrass "the first clear-cut orchestral form in 500 years of Anglo-American music." Bluegrass arrived just as country music was threatened with homogenization. Bluegrass reintroduced a reverence for ancient country styles, songs, and tunes. Bluegrass also resurrected the five-string banjo and dobro steel guitar, and brought the fiddle back into the limelight at a time when other country musicians seemingly were abandoning it.

Bluegrass vocals recall mountain folk-singing traditions, while the sacred repertoire of bluegrass songs ranges from old spirituals to gospel. Bluegrass has its roots in the mountain string-band sound. Although it emerged in the 1940s—around the same time as honky-tonk—bluegrass was everything that honky-tonk was not. Where honky-tonk celebrated modern living (and the rowdier the better), bluegrass looked inward, turning the clock back to a simpler time.

The classic bluegrass band consists of fiddle, guitar, mandolin, bass, and banjo; all instruments are acoustic. The guitar is used as a rhythm instrument, while the fiddle and the banjo are primarily solo. The mandolin sometimes is used as a lead or percussion instrument. But whatever the instrumentation, the music is played at a rapid, breakneck speed, often with many improvised solos. The vocals are renowned for their high pitch, and two-, three-, and four-part harmonies are common. In fact, most bluegrass bands have lead, tenor, baritone, and bass singers.

Originally, bluegrass didn't even have a name; the term simply referred to the music of one man, Bill Monroe, and to the three-finger banjo style of Earl Scruggs. Monroe's band was known as the Bluegrass Boys, and he described his music as "the old southern sound that was heard years ago—many, many years ago—in the backwoods, at country dances . . . . Bluegrass brings out the old, ancient tunes."

William Smith Monroe was born near Rosine in central Kentucky, the eighth and last child of James Buchanan (Buck) and Melissa Vandiver Monroe. His father owned a six-hundred-acre farm and his family, of Scots heritage, had been a part of the great migration into Appalachia that had begun in the eighteenth century. Bill, with this background of the American frontiersman—bold, individualistic, and hardy—grew up in a tight-knit Kentucky community, where neighbors knew one another and everyone seemed to be somebody else's cousin. Because of poor eyesight, young Bill did not participate in such typical boyhood pastimes as baseball and other outdoor activities. Some historians, in fact, believe that his physical impairment helped in the development of his musical ability.

Like the Irish and Scottish harpers of old—such as the great Irish harper Turlough O Carolan—many of whom were blind or had other physical ailments, Monroe turned his handicap into an advantage and developed an acute sense of hearing. He had to learn by ear, for example, the harmony parts in church music and soon developed an impeccable knack of knowing what "sounded" right. It was an instinct that served him well.

Monroe's original compositions employ much of the mythical framework that is found in the old Scottish or Irish ballads—an infectious melody, simple lyrics, well-structured narrative form, magical or vaguely supernatural events, and universal emotions. Much of his language is drenched in stark religious symbolism. His lyrics are preoccupied with death and couched in a formal, almost archaic language that occasionally employs modal scales. He wrote songs with titles like "Sweetheart, You Done Me Wrong," "Memories of Mother and Dad," "When the Golden Leaves Begin to Fall," "My Dying Bed," "I'm Blue, I'm Lonesome," and "On the Old Kentucky Shore." In Monroe's world, the highways are populated with rogues and scoundrels and the southern landscape littered with desolate crossroads and lonely graveyards. He looked beyond his earthly existence to the gates of heaven, where he hoped to find peace and solitude, far from the wicked path of sin.

"The bluegrass singer," wrote folklorist Alan Lomax, "hollers in the high lonesome style beloved in the American backwoods." Bluegrass turned for inspiration to the songs and tunes that ancestors had brought with them before the Revolutionary War. To quote Lomax again: "A century of isolation in the lonesome hollows of the Appalachians gave them time to combine strains from Scottish and English folksongs, and to produce a vigorous pioneer music of their own."

This high lonesome sound of bluegrass has its roots, too, in traditional psalm singing; its links with Gaelic psalm and shape-note singing are particularly strong. The singing is done in a tense, high-pitched style that often turns into a falsetto, and songs are frequently shouted and ornamented with rising and falling notes as well as with grace notes. According to his biographer Richard D. Smith, Monroe's "high lonesome" sound derived from Methodist, Baptist, and Holiness church singing.

In theme alone, bluegrass—and for that matter, many of the old country ballads—evokes a peculiarly Celtic feeling in its intense longing for home that is almost evangelical in tone, as if the singer is pining for some childhood Eden or mythical Paradise Lost. The music of the Stanley Brothers, a seminal bluegrass band, is very much in the English and Scottish tradition with its minor keys, somber arrangements, and pentatonic scale. At the same time, a selection such as Bill Monroe's "Scotland" recalls the old country not only in name but also in sound. Smith describes the tune's twin fiddles (performed by Kenny Baker and Bobby Hicks, members of Monroe's band) as "providing bagpipe-like airs."

Bluegrass is, says historian Robert Cantwell, "close to the religion and culture of the original Scots-Irish who began to settle in America early in the eighteenth century." He particularly pointed to an emotional link with the Gaelic psalm-singing tradition of the Hebridean island of Lewis. His analogy is so evocative that I will quote at length:

> The deacon of a tiny country church, a raw-boned man wrapped in a tight black suit, with a head of wooly, storm-colored hair, has just risen out of the group of men who sit behind the altar in order to line out the concluding song of this morning's service, a psalm; he begins to sing even before the last periods of the preacher's sermon have died away. Out comes a shrill, declamatory call, answered almost instantly by a swelling pentatonic chant that gathers in the air like pilgrims from many far-flung cities convening upon a holy place, ascends in harmonious steps to a kind of gale that seems filled with the laughter of young women, and gradually descends until it meets a reiterated cry from the deacon. As the song develops, deacon and congregation encroach upon one another ever more deeply, until the surf-like alternation of their voices, each washing over the other, locks them together in the rhythm of spiritual embrace.
>
> We might be among the African Methodists of Alabama or in Kentucky, among the Old Regular Baptists. By itself the sound is exotic and timeless . . . . Even a bluegrass gospel song comes to mind: Flatt and Scruggs's "Cabin on the Hill." In fact, though, we are in the Irish Sea, on the greatest of the Hebrides, the thorny Isle of Lewis, where lives a lean race of Scots Presbyterians whose intensely introspective and strict Calvinism, and whose tradition-bound way of life, is as close to anything in Britain to the religion and culture of the original Scots-Irish who began to settle in America early in the eighteenth century.

If the "high, lonesome sound" of bluegrass music has British roots, they are probably here, in a tradition part Gaelic, part medieval and ecclesiastical, whose primitive vigor was reawakened in America by the touch of Afro-American song, with which it shared an uncompromising adherence to the aural laws of harmony and melody.

The popularity of bluegrass music remains as strong as ever; we need only look at the success of Alison Krauss and Union Station as proof. Krauss, a young fiddler from central Illinois and barely out of her twenties, has already earned many accolades for her confident stage presence, traditional-sounding vocals, and sweet long-bow style of fiddling. Truly at home with the fiddle, she has turned to the traditional tunes of the vast bluegrass repertoire as well as to the master himself—the late Bill Monroe—for inspiration. And there are others. In the early 1970s musicians like Sam Bush and Bela Fleck and other members of the New Grass Revival, innovators who respected the foundations of Monroe and Stanley, electrified their acoustic guitars and found scores of new fans among the rock generation. More traditional artists include Hot Rize, Jerry Douglas, and Mark O'Connor, as well as the Johnson Mountain Boys and the Cox Family or the urban bluegrass of the Greenbriar Boys.

MANY LINKS

Without going into the technicalities of the scales used in Appalachian folk melodies, bluegrass, and African-American spirituals, suffice it to say that all bear a relationship to the music of such diverse ancient cultures as Chinese, Polynesian, African, Native American, as well as to Celtic music and Gregorian chant. One scholar, for example, noted that the African scale has much in common with Scottish music in America. Another adds that African rhythm found a home in off-beat accentuation, which was in the gait of Scots songs and a favorite device of Irish fiddlers. African scales found an echo in those of the Gaelic tradition. And no less an authority than the Czech composer Antonín Dvořák commented as far back as 1895 that he had found that the so-called plantation melodies of the South, with their unusual and subtle harmonies, bore a striking resemblance to the indigenous music of Scotland and Ireland. Interestingly, traditional English folk singers also prefer to sing at the highest possible pitch. Some link this tendency with early church singing—the practice of trying literally to reach heaven by raising the voice upward.

Psalmody—in the Catholic Church, at least—evolved into the Gregorian chant, which has certain vowel sounds (such as the final *a* in *alleluia*) drawn out. This elongation of vowels has much in common with Irish *sean-nós* singing. And it was in the southern uplands and in the remote areas of Appalachia, strongholds of the Baptist and Methodist churches, where psalm singing found its greatest proponents. Hymns were still "lined out," with the pastor chanting a line or two and then the congregation joining him in song at a slower and more drawn-out pace.

Such a practice, noted the religious historian Deborah Vansau McCauley, "was predominant among the Welsh American churches of seventeenth- and eighteenth-century America as well as in Puritan churches and goes back to sixteenth-century Scotland and England." Today, she said, it still exists in the United States "among white Christians only in Appalachia and only among the Old Regular Baptists in particular, in some Primitive Baptist and Regular Baptist churches, as well as in many African-American Baptist churches throughout Appalachia and the rural South." Significantly, McCauley described Old Regular Baptist hymn lining as sounding like "the droning of bagpipes in a human voice."

Some scholars have gone so far as to say that the mountain people of Kentucky were singing an American version of sixth-century Gregorian chants, although recent scholarship disputes such a claim. Others hear melodies reminiscent of ancient Chinese music. Perhaps what people are hearing is music built on the pentatonic scale, for a number of musical detectives have noticed a similarity in style and idiom between Scottish and Irish melodies and the liturgical melodies of the early Western church.

THE NEW TRADITIONALISTS AND BEYOND

After World War II country music continued to move further and further away from its rural and Anglo-Celtic roots, even as it enjoyed runaway commercial success. Western swing bands, led by Bob Wills and others, were especially popular on the West Coast. Country performers did a booming business in much of the United States. And even the name changed. By the late 1940s *Billboard* magazine, the bible of the music industry, preferred the *country* or *country-western* label to that of *hillbilly*, which, to many, had pejorative connotations. Country's newfound respectability was cemented in 1947 when Ernest Tubb and Friends became the first country group to play Carnegie Hall. By then the Grand Ole Opry had become synonymous with country music. By 1950 the "official" uniform of Stetson hat and cowboy-style clothes had become fully accepted, and a new generation of professional songwriters had begun to supply songs for country entertainers.

During the 1960s and 1970s, however, there were attempts to return to country's older roots. Musicians such as the New Lost City Ramblers were credited with creating an interest in "old-timey" music. Formed in 1958 by a trio of dedicated New Yorkers—Mike Seeger, Tom Paley, and John Cohen—the Ramblers successfully re-created the authentic sound of the original string bands while remaining true to their own distinctive voice. They explored the origins of traditional American folk music by turning to Appalachian balladry.

Like old-timey music, bluegrass also appealed to 1960s youth—a rock and roll surrogate, as Neil Rosenberg called it, for young intellectuals who wanted more from their music than a steady beat and saccharine lyrics.

Today, a younger generation of country artists—the so-called neotraditionalists—have also looked to country's Celtic roots for inspiration. In recent years entertainers such as Reba McIntire, George Strait, Randy Travis, and the Judds have tried to recapture the spirit of country music by turning to a classic country repertoire or by writing new material in a more traditional vein. Garth Brooks, one of the reigning country superstars, has become a pop phenomenon by, ironically, remaining defiantly country. From rural to urban, North to South, Nashville to Chicago, these artists and others like them have proven that the market for traditional-styled country music remains as strong as ever.

But few have done more to return country to its old-time roots than Ricky Skaggs. He grew up on old classics and bluegrass standards; by the time he was a teenager he was already playing with the Ralph Stanley Band. If the Judds had the mountain harmonies down cold, Skaggs knew how to hit the right notes and create the right tone. Skaggs was keenly aware of the Celtic connection, too.

Another artist who has dared to be different is Steve Earle, who continues to blur the lines between country and rock. Despite his rock arrangements, there is little doubt where he comes from; his voice is pure country. Just listen to the opening chords of "Copperfield Road" and you're almost certain to hear something that sounds suspiciously like the drone of bagpipes. Perhaps it was Earle's subtle yet deeply rooted Celtic influences that led to his successful appearance at Glasgow's Celtic Connections festival with few or no objections.

Outside the United States, country music finds its greatest and most enthusiastic support in the British Isles, especially in the Celtic regions. Indeed, a healthy and vibrant cross-pollination is taking place between the Celtic countries and the country music community. From the Outer Hebrides of Scotland to Cape Breton, musicians are exchanging songs and tunes or creating their own compositions, frequently inspired by melodies written down generations ago. In the early 1980s the versatile Scots fiddler John Cunningham, formerly of Silly Wizard, recorded *Thoughts from Another World*, which commemorated in music the crossing of thousands of Celts to America and the influence they exerted on American music. A decade or so later, in 1992, the Chieftains recorded *Another Country*, which featured a Who's Who of contemporary country greats, including Ricky Skaggs, Bela Fleck, Kris Kristofferson, Willie Nelson, Chet Atkins, Don Williams, and Emmylou Harris, and which explored the strong link between Celtic and country music.

There are many other examples of the fertile Celtic-country connections. Consider just a few: Maura O'Connell, the Irish soprano from County Clare, has made quite a name for herself in Nashville; Kathy Mattea, the popular country singer from the West Virginia mountains, collaborated with Scottish singer, songwriter, and fiddler Dougie Maclean. And north of the border, there has always been an overt appreciation of country music: Anne Murray, the Canadian songster and songwriter from the coal-mining town of Springhill, Nova Scotia, got her big break performing with Glen Campbell— himself of strong Scots roots—and has enjoyed some of biggest successes on the country charts; k.d. lang, the Alberta iconoclast, may have bolted from the Nashville scene but not before creating a series of stunning country-drenched records in which she paid musical homage to her idol, Patsy Cline; and such singer-songwriters as Gordon Lightfoot, Bruce Cockburn, and the late Stan Rogers also have been greatly influenced by American country music.

A number of years back the BBC television series *Bringing It All Back Home* brought Celtic music full circle: from the Celtic lands to the South and back again. The recording features as good an example as any of the transatlantic transformation that often occurred: "Rose Connolly" (also known as the bluegrass murder ballad "Down in the Willow Garden"). Collected by Edward Bunting in County Derry, it made its way across the ocean and surfaced in Kentucky as "Rose Connolly," a grisly ballad told from the murderer's point of view of the death of the unfortunate Ms. Connolly, who is poisoned, then stabbed, and thrown into the river. It is sung on the recording by the Everly Brothers, who learned it from their father.

Celtic music, when brought to the New World, had to reinvent itself in order to grow and survive. And it did, of course, in the form of country music. Despite the distance in years and miles one thing has never changed—a certifiable Celtic spirit. It is this spirit, this spark, that identifies the music as Scottish or Irish—Celtic, if you will—whether it originates across the ocean or deep in the heart of the Old South. Like its Celtic counterpart, the southern landscape is surrounded by the sounds of music; music permeates virtually all aspects of southern life. Whether it be the radio blasting lonesome country laments on a steamy southern night or a bluegrass band playing at some roadside honky-tonk cafe, music fills the air.

Country music in the South cuts across class and economic lines. But for many years, it was the music of a specific community—*the* music of the South—and served as a proud and honorable badge of regional identity. Now it has shed its regional status to become simply American music. Indeed, the persistent popularity of country music is but one example of the continuing Celtic influence on contemporary American life.

RECOMMENDED LISTENING

Bringing It All Back Home (BBC). Traces the musical history of country music from its traditional Irish roots to its reinvention in America. Features the music of Hothouse Flowers, Elvis Costello, the Everly Brothers, An Emotional Fish, Emmylou Harris, Ricky Skaggs, the Waterboys, Dolores Keane, Dé Danann, Paul Brady, Mary Black, Luka Bloom, Maura O'Connell, and others.

The Bristol Sessions: Historic Recordings from Bristol, Tennessee (Country Music Foundation). This classic two-CD package features the first recordings by the Carter Family and Jimmie Rodgers and includes a cross section of early country music—from fiddle tunes to blues, from ballads to gospel. These 1927 sessions have been called by no less than Johnny Cash "the single most important event in the history of country music." Among the standout cuts are the chilling urgency of Ernest Phipps and His Holiness Quartet's "I Want to Go Where Jesus Is," which captures the fire of the holiness church style and the Carter Family's rendition of "The Storms Are on the Ocean," with lyrics based on an old Scottish ballad.

Ceilidh Menage. *Plaids & Bandanas: Song Links from Scots Drovers to Wild West Cowboys* (Blue Banana Music). A wonderful selection of songs and tunes that explores the connection between the Celtic lands and the American West from the cattle culture of early Celtic society (best exemplified by the ancient "The Cattle Raid of Cooley") to the drovers of Scotland to the huge cattle drives of the Wild West. Includes "Oran nan Drobhairean/The Drover's Song," which was written in the late eighteenth century and is one of the few songs in the tradition that captures the excitement and anticipation of the annual arrival of the drovers to buy cattle in the Scottish glens. A fun, provocative, and unusual recording.

The Chieftains. *Another Country* (RCA Victor). Country music done up, Chieftains-style. Guest artists include Ricky Skaggs, Chet Atkins, Emmylou Harris, Willie Nelson, Jerry Douglas, and Bela Fleck.

Classic Country Music (Smithsonian). Two vols. A *Who's Who* of country music from Gid Tanner and his Skillet Lickers to the Judds. Selected and annotated by country music historian Bill C. Malone.

John Cunningham. *Thoughts from Another World* (Shanachie). Celtic music from both sides of the Atlantic. Scots fiddler Cunningham follows the traditional music of Scotland and Ireland to America. Cunningham wrote the last selection, "Further along the Line," to show how the Celtic peoples influenced American music.

Steve Earle. *Guitar Town* (MCA). In a truly mysterious way, Steve Earle embodies the Celtic tradition in the most natural way possible—as an extension of myself. His music bridges Celtic and country, Old World and New. Like his spiritual partners Guthrie, Dylan, and Springsteen, the country-edged rock of *Guitar Town* is full of stubborn dreamers who yearn to escape their narrow lives, if only they knew how. In *The Mountain* (E-Squared), Earle joins forces with the Del McCoury Band to create a near-classic recording of original bluegrass songs and tunes with strong Celtic overtones from the Civil War–era tale of an Irish soldier fighting for Colonel Joshua Chamberlain (complete with tin whistle) to two Irish-flavored instrumentals, "Connemara Breakdown" and "Paddy on the Beat," and the sublimely haunting "Pilgrim." One imagines a beaming Bill Monroe smiling down from heaven, nodding approvingly of the results.

The Gospel Ship: Baptist Hymns & White Spirituals from the Southern Mountains (New World Records, 1977). Historian Deborah Vansau McCauley compares this recording by Alan Lomax of Old Regular Baptist preaching and hymn lining with the Gaelic psalms from Lewis— "the only known location for hymn lining outside of the region between the Cumberlands and the Blue Ridge mountains in the United States."

Alison Krauss and Union Station. *Two Highways* (Rounder). Boasts the sublime vocals and passionate fiddling of Krauss, the bluegrass wonder of central Illinois.

Bill Monroe. *The Essential Bill Monroe and His Blue Grass Boys 1945–1949* (Columbia). Includes such Monroe classics as "Bluegrass Special," "Come Back to Me in My Dreams," "Blue Moon of Kentucky," "Wicked Path of Sin," and "The Old Cross Roads."

Rhythm of the Mountains: The Music of Appalachia (CMH). This eighty-song, four–CD boxed collection explores the origins of country, bluegrass, and folk through contemporary selections and archival material. Selections include Bradley Kincaid's version of the classic Scottish ballad "The House Carpenter."

Jean Ritchie. *Child Ballads in America*. Two vols. (Folkways). The ancient ballads come alive in these seminal recordings. Eerie, spine-tingling performances by an American original.

Ricky Skaggs. *Ancient Tones* (Skaggs Family Records). Skaggs evokes the spirit of Bill Monroe and the Stanley Brothers, resurrecting such classics as "Walls of Time" and "Mighty Dark to Travel" as well as offering up original instrumentals with his own "Connemara." Listen to his a cappella singing of "Little Bessie" and you will hear a distillation of what Bill Monroe himself referred to as the "old sounds": traditional balladry, hymns, white spirituals, even a hint of the *sean-nós* all come together. Ancient tones, indeed.

The Sound of the Dove: Singing in Appalachian Primitive Baptist Churches (University of Illinois Press, 1995). Numerous examples of singing in mountain churches and other primitive Baptist song traditions.

Southern Traditional Singers. *The Social Harp: Early American Shape-Note Songs* (Rounder). One of the few recordings in which nineteenth-century shape-note compositions are heard in their original three-voice settings. Enlightening.

Ralph Stanley and the Clinch Mountain Boys. *Hymns and Sacred Songs* (King). Haunting selection of classic sacred music from one of the seminal bluegrass bands.

Doc Watson and Clarence Ashley. *The Original Folkways Recordings: 1960–1962* (Smithsonian Folkways). A stunning recording of the banjo-picking vocalist Clarence "Tom" Ashley and the legendary blind banjo picker and singer Doc Watson. Watson's version of "Amazing Grace"—with accompaniment by Ashley, Jean Ritchie, Fred Price, and Clint Howard—recalls the Gaelic psalm singing of the faraway Hebrides in mood and phrasing. It truly captures the sound of another era.

David Wilkie and Cowboy Celtic. *Cowboy Ceilidh* (Red House). Cowboy and western classics given the Celtic treatment. Highlights includes Michael Martin Murphy's guest vocals on "The Cowboy's Lament," a lovely instrumental version of "The Water Is Wide," and Arthur Cormack's evocative rendition of the Gaelic lament "Farewell to Coigach." Another excellent selection is Wilkie and cowriter Stewart MacDougall's "Wind in the Wire," which was inspired by the true story of a Scottish Highlander named Angus MacDonald who worked as a Hudson's Bay Company clerk, as many Scots did, and married a woman from the Nez Perce tribe.

Lucinda Williams. *Car Wheels on a Gravel Road* (Mercury). A great country record. Williams digs down deep into her roots to create a timeless and immensely satisfying work.

Recommended Videos

Chase the Devil: Religious Music of the Appalachians (Shanachie). An engrossing and often unsettling portrait of mountain music and culture.

High Lonesome: The Story of Bluegrass Music (Shanachie). Traces the evolution of bluegrass music from its folk roots in the Kentucky hills to its current popularity. Features the music of Bill Monroe, the Stanley Brothers, Mac Wiseman, Flatt and Scruggs, the Seldom Scene, Alison Krauss, and others.

8

The Other Edge of the Atlantic

From Coffin Ships to the New Golden Age

Emigration and exile, the journeys to and from home, are the very heartbeat of Irish culture. To imagine Ireland is to imagine a journey.

—FINTAN O'TOOLE, IRISH JOURNALIST

They came in droves, shipload after shipload of ragged, hungry, eager faces to a land whose welcome seemed tepid at best and downright hostile at worst. Exhilarated by hope and exhausted by anxiety, most made the long Atlantic crossing to better themselves, and, perhaps, to find the happiness and peace of mind that so eluded them back home.

In the eighteenth century about 250,000 people had already left Ireland for North America, mainly Protestants from Ulster—descendants of Presbyterian Scots. The musical tradition these immigrants brought with them, as Rebecca Miller has pointed out, was decidedly non-Celtic and "more closely related to a Lowland Scottish style." Hardy types accustomed to a difficult life, they set-

tled the frontier, fighting for the American cause during the Revolutionary War and epitomizing the rugged individuality that many
to this day still associate with the Appalachian backcountry.

At the same time, Gaelic-speaking Highlanders sailed in ships
like the *Hector* to the Canadian Maritimes, cutting down forests
and erecting log cabins in the clearings, or, through the largesse of
the colonial government, receiving land grants and establishing
small, scattered communities in the sand hills of North Carolina's
upper Cape Fear River.

In contrast, the roughly seven million who left Ireland in the
nineteenth century were mostly Catholic. Although they came
from a rural environment they chose to settle in the cities—New
York, Boston, Philadelphia, Chicago, New Orleans, and other
places—where jobs were more plentiful and they could find kin-
dred spirits in most every port or urban center.

MAKING WAY TO A
FAR DISTANT STRAND

The early years of many Irish emigrants were spent combating an
insurmountable loneliness, engulfed in a black despair that derived
from what they perceived to be their own insignificance in the vast-
ness of the New World. It must be said that these traits were especially strong among emigrants who came from a rural background
and found it difficult, if not impossible, to adapt to the chilly
anonymity of city life.

The great majority of the people who left Ireland during the
1840s did so for a specific reason—to escape the horror of the
Great Famine, one of the most calamitous and tragic events in the
long and often sad history of the human race. The famine was a
defining moment in Irish history. It remains very much a part of
the Irish folk memory.

PRELUDE TO DISASTER

On the eve of the Great Famine the everyday language of the Irish
people was Gaelic. About 80 percent of the population was

Catholic. Unfortunately, the vast majority lived in dire poverty in rural communities called *clachans* while landlords and government officials lived in the "big houses." At the top of the social ladder was the Anglo-Irish Protestant Ascendancy, the English and Anglo-Irish families who owned most of the land.

Next came the farmers themselves, the people who rented the land they worked on. Those who could afford to rent large farms divided the property into smaller plots. In turn, these plots were leased to cotters (laborers who occupied a cottage or small holding of land usually in return for services). Yet the rents were high, and no one had security of tenure. It was an uncertain existence. There was no welfare system, no safety net. If a person or a family became destitute, the only place to turn was the work-house.

Living conditions were dreadful. Most people either lived in thatched cottages or one-roomed huts made of stone and turf. The huts had no windows and no sources of light except for a hole in the roof for the smoke to escape.

THE POTATO

The potato has been a staple of the Irish diet since the late seventeenth century, although, according to some accounts, it may have been introduced to the island as early as 1590. The potato was usually planted in April and May and came into season in late August; they were then stored in pits. If a shortage occurred, families would rely on oatmeal until the new potato crop arrived. Oatmeal, however, was more expensive. Those who couldn't afford it were reduced to begging.

Yet the potato adapted perfectly to Ireland's mild, damp, and rainy climate. It even grew in Ireland's notoriously acid soil. Best of all, the potato was not only cheap but also nutritious. With a splash of milk added, the lowly potato provided a balanced diet, containing protein, carbohydrates, and minerals. Some three million people—of Ireland's total population of eight million—relied on the potato as their primary food source, a dangerous dependency for which the country would pay dearly.

Ireland had witnessed numerous potato famines before. A major famine occurred between 1739 and 1741, and there were sporadic crop failures in 1816–1817, 1822, 1826, and again in 1831. But nothing could prepare anyone for the devastating impact of the Great Famine. The potato blight reached Ireland in the summer of 1845; between 1845 and 1849 the potato crop in Ireland failed in three seasons out of four. "Black '47" was the worst year of all.

By the time the crisis had ended, over a course of five or more years, some one and a half million people had died of starvation and disease and a million more had emigrated, mostly to America.

The place that is forever linked with the worst excesses of the famine, the place that lives on in Ireland's collective memory—much like Strathnaver during the height of the Highland Clearances in Scotland, where another kind of nightmare was taking place around the same time—is Skibbereen in County Cork. Here the first famine death was reported, and here the suffering and agony became all too real. The very word *Skibbereen* became synonymous with death.

Not many songs were written during the famine years—for most the memories were simply too horrible to bear—yet a generation or so later, some anonymous scribe jotted down a few words that evoke, in their simplicity and directness, the immense tragedy of that time. The scene is set years later and a safe distance away, presumably America. A son asks his father why he left his native village of Skibbereen.

> *Oh, father dear, I often hear you speak of Erin's Isle,*
> *Her lofty scenes and valleys green, her mountains rude and wild,*
> *They say it is a lovely land wherein a prince might dwell,*
> *Oh, why did you abandon it? The reason to me tell.*

The father explains that the potato famine robbed him of his livelihood and his ability to pay the exceedingly high rents and taxes.

Oh, son! I loved my native land with energy and pride,
Till a blight came o'er my crops—my sheep, my cattle died;
My rent and taxes were too high, I could not them redeem,
And that's the cruel reason that I left old Skibbereen.

Eviction was common during the famine years, since landlords, not the government, were held responsible for maintaining the welfare of their tenantry, the vast majority of whom were impoverished. It was much easier to evict than help. Cottages were burned and torn to the ground, quite often with inhabitants still inside.

Oh, well do I remember the bleak December day,
The landlord and the sheriff came to drive us all away;
They set my roof on fire with their demon yellow spleen,
And that's another reason that I left old Skibbereen.

A large number of the emigrants were Irish speakers from the west of Ireland, a home for traditional Irish music. Not only did Ireland lose a good portion of its music, but it also suffered a devastating blow with the irretrievable loss of the Irish language.

SAFE PASSAGE

Many of the early emigrant ballads were usually sad laments steeped in nostalgia, and self-pity, and singing the praises—literally—of their native soil while bitterly condemning the land of the stranger.

Some simply regret leaving.

The narrator of the well-known "Shamrock Shore," Edward Connors, is "deluded" by cheery letters sent from Canada that paint a wildly optimistic picture of people who live "like princes and earning gold galore." Determined to follow his comrades across the ocean, Connors and his wife and family travel to Belfast to book a passage on a ship bound for Quebec. Barely three days at sea they are lashed about by a fierce storm and watch their already limited food supplies dwindle with every passing day, threatening them with the very real possibility of starvation before even arriving safely in the New World.

My name is Edward Connors and the same I'll ne'er disown
I used to live in happiness near unto Portglenone
I sold my old farm as you will hear which grieves my heart full sore
And I sailed away to Amerikay I left the Shamrock Shore
                                                    –TRADITIONAL

Finally, after much struggle and suffering, the family lands in Quebec, where they are greeted by the pathetic sight of three hundred poor young Irish boys, hoping for a bit of charity. For three weeks they look for work. With no place to turn and no one to ask ("For I had friends when I had cash but none when I was poor"), they stay until their money runs out. Connors and his family find little solace in knowing that many others suffer the same predicament.

The hero of "By the Hush" suffers an even greater misfortune. Poor and hungry, he decides to sell his horse, cow, pigs, and a plot of land to make the journey to America, leaving behind his sweetheart, Biddy McGee. But our hero's fate is not a good one—he "and a hundred more" arrive during the middle of the American Civil War. Told to fight for Lincoln ("When we got to Yankee land, they shoved a gun into our hands"), he loses his leg, which prompts him to offer a piece of advice to his fellow Irishmen:

Here's to you boys, now take my advice
to America I'll have you not be comin'
There is nothing here but war where the murderin' cannons roar
And I wish I was at home in dear old Dublin.
                                                    –TRADITIONAL

The song appears as "Paddy's Lamentation," sung by Mary Black, on *Long Journey Home* (BMG), while Andy M. Stewart offers a particularly heartwrenching version in *By the Hush*.

A similar fate faces another Irishman in yet another war. Our hero soon rues the day when he made the fateful decision to leave Ireland. He searches for work and, in a display of lyrical ingenuity, even engages in a boxing match with the likes of the great Irish-American boxer John L. Sullivan. Ultimately, he joins the army as an Irish volunteer in the war against Spain and is put on board a battleship, which the Spanish capture at Santiago Bay. In the melee that follows, he is wounded in battle and is permanently disabled. From his hospital bed he composes a word of warning to all Irishmen intent on emigration:

> *To all intending emigrants I pen this simple lay;*
> *Let one who lies in hospital three thousand miles away*
> *Now warn you of the dangers that you may read and see*
> *And the fate of a young Irishman in the great land of the free.*
> —TRADITIONAL

Thousands of Irish immigrants died in battle while serving in the American armed forces. More than 150,000 Irish-born immigrants fought on the Union side during the American Civil War. Many were forced to fight for a cause and a country that they knew little, if anything, about. Many more, such as Mulligan's brigade in Chicago, served in all-Irish units.

In the nineteenth-century exile song, "A Scarborough Settler's Lament," all the action takes place in the narrator's mind.

> *Awa' wi' Canada's muddy creeks and*
> *Canada's fields of pine*
> *This land o' wheat is a goodly land, but*
> *oh, it isnae mine*
> *The heathy hill, the grassy dale,*
> *the daisy spangled lea*
> *The purling burn and craggy linn*
> *Auld Scotia's glens gi'e me*
> —TRADITIONAL

A Scots emigrant, even after living on the Canadian plains for thirty years, continues to pine for the old country, vividly recalling each "well known scene" from childhood only to awake one morning, in a bolt of recognition that he is still three thousand miles "frae hame."

THE AMERICAN WAKE

*In them uncover the destiny
of everyone,
for all who are exiled & in search
of a home. . .*
—GREG DELANTY, *AMERICAN WAKE* (1995)

The American wake is unique to Ireland, yet its roots are old.

"The practice of 'waking' (that is, watching) the dead had its origins in Irish antiquity," wrote historian Arnold Schrier. "Essentially it meant watching by the corpse all through the night until burial time the next day. This night-long vigil was supposed to ward off evil spirits and prevent them from entering the body."

Occasionally an old woman of the community would keen over the dead "in a form of a long, sorrowful elegy . . . delivered in a shrill, piercing voice that resembled a continuous high-pitched wail," wrote Schrier.

After the appropriate mourning period had elapsed, the "grieving" would indulge in a display of revelry and merrymaking. The church, which was not amused, thought such behavior clearly sacrilegious.

The American wake is a variation of waking. It symbolized death, for in all likelihood it was assumed that the nineteenth-century emigrant would never return. To loved ones and friends back home, departing was equivalent to death. There was, they reasoned, little difference between going to America and going to the grave.

"It's a sad occasion when a person leaves for America," Peig Sayers, the writer and noted storyteller from the Blasket Islands once said. "It's like death for only one out of a thousand ever again returns to Ireland."

Schrier believes the American wake began as early as 1830, if not before, and was especially strong in the south and west of Ireland, and, in particular, in northwest Donegal.

In typical Celtic fashion the American wake combined a mixture of sadness and joy. Usually the festivities began in the evening before the emigrant was ready to depart; they lasted through the night and into the wee morning hours.

Most wakes were convivial affairs, though, with much fiddle music, dancing, and hearty singing. Typically, traditional and popular songs as well as broadsides were sung at an American wake.

By the turn of the century the finality of the Atlantic crossing had subsided, and the ritual became, said Schrier, less a wake and more a long farewell.

"The airplane," wrote Irish-American journalist Pete Hamill, "ended the America Wake [sic], because the journey was no longer final; the Irish young could now go off for a year or two and fly home for Christmas."

An altogether different song of emigration—that of forced emigration—is told in "Jamie Raeburn," where the hapless protagonist is banished to some far-off land, presumably Australia, for some unspecified transgression. Although he doesn't specify his act of transgression, quite often petty criminals were sent off to Botany Bay for as little as filching a loaf of bread. It's been said that Jamie's crime was stealing a hen.

Jamie leaves his native Glasgow in shame, never again to see the "hills and dales of Caledonia":

> *Oh, my name is Jamie Raeburn*
> *From Glasgow town I came*
> *My place of habitation*
> *I'm forced to leave wi' shame*
> *from my place of habitation*
> *I noo mon gang awa*
> *far frae the bonnie hills and dales of Caledonia*
> —TRADITIONAL

Just as many, if not more, songs praised the newfound home across the ocean, the consensus being that it was better starting over in wealthy America than struggling in poor Ireland.

The author of "The Green Fields of America" recalls the good old days when Ireland's economy flourished, but now laments that everyone is off to America. He decides to join them, refusing to stay "in this land of taxation." With his sweetheart at his side, he waits for the emigrant ship that will take him away to the land of liberty where they will "never know misery or strife" and toasts "every man that has [the] courage" to go to America.

> Farewell to the land of shillelagh and shamrock,
> Where many a long day in pleasure I spent;
> Farewell to my friends whom I leave here behind me,
> To live in poor Ireland if they are content;
> Though sorry I am to leave the Green Island,
> Whose cause I supported both in peace and war,
> To live here in bondage I ne'er can be happy,
> The green fields of America are sweeter by far.
>   –TRADITIONAL

Many Irish emigrant songs revolved around that old Irish standby—guilt. These songs scolded the emigrants for not sending enough money back home to their poverty-stricken parents. Other songs expressed anger and a sense of sadness at their loss. By the mid-nineteenth century, though, many of the exile ballads sung at American wakes had a very strong political edge to them. Song after song told the emigrant in no uncertain terms that emigration from Ireland would never end and their sense of guilt for having left home would never go away until Ireland was an independent nation once again.

The emigrant song remains very much a part of the tradition today. One of the most moving of contemporary emigration ballads is "Kilkelly," written by Washington, D.C., songwriter Peter Jones and based on letters written by his great-great grandfather in County Mayo between 1860 and 1890 to relatives in America.

This heartfelt ballad is devastating in its sadness and palpable in its sense of loss, capturing beautifully the pain of separation and its long-lasting effects. The definitive version appears on the recording of the same name and is performed with great compassion and understanding by Robbie O'Connell.

And in a play on the nineteenth-century emigrant ballad, "Thousands Are Sailing to America," the entire pantheon of Irish and Irish-American popular history come together as Pogues guitarist Philip Chevron invokes the spirit of everyone from Charles Stewart Parnell ("The Blackbird") to literary bad boy Brendan Behan while giving his regards to George M. Cohan's Broadway and weeping at the death of J.F.K. "Did you work on the railroad?" he asks, "Did you rid the streets of crime?" The answers are not entirely forthcoming, for "thousands are sailing again across the ocean," even if the modern equivalent of the coffin ships is now a safer and more luxurious jet.

We have grown so accustomed to emigrants leaving the Celtic lands that it comes as a bit of a shock to acknowledge that sometimes it's the other way around. Contemporary Scottish singer-songwriter Andy Mitchell's bittersweet song "Indiana" tells of emigration *from* rather than *to* the New World. Although the narrator has lived for many years in the States—indeed long enough to raise a family—he harbors a perpetual homesickness.

> *Fare thee well now, Indiana;*
> *your green land's been good to me.*
> *There I travelled, there I settled,*
> *there I raised up my family.*
> *But the cord has never severed,*
> *and the longing each day has grown,*
> *So tomorrow, I'll be leaving*
> *for the land I call my home.*

In this case "home" is Scotland. His friends question his judgment, insisting he is "crazy" to go back to poverty. Yet the narrator much prefers the pastoral pleasures of the Highlands—from the red deer to the heron—than the considerable riches that America promises.

> *Friends they tell me I am crazy*
> *going back to just poverty.*
> *America is, so they say now,*
> *the rich land of opportunity.*
> *But the red deer runs so freely,*
> *and the heron slowly flies—*
> *These are treasures of my homeland*
> *all your money couldn't buy.*

The Ullapool-based Mitchell wrote the unusual story based on the experiences of a real couple, Tom and Valerie Bryan. She was a music teacher at a high school in the Highlands, he is a Canadian of Scots and Irish ancestry and they met in, of course, Indiana. The song has been recorded by Andy Irvine and Mairi MacInnes and has already entered the tradition.

THE POLICE CHIEF WHO CHANGED IRISH MUSICAL HISTORY

Francis O'Neill assembled the largest collection of Irish traditional music ever published. For that we should be forever grateful. His is the story of the Irish emigrant who did well and yet did not forget his origins. He devoted most of his life to playing, studying, and collecting the traditional music of his native land. His main instrument was the flute, although he also played the fiddle, the Lowland pipes, and the Highland pipes.

Born on August 28, 1848, in Tralibane, O'Neill was the youngest of seven children. He grew up in a largely Irish-speaking rural area of western Cork surrounded by the music of pipers, fiddlers, and flute players at crossroad dances during the long summer months or, in the dead of winter, in the barns and farmhouses.

Like many young Irish boys of his time and temperament, he sought excitement. Although he loved his native land, he longed for more. Thus in March 1865 O'Neill secured passage to the north of England by signing on as a cabin boy under a Captain Watson, according to his biographer Nicholas Carolan, "sailing during the following years to Russia, Egypt, the United States, the West Indies, Mexico, South America, Hawaii, and Japan, and rounding the Cape of Good Hope."

Eventually he settled in Chicago. The year was 1873, and he was twenty-two.

O'Neill joined the police force in August of that year, after various stints at other jobs, including work as a laborer in a Chicago freight house. He became desk sergeant in the Deering community in 1878, an Irish neighborhood where traditional musicians were common.

The Irish first settled in Chicago in the 1830s, when they arrived in large numbers to dig the Illinois and Michigan Canal, which connected Lake Michigan to the Illinois River and beyond to the Mississippi. The majority of these early settlers were from County Cork, living in shanties along the Des Plaines River. Many had already gained experience building the Erie Canal in Pennsylvania.

Large numbers of Chicago's Irish-born population congregated in the area near the south branch of the Chicago River. Neighborhoods like Conley's Patch, Healy's Slough, Canaryville, Bridgeport, Brighton Park, and Back of the Yards became known as Irish strongholds.

By the time O'Neill arrived in the early 1870s, the native Irish formed about 13 percent of the population or some forty thousand people, according to Carolan, many of them traditional musicians. Added Carolan, "Living within its 200 square miles were musicians from all the thirty-two counties of Ireland and many American-born musicians of Irish descent, and a stream of visiting Irish professional musicians, especially pipers, was constantly passing through the city . . . ." By the turn of the century the figure rose to more than 235,000—including American-born children of Irish emigrants.

THE WORKING LIFE

So, bid farewell to famine, it's off to Amerikay
To work as a navigator for 90 cents a day
And hope to dig a fortune by the time they reach LaSalle
On the Illinois and Michigan Canal

–KEVIN O'DONNELL
(C. 1987 ARRANMORE MUSIC)

Most of the famine Irish who arrived on America's shores were unskilled, with little or no funds, and few immediate concerns beyond feeding their hungry bellies and securing a roof over their heads.

The vast majority found work at the bottom of the economic ladder: women as millworkers, servants, and cooks; men as unskilled factory workers, lumberjacks, miners, and dock hands. It was the Irish who dug the nation's ditches and built the nation's railroads. In a real way they crafted—literally brick by brick, stone by stone, piece by piece—the very foundation upon which the American republic rested.

In "When New York Was Irish," Terry Winch, cofounder of the Irish-American folk group, Celtic Thunder, recalls the days when the Irish in New York "worked on the subways" and "ran the saloons," "put out the fires and controlled City Hall"—how in fact they had "started with nothing and wound up with it all."

Francis O'Neill became chief of police in 1901. As chief, he supervised more than three thousand officers, some two thousand of whom were reportedly Irish. One of those officers, a certain James O'Neill (no relation) became his right arm. A fiddle player from County Down, he had lived in Belfast. "James O'Neill," wrote Nicholas Carolan, "had what Francis lacked, the ability to note down tunes quickly and accurately from the playing and singing of others." Born in 1863, James O'Neill worked in the Bridgeport pumping works.

In the late nineteenth century there existed a lively traditional scene, one of packed dance halls, saloons, and vaudeville theatres where skilled musicians could earn a living from traditional music. It was found not only in Chicago but also in New York, Philadelphia, Boston, and other pockets of Irish settlement.

Even as the police chief, O'Neill had tried to balance work with pleasure. Sometimes the latter won out. One day when the chief could not be located, rumors began circulating that he had been assassinated. In a near panic, a battery of officers was dispatched to try to find the errant chief. After the initial search proved fruitless, one officer, who knew O'Neill's love for music, suggested a fiddler friend's home in Brighton Park. Sure enough, when the officers arrived they found the two musicians in the living room in the throes of a mini music session, the chief with his flute and the friend with his fiddle.

O'Neill left the force in July 1905 to pursue his avocation seriously. He collected music wherever he traveled, from local Irish immigrants as well as from Irish musicians who passed through town. By the time his life had ended he had spent close to three decades collecting tunes, sifting through musty old manuscripts, and socializing with musicians. In 1903 he published, at his own expense and in a bound edition of two thousand copies, his greatest work: *O'Neill's Music of Ireland*. With 1850 melodies this was the largest collection of Irish music ever printed, and it's still considered the bible of traditional Irish music. It contains 625 song airs, 75 Carolan harp tunes, 415 double jigs, 60 slip jigs, 380 reels, 225 hornpipes, 20 long dances, and 50 marches and miscellaneous.

Francis O'Neill died of heart failure on 28 January 1936 in his home at 5448 Drexel Avenue on Chicago's South Side. He is buried in the family mausoleum in the mostly Irish Mount Olivet Cemetery in Mount Greenwood, a still-largely Irish neighborhood on the southern tip of the city.

O'Neill's legacy within the Celtic tradition seems assured. Nicholas Carolan has called him "the greatest individual influence on the evolution of Irish traditional dance music in the twentieth century."

SEARCHING FOR RESPECTABILITY

Despite some stubborn problems, turn-of-the-century Chicago could take pride in its vibrant and lively Irish-music community. Yet even in Francis O'Neill's day there wasn't much motivation to study or perform Irish music other than applause and good intentions. Not one of the many musicians that he knew, for example, depended on music for their livelihood. Naturally, this apathy disturbed him. "If neglected by our own people," he asked, "what can we reasonably expect from others?"

It was a problem that reflected the changing status of the Irish immigrant in American society. Immigrants, eager to be accepted by the Anglo-American Protestant majority, adopted mainstream tastes in pursuit of respectability. Countless hours were spent listening to the popular music of the day or, for those with higher pretensions, classical music, rather than the traditional music of their forebears. "Irish folk music and song," wrote musician and historian Lawrence McCullough, "came to be regarded as relics of a past best left forgotten; the older Irish music was intimately bound up with the history of an Ireland most emigrants wished to forget or alter."

By the time Chicago's World's Columbian Exposition took place in 1893, traditional Irish music was already losing ground among some members of the Irish community while, ironically, drawing considerable public attention. O'Neill himself talked of a lack of proper respect and appreciation accorded the traditional Irish musician.

Many factors helped explain this decline in popularity of traditional Irish music within the Irish community during the early years of the twentieth century: an overall decline in Irish emigration to Chicago, a collapse of "spirit" within traditional neighborhoods, and, most of all, changing musical tastes. The vast majority of Irish-Americans preferred the stage Irish music that had begun to attract attention in the city's music and vaudeville halls. In both America and throughout the British Isles, people preferred to listen to the melodies and ballads of Thomas Moore and Percy French rather than the authentic music of the homeland.

During the first few decades of the twentieth century, small, independent record companies like Decca, Victor, Celtic, Gennett, and Columbia produced hundreds of 78 RPM recordings. In Chicago they included the music of pipers Eddie Mullaney, Tom Ennis, and Joe Sullivan; fiddlers Francis Cashin and Selena O'Neill; flute players Paddy Doran and Tom Doyle; and pianists Frances Malone and Kathleen Kearney. And, in the 1930s a new generation of musicians, including Eleanor (Kane) Neary and John McGreevy, entered the studio. Unfortunately, they were the last commercial recordings of Chicago Irish musicians for almost forty years until McGreevy, who died in 1990, and flute player Séamus Cooley recorded for Philo Records in 1974.

Other important Irish and Irish-American musicians to record in the 1920s included the Sligo fiddler Paddy Killoran as well as the Chicago-based Bowen's Irish Orchestra.

In 1934 step dancer Pat Roche arrived from County Clare; he would eventually form the Harp and Shamrock Orchestra, one of the early American bands to model themselves on the Irish *ceilidh* band. Included in the lineup were John McGreevy and Jimmy Devine on fiddles; John Gaffney on accordion; Pat McGovern on flute; Joe Shannon on uilleann pipes; Eleanor Kane on piano; and Pat Richardson on drums. Roche himself provided the step dancing.

Meanwhile, in New York, a thriving scene was underway.

THE GOLDEN AGE IN THE BIG APPLE

The first three decades of the twentieth century saw hundreds of thousands of new Irish emigrants arrive on American shores, most from northern and western Ireland. A growing emigrant population meant the formation of many Irish-American societies, which in turn sponsored regular *ceilidhs* (informal parties) and concerts. "At the turn of the century it was reported that there was more Irish traditional music being played in New York, Boston, Philadelphia or Chicago than there was in Ireland," wrote P.J. Curtis.

In this fertile ground, traditional musicians were treated with respect. Support for Irish music and dance was so strong that the 1890s are considered, at least on the East Coast, the "Golden Age of Irish Music." Most of the fine traditional Irish musicians in America at the time either lived or at least spent some time in New York. It was a grand time to be both Irish and a musician. Probably the grandest place to be was in New York City's Celtic Hall, a major venue for Irish music and dance on West Fifty-Fourth Street that thrived during the golden era.

In addition to the venues and dance halls, regular house *seisuns* (sessions) allowed the musician the chance to bask in the company of fellow musicians but also offered a place to simply relax, have a good time, perpetuate the music of the homeland with like-minded folk, and relieve the sense of isolation of being a stranger in a big country.

The golden age in New York peaked in the 1920s. By the early 1930s a decrease in Irish immigration, the advent of the Great Depression, and the outbreak of World War II seriously disrupted the Irish-music community. In addition, the wartime ban on shellac negatively affected the entire ethnic recording industry.

 ## MICHAEL COLEMAN AND JAMES MORRISON

Two of Ireland's finest fiddlers of the early decades of the twentieth century both hailed from County Sligo, and, coincidentally, both were born a few miles apart. Moreover, they emigrated to the United States around the same time and settled in the same city—New York.

Michael Coleman is one of Ireland's greatest fiddlers and one of the greatest influences on contemporary fiddlers. Born in 1891, Coleman emigrated to the United States in 1914 when he was in his twenties. He also influenced pipers, flute players, and accordion players both in Ireland and the U.S. His major recordings were made in the 1920s and 1930s. He died in 1945.

James Morrison was born in 1893 and arrived in the States in the 1920s. Both men played in the fast, highly ornamented style of Sligo.

They may have recorded in the States but their recordings made their way back to Ireland, deeply affecting the playing style of countless men and women, on both sides of the Atlantic.

Not only were their style and technique emulated, but their repertoire was adopted too. Indeed, both men, but Coleman in particular, are credited with cementing the trend toward musical standardization that had started with the publication of Francis O'Neill's *Dance Music of Ireland* and continues to this day. As a result, regional variations diminished, especially in areas where they were not that strong to begin with.

Dance music would literally never be the same.

Dozens of Irish-American dance halls thrived in New York City during the golden age. The bands played both traditional Irish dance music and the popular dances of the day, from foxtrots to quicksteps. Many of the bands moved closer toward a big-band sound, adding brass and reed instruments and playing popular American standards.

The 1950s saw the arrival in New York of yet another generation of fine Irish musicians. They included accordionists Joe Cooley from County Galway and Paddy O'Brien from Tipperary; flute player Jack Coen from East Galway and his brother, concertina player Father Charlie Coen; fiddlers Johnny and Paddy Cronin from Kerry and Longford fiddler Paddy Reynolds.

Like Celtic Hall in an earlier era, the City Center Ballroom, which opened in 1956 on West Fifty-Fifth Street, became the premier Irish dance hall in New York—"arguably," said Rebecca Miller, "in the United States." What made it so successful was its combination of big-band music, courtesy of Brendan Ward and his All-Star Orchestra, and *ceildih* dance sets. City Center offered the best of the New World with a smattering of the Old.

IRELAND OF THE SONGS

The Irish-American popular song tradition dates from the early years of the nineteenth century, when popular entertainment swept across the country. By the end of the century, Tin Pan Alley had written countless nostalgic songs with homesick immigrants in mind.

Or as musician and folklorist Mick Moloney has observed: "Irish-American songs romanticizing the homeland became a staple feature of the commercial songwriting industry in the early years of the twentieth century when the Irish were achieving a new respectability in American society."

Earlier, the popularity of sheet music grew with the popularity of the piano. Lyrical parlor songs, with their simple harmonies and appealing melodies, also found a ready market. As early as the post–Civil War era emigration songs were already painting a rosy picture of Irish domesticity—"I'll Take You Home Again, Kathleen" in 1876 is a prime example.

Even the traditional fiddler James Morrison could not ignore the immense influence of the American pop music-making machinery. "Along with traditional reels, jigs and hornpipes," said William H. A. Williams, "Morrison recorded popular American two-steps such as 'The Wreck of the 99' and 'Oh Dem Golden Slippers,' as well as such nontraditional Irish-American favorites as 'When Irish Eyes Are Smiling' and 'My Wild Irish Rose.'

"The Ireland of American popular songs," continued Williams, "is more a place of dreams and memories than of mountains and lakes. It is a dreamland that, in the imagination of the singer, is always calling him home." In other words, this mythical place is vastly different from the urban multiethnic America where most of the Irish emigrants and their offspring lived. The songwriters of Tin Pan Alley were writing about a land that only existed in their fertile imaginations. But it was a version that was easily accepted by Irish and Irish Americans alike.

Williams went on to say that meeting on the same musical plain were two Irish stereotypes: the patriotic, but sentimental, stereotype, crafted by ballad collector Thomas Moore, and the straightshooting, affable, and reliable Irish American, whom Williams called "the direct, albeit a greatly reformed descendant of the stereotypical Paddy."

This sanitized but widely popular version of Ireland was especially appealing to the children of the Irish emigrants, who had given up so much and suffered tremendously to arrive on American shores. Concluded Williams:

The Ireland of the songs was, in the end, an aspect of America, an isle of American-born dreams. The Emerald Isle provided an uncomplicated, usable 'homeland' for those who had not been born in Ireland and who had little inclination to visit it, yet who needed something more than the vast, grimy industrial cities to call 'home.' The Ireland of song was a cleaned up, pretty place, where decent, rural simplicity replaced poverty.

In short:

. . . Americans came to love the blarney and shamrocks, Killarney's rocks and fells, and Macnamara's Band. Within American popular culture, the Irish were defined as a patriotic, hardworking, happy people, exemplars of the old verities of family and community. The image of Ireland became an appendage of the American myth of the rural Eden.

 ## TYPICAL IRISH TIN PAN ALLEY SONGS

Ireland was a favorite subject of Tin Pan Alley writers around the turn of the century and beyond. A smattering of better-known Tin Pan Alley–penned songs with Irish themes includes the following:

"Sweet Rosie O'Grady (1896)
"My Wild Irish Rose" (1897)
"Where the River Shannon Flows" (1905)
"Mother Machree" (1910)
"When Irish Eyes Are Smiling" (1912)
"Too-re-loo-ra-loo-ra (That's an Irish Lullaby)" (1912)
"Top of the Morning" (1920)

Similarly, the recordings by opera singer John McCormack of Irish-American popular songs found an audience beyond the Irish community and hence gave the Irish the respect and legitimacy they had so longed for. His records of course had little to do with traditional singing; rather, they belonged to a manufactured image of Ireland defined by the popular culture of the day. They were Irish songs written by Americans.

Today the Irish-Canadian tenor John McDermott and the wildly popular Irish singer Daniel O'Donnell sing the standards made famous by earlier generations including such old war-horses as "Galway Bay," "Danny Boy," "I'll Take You Home Again, Kathleen," and "The Fields of Athenry." McDermott, who also has Scottish connections, is a bit more flexible, performing the songs of Robert Burns ("My Love Is Like a Red, Red Rose"), Jacobite-inspired compositions ("The Skye Boat Song"), modern classics (Eric Bogle's "And the Band Played Waltzing Matilda"), and other hoary favorites ("Annie Laurie," "The Bluebells of Scotland").

Singer Tommy Makem has commented on the tendency of Irish audiences during the late 1950s to prefer American Irish pop songs over authentic songs from the tradition. "When we started out, we refused to sing for Irish audiences because they would all be into Bing Crosby, 'Danny Boy,' things like that. That's what they were being fed by the radio programs at the time. . . . They had left Ireland and sort of looked down on Irish music. You were a peasant if you sang that kind of thing."

THE NEW GOLDEN AGE

Yet attitudes would soon change. Another wave of Irish immigrants arrived in America during the late 1950s and early 1960s. And even in Ireland itself, the tide was slowly turning. The 1960s saw the emergence of Comhaltas Ceoltoiri Eireann, the Dublin-based organization formed by Irish musicians to support and promote Irish music.

The folk revival of the 1960s and the impact of the Clancy Brothers' popularity all played their part in making people on both sides of the Atlantic sit up and take notice of the musical treasure that waited behind their own front door.

The music of contemporary Celtic America is a cross-fertilization of styles, regions, and repertoires.

One of the leading figures of this new golden age is Mick Moloney. Singer, banjo player, folklorist, he seems to have been involved in virtually every significant project that involved traditional Irish music in the past two decades. Emigrating from Ireland to Philadelphia in 1973, Moloney grew up in County Limerick and learned many of the old tunes from older traditional musicians in the area. He played professionally with several folk groups in Dublin in the early 1960s and later he was a member of the Johnstons, a popular folk group of the time, with whom he played tenor banjo.

Moloney has produced or played on more than forty recordings and documentary films, as well as organizing various Irish-music festivals and workshops. He obtained a doctorate in folklore and folklife from the University of Pennsylvania and lectures widely on Irish music and culture. In his spare time he also runs his Irish Folklore Tours from May to September, serving as guide, storyteller, and all-in-all Irish raconteur.

In 1977 Moloney founded Green Fields of America, whose purpose was to showcase some of the finest musicians working within the diverse Irish-American community. The lineup included both native Irish and American-born Irish: singer Robbie O'Connell, nephew to the Clancy Brothers; piano accordionist Jimmy Keane; fiddler Eileen Ivers, uilleann piper Séamus Egan; and dancers Donny and Eileen Golden.

In the mid–1980s Moloney teamed up with singer Robbie O'Connell and piano accordionist Jimmy Keane to record *Kilkelly*. It contains the great emigration ballad of the same name but also an operetta, "The Green Fields of America," which links the themes of emigration, settlement, and assimilation through 150 years of music drawn from broadsides, vaudeville, music hall, radio, and the old 78 rpm recording industry. The recording addresses various themes in emigration history—the American wake with "The Farewell Reel" and a spate of Irish-American labor songs, including "No Irish Need Apply," "The Rambling Irishman," "Paddy on the Canal," and "The Hod Carrier's Song."

Arguably the most innovative, certainly the most daring, of contemporary American-born Irish musicians is Eileen Ivers. Born in 1965 of Irish parents in the Bronx, Ivers started playing fiddle at the age of nine. Her mentor and teacher was the acclaimed Irish fiddler Martin Mulvihill. She has made numerous solo recordings and is a member of the popular Irish-American all-female band Cherish the Ladies. Her biggest claim to fame, though, is being a member of the cast of *Riverdance*.

Another contemporary musical firebrand is multi-instrumentalist Séamus Egan. Adept on the flute, tin whistle, banjo, mandolin, and uilleann pipes, Egan was born in Philadelphia in 1969. At a young age he returned to Ireland with his parents and family. They settled in in County Mayo, where Egan started to learn traditional music at the age of eight from a local teacher and musician, Martin O'Donoghue. He made his first solo recording for Shanachie when only sixteen. One of his striking original compositions, "Weep Not for the Memories," pays musical homage to some of the great traditional Irish musicians who have passed on, including Ed Reavy and Martin Mulvihill. Now a member of the Irish-American supergroup, Solas, Egan created a splash with his score for the quirky Irish-American film *The Brothers McMullen*.

One of the finest fiddlers living in the United States, Séamus Connolly moved to the Boston area in 1976 from Killaloe, County Clare. He picked up the fiddle at age twelve, inspired by the classic recordings of James Morrison, Michael Coleman, and Paddy Killoran. Later he found additional inspiration from the likes of Bobby Casey, Tommy Potts, and piper Willie Clancy. He is the musical director of Comhaltas Ceiltoiri Eiream, an Irish-traditional-music organization in Massachusetts.

Chicago-born John Williams is one of the few American-born musicians to specialize on the concertina. His father and grandfather—both concertina players—came from Doolin, a small fishing village and the traditional music capital of County Clare. Williams spend summers there as a teenager, soaking up the considerable atmosphere, playing with legendary locals such as the late whistle player Micho Russell, fiddler P. J. Hayes, and piper Davy Spillane.

It was in Doolin that he picked up most of his repertoire. Heavily influenced by the distinctive Clare style of concertina playing, he has also found inspiration in the music of uilleann piper Joe Shannon, flautist Séamus Cooley, and fiddler John McGreevy.

Like Séamus Egan, Williams is also a member of the supergroup Solas, whose individual members sounds like a Who's Who of traditional Irish-American music. Culled from Chanting House, Cherish the Ladies, the Sharon Shannon Band, Green Fields of America, and Atlantic Bridge, Solas also consists of vocalist Karan Casey, ex-Chanting House guitarist John Doyle, and fiddler Winifred Horan.

Someone who comes firmly from within the tradition yet is not afraid to stand outside it is Maura O'Connell. She feels equally at ease singing traditional Irish songs as she does the songs of John Hiatt, Janis Ian, Tom Waits, Shawn Colvin, and Mary-Chapin Carpenter.

O'Connell grew up in County Clare and began singing with another young musician from her hometown of Ennis named Mike Hanrahan, who later became a member of Stockton's Wing. She then joined the traditional Irish group Dé Danann and as lead singer appeared on *Star-Spangled Molly*, one of the band's most successful recordings in its long career. She quit to record her first solo album.

While with Dé Dannan, she met members of the American band New Grass Revival. Suitably inspired, she decided to make the big move to Nashville in 1987. In the course of her peripatetic career she has worked with the likes of Mark O'Connor, Jerry Douglas, Edgar Meyer, and Bela Fleck—all unofficial members of the so-called new acoustic-music scene that fused jazzy elements with country. With numerous recordings under her belt—*Just in Time* in 1988, *Helpless Heart* in 1989, *A Real Life Story* in 1991, *Blue Is the Colour of Hope* in 1992—she returned to Ireland long enough to record two tracks, "Living in These Troubled Times" and "Summer Fly" for *A Woman's Heart* (1993), a compilation of Ireland's leading female performers that turned out to be the biggest-selling Irish album of modern times.

"I have a mandate," she has stated, "and that is to bring back honor to the art of singing. Not every singer can write, just as not every writer can sing. Historically, what I do has been proven as an art form on its own. Nobody says to an opera singer, 'Why didn't you write that?' To me, being an interpreter is a tremendous art."

To O'Connell, a good song is simply a good song, no matter where it comes from.

RECOMMENDED LISTENING

The Barra MacNeils. *The Traditional Album* (Polygram). Mostly traditional Cape Breton and Scots tunes from this popular Cape Breton band.

Joe Burke, Andy McGann, and Felix Dolan. *A Tribute to Michael Coleman* (Green Linnet). This new digital master of the classic 1965 recording features Burke on button accordion, McGann on fiddle, and Dolan on piano.

Liz Carroll (Green Linnet). The definitive recording by the amazing Irish-American fiddler. In her latest CD, *Lost in the Loop* (Green Linnet), Carroll offers more than a dozen gems from the first jig she ever wrote to the newest tune, the irresistible title cut (about driving on the congested streets of downtown Chicago). It's a mature and immensely satisfying work from someone at the very peak of her profession.

Celtic Thunder. *The Light of Other Days* (Green Linnet). Seminal recording from the popular Washington, D.C.–Baltimore Irish band whose roots lie in the Irish dance halls of the old Irish-American enclaves. With songs by Bronx-born Jesse and Terry Winch, it includes the wistful "When New York Was Irish" and "The Galway Ghost," the latter about an Irishman forced to flee Galway for the New World after killing a man in a drunken brawl.

Cherish the Ladies. *One and All: The Best of Cherish the Ladies* (Green Linnet). All-female band of great Irish-American musicians who work well together without sacrificing their distinctive personalities.

Michael Coleman. *Classic Recordings* (Shanachie). Coleman made a profound impact on generations of Irish fiddlers on both sides of the Atlantic; listen to this recording and you'll understand why.

Dear Old Erin's Isle: Irish Traditional Music from America (Nimbus). A marvelous sampling of Irish traditional music as experienced in America. The musicians are fiddlers Seamus Connolly, Eileen Ivers, Liz Carroll, Kevin Burke, Brendan Mulvihill, button accordionist Billy McComiskey, flute player Séamus Egan, melodeon player Tom Doherty, uilleann piper Joe Shannon, piano accordionist Jimmy Keane, and button accordionist and concertina player John Williams. Simply the best of the best.

Séamus Egan. *When Juniper Sleeps* (Shanachie). Wonderful piece of musical virtuosity from one of the younger generation's finer musicians.

Alasdair Fraser and Jody Stecher. *The Driven Bow* (Culburnie). Fraser is one of the most expressive fiddlers of his generation. Any Fraser recording is worth picking up, but *The Driven Bow* is especially significant. Here he and his American colleague Jody Stecher trace the Scottish influence on the Cape Breton fiddling tradition. A lovely thing to behold.

4 Yn Y Bar. *Stryd America/America Street* (Fflach). Emigration to America from a Welsh perspective. In the lovely title cut, so many people who lived on a particular street in the Welsh village of Gaerwen in Anglesey have emigrated to America that the local postal carrier refers to it as "America Street."

Hugh Gillespie. *Classic Recordings of Irish Traditional Fiddle Music* (Green Linnet). County Donegal fiddler who emigrated to New York in 1928. A contemporary of Michael Coleman, Gillespie is considered one of the greatest traditional fiddlers to emerge from the Emerald Isle.

The Green Fields of America. *Live in Concert* (Green Linnet). Some of the finest Irish-American talent live. Features Mick Moloney, Robbie O'Connell, Jimmy Keane, Eileen Ivers, Séamus Egan, and Donny and Eileen Golden.

Hidden Treasures: Irish Music in Chicago ("Big Chicago" Records). Irish music in Chicago has a rich and colorful pedigree. This wonderful collection proves why. It includes selections by such Windy City traditional music stalwarts as Liz Carroll, John Williams, Baal Tinne, Laurence Nugent, and Jim Dewan as well as the more modern sounds of the Drovers and the Muck Brothers. Among the standouts is a particularly haunting *sean-nós* vocal by Aine Meenaghan and an original piece by the multitalented Joseph Sobol, a non-Celt who has transformed the ten-string cittern into a masterful Celtic instrument. Added bonus: a descriptive listing (and locator map) of twenty-three Chicago-area Irish and Scottish pubs and venues that regularly feature live music from the durable Abbey Pub to a fairly new addition, Chief O'Neill's, which is owned and operated by musicians Brendan and Siobhan McKinney and of course is named after the legendary Chicago police chief/musician/collector. Indeed, the spirit of O'Neill is very much evident throughout.

Eileen Ivers. *So Far: The Eileen Ivers Collection 1979–1995* (Green Linnet). A collection of the best from a fiddler with plenty of life in her yet.

Dolores Keane and John Faulkner with Eamonn Curran. *Farewell to Eirinn* (Mulligan). Irish emigration ballads sung with typical passion by the great Dolores Keane. Includes "Paddy's Green Shamrock Shore," "Edward Connors," "The Kilnamartyr Emigrant," "The Farmer Michael Hayes," and "Sliabh Gallion Braes."

Kips Bay Ceili Band. *Digging In* (Green Linnet). Modern-day *ceilidh* band from New York City; features ex-Battlefield Band Pat Kilbride on guitars, cittern, lead and backing vocals, and lilting and John Whelan on button accordion and keyboards. Special guests include Joanie Madden on whistle and flute.

Long Journey Home (BMG). Features Mary Black, the Chieftains, Elvis Costello, Vince Gill, Van Morrison, Sinéad O'Connor, Liam Ó Maonlaí, Sissel, and the Irish Film Orchestra.

Natalie MacMaster. *My Roots Are Showing: Traditional Fiddle Music of Cape Breton Island* (Greentrax). The Canadian fiddler shows off her Scottish roots with masterful versions of "Hey, Johnnie Cope," "Willie Fraser," "Balmoral Highlanders," and others. Includes both Scottish and Cape Breton tunes.

Mick Moloney, Robbie O'Connell, Jimmy Keane. *Kilkelly* (Green Linnet). Features the classic emigration ballad "Kilkelly" and the wonderful "Green Fields of America" operetta.

Brian McNeill. *The Back o' the North Wind: Tales of the Scots in America* (Greentrax). This concept album from the ex-Battlefield Band singer, songwriter, and fiddler profiles in song the lives of six Scots and their impact on America. Some are famous (Andrew Carnegie, John Muir, and Flora MacDonald); some are obscure (including Ewen Gillies, an adventurer from St. Kilda).

Jerry O'Sullivan. *The Invasion* (Green Linnet). One of the few American-born uilleann pipers.

Out of Ireland: The Story of Irish Emigration to America (Shanachie). Film soundtrack featuring Mick Moloney, Eileen Ivers, Séamus Egan, Jerry O'Sullivan, Jimmy Keane, Tommy Hayes, Eugene O'Donnell, and John Williams.

Ossian. *Light on a Distant Shore* (Iona). Contains the great emigration ballad "Jamie Raeburn," sweetly sung by Tony Cuffe and an extended emigration suite: "Light on a Distant Shore," "Arrival," "At Work on the Land," and "In the New World."

Solas (Shanachie). Debut record from the Irish-American supergroup.

Thousands Are Sailing: Irish Songs of Immigration (Shanachie). Classic Irish immigration songs ("Shamrock Shore," "Galway Bay," "Thousands Are Sailing," "Paddy's Green Shamrock Shore") performed by masters of the genre (including Dolores Keane, Planxty, Boys of the Lough, Dé Dannan, Wolfe Tones, and Liam Clancy).

Traditional Music from Cape Breton Island (Nimbus). The best of Cape Breton's rich musical heritage: Jerry Holland, Buddy MacMaster, Natalie MacMaster, Carl MacKenzie, Brenda Stubbert, Dougie MacDonald, Howie MacDonald, the late John Morris Rankin, Dave MacIsaac, Tracey Dares, Hilda Chiasson, Paul MacNeil, and Jamie MacInnis.

RECOMMENDED VIDEOS

Far Away from the Shamrock Shore: A History of Irish Music in America (Lake Productions). Musical and historical documentary that traces Irish influence on American music and culture. Features the music of the Clancy Brothers and Tommy Makem, Boiled in Lead, Cherish the Ladies, and others.

From Shore to Shore: Irish Traditional Music in New York City (Cherry Lane Productions). Combining archival photographs and film footage with contemporary interviews and performances, this video documents the effects of Irish immigration on the traditional music of New York. Features performances and interviews with Eileen Ivers, Andy McGann, Jerry O'Sullivan, Paddy Reynolds, John Whelan, and others.

9

Full-Force Gaels

Planxty to U2

I started with rock 'n' roll and . . . then you start to take it apart like a child with a toy and you see that there's blues and there's country. . . Then you go back from country into American music, and you go back from American folk music and you end up in Scotland or Ireland eventually.

—ELVIS COSTELLO

The sweaty bodies sway back and forth, rocking to the incessant beat. Some of the more inebriated celebrants bounce off each other, like sailors coming off an all-night binge, while the ubiquitous drums pound out a throbbing rhythm. The singer steps up to the microphone, clearly caught up in the passion of the moment. Then the unexpected occurs. Out of the singer's mouth comes a torrent of words that few in the room can understand, since she is singing in one of the world's oldest languages: Gaelic. And what is that subtle but unmistakable sound in the background? Could it be bagpipes?

SOMETHING REMARKABLE IS happening in the fickle rock and roll landscape. Rock is looking to the past for inspiration, to music usually associated with heather moors and green rolling hills, with Aran sweaters and lilting tin whistles.

What do you get when you mix together one of the world's oldest forms of music with a brash twentieth-century upstart? Celtic rock, of course. Take the spontaneity of an Irish pub session, the wisdom and utter beauty of a Gaelic love song, and the raw energy of an eclectic guitar and you'll get an idea of what's going on. From the fiery anger of the Irish-American band Black 47 to the Highland funk of Mouth Music, a quiet revolution is taking place, and the future looks bright indeed.

"If you have a strong core foundation," says Irish musician and scholar Mick Moloney, "you can do anything with a tradition, because it's not endangered . . . . [P]eople are attracted to it not only because it is quite compelling and passionate music but also because it is tied to a living, breathing tradition. . . ."

Echoes Scottish fiddler John Cunningham, "Anyone can take hold of the music; it's very primal in nature. Any of us who play Celtic music can tell you: Once you play this music, it's part of your life. It's who you are."

And, I might add, when you have heard it for the first time, you might never listen to music in quite the same way again, for once its gets into your system Celtic music is hard to shake. It appeals to people's gut instincts, to their sense of the ineffable. It is both sacred and profane, timely and timeless, a music for the ages *and* for the moment.

A HYBRID WITH A DIFFERENT NAME

Celtic rock is essentially rock rhythms wedded to traditional music, chiefly Irish or Scottish in origin. Traditional instruments and electric guitars, traditional themes and modern themes live side by side—if not in blissful harmony at least in a mostly happy accommodation of each other's differences and similarities. In its broadest sense, though, Celtic music can include music that is influenced by traditional Celtic material, music whose lyrics address Celtic themes, or material composed in a Celtic language (most commonly Irish, Scots Gaelic, or Welsh).

A "typical" Celtic rock band may employ the usual electric guitars and drums but it might also have fiddle, tin whistle, mandolin, bagpipes, *bodhran* (Irish drum), and occasionally *bombarde* (Breton horn)—not to mention harps or even synthesizers.

Clearly, Celtic music is a remarkably resilient art form. More than just sad laments and fast reels, it is a complex music that has deep roots in a particular time and place yet is confident enough to embrace other forms under its increasingly diverse umbrella.

Don't Step on My Blue Suede Brogans

The current Celtic rock scene owes a very large debt to the Celtic revival of the 1960s and 1970s, which coincided with a similar interest in folk roots in America. Bands and individuals began to experiment with traditional music—to explore their own roots in order to come up with something new and exciting. Whether then or now, though, the traditional music of the Celtic peoples was being presented with a new twist.

The roots of the Celtic revival can be traced back to the late 1950s, when the Clancy Brothers and Tommy Makem—Irishmen trying to make a living in New York—began to rediscover their own national music. They were among the first to adapt traditional songs to a contemporary setting by using to best advantage harmonies, guitar, and a five-string banjo and other musical examples inspired by the American folk boom. A similar interest was taking place in Britain with the likes of Ewan MacColl and Peggy Seeger, the Copper family, the Young Tradition, the Watersons, Dave Swarbrick and Martin Carthy, Donovan and Ray and Archie Fisher, among others.

Unfortunately, it set off something of a folk explosion—an ersatz authenticity—with scores of young people throughout the British Isles invading pubs, strumming a guitar, wearing fishermen's jerseys, singing watered-down versions of ancient ballads, and, in essence, passing themselves off as the real thing to anyone willing to listen.

Another down side of the revival in Ireland was the proliferation of *ceilidh* bands, ubiquitous show bands with a penchant for bad American country-western rhythms who were more concerned with finding the next gig than sharing the authentic music of their native culture. The typical *ceilidh* band lineup consisted of piano, drum, fiddle, accordion or piano, and every pub in Ireland seemed to have one.

The folk music revival in Scotland also got its start in the 1950s but, unlike the case with Ireland, much of it was politically inspired. Like some latter-day Sir Walter Scott, folk-music scholars, ranging from the American Alan Lomax to native Scot Hamish Henderson roamed the countryside in search of authentic folk culture, collecting traditional songs and tunes. In 1951 the School of Scottish Studies was established in Edinburgh. Its purpose was to study not only traditional Scottish music and song but also the greater traditional Scottish culture. It is still going strong to this day.

The roots of Scottish rock lie in the ballrooms and folk clubs of the 1950s when American-style country and R&B began to replace traditional Scottish music. Lonnie Donegan launched skiffle in the mid-1950s. Its heyday culminated with Donegan enjoying a top-ten British and American hit with his cover of Leadbelly's "Rock Island Line" in 1956. Significantly, some scholars trace the melody on the flip side, "John Henry," an American work song, to Scotland.

Born Anthony Donegan in Glasgow, Donegan was so smitten with American music that he changed his first name in honor of the American bluesman Lonnie Johnson. With its New Orleans-style rhythm and delivered in a surprisingly authentic-sounding American accent, "Rock Island Line" took Britain by storm. Everyone wanted to become part of the skiffle phenomenon. Skiffle bands sprouted up from Glasgow to London. Scores of legendary English singers from Ringo Starr and Elton John to Albert Lee and Ron Wood would later admit Donegan's influence.

Skiffle's very success proved its undoing. Recording companies jumped on the skiffle bandwagon—in effect, taking the spontaneity out of a very grassroots music—and skiffle veered into two opposite directions, folk and rock and roll.

In the mid-1960s another alternative scene emerged in the youth market in Ireland and Scotland. Beat clubs catered to teenagers and the changing world that swirled all around them. With names like Bluesville, the Chessmen, the Chosen Few, Granny's Intentions, and the Greenbeats in Ireland or the Poets, the Beatstalkers, and the Pathfinders in Scotland, they appealed to a largely urban crowd. The beat bands adopted a modern look and wore snappy clothes. Of course, there was nothing particularly Irish or Scottish about them, except for the fact they were products of an Irish or Scottish upbringing. The beat groups looked to America for their musical influences—especially to Motown, soul, and R&B—not to the indigenous music of their native lands. African-American influences were so strong that a band like Lulu and the Luvvers—fronted by the full-throttle vocals of Glasgow-born Lulu (real name: Marie McDonald Mclaughlin Lawrie)—was thought to be American. Their cover of the Isley Brothers' "Shout" spawned the first Scottish hit of the Beat era.

Around the same period, a loose confederation of pop-culture iconoclasts caused a stir in Scottish folk circles and beyond. Defying all categories, the members of the Incredible String Band didn't just break barriers. They flagrantly, joyously ignored them, relishing in the sometime bizarre merging of incongruous forms. Established in 1965 by two Scots, Robin Williamson and Mike Heron, their increasingly international music borrowed heavily from Indian, Middle Eastern, and Scottish traditions. Truly ahead of their time—and, with their acid trips and imagery steeped in psychedelia, also truly *of* their time—these two mystics defiantly mixed traditions at a time when convention in the folk world was uniformly followed. In effect, they created world music before the term was even coined. Pipes, sitars, myth, folklore, Celtic, Asian, Arabic—they all come together in one glorious, if rather chaotic, palette of sounds and textures. On *The Hangman's Beautiful*

Daughter (Elektra), the band's most cohesive work, Williamson played more than a dozen acoustic instruments. In recent years, Williamson has become known for his harp playing and, indeed, he has spent valuable time researching the repertoire of early Scottish harp music.

Yet musical experimentation within genres has not been strictly confined to the Celtic world. As early as 1965 English vocalist Shirly Collins, who played a pivotal role in the English folk revival, was experimenting with jazz, blues, and folk fusions.

The die had been cast. There was no turning back.

PLUGGED IN

With seemingly limited room to maneuver—traditional music in general is notorious for its inbred conservatism—the range that exists in Celtic music is all the more astonishing. Essentially, Celtic rock is a subgenre of the contemporary world-music explosion. Yet aspects of Celtic music have had a subtle influence on contemporary popular music for decades, especially on the British invasion of the 1960s and 1970s.

The Scottish impact of the invasion reaches from Donovan and Jack Bruce to Gerry Rafferty, the Average White Band, and the underrated Frankie Miller in the 1970s. Another survivor is Ian Anderson, the Edinburgh-born flautist who led the supergroup Jethro Tull to rousing international success in the 1970s and 1980s and even into the 1990s has filled stadiums with his retro band of heavy-metal folk.

Formed in 1968, Jethro Tull is a remarkable success story. Whatever one thinks of his skill on the flute, Anderson remains one of the most charismatic characters—certainly one of the most eccentric—in rock. If nothing else, his persistence and determination to keep the band going is at least worthy of some kind of grudging respect. From its earliest incarnation, the band and Anderson in particular had a strong appreciation of the folk tradition. Steeleye Span was a major influence on the band, especially evident in the late 1970s with the release of *Songs From the Wood* (EMI). In cuts such as "Jack-in-the-Green," "Cup of Wonder," and "Pibroch (Cap in Hand)," Anderson taps into English and Scottish folklore; the overall effect is of (relative) light and playfulness. To my mind, though, much of Jethro Tull's material sounds terribly dated—overblown and pretentious and downright silly at times—and is best appreciated more as an intellectual exercise than for sheer musical enjoyment.

The 1980s brought a new generation of Celtic rockers—Midge Ure, Bronski Beat, Simple Minds, Roddy Frame and Aztec Camera, and the Eurythmics, to name a few. And who can forget the first time they heard the anthemic and distinctively Scottish sound of Stuart Adamson's guitar-driven Big Country? Guitars would never sound the same again.

More recently, the Waterboys, Jesus and Mary Chain, Texas, Deacon Blue, Hue and Cry, the Silencers, the Proclaimers, the Blue Nile, Edwyn Collins, Teenage Fanclub, and Del Amitri have all added their voices to the collective chorus. Most, if not all, offer more than a touch of Celtic melancholy in their bag of musical tricks (such as Justin Currie of Del Amitri's appropriately weary voices) or lyrics (The Eurythmics' "Here Comes the Rain Again" could only have been written by a Celt).

From Ireland one need only think of the Celtic-tinged melodies of Van Morrison, Thin Lizzy, Horslips, the Boomtown Rats, Sinéad O'Connor, That Petrol Emotion, Cactus World News, and the Cranberries. Probably the most controversial band to emerge from Ireland in recent years has been the rowdy, whisky-drenched sound of the Pogues. In the early 1980s, the English-based yet strongly Irish-influenced Dexys Midnight Runners had an international hit with the infectious "Come On, Eileen." At one point the band's lineup they boasted three fiddles as well as banjoes and tin whistles. The rage for all things Celtic was on.

Wales, often a sorely neglected member within the loose Celtic configuration, has given us Dave Edmunds and the Alarm as well as numerous English and Welsh-language groups not generally known outside Welsh borders. The all-Welsh lyrics of the Alarm's *Tan* (Raw) (Crai) sounds perfectly natural set against the band's hard rock guitars and Mike Peter's strong lead vocals. Novelty also plays its part. How often do you get the opportunity to hear Neil Young's "Rocking in the Free World" ("Rocio Yn Ein Rhyddid") or John Lennon's "Merry Christmas, War Is Over" ("Nadolig LLawen") in Welsh?

Across the Irish Sea a few of the leading names on the Irish folk circuit—including Johnny Moynihan, Andy Irvine, and Terry Woods—formed an electric outfit called Sweeney's Men in Galway during the summer of 1966. Meanwhile, on the continent, there were rumblings in Brittany when the Breton harpist Alan Stivell founded the first folk-rock band in Europe. Along with guitarist Dan Ar Bras, he drew inspiration from the larger pan-Celtic world and, indeed, was among the first of the Celtic musicians to promote the spirit of musical camaraderie among the Celtic peoples.

The Irish folk-music bloom began in earnest in the 1960s and 1970s. The influence of the Clancy Brothers and Tommy Makem remained strong, as did the impact of the American folk boom and such acts as the Kingston Trio and Peter, Paul, and Mary.

Irish bands like Sweeney's Men, the seminal Irish electric folk band of the 1960s, and the Johnstons provided a link between the pub ballad bands of the early 1960s and the more sophisticated music of the folk groups that would emerge in the 1970s. Formed in Galway during the summer of 1966, the original lineup consisted of Johnny Moynihan, Andy Irvine, and Joe Dolan. The banjo player, Terry Woods, who relied heavily on American folk music for inspiration, joined later. Their debut recording contained a version of two traditional ballads, "The House Carpenter" and "Willy o' Wimsbury." Although a short-lived outfit, they were immensely influential.

With the 1972 formation of Planxty the Irish folk revival was in full bloom. One of the most important bands of the Celtic revival was Planxty. Some even say that without their considerable presence there would not have even been a revival. Combining traditional music with original compositions, they had a multilayered sound yet remained primarily acoustic. Although they were together only a brief three years—they made their last public appearance in London in 1975—their influence was immense. They were among the first to experiment with Irish music—not only to popularize traditional music without diluting its essence but also to prove that an acoustic band could pack as much emotional punch as any rock outfit. Rather than diminishing the tradition, they enhanced it.

Planxty drew on influences that ranged from rock to eastern European folk music, reflecting the varied interests of their talented members. The shifting lineup included at various times vocalist, guitarist, and bodhran player Christy Moore, keyboardist Dónal Lunny (later replaced by Johnny Moynihan, late of Sweeney's Men), uilleann piper Liam O'Flynn, and vocalists Paul Brady, who took Moore's place, and Andy Irvine—names that resonate throughout the history of Irish traditional music to this day. Lunny seems to have been a member of almost every important traditional Irish band. O'Flynn, a traditional piper from County Kildare, had learned the pipes from such earlier masters as Leo Rowsome, Willie Clancy, and Seamus Ennis.

The chief figure behind the success of Planxty—indeed, the reason for its very existence—was Moore, the scruffy, vest-wearing Irishman who, in the opinion of music writer Mark J. Prendergast, "changed the entire history of Irish traditional music." Moore broke down barriers of traditional and modern by virtue of his larger-than-life ego, his unimpeachable integrity, and his absolute commitment to the music. Audiences knew they were getting the real thing, not some treacle-coated alternative. A great folk singer, he brought respect and popularity to the tradition; he breathed new life into an old song.

Born in County Kildare in a rural environment, he spent a good part of the early 1960s in a stable but ultimately dead-end job as a bank clerk. A strike in 1966 led to unemployment, and he looked elsewhere. He had always had a way with a song, so he emigrated to England and found work in the booming folk circuit. Returning to Ireland, he felt refreshed and inspired to give the dusty old Irish ballads he grew up with new life.

Moore recruited a bunch of like-minded Irishmen—acoustic guitarist and *bouzouki* player Dónal Lunny, mandolin player Andy

Irvine, and uilleann piper Liam O'Flynn—as backup musicians for his breakthrough recording, *Prosperous* (Tara). Recorded live in Prosperous, County Kildare, it was full of youthful and exuberant energy and passionate spontaneity, presenting a whole new face of traditional Irish music to the nation. Significantly, it also included covers of Woody Guthrie's "Ludlow Massacre" and Bob Dylan's "Tribute to Woody," evidence of Moore's sympathy with the two great eras of American protest music, the pro-labor period of the 1930s and the youth-fed movement of the 1960s.

Wishing to push the envelope of Irish traditional music even farther, he brought most of the lineup of the *Prosperous* album with him to form what would become Planxty. In 1973 they released their debut recording.

In essence Planxty gave tacit permission for later generations to experiment and explore within the previously confined box of traditional music. The joy and excitement they brought to their live performances was palpable and legendary, especially in their use of the *bouzouki* as a rhythm instrument, and the manner in which they effortlessly integrated uilleann pipes with guitar, mandolin, and fiddle. Their arrangements of old airs and tunes gave a much-needed shot in the arm to the music. With their fresh approach, it is not surprising that the band siphoned a great share of their support from a huge rock audience. Planxty changed forever the way Irish music was heard and the way people, especially younger generations, perceived it. No longer would it be the music of an older generation; rather it became a very living and vibrant music of Irish youth.

Like Planxty, the Bothy Band was also short lived—1975 to 1979—yet their impact was also as considerable; in many ways it was a forerunner of the world-music groups that are with us today. Years after their demise, many still warmly recall their innovative mixture of traditional material and modern-style arrangements, with elements of jazz, classical, and rock, all performed in a sophisticated and passionate style. Their melody section, for example, was provided by pipes, flute, whistles, and fiddles, while the rhythm consisted of guitars, *bouzouki*, and *bodhran*.

The Bothy Band was more rooted in the tradition than was Planxty. The original lineup consisted of Dónal Lunny on *bouzouki*, Paddy Keenan on uilleann pipes, Matt Molloy on flute, and Paddy Glackin on fiddle; the group was later joined by the brother-and-sister team of Mícheál and Tríona Ó Dhomhnaill on guitar and clavinet, respectively. Accordionist Tony MacMahon was involved early on but left before the band made its debut at Trinity College, Dublin, in February 1975. By the end of the year Glackin had left to be replaced by the fiery style of Donegal fiddler Tommy Peoples. Peoples in turn was replaced by Kevin Burke.

Both Planxty and the Bothy Band helped popularize Irish folk music by introducing electric instruments and innovative arrangements into the fold. In particular, Planxty's lusty vocalist Christy Moore brought a level of spontaneity and a vibrant spirit to folk heretofore unknown, proving that a traditional band could play with all the power and passion of rock.

In the early 1980s Moore and Lunny turned their gaze toward even broader vistas when they founded Moving Hearts. Although drawing its surface inspiration from rock and jazz arrangements, the sound of the band was still steeped in a decidedly Irish mentality. Since then, others have moved comfortably between the traditional and rock worlds, including Clannad and the Saw Doctors.

When Moore founded Moving Hearts in 1981, he wasn't quite sure what the reaction would be to his experiments in folk rock. He apparently struck the right chord, though, for the band's debut recording reached the top of the Irish charts. With a lineup consisting of Moore on vocals, guitar and *bodhran*; the ubiquitous Dónal Lunny on electric and acoustic *bouzouki*, synthesizer, and vocals; Declan Sinnott on lead guitars; Eoghan O'Neill on bass and vocals; Davy Spillane on uilleann pipes and whistle; Keith Donald on tenor and soprano saxophones; and Brian Calnan on drums and percussion, everything jelled. Undeniably Celtic in spirit, it reverberated with strong jazzy overtones and brimming over with edgy topics from emigration to war.

Moving Hearts was yet another one of those short-lived Irish outfits. Moore went on to concentrate on a solo career. *Ride On*

(WEA) is a collection of songs by such diverse composers as member of parliament and martyr to the IRA cause Bobby Sands and compositions by W. B. Yeats. Moore is backed up by ex-Hearts, Lunny and Sinnott. Another solo recording, the well-received *Ordinary Man* features help from some of Moore's most illustrious friends, including Arty McGlynn, Dónal Lunny, Andy Irvine, and Liam O'Flynn. Even a very young Enya makes an appearance.

Newer bands such as Patrick Street and Solas are latest in this long line of Celtic supergroups.

CELTIC STORY TELLERS

The Celt has always been a grand storyteller, and this love of the written word applies to traditional- and folk-music circles. One of the best of the modern storytellers is singer-songwriter Paul Brady.

Born in Strabane, County Tyrone, he has comfortably moved from folk to traditional to rock. In 1967 he joined the Irish folk group the Johnstons, known for their harmonies and interpretations of traditional songs as well as modern folk songs by the likes of Joni Mitchell and Ralph McTell. By 1974 uilleann piper Liam O'Flynn invited Brady to join Planxty, which by then had earned a reputation as the most important traditional Irish group around. Now the lineup consisted of Brady, Christy Moore (who left two months later), O'Flynn, Andy Irvine, and Johnny Moynihan.

When the supergroup broke up the following year, Brady and Irvine decided to team up on their own projects. Their record *Andy Irvine/Paul Brady* (Mulligan), released in 1976, met with immediate critical acclaim. Folk based yet somehow cosmopolitan, it offered an intoxicating mix of exotic instruments—exotic, that is, in traditional-Irish-music circles at the time—including the harmonium, *bouzouki, cittern,* and hurdy-gurdy and contained masterful performances of traditional classics "Arthur McBride" and "Lough Erne Shore." Traditional musicians Matt Molloy and Tommy Peoples guested on the record.

Brady also made several traditional fiddle records with Tommy Peoples, Andy McGann, and Kevin Burke in the late 1970s, but *Welcome Here, Kind Stranger,* voted the best folk album of 1978 by *Melody Maker*, cemented his reputation as one of the finest interpreters of traditional material. Its collection of folk songs, including "The Lakes of Pontchartrain," was given a modern treatment with rock rhythms bubbling under the surface.

Feeling restrained by the limits of traditional music, he began writing original material. His 1981 rock debut *Hard Station* (Polydor) revealed a rock and roll heart; the album was full of biting lyrics and hard-edged instrumentation. He soon earned an international reputation as a fine songwriter and became a favorite of numerous big-league singers. Everyone from Carlos Santana to Tina Turner wanted to record Brady's songs. *Back to the Centre* (Mercury), released in 1986, featured a stellar cast of guest artists, including Eric Clapton on electric guitars, Larry Mullen, Jr., on drums, and Loudon Wainwright III on backup vocals. It also contained the compassionate anti-war song "The Island," which traditional Irish singer Dolores Keane sings so beautifully on the best-selling *A Woman's Heart*.

DIPPING INTO THE CELTIC WELL

The first truly Celtic rock band to gain international attention, however, was Horslips, which first emerged on the Irish scene in the early 1970s. A somber bunch of musicians with a scholarly bent, the members of Horslips intertwined Celtic myth with sturdy—some said heavy-handed—rock. They saw no inconsistency with combining the power and immediacy of rock with the vibrance and emotional depth of their Irish heritage. In March 1972 their potent version of "Johnny's Wedding" topped the Irish charts. Although they created an essentially Irish music, it was music that could appeal to the non-Irish as well.

Drummer Eamon Carr had spent his childhood in Kells, County Meath, an area associated with the great Irish illuminated medieval manuscript *The Book of Kells*. Carr, experimenting with music and poetry, and a friend named Peter Fallon started a quarterly literary magazine in Dublin. Eventually they met graphic designer Charles O'Connor, who professed an interest in traditional music and played concertina, mandolin, and fiddle. Johnny Fean, a

fiery guitar player from the Shannon area, replaced original guitarists Declan Sinnott and Gus Guiest. Tin whistle player Jim
Lockhart and bass guitarist Barry Devlin rounded up the roster. Intent on maintaining artistic control, the success of several singles
allowed them to form their own record label, Oats.

Much of their earlier work was based on Irish myth and legend,
yet their music was also an intentional effort to fully embrace the
larger Celtic consciousness. In *The Tain* and especially *The Book
of Invasions: A Celtic Symphony*, a concept recording based on a
twelfth-century Irish chronicle, they dipped deeply into the well of
Celtic folklore. Side two was divided into two categories of the traditional Celtic types of music, *goltrai* (lament) and *suantrai* (sleep).

The Irish reaction to this unusual mix of myth and rock was uniformly ecstatic. The band's first record, *Happy to Meet, Sorry to
Part*, was a mix of mostly traditional airs and folk tunes. When
asked by Dublin's famous Abbey Theatre to provide background
music for the stage adaptation of the Irish legend *The Tain*, the
band was eager to accommodate. From this experience came its
second recording, of the same name, and its first concept album,
which featured Lockhart on flute, whistles, uilleann pipes, and vocals; Carr on drums, *bodhran*, and percussion; O'Connor on fiddle, mandolin, concertina, and vocals; Fean on banjo and vocals;
and Devlin on bass and vocals.

"Our wish was to provide an essentially Irish rock music, some-
thing distinctly our own," Eamon Carr once told rock journalist
Mark J. Prendergast. "We felt it was very important to convey our
Irishness—a sense of our own identity and our heritage."

Drive the Cold Winter Away (Oats) was in a very folky vein and
included a medieval arrangement of a traditional carol in Irish, a
hornpipe, reels, a Manx carol, and a Carolan tune. Later records
were more straightforward guitar rock with very little, if any, traditional instrumentation; these included *Aliens* (RCA) in 1977,
about the Irish in America in the mid-nineteenth century, and the
follow-up *The Man Who Built America* (RCA) in 1979, about
Irish immigration to the United States.

Horslips spawned a lot of imitators, most of the dreadful variety
and, fortunately, long forgotten.

Meet Me on the Ledge

The revival was not just taking place in the Celtic world, however. The English revival was also in full throttle. Two English folk-rock bands that were very influential on the Irish and Scottish musical scenes and made significant headway in America were Fairport Convention and Steeleye Span.

Initially an electric folk band, Steeleye Span wrote original songs taken from English and Scots folklore and balladry. Fairport, on the other hand, was primarily a rock band whose members, inspired by the burgeoning American folk-rock movement of the 1960s, began tapping into their own rich heritage and composing extraordinary songs in the folk tradition.

Fairport Convention has been called an English national treasure. Many years after forming back in the 1960s, the band still survives, albeit in a radically different form. Moreover, they book their own tours, run their own label (Woodworm), and each year sponsor the popular Cropready Festival in Oxfordshire. Veterans of the band include founding member Simon Nicol and bassist Dave Pegg. Longtime drummer Dave Mattacks recently left the band after many years.

The original Fairport lineup consisted of Simon Nicol on guitar and vocals, Richard Thompson on guitar and vocals, Ashley Hutchings on bass, Martin Lamble on drums, and Judy Dyble on autoharp and vocals. Other important members included Sandy Denny, Ian Matthews, Dave Swarbrick, Dave Mattacks, and Bob Pegg.

To many people Fairport represents the quintessential English folk-rock group, with spirit of a rock band. At various times the group could boast the talents of a great singer, the glorious Sandy Denny; a brilliant guitarist, Richard Thompson (who was no slouch as a singer and writer); and a wonderfully expressive fiddler, Dave Swarbrick.

Although grounded in traditional music, the band's collective efforts never sounded stilted or artificial. Instead everything came together—the gorgeous vocal harmonies, the solid musical craftsmanship—and the level of care was evident throughout.

Denny, a folk singer making the rounds of the English club circuit, played a stint with English folk-rock group the Strawbs before joining Fairport. To many of her fans she was the voice of Fairport, a honeycombed jewel equally at home with older and contemporary material. But it was with the traditional that she shone her brightest. Even Denny originals like "Fotheringay," about the imprisonment of Mary, Queen of Scots, in Fotheringay Castle on the eve of her execution, sound as if they emerged full blown from the Middle Ages, so thoroughly and yet naturally were they conceived. With its harpsichordlike guitars and angelic background harmonies, the song could easily be thought an authentic piece of sacred medieval music.

 ## DUELING VOCALS

Many contemporary rock stars appreciated what Fairport Convention was trying to do. In what must be one of the more unusual duets in modern musical history, Denny traded off vocals with Led Zeppelin singer Robert Plant on "The Battle of Evermore" (*Led Zeppelin IV*, the so-called Runes album). Despite its heavy-metal reputation, Led Zeppelin had a soft spot for folk material. In addition to the Denny duet, the band included acoustic songs on early recordings. And even its signature song, "Stairway to Heaven," begins on an acoustic note. They were also big fans of such Scottish folk figures as Robin Williamson and the Incredible String Band, and the innovative guitarist Bert Jansch.

Among Fairport's many recordings, *Unhalfbricking* and *Liege and Lief* (both A&M) contain the most traditional material; the latter is generally acknowledged to be its finest work. Subsequent records, sometimes with different lineups, would continue to explore traditional material sporadically, including *Babbacombe Lee* in 1972 and *Bonny Bunch of Roses* in 1977.

The Fairport roster was more fluid than most. Denny quit to form the short-lived Fotheringay, Hutchings to form Steeleye Span, while Thompson departed in 1971 to pursue a successful solo career, first with his wife, Linda, and then, following the breakup of their marriage, on his own. Tragically, Denny died in 1978 of a brain hemorrhage after falling down a flight of stairs at a friend's house.

Of all the Fairport veterans, Thompson is the best-known and indisputably one of the finest guitarists of his generation, as well as an excellent songwriter. His singular guitar work and brooding, fatalistic lyrics drenched in despair have set him apart from the conventional rock world. With Linda, a native of Glasgow, Thompson created some of the most satisfying recordings of the modern rock era. Yet much of their sensibility and emotional colorings derived from ancient Celtic roots.

The most commercially successful of the English electric folk bands, Steeleye Span originally consisted of Tim Hart on guitar, dulcimer, and vocals; Maddy Prior and Gay Woods on vocals; Terry Woods on guitar, mandolin, and vocals. Later Martin Carthy replaced both Woods (Carthy later left then rejoined, the latter time bringing aboard singer, button accordionist and concertina player John Kirkpatrick). Other members have included Peter Knight on fiddle, Rick Kemp on bass, and Bob Johnson on guitar.

They adopted, arranged, and occasionally rewrote traditional material. Sometimes, though, in their zealous attempt to relate to a contemporary audience, their modern arrangements veered toward the heavy handed, overwhelming the original material in a deafening crescendo of drums and electric guitars and, in essence, creating an unnatural musical alliance.

Hark! The Village Wait (RCA) contained mostly traditional songs and ballads with rock arrangements: classics such as "Dark-eyed Sailor" "Lowlands of Holland," and "Twa Corbies" got the full Steeleye treatment. Other records with considerable traditional material include *Below the Salt* (Chrysalis) and *Parcel of Rogues* (Chrysalis). The latter featured "Alison Gross," "The Wee Wee Man," "Cam Ye O'er Frae France," and the title cut.

In another example of the rock-folk connection, Jethro Tull's Ian Anderson produced *Now We Are Six* (Chrysalis), which featured not only the group's version of the classic Scots ballad "Thomas the Rhymer" but also, inexplicably, David Bowie playing saxophone on one of the cuts. Yet another recording, *Commoner's Crown* (Chrysalis), included even more Scots ballads—"Demon Lover" and "Long Lamkin"—and the just plain weird appearance of Peter Sellers playing ukulele on the shanty "New, York Girls." Their most commercially successful record, *All Around My Hat* (Chrysalis) made some inroads into the American market.

Singer, guitarist, and mandolin player Martin Carthy is considered the single most important figure to emerge from the modern English folk revival. In addition to his work with the Albion Band, Steeleye Span, Brass Monkey, and, more recently, the Watersons, it is his solo output—recordings like *Prince Heathen, Sweet Wivelsfield*, and *Out of the Cut*—that marked him as an exceedingly talented interpreter and crafter of traditional material, while his distinctive percussive guitar style made him stand out above the crowd.

The uncrowned queen of the modern English folk revival is June Tabor. Influenced by traditional English and Scottish performers from Anne Briggs to the Blairs of Blairgowrie, she has long been a personal favorite of many rock singers, Steve Winwood and Elvis Costello among them. In *Angel Tiger* (Green Linnet), her 1992 recording, she performed Costello's "All This Useless Beauty" and Billy Bragg's "Rumours of War." Early recordings were particularly strong on traditional and folk songs. *Airs and Graces* (Shanachie), her solo debut, features her rightly famous version of Eric Bogle's "And the Band Played Waltzing Matilda" as well as the beautiful Scots ballad "Queen Among the Heather."

And just to prove that she doesn't have any desire to be boxed into a musical corner, in the early 1990s Tabor teamed up with the English folk-rock group the Oyster Band, making a record (*Freedom and Rain*), going on tour, and performing revved-up versions of "Dives and Lazarus" and "Susie Clelland."

Clearly undefinable is the work of Nick Drake, one of the most enigmatic figures to have emerged from the English folk scene. In recordings like *Five Leaves Left* (1969) and *Bryter Later* (1971), he created a truly personal vision, melancholy works that were part folk and part jazz with elements of blues and pop delivered in consciously poetic style. Drake died from a drug overdose in 1974, but despite his all-too-brief life and small recorded output, he influenced many folk and pop musicians, including Peter Buck of R.E.M., Kate Bush, Richard Thompson, and John Cale.

SINGING IN TONGUES

One of the most significant developments in the contemporary Celtic revival is the decision of a growing number of younger singers, both traditional and rock, to perform songs in their native Celtic tongue. In Scotland these traditional singers include Christine Primrose from Lewis, Catherine-Ann MacPhee from Barra, and Arthur Cormack from Skye. Such choices have had considerable consequences on contemporary Celtic rock musicians as well.

In the mid-1980s the Dublin quartet Na Firein was one of the few, if not the only, contemporary Irish rock bands to write and perform entirely in the Irish language. Themes ranged from the universal dilemma of young love, to more politically tinged subject matter such as war and alcoholism, to the timeless discovery of Celtic mythology. A few years earlier, in 1983, Barry Ronan, a singer from the Irish-speaking Aran Islands, released *Trath* (Gael-Linn), a collection of songs written and performed in Irish.

In Tua Nua got their start in County Howth in 1982 and mixed Celtic instrumentation with a rock beat set to the evocative vocals of Leslie Dowdall, a native of Dublin. More important, perhaps, at least for the future of Celtic rock, the band featured a very young Sinéad O'Connor. Even at the tender age of fourteen, O'Connor was a musical revelation. Blessed with the purest of voices and a vocal range that could shift from soft and gentle purring to high-pitched screaming in a matter of seconds, O'Connor was and is a Celtic original, determined to do things her own way even when the rest of the world could only shake its head in collective bewilderment or dismay. O'Connor made her solo debut with *The Lion and the Cobra* (Chrysalis). With her shaved head and intense, humorless public persona, she cut an enigmatic swath through modern pop music. Her influences are many and seriously eclectic—Asian, African, classical, disco, and funk—all suffused with an essential Irish quality.

The duo of Sonny Condell from County Wicklow and Leo O'Kelly from County Carlow made up Tir na nÓg (which means Land of Eternal Youth). With its acoustic guitars and warm, pastoral sound, the band dressed up the whole notion of Irish mythology and presented it in modern guise to a contemporary audience.

The most important rock band to emerge from the Scottish Gaidhealtachd, however, remains Runrig, a six-man outfit from the Isle of Skye (their name refers to the old Highland method of farming) that formed in the mid-1970s. Even when sung in English, the group's songs revolve around Celtic themes, from the survival and maintenance of the Gaelic language to emigration to the New World to coming to terms with your heritage and culture.

Runrig began as a traditional folk group (its first recording was entirely in Gaelic), but recent releases have openly tried, with mixed success, to court the international market. Although one of the most popular rock bands to emerge from Scotland, they have barely made a dent in the vast North American market and, in fact, have never even bothered to tour the United States. They have met with greater acceptance in Canada and has toured the Great White North numerous times, even writing songs about the experience in songs like "The Cutter," "Ard" (High), and "Canada." From its mostly acoustic debut, *Play Gaelic*, to *In Search of Angels* (both Ridge), the best of their recent recordings, Runrig's output has been consistently solid. Until recently it was led by the golden-voiced Donnie Munro; he has since left to pursue a career in politics and replaced by Cape Bretoner Bruce Guthro. Most of the band's repertoire is written by the brother team of Calum and Rory MacDonald, whose literate and intelligent lyrics resonate strongly with the often sad but just as often defiant history of the Gael.

Clearly, the influence of traditional Gaelic singing on rock singers is a subtle yet persistent presence. Younger generations of singers such as Mary Black or Liam Ó Maonlaí are gifted unaccompanied vocalists in their own right—Black from the English-speaking Irish tradition and Ó Maonlaí from the Irish-speaking tradition. The language of the Gael and, in particular the influence of *sean-nós* can be heard not only in the vocal inflections of an

O'Connor or Van Morrison but also in the work of such diverse Irish bands as the Cranberries, the Pogues, and Hothouse Flowers. Liam Ó Maonlaí and Fiachna O Braonain of the latter are, as their names indicate, native Irish speakers, and Ó Maonlaí, in particular, was at one time the all-Ireland champion *bodhran* player.

Perhaps the most exciting development in Celtic music, though, is the number of new songs being written today in English and in the Celtic tongues. New tunes are being composed, too, and entering into the tradition.

Of all the contemporary groups with traditional roots, the Scots band Capercaillie offers the most aggressive and tasteful, not to mention commercial, example of combining the new with the old. Called "the most exciting and vibrant band in Celtic music today" by *Billboard* magazine, along with boasting the sublime talents of vocalist Karen Matheson and reworking age-old Gaelic melodies and songs, Capercaillie bridges the gap between musical eras and musical genres. Several years ago its rendition of the ballad "Coisich A Ruin" became the first Gaelic song to crack the United Kingdom's top forty. The group has been experimenting with cinema as well—Matheson not only sang on the soundtrack of the motion picture *Rob Roy* but also appeared on screen, singing a haunting Gaelic lament.

The best-known Irish band to emerge from the Irish Gaeltacht, Clannad, is still going strong. Formed in 1970, the band is an all-family affair, consisting of the families Brennan and Duggan, who grew up in Irish-speaking Gweedore, in County Donegal. Ciaran plays bass and guitar; his sister Maire, harp; brother Pol, tin whistle, flute, and guitar. Padraig Duggan plays mandolin, harmonica, and guitar and brother Neel plays guitar. Maire sings lead and all members sing harmony.

Their father, Leo, played saxophone, clarinet, and accordion and had his own show band before settling in Gweedore, where he opened a tavern. Their mother was a music teacher and played organ and harmonium. In the rural setting of their father's country pub they grew up listening to a wide variety of music, from Gaelic songs to jazz and popular songs. From their maternal grandparents they learned Gaelic songs and myths, folklore, and legends.

Never traditionalists, band members do things their own way, not because of any inherent rebellious streak but rather because that's the way they've always treated music. They don't discriminate—good music is good music, no matter where it comes from or what category it may happen to fall into. Their early output cheerfully mixed folk with jazz and classical, which made it different enough; but what really made it stand out was that, especially in the early years, most of the songs were sung in Irish.

Their debut recording featured folk and original material and boasted the fine vocals of Maire Brennan and virtuoso instrumentation from her band members, which featured upright bass, flutes, guitars, and various percussion. *Dulaman* (Gael-Linn), the follow-up, continued the traditional theme and contained a Carolan tune, a Breton song, and a Welsh tune.

Later recordings saw the group experimenting increasingly with modern arrangements, including forays into moody, electronic folk and jazz-influenced contemporary music. Its big hit, "Theme from Harry's Game," is all modern atmospherics, while *Macalla* (RCA) is its definitive fusion recording, with modern rock, jazz, and pure pop songs. "In a Lifetime" featured guest vocals by Bono. Bruce Hornsby has also offered his services. Unfortunately, much of its recent output has consisted of mostly bland and unimpressive pop songs, a far cry from the excitingly progressive folk-jazz-traditional combination that the group initiated so many years ago.

The youngest member of the family, Enya, didn't get billing on Clannad recordings until *Fuaim* was released in 1982. By that time, though, she had her eye set on her own career. Enya has sold more than thirty-three million recordings worldwide—and that's a conservative estimate. She has been called the world's most anonymous superstar. Trained in the classical music, her roots are firmly rooted in the Irish folk tradition.

After leaving Clannad she created her own particular music, with her own sound. Much criticism has been directed her way, as if the whole ethereal, wispy Celtic New Age scene is entirely her fault. In some significant ways she did contribute to it—but that's a roundabout way of saying that she has been successful beyond most everyone's imagination. Her debut, *Enya* (BBC Records), which is essentially the soundtrack of the BBC television documentary *The Celts*, is a wonderfully atmospheric musical history of the Celtic peoples, evoking all manner of Celtic imagery. Accompanied by Liam O'Flynn on uilleann pipes and Arty McGlynn on guitar, her voice (or should I say voices, since much overdubbing occurs) is surrounded by the sound of acoustic piano, drum machine, and synthesizers, to mesmerizing effect.

POLITICAL BEDFELLOWS

More and more, Celtic rock bands are unafraid to admit having a social conscience. U2 was one of the first 1980s groups to inject politics into its music; along the way it brought an inestimable Celtic spirit to rock. The Pogues, the Alarm, Runrig, and the Proclaimers have continued in that tradition.

The Proclaimers, consisting of the fair-haired, bespectacled Reid twins, grew up listening to Chicago jazz, 1960s R&B, and country-western, as well as traditional Scottish music. Their sound is utterly original, a mix of gorgeous harmonies and passionate vocals. In songs like "Throw the 'R' Away," "What Do You Do?," and "Cap in Hand," they address such thorny issues as language and the social price you pay for speaking in the "wrong" accent, the search for national identity, and the need of a people to determine their own destiny.

The most notorious entry in the Celtic rock genre must be the Pogues. Steeped in the hard-drinking culture of Ireland's working classes, these Londoners of Irish descent were the first group to mix traditional folk and punk rock, infusing the usually conservative milieu of Irish music with a rare brand of raw, unadulterated anger. And in Shane MacGowan, their charismatically scruffy lead singer—in recent years he has left and been replaced with a rebel from an earlier era, Joe Strummer of the Clash—they had a surprisingly literate and sensitive, if frequently profane, songwriter. MacGowan earned a well-deserved reputation—and reams of scathing criticism—for his sloppy stage presence and unpredictable behavior, much of it due, it turns out, to heavy drinking, both on and off the stage. Yet personal problems aside, his interpretation of band member Philip Chevron's "Thousands Are Sailing" is a modern Irish immigration ballad in the tradition of the old ballads but updated with a dark, street wisdom, while "Streets of Sorrow/ Birmingham Six" confronts the seemingly intractable struggle in Northern Ireland. Originally dismissed by some critics as a novelty act, the Pogues have probably done more than any group in introducing traditional material to contemporary audiences.

The group started out in North London in 1983: MacGowan, Jem Finer, and Spider Stacey, a trio of natural-born troublemakers singing and playing rebel songs in local pubs. MacGowan was reared in County Tipperary but sent to public school in London, which did not sit too well with him. He was working at a succession of menial jobs when the London punk rock scene came to life. It was a match made in musical heaven and perfect timing for both MacGowan and the scene. The terrible trio were later joined by electric bassist Cait O Riordan as well as Terry Woods and guitarist Phil Chevron.

Early records consisted of mostly Irish drinking songs and emigrant ballads. Their notoriety and irreverence caught the attention of Elvis Costello, who produced their second record, *Rum, Sodomy, and the Lash* (Stiff). This featured some of MacGowan's most mature songwriting to date, including "The Sick Bed of Cuchulainn" and "The Old Main Drag," the first about alcoholism, the second about male prostitution. Other highlights included MacGowan's idiosyncratic take of Ewan MacColl's "Dirty Old Town" and O Riordan's fine ballad "I'm a Man You Don't Meet Every Day."

Honing their live act, they attracted vociferous crowds in both Britain and America. The EP *Poguetry in Motion* (Stiff) contained a scathing indictment of Irish-American sentimentality in "The Body of an American," while *If I Should Fall from Grace with God* (Island) was perhaps their finest effort to date, a compelling range of swaggering, rakish songs including the aforementioned "Thousands Are Sailing" along with "Fairytale of New York," "Turkish Song of the Damned," and "The Broad Majestic Shannon," full of provocative lyrics and sinuous melodies, all performed with MacGowan's patented growl.

 ## SNEERS ON THE ROCKS

One of the most important rock bands to emerge from Ireland in the 1970s was Thin Lizzy, a blues, folk, and progressive-rock outfit led by a tall, angular chap named Phil Lynott. Born in England but raised in suburban Dublin of Brazilian and Irish parentage, Lynott, like many Irish musicians at the time, looked to America and England for his musical role models. The archetypal great American rock guitarist was a particular favorite. Thin Lizzy's output was not particularly Irish—indeed, you would be hard pressed to find anything that hinted of their Irish connection—but the band's debut recording did contain the song "Eire," which was chock full of Irish historical allusions, from the Vikings to the great Irish patriot Hugh O'Donnell. More than content or feeling, it was attitude that Thin Lizzy projected in ample doses. Here were rockers who made no bones about their Irish upbringing. They took their Irishness for granted, expecting the rest of the world to accept them at face value.

Larry Kirwan is very much cut from the same emotional cloth as MacGowan, a soul spirit lost not on the streets of London but rather of New York. As lead singer, song lyricist, and poet of the Irish-American rock band Black 47, Kirwan is a major force on the contemporary Celtic rock scene. His lyrics are packed with venom and passion; his music a full-throttle attack on complacency, both in his native Ireland and his adopted homeland. Indeed, the band's very name—referring to 1847, the worst year of the Great Irish Famine—is indicative of its general artistic philosophy. Kirwan's worldview may be bleak—America as seen through the bloodshot eyes of a contemporary Irish immigrant—yet he remains defiantly hopeful.

Fire of Freedom is perhaps the group's most fully realized release. "We're all mad over here/living in America," Kirwan shouts, at the top of his lungs. In "Maria's Wedding" he sounds like an Irish-American Springsteen stoned out of his mind on a bottle of Guinness, all working-class confessions and empty promises to change. "Rockin' the Bronx" is cheeky Irish rap, while the melody of "Down by the Sally Gardens" becomes a revamped "40 Shades of Blue" that stretches across the Atlantic from New York's old punk hangout CBGB's to the green fields of Ireland. With a voice that sounds constantly on the verge of tears, Kirwan sometimes allows his emotions and his often strident lyrics to get the best of him, where a bit more control and subtlety would have served the songs better.

SEARCHING FOR SOMETHING

No Irish rock band—indeed, no rock band from any part of the Celtic world—has reached the level of success that U2 has enjoyed. The members have earned their success through good fortune and sheer hard work but, more than this, it is their commitment to a greater good—to the rock and roll ideal—that has made them so appealing to millions of people around the world. The music they create is bigger than themselves. Call it their larger-than-life Celtic spirit, if you want, but there is no denying their commitment to the better instincts of rock and their firm belief that it can, in some small way, make the world a better place.

Drummer Larry Mullen, Jr., formed U2 back in 1976 when he was only fourteen. He placed an advertisement in a Dublin paper, asking for potential band members to step forward. More than a dozen hopeful musicians, or wannabe musicians, appeared at his doorstep. Three were ultimately chosen: guitarist David Evans (the Edge), bassist Adam Clayton, and singer Paul Hewson (Bono). Evans, son of a Welsh engineer, had spent his early childhood in east London. The English-born Clayton was the son of a RAF pilot who had moved to Ireland when Clayton was eight. Clayton had bummed around Europe for a while and thus was the most worldly of the bunch. Hewson was born in North Dublin of a Protestant mother and a Catholic father. He professed a strong belief in Christianity and seemed a natural leader.

After many years paying their dues on the Irish music scene, the band made a prophetic career choice by choosing to concentrate on the American market early on rather than, like most Irish bands at the time, trying to "conquer" England before moving to points farther west. More important, members decided to stay in Ireland and use Dublin as their base of operations.

U2 met with almost immediate success. Early recordings such as the debut *Boy* and its followup *October* already showed the passion and commitment that each member brought to the band, and displayed their individual strong points: Bono's soaring vocals, the Edge's searing guitar licks, Mullen's muscular drumming, and Clayton's sturdy rhythm section.

The next recording, *War*, contained the powerful antiwar single "New Year's Day" and the politically charged and instantly controversial "Sunday Bloody Sunday." Yet it is *The Joshua Tree*, released in 1987, that remains their unqualified masterpiece. Taking their cue from the Joshua tree itself, a cactus that is said to symbolize both the emptiness of the physical world and its spiritual expansiveness, they created a beautiful, fully realized and often very spiritual work. The themes were hardly Irish—America as the Promised Land, life in the modern world, personal despair, spiritual yearning—nor were the musical influences—blues, gospel, and even country blues. Yet somehow the group's Irish spirit shone through. It sounded both Irish and American—but it also transcended nationality and musical boundaries. In a way, this was soul music. Irish soul music.

CALEDONIA SOUL MAN

No one quite epitomizes the broad expansiveness of the Celtic spirit more thoroughly than Van Morrison, who can easily slide from a piece of delicate Celtic mysticism to raunchy American R&B. Indeed, his Celtic mixture of folk, blues, rock, jazz, and classical is unique in contemporary pop music.

More jazz artist perhaps than rock 'n roll warrior, Van Morrison in recent years has delved deeper into his Celtic roots to emerge musically rejuvenated. In songs like "Celtic Ray" and tunes like

"Celtic Swing," Morrison, like a true Celt, finds spiritual bliss in the earth's rivers and valleys, in the natural rhythm of nature.

Born in Belfast in 1945, Morrison, an only son, was raised a Jehovah's Witness and grew up surrounded by music. His mother was a jazz singer who felt equally at ease with gospel and country. His father was a big fan and collector of American blues, especially Muddy Waters, Ray Charles, and John Lee Hooker. When Morrison was only twelve he joined local skiffle bands, and by the time he was thirteen he had already mastered the guitar, harmonica, and saxophone.

Much of Morrison's early output was R&B–inspired. In bands like the Monarchs and, in particular, Them, R&B and rock came together, Irish style: Extended jams combined with Morrison's raw, ferocious delivery. Them's big hit of the 1960s, the edgy "Gloria," became a favorite of every garage band in America. His versions of Dylan's "It's All Over Now Baby Blue" and Paul Simon's "Richard Cory" convey bile and barely controlled anger. In 1967 he recorded one of the great pop singles of the modern era, the infectious "Brown-Eyed Girl," which topped the charts and remains a favorite of American radio stations to this day.

Then over two days in the summer of 1968, he recorded what many critics regard as one of the most extraordinary recordings of the modern era. The dreamlike *Astral Weeks* is inscrutable, enigmatic, dense, full of layer after layer of Celtic mysticism that weaves jazzy, classical, and folk elements into its incandescent whole. At times Morrison's trancelike vocals recall the litany of ancient Gaelic poetry. The recording contains songs about the creative spirit, fleeting images of childhood, young love, heroin addiction. It is a record of memories and lived experience, even of spiritual grace—and by a man who was all of twenty-two when he recorded it. In short, it's an astonishingly mature and self-assured piece of work.

Morrison's next release, *Moondance* (Warner Brothers), has an overall, jazzier sound with the occasional acoustic pieces ("And It Stoned Me," a paean to childhood memories and the simple joys of two boys fishing); the title song is a hopelessly romantic tribute to lusty young love, while the lyrical "Into the Mystic" is, quite simply, a perfect song. *Tupelo Honey* (Warner Brothers) has an altogether lighter and more playful sound, with a country accent, highlighted by the lovely acoustic title track.

The acoustic-based *St. Dominic's Preview* (Warner Brothers) returned to darker themes, including the eleven-minute acoustic blues of "Listen to the Lion," bristling with rage, and the nearly equally long "Almost Independence Day." *Veedon Fleece* (Warner Brothers) with its gorgeous mystical streaks is redolent of lush Irish romanticism, and features such classic Morrison songs as "Linden Arden Stole the Highlights," "Who Was That Masked Man" (about highwaymen), "Streets of Arklow," and the pastoral "Country Fair."

The straight-ahead rock of *Wavelength* (Warner Brothers) turned into the easy listening *Into the Music* (Warner Brothers), which featured Robin Williamson playing a wistful penny whistle on "Troubadours," which reeks of medievalism, and "Rolling Hills," infused with gentle Christian spirit and bucolic, Celtic-like imagery.

The peaceful *Common One* (Warner) contains four long pieces, including the lovely "Haunts of Ancient Peace"; the massive, fifteen-minute "Summertime in England" celebrates the spirit of T. S. Eliot, William Wordsworth, Samuel Coleridge, William Blake, W. B. Yeats, James Joyce, and even the voice of Mahalia Jackson, as meandering as a mountain stream.

Since the early 1980s Morrison has occasionally turned to his Celtic roots for inspiration. *Beautiful Vision* (Mercury), a lovely record, features uilleann pipes on "Celtic Ray" and such mystical touches on "Dweller on the Threshold" and "Aryan Mist." Especially touching is the childlike innocence of "Across the Bridge Where Angels Dwell."

Inarticulate Speech of the Heart (Warner) has more of a traditional folk mood with its procession of flutes, uilleann pipes, and acoustic guitar. "Celtic Swing" and "Connswater" are especially evocative. Davy Spillane plays the uilleann pipes and low whistle, Arty McGlynn, the acoustic guitar. Spillane again appears on the title track of *A Sense of Wonder* (Mercury). Here the Irish atmosphere is joined by jazz and folk rock. In *No Guru, No Method,*

No Teacher (Mercury), the classical arrangements feel thoroughly cloaked in an Irish spirit coupled with strong Christian sentiments. "Tir Na nÓg" recalls the ancient Irish myth, while the more-down-to-earth "One Irish Rover" is about Irish emigration. In *Poetic Champions Compose* (Mercury), Morrison comes full circle with the instrumental "Celtic Excavation," which brings Ireland and Scotland together on a musical soundscape.

After years of flirting with Celtic traditional music, Morrison decided in 1988 to devote an entire record to exploring his Celtic roots by teaming up with the Chieftains to produce *Irish Heartbeat* (Mercury). It contained singular renditions of such Irish classics as "Star of the County Down," "Raglan Road," "Maire's Wedding," and "She Moved through the Fair." Blues, soul, and Irish traditional come together in typically Morrisonesque fashion, which is to say unlike any other recording around. Purists would likely cringe at Morrison's artistic deviations—sort of a Celtic litany meets blue-eyed soul. Chieftain harpist Derek Bell, who absolutely adored the record, offered his take on it. "It's a classic," he told biographer John Glatt. "An absolute classic. In a sense from the purist's folk point of view it's grotesque, to put it at its most kind. Some critics don't think the collaboration came off at all.

"I mean no purist is going to sing things like 'She Moved Through the Fair' repeating 'our wedding day' three times. That's an element of soul music. The repetition and jazz-like style of words for the sake of emphasis. That belongs to soul. It has nothing to do with our tradition at all."

In other words, Morrison does his own thing, in a style that incorporates elements from various musical traditions—rock, blues, soul, jazz, folk, and, yes, Irish traditional—but a mixture, a Celtic mixture, that is uniquely his own.

GROWING POPULARITY

Who knows where it will end? The Celtic tradition love to wink a jaundiced eye at convention. One moment Mary Black, Ireland's top female singer, performs a stinging rendition of the jazz classic

"Don't Explain," while another, smoky-voiced Mary Coughlan, sings the blues—the Irish kind—with as much conviction as any deep-fried southern mama. Meanwhile, Maura O'Connell comfortably flits between Nashville and Dublin. And even an artist as mainstream as Sting has drawn from the Celtic tradition to create his own blend of smooth and sophisticated pop from the Celtic touches of his *Mercury Falling* recording to, more recently, his spirited vocal salute to Bonnie Prince Charlie in the Jacobite rallying cry, "No Ghile Mear." Last we heard from Capercaillie's Karen Matheson, she was swapping Gaelic mouth music with Spanish/North African traditional chants, an ecstatic combination made in world-music heaven. Who knows, indeed.

The Waterboys were a conventional rock band until leader Mike Scott caught the traditional Celtic music bug and they transformed their sound into an appealing pan-Celtic mixture of mandolin, fiddle, saxophone, keyboards, and drums. Their breakthrough recording *Fisherman's Blues* (Chrysalis) contained many original songs written in a folk vein, including a swinging version of the traditional "When Will We Be Married?" and a brilliant interpretation of William Butler Yeats' fairy ode "The Stolen Child."

The 1990s has witnessed the considerable popularity of the Corrs, consisting of sisters, fiddler Sharon, drummer Caroline, and lead singer Andrea, and older brother, keyboardist-guitarist Jim who hail from Dundalk, on Ireland's east coast. Unabashedly commercial, their mixture of pop and Celtic sounds has proven an irresistible draw for people who like their music to be different (but not too different), traditional (but not too traditional). As of this writing, this Irish supergroup is already making major inroads into the vast and hard-to-crack North American market.

Other rock performers have created music that emerges directly from their Celtic roots. The enigmatic Scots band Cindytalk uses pipes and choirs, guitars and, on one recording, a reading by the otherworldly Glasgow novelist Alasdair Gray to make their musical statement. Just as enigmatic, if not more so, are the Cocteau Twins, who have gone a step farther by turning to the old Scots tongue, with its lively mixture of robust vernacular and earthy poetry, as their equivalent of a musical instrument.

For in the brave new world of Celtic rock, nothing is sacred, everything is fair game, and most anything can happen. Despite the tinkering with tradition, the meddling into age-old melodies and rhymes, what is indisputable is the genuine respect that the musicians bring to the music. Borrowing from the past, they have created a music of and for the future.

RECOMMENDED LISTENING

Big Country. *The Crossing* (Polygram). Debut recording by this Scottish quartet and still their finest work. Part urban angst and heart-on-your sleeve vulnerability, *The Crossing* manages to be hopeful and somber at the same time—clearly a Celtic talent. Stuart Adamson's vocal style and intelligent lyrics recall a Scottish Springsteen. Uniformly excellent songs, especially the anthemic "In a Big Country," "Fields of Fire," and "Chance."

Black 47. *Fire of Freedom* (EMI). Politically charged Irish-American rock from the always passionate pen of singer Larry Kirwan. Truly New World music.

The Blue Nile. *Hats* (A&M). A darkly brooding, richly atmospheric, and intensely introspective recording by three former University of Glasgow students—Paul Moore, Paul Buchanan, and Robert Bell. Moody music for a rainy evening.

The Bothy Band. *The Best of the Bothy Band* (Green Linnet). The best from Ireland's seminal traditional band.

Paul Brady. *Welcome Here, Kind Stranger* (Mulligan). The definitive folk album from one of the best of the modern Irish rockers.

Martin Carthy. *The Collection* (Green Linnet). Compiled from *Sweet Wivelsfield, Crown of Horn, Because It's There, Out of the Cut*, and *Right of Passage*; features traditional and original songs and tunes, including his masterful version of the old ballad "Lord Randal."

Clannad. *Rogha: The Best of Clannad* (RCA). Includes Gaelic songs as well as the band's patented blend of atmospheric vocals and haunting instrumentation in addition to the pure pop of more recent recordings.

Cocteau Twins. *Treasure* (Capitol). If anyone deserves to be called otherworldly, surely it is the Cocteau Twins, a Scottish duo who create weirdly wonderful, strangely maddening music, music that is thoroughly modern yet exists outside time. Cryptic lyrics, eerie sound effects, hypnotic repetition, floating angelic vocals all add to the intoxicating mix. Uniquely unique.

The Corrs. *Forgiven, Not Forgotten* (143 Records/Lava Records). It's hard to resist the Corrs. Their patented mixture of traditional and modern, slickness and sincerity, infectious melodies and luscious harmonies, coupled with a wholesome sexiness have made them genuine crowd-pleasers on both sides of the Atlantic. *Forgiven, Not Forgotten* goes a long way towards explaining their broad appeal.

The Cranberries. *Everybody Else Is Doing It, So Why Can't We?* (Island). Haunting and moody melodic pop by one of Ireland's most popular bands. Includes their signature songs "Dreams" and "Linger."

Sandy Denny. *Sandy* (A&M). Lovely collection of ballads and songs that includes the shimmering "Listen, Listen." *Who Knows Where the Time Goes* (Island) is a four-disk boxed set of music before, during, and after Denny's Fairport period. As always, Denny's aching, vulnerable vocals captivate, bringing us entirely into her world.

Nick Drake. *Fruit Tree* (Rykodisc). The complete set of his recordings, available individually or in a boxed set.

Hothouse Flowers. *People* (London). Jazzy Irish rock band with a cool, sophisticated feel.

Christy Moore. *Christy Moore* (Atlantic). Everything comes together in this classic collection: Christy Moore's compassionate voice, powerful songs by some of his Ireland's best songwriters (Jimmy McCarthy's "Lisdoonvarna" and "Ride On," Barry Moore's "The City of Chicago," Peter Hame's "Ordinary Man," and Christy Moore's own "Delirium Tremens"), and tasteful arrangements by a host of legendary Irish musicians from Dónal Lunny and Arty McGlynn to Liam O'Flynn and Declan Synnott.

Van Morrison and the Chieftains. *Irish Heartbeat* (Mercury). Van meets Paddy, which results in more than a few surprises.

Van Morrison. *Astral Weeks* (Warner Brothers). Stream of consciousness; the James Joyce of pop records. A masterpiece of the modern recording era.

Moving Hearts (WEA). Contains "Irish Ways and Irish Laws" and Phil Chevron's "Faithful Departed."

Planxty. *The Planxty Collection* (Polydor). Includes "The Lakes of Pontchartrain," "Cliffs of Dooneen," "Raggle Taggle Gypsy," and other favorites.

The Pogues. *If I Should Fall from Grace with God* (Island). Shane MacGowan at his most lyrical; an irreverent romp through Irish and Irish-American life. Worth it if only for the hilarious exchange between MacGowan and guest singer Kirsty MacColl as unsentimental lovers who have seen better times together and make sure the other knows it!

The Proclaimers. *Sunshine on Leith* (Chrysalis). Gorgeous harmonies, grand passion, and irresistible hooks by Craig and Charlie Reid combine to create a truly wonderful sound. The beauty of the profoundly humble and deeply spiritual title cut simply takes your breath away. Includes the Reid brothers' inimitable rendition of Steve Earle's "My Old Friend the Blues."

Runrig. *Long Distance: The Best of Runrig* (Chrysalis). A good introduction to the band although early releases, such as *Play Gaelic*, are completely ignored. The recording does include two of their finest songs, though: "Rocket to the Moon" and "Protect and Survive." In 1998 the band released an all-Gaelic anthology, *Runrig: the Gaelic Collection 1973–1998*. Their latest recording, *In Search of Angels* (Ridge), features the vocals of Bruce Guthro, Donnie Munro's replacement. With Guthro, they have found a worthy successor to the golden-voiced Munro. Indeed, *In Search of Angels* is the band's most memorable release in recent years, a recording that celebrates second chances and the inevitability of change, full of finely-crafted songs by Calum and Rory MacDonald from the cautious optimism of "Life Is" to the mystical "Travellers."

The Saw Doctors. *Sing a Powerful Song* (Paradigm). A compilation of the first three Saw Doctors recordings issued in Ireland and the U.K. In essence, they represent the best of this popular and uniquely Galway band. Catchy hooks and infectious melodies, passionate vocals and a deadly rhythmic section make them instantly likable. Seventeen mostly short gems, songs of roots rock, Irish style. My vote for the friendliest band on any side of the ocean. Includes the country jaunt of "N17" and the randy "I Useta Lover." Many of the titles sound like timeless rock 'n roll classics but with strong Irish themes from bringing in the harvest to going to mass.

Steeleye Span. *Portfolio* (Shanachie). This best-of collection includes "Alison Gross," "Thomas the Rhymer," "Long Lamkin," and "All Around My Hat."

Straight Outta Ireland (Scotti Bros.). Features the work of numerous up-and-coming Irish rockers, including the Would Be's, the Young Dubliners, Katell Keineg, the Golden Horde, the Spirit Merchants, the Chanting House, Lir, Leslie Dowdall, The Men They Couldn't Hang, Diesel Heart, and Fatima Mansions.

June Tabor. *Airs and Graces* (Shanachie). Nobody does it better. Tabor at her glorious best.

June Tabor and the Oyster Band. *Freedom and Rain* (Rykodisc). What happens when Tabor, the dusky-voiced queen of English folk, meets up with a bunch of raggle-taggle Englishman and one Scotsman? Just listen.

Richard and Linda Thompson. *Shoot Out the Lights* (Hannibal). Great collection of bang-up songs from Richard Thompson, the modern-day troubadour of angst. Highlights range from Linda's tremulous vocals on "Walking on a Wire" to Richard's sublime "Wall of Death." Features backup vocals from the Watersons, including Martin Carthy.

U2. *The Joshua Tree* (Island). The Irish supergroup's finest hour. Great songs, memorable lyrics, and the soaring vocals of Bono.

The Waterboys. *Fisherman's Blues* (Chrysalis). Definitive Waterboys, from jaunty Celtic-inspired melodies to a rendition of a W. B. Yeats poem.

Wolfstone. *The Half Tail* (Green Linnet). Crisp, intelligent lyrics and tight arrangements characterize the best of this Scots band's work. Strong vocals by Orcadian Ivan Drever.

10

No Boundaries

Forging Old Links,
Creating New Traditions

Of all the interest in world music, the appeal of Celtic music is arguably the strongest.

–PETE HEYWOOD,
LIVING TRADITION MAGAZINE EDITOR

[T]here can be no tradition without innovation.

–LINER NOTES, *CELTIC CONNECTIONS,*
EARLE HITCHNER, IRISH MUSIC JOURNALIST

I believe that Irish music, the tradition, is so robust, so strong, you can sit and hear somebody play a slow air on a tin whistle and it can move you, but you should equally be able to take that and express it in a contemporary way without damaging the tradition.

"Otherwise, we just restate the past."

So stated Irish musician John Whelan, another musical rebel with a cause, the cause in this case finding new ways of expressing a very old music without inflicting damage.

In 1990 *Billboard* magazine introduced its world-music chart. From this rather humble beginning world music has become a veritable industry all its own. From "global" record labels like David Byrne's Luaka Bop and Peter Gabriel's RealWorld to the music of Marta Sebestyen or the Gypsy Kings, world music has created its own niche in the notoriously fickle musical marketplace.

Five years later, in 1995, two-thirds of world-music chart toppers were Celtic. Now a major record label, Atlantic, distributes a strictly Irish-music label, Celtic Heartbeat. This is, of course, in addition to the numerous small and independent labels on both sides of the Atlantic—such as Narada in the United States, Claddagh in Ireland, and Greentrax in Scotland—that specialize in Celtic music.

 ## Ian Green of Greentrax

Launched by ex-police inspector Ian Green in 1986, Greentrax is now regarded as Scotland's premier traditional-music label. With more than 150 releases to its credit, Greentrax specializes in folk, instrumental, Gaelic, and piping. It also distributes the important Scottish Tradition Series from the School of Scottish Studies archives (previously released by Tangent Records).

Green is more than willing to push traditional music beyond its previous boundaries. Among the more adventurous artists on his roster are Shooglenifty, Peatbog Fairies, Seelyhoo, and Natalie MacMaster. Well-established performers are not slighted either: Aly Bain, Eric Bogle, Dick Gaughan, Jean Redpath, Catherine-Ann MacPhee are just a few.

Born in Forres, Morayshire, in 1934, the son of a head gardener who played the Highland pipes, Ian and his family moved to Edinburgh when he was fourteen. He spent three years in the regular army, serving in Korea. On leaving the army Green joined the Edinburgh City police force, where he stayed for some thirty years. He retired with the rank of police inspector in 1985.

During his time there he started the Police Folk Club; he was also one of the founding members of the Edinburgh Folk Club as well as coeditor, for ten years, of Sandy Bell's *Broadsheet*.

The origins of Greentrax lie in Discount Folk Records, a small mail-order and festival-stall service that Green started and quickly expanded. Encouraged by the positive response, Green thought he saw a solid future in the music that he loved so much. Against the wishes of some of his more practical colleagues, he invested half of his police pension into a new record label, which he decided to call Greentrax. And why not? For Greentrax is very much a family affair. The Green family has invested not only money but also plenty of blood, sweat, and tears to this grand scheme that, to the surprise of many, has actually succeeded.

In early June 1998, Greentrax announced the launching of their newest label, called G2, which will release the work of artists who fall outside the confines of Scottish traditional music.

Just as the term *world music* serves as an umbrella for different styles and genres of music, so functions the term *Celtic music*. For better or worse, both are marketing tools.

There is a growing concern that by throwing everything into the Celtic-music washer, the power of the original music will be diffused, if not extinguished entirely. Put another way, taken out of context and packaged into a bland and nebulous entity, a good chance exists that the music will become nonthreatening, pleasant, innocuous, inconsequential—in a word, forgettable.

Can the success of Celtic music worldwide—however you wish to define it—destroy the admittedly fragile infrastructure and social system that nurtured the music in the first place? And what does it mean when so-called Celtic-music festivals that play to upwards of fifty thousand people at a time include such decidedly non-Celtic performers as Los Lobos or the Indigo Girls? How then do we define *Celtic*? Is ersatz Celtic threatening to overrun the market? To dilute the real thing?

These are questions with no easy answers. Time will reveal where the music leads us.

No Boundaries

Boundaries between musical genres have grown increasingly fuzzy in recent years. The Chieftains have been appreciated by a rock audience for decades—Paul McCartney and Eric Clapton were fans even before the Irish group gained mainstream recognition—opening for the likes of the Rolling Stones and U2 and collaborating with everyone from Van Morrison to Marianne Faithfull.

A band that broke all the rules long before musicians even knew there were rules to be broken is folk-rock pioneer Pentangle. Originally formed in 1967 by Bert Jansch, Jacqui McShee, John Renbourn, Danny Thomson, and Terry Cox, the band was a fusion of folk, jazz, and blues. It disbanded in 1973 but reformed a decade later and, in yet another reincarnation, came together again in 1990.

Born in Glasgow but raised in Edinburgh, songwriter and guitarist Bert Jansch hitchhiked across Europe as a young man. Somewhere he developed an interest in American blues. By the time he moved to London in the early 1960s, he became known for his so-called folk-baroque style. This popular and influential folk-rock group, wildly eclectic before it was fashionable, paved the way for the likes of Fairport Convention, Steeleye Span, and similar bands that I discussed in chapter 9. Blues, jazz, folk, rock, Celtic, classical, Indian—whatever the genre, Jansch had a knack for fusing musical traditions not typically found together.

The Irish band Clannad, eclectic from the start, mixes jazz, classical, and rock influences but, even in its folkier days the group indulged in some serious and extended improvisation during concert appearances—extremely rare in traditional Irish music circles.

Several years back Maire Brennan, Clannad's lead singer, performed a duet with U2's Bono on the track "In a Lifetime." More recently she has continued her penchant for experimentation by incorporating rhythms from Africa, India, and eastern Europe on her solo debut *Misty-Eyed Adventures* (Atlantic), which, in another example of Celtic camaraderie, was produced by the critically acclaimed Glasgow cult rock favorite, the Blue Nile.

Defying categories comes naturally to Brennan. "When we started off," she once said, "we used to get up and sing Gaelic, then a Beach Boys song, then a Beatles song. We never saw the difference."

For better or worse, anything goes.

A SOUL SO RARE

One of the great innovators of Irish music was the late Séan Ó Riada. Ó Riada contributed greatly to the Irish traditional-music revival in the late 1950s and early 1960s. He also is credited with bringing traditional music to a modern Irish audience by making it more accessible.

In the 1950s Irish traditional music had a small following, confined mostly to rural areas or appreciated by a few token traditional musicians in scattered urban settlements. It was the less traditional *ceilidh* band that was the rage; even Turlough O Carolan was little known. In fact, the vast majority of Irish people had little day-to-day contact with traditional music, period.

As musical director of the Abbey Theatre, Ó Riada composed original music based on Irish traditional musical styles. More than this, though, he composed for orchestras, penned original film scores, and even wrote a mass in Irish based on the *sean-nós* tradition.

Born John Reidy in County Cork, Ó Riada was brought up in a small town in County Limerick surrounded by music. He learned to play the fiddle as a child and later studied music at University College, Cork. The academic setting nurtured his interest in other cultures and other musical forms, especially jazz and avant-garde music. Fascinated by Gaelic history and culture, he adopted the Irish form of his name in the late 1950s. Later, he moved from his Dublin base to live in the Irish-speaking area of western Cork in the village of Cuil Aodha on the banks of the Sulan River.

Ó Riada was commissioned to write the background music for two radio programs on an Irish radio station in Cork in 1958. He did what no one had done before: He scored *sean-nós* and other traditional themes for orchestra in a way that bridged Gaelic and European music. It was considered both revolutionary and successful.

After serving as director at the Abbey for five years, he was given a golden opportunity. In 1960 Gael-Linn, the Irish-language organization, asked him to compose the soundtrack for the documentary film *Mise Eire (I Am Ireland)*, about the founding of the Irish Republic. Using traditional songs as a foundation, he went about composing music that would be worthy of his subject yet able to adapt to an orchestral setting. Expectations were high. Ireland had no Mozart, no Beethoven as musical mentor. In fact, with the exception of John Field and perhaps a few others, it had very little in the way of a classical tradition to speak of. Ó Riada was left to his own devices and to a rich centuries-old oral culture as his chief source of inspiration.

He did not disappoint. The music he created was both majestic and humble—a score born from a land that had known all too well what it meant to suffer but also understood the sense of relief that comes with a joy worth struggling for.

Virtually overnight, Ó Riada became a national celebrity and a national hero.

And in 1962, during a series of Irish radio programs called *Our Musical Heritage*, the forward-looking Ó Riada claimed that the structure of Irish music shared a common ancestry with Indian and Eastern musical idioms—quite a statement to make in the early 1960s.

In 1963 Ó Riada composed the film soundtrack for *The Playboy of the Western World*, which featured the music of Ceoltoiri Chualann, a chamber ensemble that he put together three years earlier. Ceoltoiri Chualann played traditional music as a group—another daring innovation. Before this ensemble, traditional music was considered a solo art, except for the popular *ceilidh* dance bands. Using traditional instruments but with classical-style arrangements, the ensemble incorporated elements of harmony and improvisation—alien concepts in Irish traditional music. In addition, it revived the compositions of the great Irish harper Turlough O Carolan.

The mission of the ensemble was clear: to return traditional Irish music to the people. Indeed, more than an ensemble, the group was a folk orchestra. The membership consisted of fiddlers John Kelly, Seán Keane, and Martin Fay; uilleann piper Paddy Moloney; flute player Michael Tubridy; accordionist Sonny Brogan and Eamon de Buitlear; singers Darach O Cáthain and Sean O Sé; and Ronnie McShane on bones. Ó Riada himself played the *bodhran* and harpsichord, which he believed was more closely related to the medieval Irish *cruit* than the modern Irish harp. This illustrious group formed the basis of what would eventually become the Chieftains.

Alas, it was not to last in its present form. Ó Riada disbanded the historic ensemble in 1969, intent on trying "something new." Perhaps he felt he had exhausted all of its possibilities; that he had no more musical roads to pursue. An inherently restless man, he was never one to stay too long in one place or on one project. Whatever the reason, he decided to move on. The last years of his life were largely spent composing liturgical music.

Ó Riada died in a London hospital in October 1971. He was only forty.

In his lifetime, though, Ó Riada in effect reintroduced traditional Irish music to the Irish people. He opened their eyes to its inherent beauty, its innate power, and its remarkable ability to be many things to many people.

Many of the traditional Irish bands that I have already discussed held Ó Riada's work in high esteem and considered the ensemble that he formed their ideal. Taking his genius as their rallying call, they freely experimented with traditional, folk, and original material, bending, twisting, extending, and reshaping the tradition so that it sometimes became all but unrecognizable. Ó Riada was the perfect role model for a new era in traditional Celtic music, for he took eclecticism to new heights. Groups like Planxty, the Bothy Band, Dé Danann, Horslips, Moving Hearts, and individuals such as contemporary Irish composers Shaun Davey and, especially, Mícheál Ó Súilleabháin, owe a huge debt to Ó Riada's creative genius and, indeed, to his courage in pursuing his singular vision—

one that for many seemed destined to failure. For Ó Riada, never one to confine himself within borders, saw music as an *international* art form. By fusing traditional themes, especially *sean-nós* singing, with European art music, he revolutionized the group playing of traditional music. Film director Louis Marcus has commented on Ó Riada's love of the Gaelic arts:

> Ó Riada reveled in the cyclic form of the Gaelic tradition, which applied layer after layer of ornamentation on the basic frame. He could argue eloquently that this was the characteristic mould of the Celtic creative imagination, citing examples as remote from each other as the Book of Kells and Joyce.

THE CHIEFTAINS

The Chieftains are the most famous traditional-Irish-music band in the world. Period. No one comes close. They also earn the honors of being the most durable and reliable. As we have seen, lineups within traditional-music circles are remarkably fluid. Musicians come and go and come back again. Unlike most of their colleagues, the Chieftains have managed to remain fairly stable. In 1998 members celebrated thirty-five years together. Very few musicians, no matter what kind of music they play, can claim such a feat.

The first Chieftains record, *The Chieftains*, was released in 1964 on the Dublin-based Claddagh label. The lineup consisted of Paddy Moloney on uilleann pipes, Seán Potts on tin whistle, Martin Fay on fiddle, Michael Tubridy on flute, concertina, and tin whistle, and the late David Fallon on *bodhran*. In 1969, when *Chieftains 2* was released, Peadar Mercier replaced Fallon on *bodran* and Seán Keane joined on fiddle. Harper Derek Bell came in the early 1970s, *bodhran* and occasional singer Kevin Conneff arrived in 1976, and the "newest" member of the band Matt Molloy joined in 1979. The lineup of Paddy Moloney, Martin Fay, Seán Keane, Derek Bell, Matt Molloy, and Kevin Conneff remains the same today.

Their career took off—their range, variation, and passion apparent to anyone who heard them—and soon they began attracting fans from decidedly non-Celtic corners, ranging from Mick Jagger to Paul McCartney. This makes perfectly good sense, for the members don't recognize boundaries. Today the world is their musical smorgasbord and they sample its exotic tastes, wherever this takes them. In October 1979 they performed for Pope John Paul I before an estimated crowd of 1.35 million in Dublin's Phoenix Park—the largest crowd of their career.

This most certainly was a far cry from the atmosphere in which Moloney had grow up. Traditional music had then received little attention from the general public, which much preferred the popular music of the day. "There was no shortage of [traditional] musicians," Moloney has emphasized. "There was a shortage of listeners. [The music] was being played. It just wasn't being heard."

After many years of struggling along on a part-time basis, the Chieftains finally decided to turn fully professional in 1975. "I never believed it would take off," admitted Paddy Moloney. "But, like Martin Luther King, I had a dream. Now Irish music has soared throughout the world. I'm tremendously proud of that."

In the mid-1970s the group began to experiment with extended suites, such as Moloney's massive fourteen-minute "Bonaparte's Retreat." But the members' interests extend well beyond Irish traditional music.

In 1982 they opened for the Rolling Stones at Slane Castle in Dublin. The following year the Chieftains became the first Western group to perform with a Chinese folk orchestra, and the first group ever to perform on the Great Wall of China. Further broadening their horizon, they recorded an album with James Galway exploring the musical link between Ireland and Scotland, and then recorded an album of Breton music, *Celtic Wedding*. More recently they recorded an album of Galician music.

In 1992 they explored the country roots of Irish music in *Another Country* (RCA Victor), and in 1995 Moloney's longtime love affair with rock music came to its natural fruition when some of the biggest names in rock performed on *The Long Black Veil*.

(RCA Victor): Sting phonetically singing an Irish Jacobite song written in honor of Bonnie Prince Charlie, "Mo Ghile Mear" (complete with Scottish pipes); Sinéad O'Connor contributed a stirring version of "The Foggy Dew" accompanied by Ry Cooder on electric guitar and Carlos Nuñez on the *gaita*, along with a particularly stark "He Moved through the Fair"; Marianne Faithfull's vocals were appropriately weary on "Love Is Teasin'"; a typically overwrought Tom Jones sang "Tennessee Waltz"; and a surprisingly effective Mick Jagger, in great voice, joined in on the richly atmospheric title cut, which evokes both the American South and rural Ireland. Van Morrison also offered "Have I Told You Lately That I Love You?," in his typically unique way, which prompted Moloney to comment, "When he goes into some of those long ending songs he could be a Connemara man singing a *sean-nós* song."

The undisputed leader of the Chieftains—the band's manager, creative spark, and guiding light—has always been Paddy Moloney, a diminutive fireball of a man with a hearty laugh and affable manner who has directed all of his professional energy into making the Chieftains not only the best traditional Irish band in the world but also the best known. The purpose of the band has never changed: to expose traditional Irish music to as many people as possible.

Moloney grew up in Dublin absolutely steeped in traditional music. By the time he was eight he was playing the uilleann pipes. His teacher was none other than the great uilleann piper himself Leo Rowsome. "There was always music in the house, singing, that kind of thing," he once told an interviewer. "At school there was a school band and I used to do everything in the band, conduct, the lot. I had this God-given gift of being able to pick up tunes having heard them once or twice." Then in one of the great understatements of Irish music he added, "It was really very handy."

The Chieftains have always been a few steps ahead of everyone else. In the mid-1980s the future sensation of *Riverdance*, Michael Flatley, performed with them and in 1990, Flatley's *Riverdance* partner, Jean Butler. And in a memorable St. Patrick's Day concert several years ago at Carnegie Hall, guest artists included Sinéad O'Connor, Ashley MacIsaac, and Carlos Nuñez.

Why the Chieftains? What have they been able to do, able to communicate, that other bands, perhaps just as talented and just as committed, have not? What is their secret?

Perhaps it all comes down to one word: party. Or, if you prefer, you could borrow a phrase from the Chieftains' songbook, *hooey*. The Chieftains love to host a party, and since they have been doing just that for more than thirty-five years, they have become quite adept at it. In 1989, in perhaps the ultimate validation of their work, they were named Ireland's official musical ambassadors.

But more than their winning ability to extend a good time to everyone within earshot is their commitment to bringing Irish traditional music to the attention of the world. Their virtuosity, playful spirit, and enthusiasm for the music is infectious. When you attend a Chieftains concert, you know it's no act. They're enjoying themselves just as much as you are.

"We are a gentle, humorous, kind people," Moloney once said to a reporter from the *New York Post*, referring to his fellow Irishmen and -women. "It is a very old nation that's produced some of the finest artists. We're steeped in the arts, despite all the occupations and wars—we've held onto our traditions."

SOMETHING NEW, SOMETHING OLD

During the 1980s and 1990s a new generation of Celtic musicians has stepped to the forefront. Some are clearly following in the path that bands like Planxty and the Bothy Band in Ireland or Silly Wizard in Scotland paved before them. Others are following their own road, looking forward to the future.

Altan, considered the best of the current traditional Irish groups, employed a back-to-the-basics approach at a time when other groups were looking frantically for the next big thing. A tightly knit ensemble of musicians who deeply care about their craft, in the eyes of many critics Altan has donned the mantle previously worn by Dé Dannan and, before that, Planty and the Bothy Band.

Flute and tin whistle player Frankie Kennedy was considered one of the finest traditional Irish musicians. A native of Belfast and a former schoolteacher, he met singer and fiddler Mairéad Ní

Mhaonaigh in her native Donegal, where he spent summer holidays learning Irish and playing music. They married in 1981. Two years later, the couple recorded their first album together, *Ceol Aduaidh* (Music of the North), which consisted mostly of tunes and Irish-language songs indigenous to the Irish north or that had come over from Scotland. The heavy Scots influence in the band's music has much to do with the labor force that migrated back and forth across the Irish Sea. Seasonal workers often shuttled from Donegal to Scotland as an economic necessity up until fairly recent times.

Ní Mhaonaigh grew up in Gaelic-speaking Gweedore, in northwestern Donegal. She learned to play the fiddle from her father, Francie, one of Donegal's premier musicians and songwriters. Her clear and unaffected vocals remain one of the highlights of any Altan record. The music of Planxty inspired her to turn to her own Irish roots. Not surprisingly, she sings mostly in Irish.

Much of the material on *Ceol Aduaidh* was indicative of the direction that Altan would ultimately pursue. The band plays mazurkas, highlands, jigs, reels, and *strathspeys*, much of it from the northern Irish tradition.

"Donegal is very isolated from the rest of Ireland," Ní Mhaonaigh says. "The music we play, I think, fits the landscape and the mountains there. It's very wild."

Altan met with critical and popular success almost from the beginning. *Island Angel* (1993), which at least one critic has called the best traditional Irish album of the decade, stayed on *Billboard*'s world-music chart for eight months.

"We really put a lot of stress on integrity, and we hope people realize that. We're not just giving them music, we're giving them a piece of our heritage," said the late Frankie Kennedy.

Diagnosed with cancer in 1992, Kennedy continued to record and perform until his death on September 19, 1994, at Belfast's Royal Victoria Hospital. He was thirty-eight.

Although the band has continued to flourish in his absence, I can't help but wonder if his generous spirit, like some Celtic guardian angel, hovers over them, watching them grow and admiring their ability to connect with an increasingly large and loyal international following. At least, I would like to think so.

SOME OF THE OLDER bands have also managed to find new life by either going in a new direction or by adding new members—or sometimes both.

One of the most durable of Celtic bands is Scotland's Battlefield Band. Employing synthesizer, electric piano, and pedal organ, Battlefield Band has been moving more and more in a decidedly nontraditional direction. Over the years it has witnessed major changes in its lineup, yet somehow the core members, including vocalist Alan Reid, find new ways of saying things that have already been said. Many thought that singer, fiddler, and founding member Brian McNeill's departure to write novels and pursue solo work would lead to the band's eventual demise.

But it forged ahead, more determined than ever. Iain MacDonald, the former piper for Ossian, replaced Dougie Pincock and was soon joined by the young fiddler John McCusker from Parcel o'Rogues. In 1984 vocalist and guitarist Alistair Russell, the band's token Englishman, came aboard. Brought up in northeastern England of Scottish parentage, Russell's easy manner proved an effective foil to Reid's somber persona and penchant for historical ballads. Today, Davy Steele of Ceolbeg and Mike Katz are the latest additions.

The secret to Battlefield Band's longevity is their chameleon-like ability to adapt. Alan Reid is credited with introducing keyboards into traditional music—first a pedal organ, then the electric piano, and still later synthesizers—at a time when modern instruments was frowned upon. Yet synthesizers and drum machines have always been an integral part of Battlefield's oftentimes larger-than-life sound. Add the mix of Highland bagpipes, fiddles, guitars, flutes, and saxophones, and you have the recipe for something altogether different. "On every album, we've done something slightly off the wall," Reid has admitted.

Another Scottish band with an impressive longevity record is the Tannahill Weavers. Taking its name from the Scots poet Robert Tannahill and the weaving industry of Paisley, the members' hometown, the band has been in existence since the late 1970s. It's known for high-energy instrumentation—if you're looking for much in the way of reflection, go elsewhere. Indeed, you may get the feeling the group has lasted so long through sheer will, or perhaps centrifugal force. In the early days the Weavers made a name for themselves based on the impressive technical skills of bagpipe wunderkind Alan MacLeod. Singer, songwriter, and fiddler Dougie Maclean was also a member, though briefly. Three-part vocal harmonies, a driving rhythm attack, and the solid singing of vocalist Roy Gullane all played their part in the band's success. Members' affable stage presence certainly helped when they were on the road, which with the Weavers is a large part of the time.

Dé Danann has been around forever, too, or so it seems. So how does it remain fresh? Rotating singers every few years helps. Most of Ireland's best traditional singers have paid their dues as a member of this legendary group—Dolores Keane, Mary Black, and Maura O'Connell all put in time. Lately, Eleanor Shanley has represented the voice of the band and quite nicely at that.

Dé Danann came together in the 1970s. Through countless personnel changes the focus of the band has remained the fiddling of Frankie Gavin and the *bouzouki* and guitar playing of Alec Finn. Other early members included Charlie Piggott on banjo and Johnny McDonagh on *bodhran* and bones. Still later came, and usually went, Johnny Moynihan, Jackie Daly, and Mary Bergin.

Although traditional in its focus, Dé Danann has been unafraid to veer off into other directions, perhaps more so than like-minded bands. Over the years it has recorded Irish versions of pop songs, klezmer music, and even gospel.

The brother-sister team of guitarist Mícheál Ó Dhomhnaill (MEhall o'DONnel) and vocalist and keyboardist Tríona Ní Dhomhnaill have been involved in among the most innovative projects and groups in Celtic music. The siblings were raised in a bilingual Dublin household, although their father hailed from Donegal. Tríona, Mícheál, and another sibling, Mairead, as well as

Daithi Sproule, formed the short-lived Skara Brae, a group in many ways ahead of its time, since it featured harmony singing in Irish accompanied by sophisticated guitar work. Its songs and style derived from the *sean-nós* of their ancestral Donegal home.

From 1975 to 1979 Mícheál and Tríona were both members of the Bothy Band. When that seminal group broke up, she emigrated to the United States, where she eventually formed Touchstone, a fertile exploration of Irish, Canadian, and American sources that took her into uncharted territory. "Take the music wherever you want to," she has said, and indeed she has.

Mícheál is just as unconventional—perhaps more so. He too came to America, settling in Portland, Oregon, where he has worked with various groups, often of a jazz-oriented nature. The acoustic group Puck Fair, which has featured John Cunningham on fiddle, Tommy Hayes on *bodhran*, Brian Dunning on penny whistle, Gordon Lee on piano, and Billy Oskay on viola, brought traditional Irish and urban American influences together. Tríona has joined him in the quartet Nightnoise, one of the first groups to blend Celtic music with New Age, jazz, and world music. Some say they brought an element of respect to New Age, an often maligned music. And in an inspired sibling match, Tríona and Mícheál joined Scots fiddler John Cunningham and his brother accordionist Phil Cunningham in Relativity, which showcased both Irish and Scottish traditional music but, once again, featured a very rich and highly modern sound.

One of the more recent of the supergroups—the last of the supergroups perhaps—is Patrick Street, founded in 1986. The original lineup consisted of fiddler Kevin Burke (ex–Bothy Band, currently with Open House), accordionist Jackie Daly (ex–Dé Danann and the short-lived Buttons and Bows); singer and *bouzouki* player Andy Irvine (ex-Planxty), guitarist and Northumbrian piper Ged Foley (ex–Battlefield Band, currently with The House Band). Guitarist Arty McGlynn replaced Foley on the second record (as of this writing, McGlynn is gone and Foley is back once again). As veteran a group of traditional musicians as you're ever likely to meet, Patrick Street thrives on the familiar exchange between musicians, the deep sense of camaraderie, that can only come with time, experience, and a profound trust and respect in each other's abilities.

The House Band plays Irish, Scottish, Breton, Bulgarian, African, and whatever else kind of music suits the members' fancy. Their music has been described as the work of "pan-Celtic renegades." "I kind of like that," Foley has admitted, "although we're not renegades. We're not punk rockers or anything, but we're not sticking to any particular tradition either." Indeed, although the majority of their material is of Celtic origin, the House Band remains defiantly eclectic. An English tune may be followed by a Romanian tune, followed by an Elvis Costello cover.

One of the finest and most pan-Celtic of the veteran bands, the Boys of the Lough, essentially introduced Celtic music to the American folk scene more than twenty years ago. Indeed, the group is said to be the first Celtic band to turn professional. All virtuoso musicians, they play mostly tunes from Scotland, Ireland, England, and Shetland, with the occasional vocal contributions by whistle and flute player Cathal McConnell and uilleann piper Christy O'Leary (as of this writing, O'Leary has since left the band). The heart of the band lies with the great Shetland fiddler Aly Bain and guitarist Dave Richardson. Early members included singer Dick Gaughan and Robin Morton, founder of the Scots-based independent record label Temple Records.

In 1988 veteran Irish musician Johnny McDonagh left Dé Danann, the band he helped found many years before, to try something different. Deciding to form his own group, he put together Arcady, which included Frances Black (sister of Mary), old friend and accordionist Jackie Daly, and a coterie of younger musicians. Other newer bands include the youthful and wonderful Déanta from County Antrim and County Derry, and the exciting Dervish from County Sligo.

And there are many others. Ossian recently regrouped after a long absence from the scene. As before, its lovely combination of harp and uilleann pipes accented by fine vocals remains its chief calling cards. Ceolbeg, an innovative traditional group, recently lost Davy Steele to Battlefield Band but has since gained veteran singer Rod Paterson. The wonderfully named Deaf Shepherd is one of the more exciting of the newer bands on the Scottish scene, as is the roots band Iron Horse. The Aberdeen quartet Old Blind Dogs, not to be confused with Four Men and a Dog from Northern Ireland, plays traditionally based music but with elements of rock, reggae, world, and especially jazz.

Meanwhile, north of the Scottish mainland, Rock, Salt, and Nails is a particularly frisky folk group from Shetland. Their southern neighbor, Wolfstone, is a terrific band with a distinctive sound that boasts the talents of Orcadian singer Ivan Drever, fiddler Duncan Chisholm, and keyboardist Stuart Eaglesham. The Cast consists of the fine singing and fiddling of Mairi Campbell and her musical partner in crime Dave Francis, who also serves as director of the Edinburgh Folk Festival.

BETWEEN WORLDS

All this ongoing experimentation over the years has created a healthy cross-fertilization between musical genres.

Contemporary composer Mícheál Ó Súilleabháin, the natural successor in both spirit and intent to Séan Ó Riada, is a modern builder of bridges between traditional and European art music. His musical piece "Between Worlds," with its lively piano, traditional rhythm provided by bones and *bodhran*, and string orchestra, is a nice metaphor for crossing to the other side, for neither being fully one nor the other. In *A River of Sound*, based on the Irish television program of the same name, Ó Súilleabháin traces the "changing course" of Irish traditional music. Controversial in its native Ireland for its bold juxtaposition of the traditional with the modern, the record is truly a marvelous panache of various musical styles that extends and deepens the Irish tradition, bringing it into contact with the wider world. It is a musical feast and, quite simply, an absolute joy to listen to. Through the work of various artists, Ó Súilleabháin explores the yin and yang of traditional music, its affinities and the marked differences from other genres. Blues and traditional Irish music, traditional and the baroque, the *bodhran* and Asian percussion instruments—all this and more indicate the brave new world that awaits the musical adventurer.

"Music has to move with the times," says Savourna Stevenson, one of Scotland's leading *clarsach* players and the daughter of classical composer and pianist Ronald Stevenson. Taking harp music to new worlds, Stevenson approaches the traditional instrument from a jazz musician's perspective. Is the world ready for *jazz clarsach?* Time will tell.

Another example of folk and classical coming together is Phil Cunningham's *The Highlands and Islands Suite*, which made its world première at Glasgow's Celtic Connections in 1997 and its Highland première at the Highland Festival. Performed by the sixty-three-piece Scottish Chamber Orchestra, the forty-member Glasgow Phoenix Choir, and the thirty-member Highland Fiddle Orchestra, it showcased the talents of traditional Scots musicians Aly Bain, Duncan Chisholm, Ian Hardie, and Bruce MacGregor, combining traditional, classical, and contemporary elements.

On the wonderful *Appalachia Waltz*, a unique collaboration between Texas fiddler Mark O'Connor, bassist Edgar Meyer, and cello virtuoso Yo-Yo Ma, the three musicians create a flowing and effortlessly expressive—not to mention fun—piece of work. Like a true native son of the Lone Star state, O'Connor manages to find artistic freedom—tastefully flaunting, if you will, his individuality—while adhering to the basic traditional framework. It is a structure that still allows room for personal expression.

According to the CD's cover notes, "You try to take the skills you have and enter into different worlds, partake of different traditions," said Yo-Yo Ma, an eclectic musician with probably the most catholic taste of any around today. O'Connor's stately title cut, which he wrote expressly for Yo-Yo, uses the open strings so common to the Shetland and Scandinavian traditions, with slight Appalachian touches.

"College Hornpipe" is a playful variation of a traditional hornpipe, using bass and cello; the Irish air "Star of the County Down" begins on a mournful note then is joined by the equally slow and soulful wail of O'Connor's fiddle; while the lively bass-and-fiddle duet of "Speed the Plow" feels equally at home at a hoedown, *ceilidh*, or, for that matter, on a concert stage!

Many many miles away from the Appalachian mountain country lie the rolling, green hills of Galicia in Spain, home to Milladoiro.

Rodrigo Romani, the band's harpist and *bouzouki* and guitar player, told writer Steve Winick: "In the beginning we wanted to do the same that the Chieftains did for Irish music, or the Bothy Band, or [Alan] Stivell with Breton music. The same, but with our music. . . . And it was a good example for us, because nobody in Galicia was doing that.

"The Celtic heritage in Galicia is very important," he maintained. "But, it's not our only exponent, our only heritage. The Latin legacy includes the Galician language, Gallego, whose speakers are mutually comprehensible with speakers of Portuguese. The Celtic influence in the language is minimal."

Milladoiro's synthesis of folk music and medieval art music has been called "chamber folk." It has a classical feel yet with discernible Celtic traces. Although the language of Galicia, Gallego, is a Romance language, Breton and Galician expert Lois Kuter detects Celtic influences in both its phonetics and vocabulary, tracing the ultimate roots of the music to the Celts from Britain who emigrated to both Brittany and Galicia in the fifth, sixth, and seventh centuries. Indeed, Galicia's links with Brittany remain very strong. Since the late 1960s Galician dance troupes and bagpipe bands have routinely played at Breton festivals. And the Galician bagpipe, the *gaita*, more than resembles the Breton bagpipe, the *biniou*, in sound and shape.

The traditional way to play Galician music is two pipes, drums, and a tambourine. Milladoiro adds tin whistle, clarinet, oboe, uilleann pipes, mandolin, flute, piccolo, fiddle, *bouzouki*, Celtic harp, ocarina, and, of course, *gaita*. Celtic in structure and style and most definitely in spirit, the group's music exudes a certain stateliness, a mix of medieval classicism, jazz, a smattering of New Age perhaps, and the occasional brush with pop. It is a lush, romantic, richly atmospheric music that garners a tremendous amount of goodwill.

Considered Scotland's finest traditional music group, the Whistlebinkies research, arrange, perform, and record Scottish traditional music and song using only authentic instruments. It led the revival of interest in the bellows-blown bagpipes in Scotland and was the first to combine the three national instruments—fiddle, *clarsach*, and pipes—in regular performance. It has been involved in various exciting projects, including a collaboration with American composer John Cage entitled "Scottish Circus." Further, the Whistlebinkies played Scottish fiddle music with Sir Yehudi Menuhin and in 1990 became the first Scottish folk group to tour China. Flute and *clarsach* player Edward McGuire is a fine composer in his own right, having written an orchestral work for bagpipes, *Calgacus*; an opera, *The Loving of Etain*; and *Peter Pan*, a piece commissioned for Scottish Ballet.

ABSORBING NEW INFLUENCES

Across the Atlantic, the Toronto-based band Rare Air played what some have called Celtic funk. Others prefer bagpipe funk, or is it Celtic jazz? The labels can get confusing, but no matter. The typical Rare Air sound, if there is such a thing, features a mix of modern and Old World instruments. Keyboards, electric bass, synthesizers, and electric guitars join a Highland snare drum, a wooden flute, and the Breton *bombarde* and *binou*. Their Celtic roots music reaches out to everything from rock and blues to free jazz and African rhythms.

More recently another Canadian has been stirring up the Celtic waters with his flagrant disregard—or shall we say celebration?—of the livelier aspects of traditional Celtic music. Ashley MacIsaac, a passionate fiddler who brings the intensity and velocity of the fiercest rock to his chosen instrument, has managed to bring together the unlikely combination of Celtic folk with electronic dance music in his own inimitable style. Considering that he is a member of Nova Scotia's most musically respected family, that is hardly surprising.

No one is quite as wild as Martyn Bennett, though. The amazingly inventive Bennett has taken up where Mouth Music left off. Mouth Music, as you may recall from chapter 5, mixed African rhythms with Gaelic songs. Bennett goes many steps further, intentionally playing an older tradition of land and sea "against the neon technology of our growing Urban culture" and watching where it takes him. *Bothy Culture* is a hybrid of traditional Gaelic music with house, hip-hop, and modern dance music and interspersed with all kinds of unusual bits and pieces oddly juxtaposed—Gaelic poetry; Punjabi folk songs; Joiking, a form of chanting from the northern fringes of Sweden; even the *pibroch* "Lament for Red Hector of the Battles," as well as several non-Celtic instruments. These include the *ud* (a fretted Turkish or North African lute) or *doudouk*—similar, said Bennett, to Scottish bagpipes and common in the Islamic lands. Throughout all this musical mayhem, Bennett projects a daft, endearing sense of humor. His tune "Shputnik in Glenshiel," for example, is about a Scottish crofter (or farmer) "who spotted the Hale Bop comet, but was fairly Shputniked at the time."

Born in Newfoundland in 1971 of Highland and Lowland Scots ancestry, Bennett spent his formative years in the Canadian province's Codroy Valley, founded by Gaelic-speaking Highland Scots in the mid-nineteenth century. (He is the son of Margaret Bennett, a Gaelic scholar and lecturer as the School of Scottish Studies in Edinburgh). He attended school in the Scotland's capital city, Edinburgh, and received a classical education on violin and piano at the Royal Academy of Music and Drama in Glasgow. After the release of his second solo recording, *Bothy Culture*, he formed the band Cuillin Music.

Paul Mounsey, founder of the band Nahoo, is another Scot who presents the traditional music through the medium of contemporary pop styles, using, like Bennett, snippets of spoken words to comment on the music. In "Passing Away" a speaker mourns the loss of the Gaelic language while the baleful *pibroch* song "MacCrimmon Will Never Return" plays softly in the background.

A fusion band that crosses barriers, the Edinburgh-based Tartan Amoebas play bagpipes, fiddle, saxophone, and trumpet with a rhythm section of drums, percussion, bass and guitars augmented by keyboard, loops, beats, and other modern wizardry. Another Edinburgh band, the funky Shooglenifty, is truly a mix of modern and traditional, with an emphasis on the former. For those who like labels, they play "hypnofolkedelic ambient trad acid-croft," a description that you're unlikely to find in any record catalogue. Its influences range from Captain Beefheart to the Fall.

More traditional is yet another Edinburgh band, Seelyhoo. (The unusual name is an old Scots word for a membrane sometimes found covering a new born baby's head. It is supposed to signify good luck.) The lineup consists of the wonderful Wrigley Sisters from Orkney on fiddle and guitar and keyboard, Sandy Brechin on accordion and vocals, Fiona Mackenzie on vocals and whistle, Aaron Jones on bass guitar, *bouzouki*, and vocals, and Jim Walker on percussion and drums. In addition to original tunes, many with an Orcadian or Scandinavian touch, Seelyhoo features Gaelic songs with modern arrangements.

The Peatbog Faeries, from Skye, play Highland war pipes backed by bass and percussion.The addition of synthesizer and keyboards gives the band a modern and very clean sound—think of Mike Oldfield's "Tubular Bells" with a bit of infectious Highland melody.

A top live act, Salsa Celtica is a ten-piece group of Celtic and Latin (or shall we say Celtino) musicians culled from the Scottish jazz and folk scenes. They play their own form of Latin American salsa, derived from a diverse range of South American styles from Cuban *son* to African-Latin jazz. Lately, the Scots Gaelic band Capercaillie have been experimenting with world music, mixing traditional chants from North Africa with Gaelic song, while Mac Umba, an eleven-piece pipe and percussion outfit, combines Brazilian and Caribbean percussions and rhythms with Scottish traditional material—including probably the first time in the history of the recording industry that a Robert Burns lyric, "A Man's a Man for a' That" ever appeared as a Afro-samba march.

Some people travel thousands of miles to go their own way, to do their own thing. Duncan McLean and the Lonestar Stone Band is led by Orcadian novelist and sometime guitarist Duncan McLean, who through the music tries to re-create the atmosphere of southwestern dance halls epitomized by Bob Wills's Texas Playboys and his electric steel guitar. Call it what you want—Scottish bluegrass?—Wills's western swing, a fusion of country, blues, and jazz, was the reason that several years ago McLean traveled across the ocean "three thousand miles from home, six hundred miles from anyone who knows more about me than the name on my credit card." He wrote about his travels in his very funny travelog, *Lone Star Swing: On the Trail of Bob Wills and his Texas Playboys.*

Among the younger generation of Scottish singer-songwriters, Carol Luala, descended from Romany gypsies, is a cool and sophisticated pop stylist with jazzy overtones, while Eddi Reader has earned a reputation as one of Scotland's finest live performers, comfortable with everything from gentle ballads to swinging melodies. In Ireland singer-songwriters Luka Bloom, Kieran Goss, Kieran Halpin, and others are continuing the strong literary tradition of earlier generations of Irish songwriters.

Many other musicians, both new and established, continue to stretch the tradition without breaking it. They include everyone from singer-songwriter Dougie Maclean, a fixture of the Celtic music scene for many years, to Anna Murray, a young Gaelic singer and piper from Lewis with a bluesy touch, who has managed to pursue careers in both music and acting.

 ## SOUNDTRACKS

In recent years, Hollywood has taken note of the upsurge of interest in Celtic music. From *Last of the Mohicans* to *Titanic*, composers have found something in the music that transcends characters and plot. Sometimes, though, as in the case of *The Secret of Roan Inish*, the score adds immeasurably to the overall effect and deepens the meaning of the story.

Some recent examples of major films with Celtic scores include:

Braveheart (London, 1995). Music composed by James Horner. Despite being set in Scotland, the instrument that really defines its sound belongs to Eric Rigler's Irish uilleann pipes. Also features whistle and bodhran. As always with Horner, the music is lush and highly emotional.

The Piano (Virgin, 1993). Music composed by Michael Nyman. Features the minimalist piano of Nyman, who uses Scottish folk and popular songs to surprisingly good effect as the foundation for his score, finding just the right combination of moody piano and earthy folk melodies. When needed, as in the windswept "A Wild and Distant Shore," he offers great romantic breadth. The simple "The Heart Asks Pleasure First" recalls a plaintive Robert Burns tune.

Rob Roy (Virgin, 1995). Music composed by Carter Burwell. Showcases the vocals of Karen Matheson, with reels performed by her band Capercaillie, and two Gaelic songs also performed by Matheson, "Theid mi Dhachaigh" (I'll Go Home) with accompaniment by fiddler Angus Grant and "Morag's Lament." Features Davy Spillane on uilleann pipes and low whistles, Maire Breatnach on fiddle, Tommy Hayes on *bodhran*, and Ronan Browne on penny whistle. To give it an additional ring of authenticity, *Riverdance* composer Bill Whelan served as music consultant.

The Secret of Roan Inish (Daring/Rounder, 1995). Music by Mason Daring. The most traditional of the bunch, *The Secret of Roan Inish* contains the old tunes "Mist Covered Mountain," "Shores of Lough Gowna," "Over the Moor to Maggie," "The Bucks of Oranmore," and original pieces by Daring. Features such fine mostly Irish musicians as Cormac Breatnach, Mark Robets, and Billy Novick on flutes and whistles, Maire Breatnach and Sandal Astrauski on fiddles, Ronan Browne and Declan Masterson on uilleann pipes, Niall o Callonain on *bouzouki*, and Mel Mercier on *bodhran*.

CROSSING BORDERS

Cross-cultural exchanges between the Celtic lands have been going on for years. Years ago Kornog made a successful attempt to broaden the music by adding such instruments as the flute, fiddle, guitar, and *bouzouki* to traditional Breton music and, due to the presence of a Scot in their lineup, Jamie McMenemy, the group often included Scots ballads as well. Indeed, they it borrowed freely from both the Scots and Irish traditions; it isn't unusual for Breton music performed Kornog-style to sound similar to Scots airs.

Increasingly, cultural partnerships transcend both political boundaries and ethnic identities.

OUT OF THIS WORLD

The unconventional and wildly successful career of Canadian singer and musician Loreena McKennitt warrants some comment. A multitude of crosscultural allusions permeate her work, from Celtic to Asian. In typically Celtic fashion, though, she often explores the music's cyclical patterns. For in McKennitt's worldview, everything is connected.

Born and raised in Morden, Manitoba, in a community inhabited by people of mostly Irish, Scots, German, and Icelandic descent, McKennitt came to appreciate Celtic music gradually. "Although my family's ancestors on the most part came from Ireland, there was very little overt 'Celticness' to my upbringing in the sense of music or storytelling.

"The first step for me was Celtic music. The whole sound drew me in an almost instinctive way and it became this vehicle to pursue history in a way I could never have imagined."

McKennitt fell in love with the music's innate lyricism, finding special affinity with the work of Breton harpist Alan Stivell and the seminal Irish traditional bands Planxty and the Bothy Band. She also had a strong affection for W. B. Yeats.

Her interests and talents all come together in her work. A sampling of her most "Celtic" recordings would include:

The Book of Secrets (1997). This is the breakaway record that includes the surprise "dance" hit, "The Mummer's Song," which links the work of a marionette maker in Palermo, Sicily, with the hobby horse of May Day celebrations in Padstow, Cornwall, and a Sufi order in Turkey. The chorus and last verse are taken from an original mummers' song traditionally sung in Abingdon, Oxfordshire. Also featured is a song about a reclusive monk on the Irish island of Skellig.

The Mask and Mirror (1994). Explores Spanish, Celtic, and Moroccan influences from Ireland to Santiago de Compostella in Galicia. Includes musical settings of poems by St. John of the Cross.

The Visit (1992). Among her most literary recordings, this features a musical setting of Tennyson's "The Lady of Shalott" and a new rendition of "Greensleeves."

Parallel Dreams (1989). Features a version of the traditional Scots ballad "Annachie Gordon" and a Native American–Celtic fusion of the "Huron 'Beltane' Fire Dance."

Elemental (1985). Fresh arrangements of Irish songs, including "She Moved Through the Fair" and "Carrickfergus," as well as musical settings of poems by Yeats and Blake.

In the liner notes to *So Far*, Mick Moloney calls Eileen Ivers "a true world musician, one who constructs a highly personal style upon impeccably crafted traditional roots, honed through generations of aural transmission in rural Ireland and urban America." Well grounded in traditional Irish music with a flair for flaunting boundaries, Ivers not only reinterprets traditional music, she circumvents it, creating in its wake her own unique sound.

Ivers has collaborated with composer Mícheál Ó Súilleabháin on his television series *River of Sound*; performed with the Irish-American rap-rock group Paddy A Go-Go; and, in probably her most publicized role, played fiddle in *Riverdance*. You never quite know what you'll hear when you listen to an Ivers recording. She is constantly experimenting with new ideas and new influences, from rock and blues to classical and jazz, from swing to eastern European.

Another Celtic band that has defied tradition is Den, the Celtic fusion band from Brittany that emerged in the the late 1980s and featured some of Brittany's finest musicians, including Patrick and Jacky Molard, formerly of Gwerz, and ex-Kornog members Soig Siberil and Jean-Michel Veillon. Founded as an outgrowth of the traditional Breton dance band Pennou Skoulm, it explored the outer limits of traditional music. From traditional and jazz arrangements to a rhythm section worthy of rock and roll, the band showcased everything from fiddle and bagpipe tunes to hypnotic suites featuring flute, guitar, and keyboards.

Similarly, Open House draws from a wide range of influences: blues, Latin American, Scandinavian, eastern European, French, bluegrass, and old-timey, to name a few. The Anglo-Irish fiddler Kevin Burke is a key member of the band's eclectic sound.

When growing up in London Burke listened to a host of players from different parts of Ireland—Kerry, Sligo, Clare. But as he told *Irish Music* magazine, you're never quite sure where the music comes from and what direction it may lead:

"[M]usic's strange—it's a Zen thing really," he mused. "I mean playing is a real discipline—but you see and hear people play things late at night when maybe they've had a few, they're not thinking about it too much and out comes this wonderful music."

It's this unpredictable quality that best captures the spirit of Open House. Like Ivers and others Burke finds new ways of interpreting the tradition while still working within it.

REINVENTING TRADITION

Innovating within the tradition can be a difficult thing. If done wrong, it can belittle the very tradition that the musician is trying to stretch. But if done right, it can be a glorious thing and a vastly rewarding exercise in creativity. In order to reinvent tradition, though, the musician must first be thoroughly grounded in it. The musician must live and breathe the tradition.

When Ashley MacIsaac, the Cape Bretoner with a major attitude, breaks the rules, he knows exactly what he is doing. Or, as he said, "I'm just a fiddler who's learned to put things different ways."

Séamus Egan is another such musician. "The whole idea of what is traditional is a constantly evolving thing," said Egan, the young wunderkind who composed the score of Edward Burns's sleeper hit movie, *The Brothers McMullen*, several years ago. "[The music] wouldn't be playing now if it didn't change. The players that my generation were influenced by were influenced by the generation that came before them. And they all changed the music. Purists who say Irish music is the way Michael Coleman played it, well, he was a revolutionary in Irish music. He created a whole new sense of what is traditional. That's why he has the stature he has today; because he was an innovator."

Egan possesses considerable knowledge and respect for the music. He admires and appreciates its natural grace, its flowing rhythm. Born in Philadelphia in 1969, he returned with his family to County Mayo for a while before venturing back to Philadelphia in 1980. Something of a child prodigy, he came to the attention of musician and folklorist Mick Moloney, who produced his solo record *Traditional Music of Ireland* (Shanachie) in 1986 when Egan was only sixteen.

Egan calls melody the heart of Irish music. "Even as I try to innovate, I don't want to lose that. Melodically, if you just read it off the page, Irish music can seem very simple. But that doesn't represent the true nature of the melody. The goal of improvisation in Irish music is different than it is in jazz. You still want to maintain the melodic sense and to improvise within that; whereas in jazz, you're taking it apart and creating new lines out of a particular melody. In Irish music, I've always felt that the idea is how much you can do while maintaining the integrity of the initial melody."

Egan constantly refers to the *feel* of the music; without the feel, there is nothing. Just an empty shell, with little or no meaning.

"You can hear people playing who you wouldn't say had prodigious technical ability," he has observed, "but you could listen to them all night because of the feel they have. With any music, it has to be the feel. An understanding of where the music is coming from, where it's been, integrated within the musician's own life experience: that all comes out in the feel. The feel of the music is really the fingerprint of the person playing."

And that in a nutshell sums up the past, present, and future of Celtic music. Somehow, too, it seems only right that a traditional musician should have the last word.

RECOMMENDED LISTENING

Altan. *The First Ten Years: 1986–1995* (Green Linnet). The best from one of Ireland's most critically acclaimed traditional bands.

Dan Ar Bras. *Acoustic* (Green Linnet). Quietly passionate recording by the Breton guitarist and singer.

Battlefield Band. *Anthem for the Common Man* (Temple). The band at its best—the voices of both Brian McNeill and Alan Reid and innovative piper Duncan MacGillivray.

Martyn Bennett. *Bothy Culture* (Rykodisc). Mind-blowing experience from a gifted and innovative musician thoroughly versed in the tradition. Dance music for the new millennium.

Brave Hearts: New Scots Music (Narada). Features music from Old and New Scotland: Capercaillie, Blair Douglas, Ashley MacIsaac, Mary Jane Lamond, Dougie Maclean, Karen Matheson, Old Blind Dogs, Anna Murray, Skyedance, Tannas, and Leahy. Highlights include MacIsaac's slyly subversive rendition of "Sleepy Maggie" (with the assistance of Mary Jane Lamond), not to mention Lamond's rich vocals on the deliciously sensuous "E Horo." The CD ends on a classy note with Dougie Maclean's touching version of Robert Burns's timeless "Auld Lang Syne."

Eliza Carthy. *Red Rice* (Topic). Daughter of Martin Carthy and Norma Waterson—two seminal figures of the English folk revival—strong-willed Eliza seems determined to bring once-staid English folk into the modern era. Fiddle and accordion playing at its most idiosyncratic.

The Chieftains. *Chieftains 5* (Shanachie). The first Chieftains recording to be released in America, its centerpiece consists of a medley of seven Turlough O Carolan tunes. Ensemble playing at its finest. An excellent example of the Chieftains' ongoing passion for musical diversity is their collaboration with flautist James Galway in *Over the Sea to Skye: The Celtic Connection* (RCA Victor), a collection of Irish and Scots tunes from a Carolan composition to a Jacobite air. The lovely *Celtic Wedding* (RCA) not only features an exquisite selection of Breton dance tunes and marches but also an extended musical medley of songs, hymns, and instrumentals associated with a traditional Breton wedding ceremony. Most recently, they have explored the Galician connection on *Santiago* (RCA Victor).

Enya (Atlantic). A selection of music from the BBC television program *The Celts*. Edgy, moody, and haunting, at times it can even be breathtakingly beautiful.

Folk 'n Hell: Fiery New Music from Scotland (Hemisphere). Wonderfully eclectic collection of some of the new sounds emanating from Scotland, from rhythm and reels to hip-hop folk. Features the music of Jim Sutherland, Burach, Shooglenifty, Paul Mounsey, Ceolbeg, Seelyhoo, Dougie Maclean, Rock, Salt, & Nails, the Poozies, the Iron Horse, Tannas, Khartoum Heroes, Old Blind Dogs, and others.

Eileen Ivers. *Wild Blue* (Green Linnet). Ivers adopts a multicultural approach—jazz, African, blues, eastern European, swing, you name it, it's here. She is joined by Kimati Dinizulu on percussion, Séamus Egan on flute, and Jerry O'Sullivan on uilleann pipes.

Kornog. *Premiere: Music from Brittany* (Green Linnet). Probably the most well-known Breton band. By virtue of the presence of vocalist, *bouzouki*, and mandolin player Jamie McMenemy, a Scot, Breton marches and dance tunes share equal space with traditional Scots ballads.

Dónal Lunny. *Coolfin* (Capitol). The chameleon of the traditional Irish music scene has reinvented himself once again. This time around his traditional sounds are accompanied by a smoking contemporary rhythm section. Guest artists include singers Maighréad Ní Dhomhnaill, Tríona Ní Dhomhnaill, Eddi Reader, and Marta Sebestyen, accordion player Sharon Shannon, and step dancer Jean Butler.

Yo-Yo Ma, Edgar Meyer, and Mark O'Connor. *Appalachia Waltz* and *Appalachian Journey* (both Sony Classical). Classical and folk come together with glorious results.

Milladoiro. *Castellum Honesti: Celtic Music From Spain* (Green Linnet). Classical, folk, Celtic, continental—the influence and associations are many. However you describe it, these Galician musicians create a lovely and lushly romantic sound.

Anna Murray. *Into Indigo* (Lochshore). Murray not only plays small and Highland pipes but is also an excellent Gaelic singer. Inventive arrangements, including traditional *waulking* songs with bluesy-jazzy splashes of acoustic guitar and harmonica.

Séan Ó Riada. *Mise Eire* (Shanachie). A majestic score; the stately main theme that weaves in and out, with its glimpses of Mozartian flute, is as melodic and emotionally satisfying as any traditional Irish air.

Ossian. *St. Kilda Wedding* (Iona). Vintage Ossian with Billy Jackson on Celtic harp, uilleann pipes, and whistles and Billy Ross on lead vocals and guitar. Contains both Gaelic and Scots songs, reels, and *strathspeys*.

Mícheál Ó Súilleabháin. *Between Worlds* (Virgin). A collection of Ó Súilleabháin's finest works. Features classic pieces ("The Fox Chase" and a particularly infectious "Brian Boru") as well as the composer's impressive title cut. Concludes with the stunning "Lumen," which features a huge cast of musicians, including Kenneth Edge on saxophone, Evelyn Glennie on percussion, Eileen Ivers on fiddle, Laoise Kelly on harp, the RTE Concert Orchestra, and the monks of Glenstall Abbey. Sophisticated, moody, romantic music—not to mention immensely listenable.

An embarrassment of riches is *A River of Sound: The Changing Face of Irish Traditional Music* (Hummingbird). Ó Súilleabháin and other artists present a musical feast for the ears, from the remarkable fluency of Ó Súilleabháin's piano to Eileen Iver's dramatic fiddling. Other artists include fiddler Frankie Gavin, singers Christy Moore and Iarla Ó Lionáird, harmonica player Brendan Power, harpist Laoise Kelly, concertina player Niall Vallely, and uilleann piper Ronan Browne.

Peatbog Faeries. *Mellowosity* (Greentrax). High tech meets traditional.

Puck Fair. *Fair Play* (Windham Hill). Puck Fair was stretching boundaries more than a decade ago. It still sounds good today. Van Morrison's "Moondance" gets the Puck Fair treatment, a jazzy mood piece on viola, violin, and harmonium.

Seelyhoo. *The First Caul* (Greentrax). Features the wonderful Wrigley sisters as well as some fine accordion work from Sandy Brechin and vocals from Fiona Mackenzie.

Shooglenifty. *Venus in Tweeds* (Greentrax). With a name like Shooglenifty, you know something's up. Wild *ceilidh* music, for the millennium and beyond.

Skara Brae. *Skara Brae* (Gael-Linn). An early attempt at traditional, jazz, and Gaelic fusion.

Tartan Amoebas. *Tartan Amoebas* (Greentrax). Another Scots band that refuses to accept things as they are. This recording features the music of Niel Gow and J. Scott Skinner as you've never heard them before, along with the sound of the fiddle, Highland pipes, trumpet, guitar, bass, drums, and percussion.

Tannahill Weavers. *The Best of* (Green Linnet). Highlights from the popular Scots band's career.

Ti Jaz. *Reves sauvages* (Escaliber). Playful, jazzy tunes from a fine Breton band.

APPENDIX

Building a Celtic Music Library:
100 Essential Recordings

The following is a very subjective list of 100 essential Celtic recordings, ranging from traditional to modern. I've tried to choose selections that are accessible to the average listener and fairly easy to locate. I hope the list indicates the sheer diversity found in this most timeless of music.

Solo, Duo, and Harmony Vocals

1. Mary Black. *Collected* (Dara)
2. Eric Bogle. *Scraps of Paper* (Flying Fish)
3. Paul Brady. *Welcome Here, Kind Stranger* (Mulligan)
4. Sandy Denny. *Who Knows Where the Time Goes?* (Hannibal)
5. *Enya* (Atlantic)
6. Archie Fisher. *Will Ye Gang, Love* (Green Linnet)
7. Dick Gaughan. *Handful of Earth* (Green Linnet)
8. Dolores Keane. *Broken-Hearted I'll Wander* (Green Linnet)
9. Ewan MacColl. *The Definitive Collection* (Green Linnet)
10. Dougie Maclean. *Real Estate* (Dunkeld)
11. Van Morrison. *Astral Weeks* (Warner Brothers)
12. The Proclaimers. *Sunshine on Leith* (Chrysalis)
13. Jean Redpath. *Father Adam* (Philo)
14. Jeannie Robertson. *The Great Scots Traditional Ballad Singer* (Ossian)
15. Andy M. Stewart. *By the Hush* (Green Linnet)
16. June Tabor. *Airs and Graces* (Shanachie)
17. Richard and Linda Thompson. *Shoot Out the Lights* (Hannibal)

Gaelic Vocals

18. Arthur Cormack. *Nuair Bha Mi Og/When I Was Young* (Temple)
19. Joe Heaney. *The Best of Joe Heaney: From My Tradition* (Shanachie).
20. Alison Kinnaird and Christine Primrose. *The Quiet Tradition: Music of the Scottish Harp, Songs of the Scottish Gael* (Temple)
21. Mary Jane Lamond. *Suas e!* (Turtlemusik/A&M Records)
22. Mackenzie. *Camhanach* (Macmeanmna)

23. Talitha MacKenzie. *Solas* (Shanachie)
24. Flora MacNeil. *Craobh Nan Udhal: Traditional Songs From the Western Isles* (Temple)
25. Catherine-Ann MacPhee. *Catherine-Ann MacPhee Sings Màiri Mhór* (Greentrax)
26. Iarla Ó Lionáird. *The Seven Steps to Mercy* (Real World)
27. Runrig. *Play Gaelic* (Ridge)

Groups

28. Altan. *The First Ten Years 1986/1995* (Green Linnet)
29. Battlefield Band. *Anthem for the Common Man* (Temple)
30. Black 47. *Fire of Freedom* (EMI)
31. The Bothy Band. *The Best of the Bothy Band* (Green Linnet)
32. Capercaillie. *Delirium* (Survival)
33. The Chieftains. *Chieftains 5* (Shanachie)
34. Cherish the Ladies. *One and All: The Best of Cherish the Ladies* (Green Linnet)
35. Clannad. *Rogha: The Best of Clannad* (RCA)
36. *Dé Danann* (Polydor)
37. Fairport Convention. *Liege and Lief* (Hannibal)
38. Kornog. *Premiere: Music From Brittany* (Green Linnet)
39. Milladoiro. *Castellum Honesti: Celtic Music From Spain* (Green Linnet)
40. Moloney, O'Connell, and Keane. *Kilkelly* (Green Linnet)
41. *Mouth Music* (Ryko)
42. *Moving Hearts* (WEA)
43. Ossian. *St. Kilda Wedding* (Iona)
44. *Patrick Street* (Green Linnet)
45. Planxty. *The Planxty Collection* (Polydor)
46. The Pogues. *If I Should Fall From Grace With God* (Island)
47. Runrig. *In Search of Angels* (Ridge)
48. Silly Wizard. *Kiss the Tears Away* (Shanachie)
49. Tannahill Weavers. *The Best of* (Green Linnet)
50. Ti Jaz. *Reves sauvages* (Escalibur)
51. The Whistlebinkies. *Anniversary* (Claddagh)
52. Wolfstone. *The Half Tail* (Green Linnet)

Instrumental (Solo or Duo)

53. Derek Bell. *Carolan's Receipt* (Shanachie)
54. Martyn Bennett. *Bothy Culture* (Rykodisc)
55. Robin Huw Bowen. *The Sweet Harp of My Land* (Flying Fish)
56. John Burgess. *King of the Highland Pipers* (Topic)
57. Kevin Burke. *If the Cap Fits* (Green Linnet)
58. *Liz Carroll* (Green Linnet)
59. Willie Clancy. *The Minstrel From Clare* (Green Linnet)
60. Michael Coleman. *Classic Recordings* (Shanachie)

61. John Cunningham. *Fair Warning* (Green Linnet)
62. Phil Cunningham. *Airs and Graces* (Green Linnet)
63. Séamus Egan. *When Juniper Sleeps* (Shanachie)
64. Alasdair Fraser and Jody Stecher. *The Driven Bow* (Culburnie)
65. Charles Guard. *Avenging and Bright* (Shanachie)
66. *Martin Hayes* (Green Linnet)
67. Eileen Ivers. *So Far: The Eileen Ivers Collection 1979–1995* (Green Linnet)
68. Ashley MacIsaac. *Hi, How Are You Today?* (Polygram)
69. Natalie MacMaster. *My Roots Are Showing: Traditional Fiddle Music of Cape Breton Island* (Greentrax)
70. Joanie Madden. *A Whistle on the Wind* (Green Linnet)
71. Brendan Power. *New Irish Harmonica* (Green Linnet)
72. Sharon Shannon. *Out the Gap* (Green Linnet)
73. Síleas. *Beating Harps* (Green Linnet)
74. Alan Stivell. *Renaissance of the Celtic Harp* (Rounder)
75. *John Williams* (Green Linnet)
76. Jennifer and Hazel Wrigley. *Huldreland* (Greentrax)

Classic Celtic

77. Aly Bain & the BT Scottish Ensemble. *Follow the Moonstone* (Whirlie Records)
78. Baltimore Consort. *On the Banks of Helicon: Early Music of Scotland* (Dorian)
79. Patrick Cassidy. *Famine Remembrance* (Windham Hill)
80. Shaun Davey. *The Pilgrim: A Celtic Suite for Orchestra, Soloists, Pipe Band, and Choir* (Tara)
81. William Jackson and the Scottish Orchestra for New Music. *St. Mungo: A Celtic Suite for Glasgow* (Greentrax)
82. Charles Lennon. *Flight from the Hungry Land* (Worldmusic)
83. Peter Maxwell Davies. *A Celebration of Scotland including An Orkney Wedding, with Sunrise* (Unicorn-Kanchana)
84. Séamus McGuire. *The Wishing Tree* (Green Linnet)
85. Liam O Flynn. *The Brendan Voyage* (Tara)
86. Séan Ó Riada. *Mise Eire* (Shanachie)
87. Mícheál Ó Súilleabháin. *Between Worlds* (Virgin)
88. Puirt a Baroque. *Bach Meets Cape Breton: Puirt A Baroque* (Marquis Classics)
89. Scott Macmillan. *Celtic Mass for the Sea* (Marquis Classics)

Anthologies

90. *Brave Hearts: New Scots Music* (Narada)
91. *Celtic Graces: A Best of Ireland* (Hemisphere)
92. *The Celts Rise Again: Contemporary and Traditional Music from Ireland, Scotland, and Brittany* (Green Linnet)
93. *Dear Old Erin's Isle: Irish Traditional Music from America* (Nimbus)

94. *Folk 'n' Hell: Fiery New Music from Scotland* (Hemisphere)
95. *Her Infinite Variety: Celtic Women in Music and Song* (Green Linnet)
96. *A River of Sound: The Changing Course of Irish Traditional Music* (Hummingbird)
97. *The Silver Bow: The Fiddle Music of Shetland* (Topic)
98. *Traditional Music from Cape Breton Island* (Nimbus)
99. *Traditional Music of Scotland* (Green Linnet)
100. *A Woman's Heart* (Darte)

Resources

CELTIC FESTIVALS

Note: Dates are approximate. Check with local tourist offices or via websites, as shown below. On-line or other publications (see listings) are also useful resources.

Ireland

Mid-April. **Pan Celtic Festival,** Tralee, County Kerry.

Early May. **Irish Traditional Music, Song, and Dance Festival,** Dungarvan, County Waterford.

Early May. **Killarney Folk Festival,** County Kerry.

Late May to early June. **Fleadh Cheoil Luimnigh,** Glin, County Limerick. Festival of traditional Irish music, song, and dance, presented by Comhaltas Ceoltoiri Eireann.

Late May to early June. **Sligo Arts Festival.** Traditional music, competitions, street music, and concerts.

Late May to early June. **Clare Festival of Traditional Singing,** Ennistymon, County Clare. Talks, concerts, and sessions.

Early June. **Writers' Week,** Listowel, County Kerry. One of Ireland's leading literary festivals, featuring reading, lectures, seminars, workshops, art, and drawing.

Mid- to late July. **Galway Arts Festival,** 6 Upper Dominic Street, Galway. Ireland's premier arts festival.

Late July. **James Morrison Traditional Music Festival,** Riverstown, County Sligo. Commemorates the great Sligo fiddle player James Morrison, who was born in 1893 in Drumfin, four miles from Riverstown. Concerts, ceilidhs, and work- shops.

August. **Fleadh Cheoil Na hEireann** The all-Ireland traditional-music festival, the largest gathering of traditional musicians, singers, and dancers from Ireland and the world. Held in a different town every year. Comhaltas Ceoltoiri Eireann, 32 Belgrave Square, Monkstown, County Dublin.

Early August. **Ballyshannon Music Festival,** County Donegal.

Early August. **Feile an Phobail,** West Belfast.

Early August. **O Carolan Harp and Traditional Music Festival,** Keadue, County Roscommon. Festival of harp music, folk concerts, and pub sessions.

Mid-August. **Feakle Festival of Traditional Music,** Feakle, County Clare. Best of traditional music, song, dance, and street theatre.

Late August. **Siamsa/Galway Folk Festival,** Taibhdhearc Theatre, Middle Street, Galway. Irish music, singing, and folk dance.

Late August. **Kilkenny Arts Week**. St. Canice's Cathedral, Watergate Theatre, and Cleere's Theatre. Classical, jazz, and traditional music, visual art, literature, film, and theatre.

Late August. **International Rose of Tralee**, Tralee, County Kerry.

Late August to early September. **Guinness Belfast Folk Festival**.

Late August to early September. **International Storytelling Festival**, Cape Clear Island, County Cork.

Late August to early September. **Leo Rowsome**. Commemorative event recalling the life and times of Leo Rowsome, the "King of the Pipers."

Early September. **Coleman Country Traditional Festival**, Gurteen, County Sligo. Fiddle competition, ceilidhs, traditional concerts, workshops, pub sessions.

Mid-November. **Sligo Contemporary Music Festival**, Model Arts Centre, Sligo.

Scotland

Mid-January to early February. **Celtic Connections**, Glasgow. Truly tremendous pan-Celtic festival, typically with the biggest names in the business on hand from Richard Thompson and Horse to Hothouse Flowers and Peatbog Faeries.

Late February to early March. **Inverness Music Festival**.

Late March. **Inverness Folk Festival**.

March/April. **Edinburgh Harp Festival**.

March/April. **Edinburgh Folk Festival**.

Early May. **Banchory Festival of Scottish Music**.

Early May. **Ceolmhor Lochaber**. Pan-Celtic festival.

Mid-May. **Buchan Heritage Festival**.

Late May. **Orkney Traditional Folk Festival**. Various locations.

Late May. **Islay Festival**. Various locations.

Late May. **Highland Harp Festival**, Balnain House, Inverness.

Late May to early June. **Highland Festival**. Various locations throughout the Highlands and Islands. Contemporary music, visual arts, dance, traditional, theatre, *ceilidhs*.

June, July, August. **Balnain House Summer Festival of Traditional Music**, Inverness.

Early June. **Isle of Arran Folk Festival**.

Early June. **Loch Lomond Festival of Gaelic Language and Culture**. Language and music workshops, literary workshops, social events.

Mid-June. **Killin Traditional Music and Dance Festival**.

Late June. **Glasgow International Folk Festival**.

Late June. **Highland Traditional Music Festival**, Dingwall.

Mid-July. **Hebridean Celtic Festival**, Stornoway, Isle of Lewis. Major summer festival of international Celtic musicians. Also workshops, pub sessions.

Mid-July. **Skye and Lochalsh Festival**.

Mid-July. **Stonehaven Folk Festival**.

Mid-July. **Isle of Bute International Folk Festival**.

Mid-July. **The Continental Ceilidh**, Lanark. Top Scots, Irish, Canadian, American, and European acts.

Late July to early August. **Skye Folk Festival**.

Late July to early August. **Aberdeen International Youth Festival.**
Late August. **Mull of Kintyre Music Festival,** Campeltown.
Early September. **Northlands Festival,** Wick and Thurso.
Early September. **Melrose Music Festival.**
Early September. **Tinto Festival,** rural Lanarkshire.
Mid-September. **From Northern Seas,** Aberdeen. Celebration of traditional fiddle music and dance from Canada, Denmark, Finland, Ireland, Norway, Sweden, and Scotland, with workshops, *ceilidh* dances, concerts, and recitals.
Mid-September. **Culross Folk Festival.**
Late September. **Highland Fiddle and Step-Dancing Festival,** Balnain House, Inverness.
Early October. **Aberdeen Alternative Festival.**
Mid-October. **The Doric Festival.** Northeast Scotland.
Late October to early November. **Scottish International Storytelling Festival,** the Netherbow, Edinburgh.

England

June. **London Fleadh,** Finsbury Park, London.
Late July. **Cambridge Folk Festival.**
Early August. **Sidmouth International Festival of Folk Arts,** Devon.

Wales

Late May. **Llanfair Folk Fayre.**
Mid-June. **World Harp Festival,** Cardiff.
July. **Gwyl Werin Y Cnapan,** Dyfed. All-Welsh festival and Wales's largest Celtic music festival to boot.
July. **North Wales Bluegrass Festival,** Trefriw.
Late July. **Fishguard Music Festival.**
Mid-August. **Pontardawe,** South Wales.

Isle of Man

Late July. **Yn Chruinnaght Inter-Celtic Festival.**

United States

Late April. **Southern Illinois Festival of Irish Music and Dance.** Carbondale, Illinois.
Early May. **Atlanta Celtic Festival.**
Mid-June. **New York Guinness Fleadh,** Randalls Island, New York.
August. **Milwaukee Irish Fest.**
Mid-September. **Celtic Fest Chicago.**

Canada

Late June. **Summerside Highland Gathering,** Summerside, Prince Edward Island.
Early July. **Nova Scotia International Tattoo,** Halifax.

Early July. **Stan Rogers Folk Festival**, Canso, Cape Breton, Nova Scotia.

Mid-July. **Newfoundland International Irish Festival**, Mount Pearl.

Mid-July. **Canada's Irish Festival on the Miramichi**, New Brunswick. Canada's largest Irish festival.

Mid-July. **Antigonish Highland Games**, Cape Breton, Nova Scotia. Reportedly the oldest continuous Highland games outside Scotland.

Mid-July. **Winnipeg Folk Festival.**

Late July. **Calgary Folk Music Festival.**

Late July to September. **Center Bras d'Or Festival of the Arts**, Baddeck, Cape Breton, Nova Scotia.

Early August. **Newfoundland and Labrador Folk Festival**, St. John's.

Early August. **St. Ann's Highland Gathering**, Cape Breton, Nova Scotia.

Early August. **Highland Village Day**, Iona, Cape Breton, Nova Scotia.

Mid-August. **Hector Festival**, Pictou, Nova Scotia.

Late August. **Edmonton Folk Music Festival.**

Mid-October. **Celtic Colours International Festival**, Cape Breton, Nova Scotia. Probably North America's most celebrated pan-Celtic gathering.

Brittany

Early to mid-August. **Lorient Celtic Festival**, Lorient.

PUBLICATIONS

Am Braighe (pronounced Uhm Bry-uh), P. O. Box 600, Port Hastings, NS, Canada B0E 2T0. Journal for those interested in Scots Gaelic language and culture in Cape Breton. Website: www.chatsubo.com/ambraighe

Bro Nevez, 169 Greenwood Avenue, Jenkintown, PA 19046. Quarterly; English-language coverage of Breton language and culture, including Breton music.

Celtic Connection, 741 West Broadway, Vancouver, BC V5Z 1K7.

Celtic Heritage, P.O. Box 8805, Station A, Halifax, NS Canada B3K 5M4. Bimonthly. Articles on history, traditions, music, and languages of all Celtic peoples.

Dirty Linen, P.O. Box 666000, Baltimore, MD 21239. Folk, electric folk, traditional, and world music. Website: www.dirtylinen.com

Folk Roots, Southern Rag Ltd., P.O. Box 337, London, England N4 1TW. Website: www.cityscape.co.uk/froots

The Irish Echo, 309 Fifth Avenue, New York, NY 10016. Website: www.irishecho.com

Irish Music Magazine, Marne Ltd., 11 Clare Street, Dublin 2, Ireland. Monthly traditional and folk magazine with features, club news, record reviews. Listings of worldwide Irish music festivals. Website: www.mag.irish-music.net

The Irish Post, 3rd floor, Cambridge House, Cambridge Grove, Hammersmith, London W6 0LE. Listings for Irish music and events in the U.K. Website: www.irishpost.co.uk

The Irish Voice Weekly, 432 Park Ave South, Suite 1503, New York, NY 10016. Website: www.irishvoice.com

The Living Tradition, P.O. Box 1026, Kilmarnock, Scotland KA2 0LG. Telephone 01563-571220. News, reviews, articles, and information on the traditional music, song, and dance of the British Isles.

The Scottish Banner, 5679 70th Avenue North, Pinellas Park, FL 33781. Reportedly the largest Scottish newspaper in the world, outside Scotland. Website: www.scotbanner.com

Scottish Life, 36 Highland Avenue, Hull, MA 02045. Four-color glossy quarterly magazine features articles on all aspects of Scottish life and culture. Regular columns include "Notes from the Outer Isles" by Kate Francis, "Scotland in Books" by Hamish Coghill, and "Scotland in Music" by Edward Scott Pearlman. Website: www.scottishlife.org

ARTS, MUSIC, AND HERITAGE CENTERS

Ireland

Comhaltas Ceoltoiri Eireann, Belgrave Square, Monkstown, County Dublin. Founded to promote the ancient heritage of Ireland, Comhaltas houses a valuable national archive of traditional music and song available to the general public. Website: www.Comhaltas.com

Irish Traditional Music Archive, 63 Merrion Square, Dublin. 10 a.m.–1 p.m. and 2 p.m.–5 p.m. Monday through Friday. Reference archive and resource center for the traditional song and music of Ireland. Promotes public education in Irish traditional music. Established in 1987, the archives contains sound recordings (cylinders, 78s, EPs, LPs, reel to reel tapes, audio cassettes, CDs), books, printed items (ballad sheets, chapbooks, sheet music, song collections, periodicals, programs, catalogs, postcards, leaflets, posters, clippings), photographs, drawings, prints, microfilm, videos for the appreciation and study of Irish traditional music, including all of Ireland, areas of Irish settlement (especially in Britain, North America, and Australia), and of non-Irish performers of Irish traditional music. The archive currently holds some 10,000 hours of sound recordings, 6,000 books, 3,000 ballad sheets, 3,000 ephemera, and more. Nicholas Carolan, the noted Irish music scholar and biographer of Francis O'Neill, is the director. Website: www.itma.ie

Irish World Music Centre, University of Limerick. Established in 1994 by Dr. Mícheál Ó Súilleabháin. Degrees offered at the masters and doctoral levels. Home of the Irish Chamber Orchestra; also research and performance in *sean-nós.* Concerns itself with research and innovation in Irish and Irish-related music worldwide. Dr. Súilleabháin has explored Irish, classical, jazz, and world-music connections. From 1975 to 1993 he worked in the music department of University College Cork; he also served as visiting professor at Boston College for a semester, where he founded the Archive for Traditional Music and partially funded the CD recording of *My Love Is in America.* He produced a series of five CD recordings of live traditional events held in Cork University from 1991 to 1995, including *Fiddlesticks, Dear Old Erin's Isle, Music from Cape Breton Island, Irish Traditional Music from England,* and *The Gathering—A World of Irish Music.* He also wrote and hosted *A River of Sound*, a series of seven television programs, in association with the BBC and RTE. Website: www.ul.ie/~iwmc/

Scotland

An Ceathramh, Muie East, Rogart, Sutherland 1V28 3UB. Gaelic language instruction in Scotland's far north. Website: www.cs.toronto.edu/~maclean/AnCeathramh.html

Aros, Viewfield Road, Portree, Isle of Skye IV51 9EU. Exhibition on the history and heritage of the Gael. E-mail address: aros@demon.co.uk

Balnain House of Highland Music, 40 Huntly Street, Inverness IV3 5HR. History of Highland music. Features concerts, workshops, sessions, and classes in fiddle, tinwhistle, *clarsach*, and stepdancing. The museum shop stocks Celtic music CDs and cassettes. Website: www.balnain.com

MacCrimmon Piping Heritage Centre, Boreraig, near Dunvegan, Isle of Skye. Exhibits on the MacCrimmons and the Highland bagpipe.

The Piping Centre, 30-34 McPhater Street, Cowcaddens, Glasgow G4 0HW. Promotes the study and history of piping in Scotland. National center for the instrument and its music. Housed in a handsome building near the Royal Scottish Academy of Music and Drama, the Theatre Royal, the Scottish Television studios, and the Glasgow Royal Concert Hall. Consists of a school with rehearsal rooms and a performance hall, museum and interpretive center, reference library, and conference facilities. Also accommodations, a small shop, and a cafe, The Pipers' Tryst. The Piping Centre offers tuition at all levels; day and evening classes are given on an individual or group basis. The National Museum of Piping displays a collection of piping artifacts and related items. Website: www.thepipingcentre.co.uk

Sabhal Mor Ostaig, Teangue, Sleat, Isle of Skye IV44 8RQ. Gaelic language courses at all levels. Also courses in piping, Gaelic song, fiddle, *clarsach*, stepdancing, tin whistle, accordion, and Gaelic culture. Instructors include some of the finest musicians in the pan-Celtic world, such as Buddy MacMaster from Cape Breton, Christine Primrose from Lewis, and Alison Kinnaird from Edinburgh. Website: www.smo.uhi.ac.uk

Taigh Arainn, Brodick, Isle of Arran. New Gaelic heritage and language center that opened in mid-June 1999. Houses the offices of Dalriada Celtic Heritage Trust. Website: www.dalriada.co.uk

Taigh na Gaidhlig, 24 Drumsheugh Gardens, Edinburgh. Proposed center for the Gaelic and Celtic arts. Including musical events, workshops, poetry readings, and Gaelic classes.

Isle of Man

The Story of Mann, Douglas, Isle of Man. Museum dedicated to the island's culture and heritage.

Wales

Celtica, Y Plas, Machynlleth, Montgomeryshire, Mid Wales. History and culture of the Celtic people. Website: www.celtica.wales.com

England

The Hammersmith and Fulham Irish Centre, Blacks Road, London W6 9DT. Extensive program of traditional and contemporary Irish music. London's premier center for Irish arts. Concerts plus sessions, *ceilidhs,* set dances, theater, comedy, art, exhibitions, film festivals, storytelling festivals, and workshops.

Cecil Sharp House, 2 Regents Park Road, London NW1 7AY. Home of the English Folk Dance and Song Society. Hosts weekly folk-dance and -music lessons and performances. Also has a music shop that sells traditional sheet music, recordings, and instruments. Website: www.efds.org

United States

Glucksman Ireland House, One Washington Mews, New York, NY 10003. Promotes Irish culture and the arts and serves as the center for Irish Studies at New York University. Website: www.nyu.edu/pages/irelandhouse

The Irish Arts Center, An Claidheamh Soluis, 553 West 51st Street, New York, NY 10019. Offers courses in Irish dance, music, acting, history, and language. Website: www.irishartscenter.org

Irish Music Foundation and Academy of Irish Music of Chicago, Chicago Music Mart, at DePaul Center, 333 South State Street, Chicago, IL 60604. Irish music classes. E-mail: seannos@aol.com

Canada

Father John Angus Rankin Cultural Centre, Glendale, Nova Scotia.

Nova Scotia Highland Village, Iona, Cape Breton, Nova Scotia. Living history museum of Gaelic culture in the New World. Website: www.highlandvillage.ns.ca

ORGANIZATIONS

Ireland

Folk Music Society of Ireland, 15 Henrietta Street, Dublin 1. Website: www.homepage.eircom.net/~shields/fmsi

Scotland

Scottish Music Information Centre, 1 Bowmont Gardens, Glasgow G12 9LR. Open 9.30 a.m.–5.30 p.m. weekdays except Wednesday. Founded in 1985, the centre houses the world's largest single collection of music by Scottish composers and information about Scottish music from all periods. The reference library contains scores, books, articles, microfilm, and news clippings; also a manuscript library and a recordings library. Visitors can buy, borrow, or rent music from the center. Also produces a monthly newsletter. E-mail: smic@glasgow.almac.co.uk

Traditional Music and Song Association of Scotland (TMSA), 95–97 St. Leonard's Street, Edinburgh EH8 9QY. Promotes Scottish traditional music by running festivals, *ceilidhs*, concerts, workshops, and competitions. E-mail: e.cowie@tmsa.demon.co.uk

SELECT RECORD OUTLETS AND MAIL-ORDER HOUSES

Ireland

Celtic Note, 14-15 Nassau Street, Dublin 2. Dublin's only Irish music store offers a full range of traditional, folk, *ceilidh*, country, and Scottish and Irish classical music; musical instruments, books; Irish film, documentaries, videos. Also serves as a resource center. Mail order and in-store database available for archive retrieval. Website: www.celticnote.ie

Claddagh Records, 2 Cecilia Street, Temple Bar, Dublin 2. Traditional music shop; large stock of traditional recordings on CD, LP, and tape. Also carries tin whistles and *bodhrans*, songbooks, and reference books on Irish music. Website: www.indigo.ie/~claddagh

Custy's Traditional Music Shop, Francis Street, Ennis, County Clare. Fiddles, banjos, concertinas, accordions, flutes, strings, traditional and folk tapes, CDs, books, photos, paintings, and crafts.

The Living Tradition, 40 Mac Curtain Street, Cork. Stocks Irish, Scottish, Breton, and world music. Website: www.ossian.ie

J. McNeill, 140 Capel Street, Dublin 1. Accordions, banjos, *bodhrans*, bones, *bouzoukis*, concert flutes, concertinas, fiddles, guitars, mandolas, mandolins, tin whistles, uilleann pipes, as well as books and recordings of traditional music.

McQuaid's Traditional Music Shop, 38 Pearse Street, Nenagh, County Tipperary. Stocks Irish recordings, books, and instruments.

Mulligan, 5 Middle Street Court, Middle Street, Galway. Large selection of Irish and Scottish traditional and folk music. Mail-order service too. Website: www.indigo.ie/~mulligan

Scotland

Blackfriars Music and The Bagpipe Centre, 49 Blackfriars Street, Edinburgh EH1 1NB. Folk and traditional specialists; stocks CDs, books, and instruments; also new and secondhand bagpipes. E-mail: scotfolk@compuserve.com

Coda Music, 12 Bank Street, The Mound, Edinburgh. One of four retail outlets in Scotland. Great selection of all types of Celtic music, with an emphasis on Scottish traditional and folk music. Website: www.codamusic.co.uk

Real Music, 23 Parnie Street, The Tron, Glasgow. Specializes in folk, country, bluegrass, jazz, blues, Cajun, Irish, and Scottish music.

United States

The Celtic Trader, 645-G Pressley Road, Charlotte, NC 28217. Celtic music, instruments, and accessories. Website: www.celtictrader.com

Devine Celtic Sounds, P.O. Box 5983, Glendale, AZ 85312.

Down Home Music, 6921 Stockton Street, El Cerrito, CA 94530. Website: www.downhomemusic.com

Elderly Instruments, 1100 N. Washington, Lansing, MI 48901. Website: www.elderly.com

Tayberry Music, 760 Ragin Lane, Rock Hill, SC 29730. Stocks LPs, cassettes, books, and small instruments.

SELECT RECORD LABELS

Ireland

Claddagh Records, Dame House, Dame Street, Dublin 2. Website: www.indigo.ie/~claddagh

Gael-Linn Records, 26 Merrion Square, Dublin 2. Website: www.gael-linn.ie

Tara Records, 4 Anne's Lane, Dublin 2. Website: www.taramusic.com

Scotland

Dunkeld Records, Taybank Hotel, Dunkeld, Perthshire PH8 0AW. E-mail: admin@dunkeld.co.uk. Website: www.dunkeld.co.uk

Greentrax, Cockenzie Business Park, Edinburgh Road, Cockenzie, East Lothian EH32 0HL. Website: www.greentrax@aol.com

Iona Records, 27–29 Carnoustie Place, Scotland Street, Glasgow G5 8PH.

Temple Records, Shillinghill, Temple, Midlothian EH23 4SH. Website: www.templerecords.co.uk

England

Celtic Records, 24 Mercer Row, Lough, Lincolnshire.

Fellside Recordings, 15 Banklands, Workington, Cumbria CA14 3EW.

Wales

Sain Records, Ffordd Llanllyful, Penygroes, Caenarfon, Gwynedd LL54 5TG. Website: www.sain.wales.com

United States

Arhoolie Records, 10341 San Pablo Avenue, El Cerrito, CA 94530. Website: www.arhoolie.com

Celtic Heartbeat, Atlantic Recording Corporation, 75 Rockefeller Plaza, New York, NY 10019.

Culburnie Records, P.O. Box 219, Nevada City, CA 95959. Website: www.culburnie.com

Green Linnet, 43 Beaver Brook Road, Danbury, CT 06810. Website: www.greenlinnet.com

Hannibal. Distributed by Rykodisc (see below).

Maggie's Music, P.O. Box 4144, Annapolis, MD 21403. Website: www.maggiesmusic.com

Red House Records, P.O. Box 4044, St. Paul, MN 55104.

Rounder Records, 1 Camp Street, Cambridge, MA 02140. Website: www.rounder.com

Rykodisc, Shetland Park, 27 Congress Street, Salem, MA 01970. Website: www.rykodisc.com

Shanachie Records, 37 East Clinton Street, Newton, NJ 07860. Website: www.shanachie.com

Taylor Park Music, P.O. Box 12381, North Kansas City, MO 64116.

Windham Hill Records, 8750 Wilshire Boulevard, Beverly Hills, CA 90211. Website: www.windham.com

SCHOOLS

Ireland

Early July. **Willie Clancy Summer School,** Miltown Malbay, County Clare. Ireland's largest traditional music summer school; held annually since 1973 in memory of piper Willie Clancy. Daily classes taught by experts in Irish music and dance; also lectures, recitals, *ceilidhs,* and exhibitions. All events are held in or near Miltown Malbay, starting on the first Saturday in July.

Mid-July. **BLAS. International Summer School of Traditional Irish Music and Dance,** University of Limerick. A ten-day course of lectures, tutorials, workshops, concerts, and step dancing. Website: www.musweb.com/blas

Mid-August. **Summer Harp School and Festival,** Kilmore House, Glengariff, Country Antrim, Northern Ireland. Set in the eighteenth-century ancestral home of the MacDonnells of the glens of Antrim, including the family home of Dr. James MacDonnell, one of the organizers of the Belfast Harp Festival of 1792. Consists of a comprehensive program of harp tuition, concerts, lectures, lecture-recitals, and harp repair and maintenance workshops. Under the direction of Janet Harbison.

Late August. **Scoil Eigse,** CCE, Belgrave Square, Monkstown, County Dublin. Telephone 01-280-0295. Dublin's summer school of traditional music. Includes workshops and lectures. Website: www.homepage.tinet/~lavinp/scoileg

Late December to early January. **The Frankie Kennedy Traditional Music Winter School,** Gweedore, County Donegal. A native of Belfast, the late Frankie Kennedy was one of the most influential traditional flute players in Ireland. With his wife Mairéad Ní Mhaonaigh, he formed Altan. He succumbed to Ewing's sarcoma in September 1994; a winter school devoted to teaching Irish traditional music was established by his family and friends in his memory. E-mail: gearoid@iol.ie

Scotland

Early July to early August. **The Piping Centre Summer School,** 30-34 McPhater Street, Glasgow G4 0HW. All aspects of performance on the Highland bagpipes, including practice routines, techniques, timing, and tuning. Website: www.thepipingcentre.co.uk

June, July, and August. **University of Stirling Summer Schools,** Airthrey Castle, University of Stirling, Stirling FK9 4LA. Variety of week and weekend sessions, including accordian playing, bagpipe, *clarsach,* Gaelic language, Highland and old-time Scottish country dancing, Scots fiddle, Scottish singing, and Shetland fiddle. Website: www.stir.ac.uk/daice/susschool

Early July. **Ceolas Music Summer School**, Daliburgh, South Uist. A music and dance summer school that explores the connections between Scottish traditional music, song, and dance. Crucial to the concept is a teaching philosophy that connects the music with the community and environment. Tutors from Scotland and Cape Breton offer classes in piping, fiddling, Gaelic language and song. Also house ceilidhs, community concerts, and dances. Piper Hamish Moore is the musical director. Tutors come from throughout Gaelic-speaking Scotland and Cape Breton, including pipers Dr. Angus Macdonald and Fred Morrison, step dancers Willie and Clare Fraser, Gaelic singers Catherine-Ann MacPhee and Mairi MacInnes, and fiddler Buddy MacMaster.

Late July. **Inter-Celtic Summer School, Voices of Our Kind, Adult Learning Project**, 184 Dalry Road, Edinburgh EH11 2EP. Two weeks of courses in Gaelic language, Scots fiddle, Gaelic, social dancing, piping. E-mail: embv74alp@btinternet.com

Royal Scottish Academy of Music and Dance, 100 Renfrew Street, Glasgow G2 3DB. In 1996 the RSAMD began offering a B.A. in Scottish traditional music, the first institution of higher learning in Scotland to do so. Website: www.royalscot.drama.ac.uk

United States

Late August to early September. **Valley of the Moon Scottish Fiddling School**, 1938 Rose Villa Street, Pasadena, CA 91107. Scottish fiddling from Shetland to Cape Breton. Also workshops on Cape Breton step dancing, Gaelic singing, guitar and piano accompaniment. Set among the redwoods of the Santa Cruz Mountains. Noted Scots fiddler Alasdair Fraser is the director.

Canada

The Ceilidh Trail of Celtic Music, Box 297, Inverness, Nova Scotia B0E 1N0. Offers workshops in fiddle, guitar, piano, and step dancing. Instructors include Natalie MacMaster, Buddy MacMaster, Seamus Connolly, Ashley MacIsaac, Dave MacIsaac, and John McCuster. The musical director is Cape Breton fiddler Jerry Holland. Website: www.ceilidhtrail.com

College of Piping and Celtic Performing Arts, 619 Water Street, Summerside, Prince Edward Island CIN 4H8. Highland summer concert series; short-term summer classes in step dancing, piping, and drumming. Website: www.piping.pe.ca

Gaelic College, St. Ann's, Cape Breton, Nova Scotia. Mailing address: P.O. Box 9, Baddeck, Nova Scotia B0E 1B0. Classes in all aspects of Scots Gaelic culture. E-mail: gaelcoll@atcon.com

TOURS

Keith and Rusty McNeil's Traditional Music & Dance Tour: Ireland, 16230 Van Buren Blvd., Riverside, CA 92504.

Mick Moloney's Irish Folklore Tours, Hemisphere Travel Service, 5 Washington Street, Biddeford, ME 04005.

GENERAL WEBSITES

Celticmusic.com. On-line magazine.

Ceolas. Independent, voluntary organization dedicated to promoting Celtic music by supplying information on all aspects of the genre through the internet. Listings include musicians, mail-order sources, and events guides. Many useful links. Website: www.ceolas.org

Every Celtic Thing on the Web. Description just about covers it. Huge range of listings, including links to sites relating to all branches of Celtic nationalities, mailing lists, magazines, musicians, newsgroups, and records. Website: www. og-man.net

Irish Music Net. Music industry directory; useful listings of events and festivals, with contact names and numbers. Website: www.imn.ie

Rec.music.celtic. Discussion forum for all issues relating to Celtic music. Website: www.collins-peak.co.uk/rmc

A Pan-Celtic Glossary

Aisling Irish mystical vision poem; usually features a woman who represents Ireland.

Aroon My darling.

Bard Poet and musician; composer and performer of laments, eulogies, and songs of praise.

Biniou A one-droned, mouth-blown Breton bagpipe.

Bodhran (bow-RAHN) Handheld Irish war drum, played with a small stick or the hand.

Bombarde Traditional Breton instrument that sounds similar to an oboe.

Border bagpipes Bellows-blown pipes with three drones.

Bothy ballad Work songs written by laborers who lived in the bothies or farm cottages in Scotland's northeast.

Bouzouki Plucked string instrument of Greek origin; increasingly popular with Irish musicians.

Box Slang for accordion.

Broadside Sheet of paper printed on a single side.

Brosnachadh Gaelic poetic incitement to battle.

Canntaireachd Ancient system of Highland bagpipe notation.

Cauld wind pipes Scottish bellows-blown Lowland bagpipes.

Caoine (keen) Death song, lament.

Ceilidh (also spelled ceili) Informal gathering; communal dance.

Ceol beg "Little music"; dance music of the Highland bagpipes.

Ceol mor "Big music"; applied to the music of the *pibroch*.

Clarsach Scottish harp.

Cranning Series of successive grace notes executed with different fingers.

Crwth Traditional Welsh harp.

Drove roads Routes by which cattle and sheep were brought to markets in central Scotland.

Eisteddfod Welsh music and cultural festival.

Erin go bragh "Ireland forever."

Fest-oz Breton dance or *ceilidh*.

Fili Poet. In pre-Christian Ireland, the *fili* were court genealogists, seers, and judges.

Fleadh Irish music festival.

Flyting Satirical poetic contest between bards.

Gaeltacht (also spelled *Gaidhealtachd*) Area where the Irish or Scots Gaelic language is spoken.

Gaita Galician bagpipes.

Granuaille Grace O'Malley, sixteenth-century Queen of Clare; a metaphor for Ireland.

Ground A slow melody (see Urlar).

Gue Early Shetland fiddle played on or between the knees.

Hardanger Norwegian fiddle that imitates the effect of "ringing strings"; the style is also popular in Shetland.

Highland bagpipes Reed instrument with three drones and an open chanter; air blown from the mouth through a bag held under the arm.

Hornpipe Traditional dance or tune in 4/4 time but played slower than reels; of English origin.

Jig Traditional dance or tune in 6/8 time.

Kan ha diskan Unaccompanied Breton dance songs performed in a call-and-response style.

Lowland bagpipes Bellows-blown bagpipes; similar to the Northumbrian and Irish uilleann pipes.

Makar Scots for "poet."

Mouth music See *Port-a-beul*.

Northumbrian pipes Small bagpipes from Northumberland (formerly known as Northumbria), the northernmost county in England.

Ogam Ancient Celtic alphabet.

Oran mor "Big song"; traditional ballads.

Piobaireachd (pibroch) "Pipe music"; the classical music of the Highland bagpipe. The *pibroch* refers to a lone tune with variations.

Planxty   Praise piece.

Port-a-beul   Translated as "mouth music"; instrumental music sung to words that are usually nonsense syllables.

Reel   Traditional dance or tune in 4/4 time.

Scots snap   Rhythmic device in which a short accented note on the beat precedes a longer note to produce a pronounced staccato effect.

Seanchai   Storyteller. In ancient Ireland, these poets held the lowest position amid the Druidic hierarchy.

Sean-nós   Traditional singing in the Irish language; means "old style."

Session   Informal gathering of musicians, usually held in a pub.

Set   Traditional group dance.

Show bands   Irish dance bands that played the popular hits of the day.

Slip jig   Folk dance or tune in 9/8 time.

Spirituals   Hymn texts set to folk melodies.

Step dancing   Traditional solo or group dancing. Considered the height of traditional Irish and Scottish dancing. Principal set dances are the jig, reel, and hornpipe.

Strathspey   A style of music, unique to Scotland, featuring the instantly recognizable Scots snap; a distinctive staccato effect; similar to a slow reel.

Triple harp   Traditional Welsh harp.

Tuath   Tribe, clan, or sept.

Uilleann pipes   Irish bellows-blown bagpipes.

Urlar   "Ground"; the theme at the beginning of a *pibroch*.

Waulking song   Scottish work song that employs alternating chorus and solo lines traditionally sung by women in the western Highlands when *waulking* or shrinking cloth.

Further Reading

Acton, Charles. *Irish Music and Musicians*. Dublin: Irish Heritage Series, 1978.

Alarik, Scott. "Solitude vs. Solicitude: The Music of Gordon Bok." *Sing Out* 36, no. 4 (February, March, April 1992): 2–9.

Armstrong, William A. *The Armstrong Ballads*. Edinburgh: Clan Armstrong Trust, 1989.

Bargainneer, Earl F. "Tin Pan Alley and Dixie: The South in Popular Song." *Mississippi Quarterly*, 30 (fall 1977): 527–75.

Barraclough, Nick. "Appalachian Swing" in *World Music: The Rough Guide*. Edited by Simon Broughton, Mark Ellingham, David Muddyman, and Richard Trillo. London: Rough Guides, 1994.

Bassin, Ethel. *The Old Songs of Skye: Frances Tolmie and Her Circle*. London: Routledge & Kegan Paul, 1977.

Bateman, Meg. "Gaelic Women Poets." In *An Anthology of Scottish Women Poets*. Edited by Catherine Kerrigan. Edinburgh: Edinburgh University Press, 1991.

Bayor, Ronald H., and Timothy J. Meagher, eds. *The New York Irish*. Baltimore, Md.: Johns Hopkins University Press, 1996.

Becker, Roland, and Laure Le Gurun. *La musique bretonne*. Spezet: Coop Breizh, 1994.

Bennett, Margaret. *The Last Stronghold: Scottish Gaelic Traditions in Newfoundland*. St. John's, Nwfld: Breakwater Books, 1989.

Berresford Ellis, Peter. *Celtic Dawn: Celtic Survival in the Modern World*. London: Constable, 1993.

Bianchi, Anne, and Adrienne Gusoff. *Music Lover's Guide to Great Britain & Ireland: Guide to the Best Venues, Festivals & Events*. Lincolnwood, Ill.: Passport Books, 1996.

Bold, Alan. *The Ballad*. London: Methuen & Co., 1979.

Boydell, Brian, ed. *Four Centuries of Music in Ireland*. London: British Broadcasting Corporation, 1979.

Brand, Oscar. *The Ballad Mongers: Rise of the Modern Folk Song*. New York: Funk and Wagnalls, 1962.

Brander, Michael. *Scottish and Border Battles and Ballads*. New York: Clarkson N. Potter, 1976.

Breathnach, Breandan. *Folk Music and Dances of Ireland*. Cork: Mercier Press, 1977.

Bronson, Bertrand. "Mrs. Brown and the Ballad." *California Folklore Quarterly* IV (1945): 129–40.

Bronson, Bertrand H., ed. *The Traditional Tunes of the Child Ballads*. 4 vols. Princeton, N.J.: Princeton University Press, 1959–1972.

_____, ed. *The Singing Tradition of Child's Popular Ballads*. Princeton, N.J.: Princeton University Press, 1976.

Bruford, Alan. "The Grey Selkie." *Scottish Studies* 18 (1984): 63–81.

Buchan, David. *The Ballad and the Folk*. Booklet. London: Routledge and Kegan Paul, 1972.

Cameron, David Kerr. *The Ballad and the Plough: A Portrait of Life in the Old Scottish Farmtouns*. London: Futura Publications, 1978.

Campbell, Angus Peter. *The Blood Is Strong*. Booklet. London: Channel Four Television, 1988.

Campbell, John Lorne. *Songs Remembered in Exile*. Aberdeen: Aberdeen University Press, 1990.

Campbell, John Lorne, and Francis Collinson, eds. *Hebridean Folksongs: A Collection of Waulking Songs*. Oxford: Clarendon Press, 1969.

Campsie, Alistair. *The MacCrimmon Legend: The Madness of Angus Mackay*. Edinburgh: Canongate Publishing, 1980.

Cannon, Roderick. *The Highland Bagpipe and Its Music*. Edinburgh: John Donald, 1988.

Cantwell, Robert. *Bluegrass Breakdown: The Making of the Old Southern Sound*. Urbana, Ill.: University of Illinois Press, 1984.

_____. *When We Were Good: The Folk Revival*. Cambridge, Mass.: Harvard University Press, 1996.

Carmichael, Alexander, ed. *Carmina Gadelica: Hymns and Incantations*. Edinburgh: Scottish Academic Press, 1983.

Carolan, Nicholas. *A Short Discography of Irish Folk Music*. Folk Music Society of Ireland, 1987.

_____. *A Harvest Saved: Francis O'Neill and Irish Music in Chicago*. Cork: Ossian Publications, 1997.

Carr, Patrick, ed. *The Illustrated History of Country Music*. New York: Random House/Times Books, 1995.

Carson, Ciaran. *Last Night's Fun: In and Out of Time with Irish Music*. New York: North Point Press, 1997.

Chambers, Robert. *The Scottish Ballads*. Edinburgh: W. Tait, 1829.

Chapman, Malcolm. *The Gaelic Vision in Scottish Culture*. London: Croom Helm, 1978.

Chappell, William. *Popular Music of the Olden Time*. London: Cramer, Beale, & Chappell, 1859.

Cheape, Hugh. *Tartan: The Highland Habit*. Edinburgh: National Museums of Scotland, 1991.

Child, Francis James, ed. *The English and Scottish Popular Ballads*. 5 vols. Boston, 1882–1898.

Clark, Alastair. *Aly Bain: Fiddler on the Loose*. Edinburgh: Mainstream Publishing, 1993.

Clarke, Donald, ed. *The Penguin Encyclopedia of Popular Music*. London: Penguin Books, 1990.

Coffin, Tristram P. "Mary Hamilton and the Anglo-American Ballad as an Art Form." *Journal of American Folklore*, vol. 70 (1957): 208–14.

_____. *The British Traditional Ballad in North America*. Austin, Tex.: University of Texas Press, 1977.

Cohen, Norm. "Tin Pan Alley's Contribution to Folk Music." *Western Folklore* 29, no. 1 (1970): 9–20.

_____. *Long Steel Rail: The Railroad in American Folksong*. Urbana, Ill.: University of Illinois Press, 1981.

Collinson, Francis. *Bagpipe, Fiddle, and Harp*. Newtongrange, Scotland: Lang Syne, 1983.

_____, ed. *Hebridean Folk-songs*. Oxford: Clarendon Press, 1969.

_____. *Traditional and National Music of Scotland*. London: Routledge and Kegan Paul, 1966.

Collis, John. *Van Morrison: Inarticulate Speech of the Heart*. New York: Da Capo Press, 1997.

The Complete Works of O'Carolan. Cork: Ossian Publications, 1989.

Cooke, Peter. *The Fiddle Tradition of the Shetland Isles*. Edinburgh: John Donald, 1988.

Corbett, John. "We are not the world: Getting a handle on music's catch-all label." *Chicago Tribune*, January 15, 1995.

Cowan, Edward J., ed. *The People's Past: Scottish Folk, Scottish History*. Edinburgh: Polygon, 1991.

Crawford, Richard, ed. *The Civil War Songbook*. New York: Dover, 1977.

Creighton, Helen, coll. *Songs and Ballads from Nova Scotia*. New York: Dover Publications, 1966.

Cunningham, Rodger. *Apples on the Flood: Minority Discourse and Appalachia*. Knoxville, Tenn.: University of Tennessee Press, 1987.

Curtis, P.J. *Notes from the Heart: A Celebration of Traditional Irish Music*. Dublin: Torc, 1994.

Daiches, David, ed. *New Companion to Scottish Culture*. Edinburgh: Polygon, 1993.

Darling, Cary. "Singer's Gaelic accent touches wide-range." *Chicago Tribune*, July 13, 1995.

Davie, Cedric Thorpe. *Scotland's Music*. Edinburgh: William Blackwood, 1980.

Davis, Arthur Kyle, Jr. *Traditional Ballads of Virginia*. Cambridge, Mass.: Harvard University Press, 1929.

Dawidoff, Nicholas. *In the Country of Country: A Journey to the Roots of American Music*. New York: Vintage, 1997.

Dean, Pamela. *Tam Lin*. New York: Tor, 1991.

Delanty, Greg. *American Wake*. Belfast: Blackstaff Press, 1995.

Denisoff, R. Serge. *Great Day Coming: Folk Music and the American Left*. Urbana, Ill.: University of Illinois Press, 1971.

Doherty, Liz. "The Music of Cape Breton: An Irish Perspective." Ó Riada Memorial Lecture 9. Cork: Traditional Music Archive and Irish Traditional Music Society, 1994.

Donaldson, William. *The Jacobite Song: Political Myth and National Identity*. Aberdeen: Aberdeen University Press, 1988.

_____. "Bonny Highland Laddie: The Making of a Myth." *Scottish Literary Journal*, vol. 3, no. 2 (December 1976): 30–50.

Dressler, Camille. *Eigg: The Story of an Island*. Edinburgh: Polygon, 1998.

Duggan, G.C. *The Stage Irishman: A History of the Irish Play and Stage Characters from the Earliest Times*. London: Longman's Green, 1937.

Duignan-Cabrera, Anthony. "Celtic Inc." *Entertainment Weekly*, March 20, 1998.

Dunlay, Kate. "A Cape Breton Primer: Canada's Old World Music." *Sing Out!* 34, no. 4 (fall 1989): 24–29.

Dunlay, Kate, and D.L. Reich. *Traditional Celtic Fiddle Music of Cape Breton*. East Alstead, N.H.: Fiddlecase Books, 1986.

Dunn, Charles W. *Highland Settler: A Portrait of the Scottish Gael in Nova Scotia*. Toronto: University of Toronto Press, 1953.

Dunson, Josh. *Freedom in the Air: Song Movements of the '60s*. New York: International, 1965.

Elliott, Kenneth, and Frederick Rimmer. *A History of Scottish Music*. London: BBC Books, 1973.

Emmerson, George S. *Rantin' Pipe and Tremblin' String: A History of Scottish Dance Music*. London: J.M. Dent & Son, 1971.

Epstein, Dena J. *Sinful Tunes and Spirituals*. Urbana, Ill.: University of Illinois Press, 1977.

Faolain, Turlough. *Blood on the Harp: Irish Rebel History in Ballad (The Heritage)*. Troy, N.Y.: Whitston Publishing, 1983.

Farmer, George Henry. *A History of Music in Scotland*. London: Hinrichsen Edition Ltd., 1947.

Ferris, William, and Charles R. Wilson, eds. *Encyclopedia of Southern Culture*. Chapel Hill, N.C.: University of North Carolina Press, 1989.

Finson, Jon W. *The Voices That Are Gone: Themes in Nineteenth-Century American Popular Song*. New York: Oxford University Press, 1994.

Fischer, David Hackett. *Albion's Seed: Four British Folkways in America*. New York: Oxford University Press, 1989.

Fiske, Roger. *Scotland in Music*. Cambridge: Cambridge University Press, 1983.

Flannery, James W. *Thomas Moore: Minstrel of Ireland*. Liner notes. Atlanta, November 1989.

_____. *Dear Harp of My Country: The Irish Melodies of Thomas Moore*. Nashville, Tenn.: J. S. Sanders & Company, 1997. (Includes two compact discs).

Flynn, Arthur. *Irish Dance*. Gretna, La.: Pelican Publishing, 1998.

Ford, Robert, ed. *Vagabond Songs and Ballads of Scotland*. Paisley, Scotland: A. Gardner, 1899.

Fowler, David C. *A Literary History of the Popular Ballad*. Durham, N.C.: Duke University Press, 1968.

Fraser, George MacDonald. *The Steel Bonnets: The Story of the Anglo-Scottish Border Reivers*. London: Harvill, 1971.

Frazer, Sir James George. *The Golden Bough: A Study in Magic and Religion*. 1 vol. Abridged ed. New York: Macmillan Publishing, 1963.

Friedman, Albert, ed. *The Viking Book of Folk Ballads of the English-Speaking World*. New York: Viking Press, 1956.

_____. *The Ballad Revival: Studies in the Influence of Popular on Sophisticated Poetry*. Chicago: University of Chicago Press, 1961.

Gammond, Peter. *The Harmony Illustrated Encyclopedia of Classical Music.* New York: Harmony Books, 1989.

Gantz, Jeffrey, trans. with introduction and notes. *Early Irish Myths and Sagas.* New York: Viking Penguin, 1986.

Gibson, John G. *Traditional Gaelic Piping, 1745–1945.* Montreal: McGill-Queen's University Press, 1998.

Gibson, Rob, and Dave Dewar. "Songs of the Cowboy Celts." *The Living Tradition,* June-July 1998, 28–31.

Glasser, Howard. "Ray Fisher: A Tremendous Sort of Feeling." *Sing Out!* 22, no. 6 (1974) 2–8.

Glatt, John. *The Chieftains: The Authorized Biography.* New York: St. Martin's Press, 1997.

Golway, Terry, and Michael Coffey. *The Irish in America.* New York: Hyperion, 1997.

Green, Archie. "Hillbilly Music: Source and Symbol." *Journal of American Folklore* 78 (July-September 1965).

———. "The Singing Cowboy: An American Dream." *Journal of Country Music* 7 (May 1978): 4–61.

Green, Douglas B. *Country Roots: The Origins of Country Music.* New York: Hawthorn, 1976.

Greenway, John. *American Folksongs of Protest.* Philadelphia: University of Pennsylvania Press, 1953.

Greig, Gavin. *Last Leaves of Traditional Ballads and Ballad Airs.* Edited by Alexander Keith. Aberdeen: University of Aberdeen, 1925.

Grossman, James R., ed. *The Frontier in American Culture.* Berkeley, Calif. and Chicago.: University of California Press and The Newberry Library, 1994.

Gummere, F.B. *The Popular Ballad.* Boston: Houghton, Mifflin & Co., 1907.

Haldane, A. B. *The Drove Roads of Scotland.* Edinburgh: Birlinn, 1997.

Harris, Bernard, and Grattan Freyer, eds. *Integrating Tradition: The Achievement of Seán Ó Riada.* Chester Springs, Penn.: Dufour Editions, 1981.

Haugen, Einar, and Camilla Cai. *Ole Bull: Norway's Romantic Musician and Cosmopolitan Patriot.* Madison, Wis.: University of Wisconsin Press, 1993.

Henderson, Hamish. *Alias MacAlias: Writings on Songs, Folk, and Literature.* Edinburgh: Polygon, 1992.

Herd, David, ed. *Ancient and Modern Scottish Songs, Heroic Ballads, Etc.* Edinburgh: Scottish Academic Press, 1973.

Hill, Christopher. "White Soul Music: A New Generation of Country Rockers." *Chicago Reader,* July 11, 1986.

Hogg, Brian. *The History of Scottish Rock and Pop: All That Ever Mattered.* Middlesex, England: Guinness Publishing, 1993.

Humphrey, Mark. "Alan Stivell. Celtic Harp: Soul of the Western World." *Frets Magazine,* October 1985.

Hunter, James. *The Fiddle Music of Scotland.* Edinburgh: Hardie Press, 1988.

———. *On the Other Side of Sorrow: Nature and People in the Scottish Highlands.* Edinburgh: Mainstream Publishing, 1995.

Ignatiev, Noel. *How the Irish Became White.* New York: Routledge, 1995.

Ireland, Liz. "No holds barred." *New City,* March 13, 1997.

Irwin, Colin. "The Curse of the White Heather Club" in *World Music: The Rough Guide*. Edited by Simon Broughton, Mark Ellingham, David Muddyman, and Richard Trillo. London: Rough Guides, 1994.

_____. "The New English Roots" in *World Music: The Rough Guide*. Edited by Simon Broughton, Mark Ellingham, David Muddyman, and Richard Trillo. London: Rough Guides, 1994.

Jackson, George Pullen. *White Spirituals in the Southern Uplands*. Chapel Hill, N.C.: University of North Carolina Press, 1933; reprint, 1965.

Jamieson, Robert, ed. *Popular Ballads and Songs from Tradition*. Edinburgh: A. Constable & Co., 1806.

Johnson, David. *Scottish Fiddle Music in the 18th Century*. Edinburgh: John Donald Publishers, 1984.

_____. *Music and Society in Lowland Scotland in the 18th Century*. Oxford: Oxford University Press, 1972.

Jones, Loyal. *Radio's "Kentucky Mountain Boy" Bradley Kincaid*. Berea, Ky.: Berea College Appalachian Center, 1980.

_____. *Minstrel of the Appalachians: The Story of Bascom Lamar Lunsford*. Boone, N.C.: Appalachian Consortium Press, 1984.

Kay, Peter, comp. *A Jacobite Legacy: From Bonnie Dundee to Bonnie Prince Charlie*. Loughborough, England: Soar Valley Music, April 1995.

Kennedy, Peter, ed. *Folk Songs of Britain and Ireland*. London: Oak Publications, 1984.

Kennedy-Fraser, Marjory. *A Life of Song*. London: Oxford University Press, 1929.

Kerrigan, Catherine, ed. With Gaelic translations by Meg Bateman. *An Anthology of Scottish Women Poets*. Edinburgh: Edinburgh University Press, 1991.

Kinnaird, Alison, and Keith Sanger. *Tree of Strings/Crann Nan Teud*. Midlothian, Scotland: Kinmor Music, 1992.

Kittredge, George L., and Child Sargent, Helen, eds. *English and Scottish Popular Ballads*. Boston, 1905.

Klein, Joe. *Woody Guthrie*. New York: Knopf, 1980.

Krassen, Miles, and Larry McCullough. "Irish Traditional Instrumental Music from Chicago." Liner notes. Rounder Records, 1975–76.

Kuter, Lois. *Guide to Music in Brittany*. Publication Series no. 7. Jenkintown, Penn.: U.S. Branch of the International Committee for the Defense of the Breton Language (ICDBL), November 1990.

Lang, Andrew. *Sir Walter Scott and the Border Minstrelsy*. New York: AMS Press, 1968.

Laxton, Edward. *The Famine Ships: The Irish Exodus to America*. New York: Henry Holt and Company, 1996.

Lockhart, G. W. *Fiddles & Folk: A Celebration of the Re-Emergence of Scotland's Musical Heritage*. Edinburgh: Luath Press, 1998.

_____. *Highland Balls and Village Halls*. Edinburgh: Luath Press, 1997.

Lomax, Alan. "Bluegrass Background: Folk Music with Overdrive." *Esquire*, October 1959.

_____. *The Penguin Book of American Folk Songs*. Baltimore: Penguin, 1964.

_____. *The Folk Songs of North America*. New York: Doubleday, 1960.

Lomax, John A. *Cowboy Songs and Other Frontier Ballads*. New York: Sturgis and Walton, 1910.

_____. *Adventures of a Ballad Hunter*. New York: Macmillan, 1947.

Lomax, John A., and Alan Lomax. *Folk Song U.S.A.* New York: New American Library, 1975.

Low, Donald A., ed. *The Songs of Robert Burns*. London: Routledge, 1993.

Lyle, Emily, ed. *Scottish Ballads*. Edinburgh: Canongate Press, 1994.

McCabe, Carol. "Cape Breton: Where the Music Never Ends." *Islands*, October 1995.

McCabe, John. *George M. Cohan: The Man Who Owned Broadway*. Garden City, N.Y.: Doubleday, 1973.

McCauley, Deborah Vansau. *Appalachian Mountain Religion: A History*. Urbana, Ill.: University of Illinois Press, 1995.

MacColl, Ewan. "The Radio Ballads." *Sing Out!* 17, no. 2 (April/May 1967): 6–15.

MacColl, Ewan, and Peggy Seeger. *Til Doomsday in the Afternoon: The Folklore of Scots Travellers, the Stewarts of Blairgowrie*. Dover, N.H.: Manchester University Press, 1977.

McCrumb, Sharyn. *Foggy Mountain Breakdown and Other Stories*. New York: Ballantine Books, 1997.

McCullough, Lawrence. "Irish Music in Chicago: An Ethnomusicological Study" (diss., University of Pittsburgh, 1978).

_____. "An Historical Sketch of Traditional Irish Music in the U.S." *Folklore Forum* 7, no. 3 (1974).

MacDonell, Margaret. *The Emigrant Experience: Songs of Highland Emigrants in North America*. Toronto: University of Toronto Press, 1982.

MacEachen, Frances. "Eighteenth century rock 'n roll." *Am Braighe*, Autumn 1994.

MacInnes, Sheldon. *A Journey in Celtic Music—Cape Breton Style*. Sydney, N.S.: University College of Cape Breton Press, 1997.

McKay, Ian. *The Quest of the Folk: Antimodernism and Cultural Selection in Twentieth-Century Nova Scotia*. Montreal: McGill-Queen's University Press, 1994.

McKay, Ian L. *The Art of Piobaireachd*. New Zealand: Comunn na Piobaireachd, 1997.

McLaughlin, Dermot. "Donegal and Shetland Fiddle Music." Ó Riada Memorial Lecture 7. Cork: Irish Traditional Music Society, 1992.

McLean, Duncan. *Lone Star Swing: On the Trail of Bob Wills and his Texas Playboys*. London: Jonathan Cape, 1997.

Maclean, Sorley, George Campbell Hay, Iain Crichton Smith, Derick Thomson, Donald MacAulay. *Modern Scottish Gaelic Poems: A Bilingual Anthology*. Edinburgh: Canongate Press, 1987.

MacLeod, Alistair. *As Birds Bring Forth the Sun*. Toronto: McClelland and Stewart, 1986.

_____. *No Great Mischief*. Toronto: McClelland and Stewart,, 1999.

MacLeod, Morag. "Folk Revival in Gaelic Song." In Ailie Munro, *The Democratic Muse: Folk Music Revival in Scotland*. Aberdeen: Scottish Cultural Press, 1996: 124–37.

MacNaughton, Adam. "Hamish Henderson—Folk Hero." *Chapman* 42 (1985): 22–29.

MacNeill, Seumas. *Piobaireachd: Classical Music of the Highland Bagpipe*. Edinburgh: BBC, 1968.

McWhiney, Grady. *Cracker Culture: Celtic Ways in the Old South*. Tuscaloosa, Ala.: University of Alabama Press, 1988.

Malone, Bill C. *Southern Music, American Music*. Lexington, Ky.: University of Kentucky Press, 1979.

_____. *Country Music U.S.A.* Austin, Tex.: University of Texas Press, 1985.

_____ *Singing Cowboys and Musical Mountaineers: Southern Culture and the Roots of Country Music*. Athens, Ga.: University of Georgia Press, 1993.

Manson, W. L. *Tunes of Glory: Stories, History, Traditions, Music, and Humour of the Highland Bagpipe*. Glasgow: Lang Syne Publishers, 1992.

Marcus, Greil. *Mystery Train: Images of America in Rock 'n' Roll Music*. New York: E.P. Dutton & Co., 1976.

Marsden, John. *The Illustrated Border Ballads: The Anglo-Scottish Frontier*. Austin, Tex.: University of Texas Press, 1990.

Matheson, William, ed. *The Blind Harper (An Clarsair Dall): The Songs of Roderick Morison and his Music*. Edinburgh: Scottish Gaelic Texts Society, 1970.

Mathieu, Joan. *Zulu: An Irish Journey*. New York: Farrar, Straus, and Giroux, 1998.

Meek, Bill. *Paddy Moloney and the Chieftains*. Dublin: Gill and Macmillan, 1987.

Miller, Jim, ed. *The Rolling Stone Illustrated History of Rock & Roll*. New York: Random House, 1976.

Miller, Kerby A. *Emigrants and Exiles: Ireland and the Irish Exodus to North America*. New York: Oxford University Press, 1985.

Miller, Kerby, and Paul Wagner. *Out of Ireland: The Story of Irish Emigration*. Washington, D.C.: Eliott and Clark, 1994.

Miller, Rebecca S. "Irish Traditional and Popular Music in New York City: Identity and Social Change, 1930–1975." In *The New York Irish*. Edited by Ronald H. Bayor and Timothy J. Meagher. Baltimore, Md.: Johns Hopkins University Press, 1996.

Moloney, Mick. "Irish Music on the American Stage." Ó Riada Memorial Lecture 8. Cork, Ireland: Irish Traditional Music Society, 1993.

Moreton, Cole. *Hungry for Home: Leaving the Blaskets: A Journey from the Edge of Ireland*. New York: Viking, 2000.

Morton, Tom. *Going Home: The Runrig Story*. Edinburgh: Mainstream Publishing, 1991.

Motherwell, Robert, ed. *Minstrelsy: Ancient and Modern*. Glasgow: J. Wylie, 1827.

Moulden, John, comp. *Thousands Are Sailing: A Brief Song History of Irish Emigration*. County Antrim, Northern Ireland: Ulstersongs, 1994.

Mueller, Karen R. "Meet Wales' Outspoken Triple Harper: Robin Huw Bowen." *Dirty Linen*, October/November 1990.

Munro, Ailie. *The Democratic Muse: Folk Music Revival in Scotland*. Aberdeen: Scottish Cultural Press, 1996.

_____. "The Role of the School of Scottish Studies in the Folk Music Revival." *Folk Music Journal* 6 (2): 132–68, 1991.

Nettl, Bruno. *Folk Music in the United States: An Introduction*. Detroit, Mich.: Wayne State University Press, 1976.

O Baoill, Colm. *Poems and Songs of Sileas MacDonald*. Edinburgh: Scottish Academic Press for the Scottish Gaelic Texts Society, 1972.

O Boyle, Sean. *The Irish Song Tradition*. Cork: Ossian Publications, 1976.

O Canainn, Tomas. *Traditional Music in Ireland*. Cork: Ossian Publications, 1993.

O'Connor, Nuala. *Bringing It All Back Home: The Influence of Irish Music*. London: BBC Books, 1991.

_____. "Irish Soul" in *World Music: The Rough Guide*. Edited by Simon Broughton, Mark Ellingham, David Muddyman, and Richard Trillo. London: Rough Guides, 1994.

O'Driscoll, Robert, ed. *The Celtic Consciousness*. New York: George Braziller, 1982.

Ó hAllmhuráin, Gearóid. *A Pocket History of Irish Traditional Music*. Dublin: O'Brien Press, 1998.

O'Neill, Francis. *Irish Minstrels and Musicians: The Story of Irish Music*. Cork: Mercier Press, 1987.

Ord, John, ed. *Bothy Songs and Ballads*. Edinburgh, 1990.

O'Sullivan, Donald. *Carolan: The Life, Times, and Music of an Irish Harper*. 2 vols. London: Routledge and Kegan Paul, 1958.

O'Toole, Fintan. *The Ex-Isle of Erin: Images of Global Ireland*. Dublin: New Island Books, 1997.

Patterson, Beverly Bush. *The Sound of the Dove: Singing in Appalachian Primitive Baptist Churches*. Urbana, Ill.: University of Illinois Press, 1995. Accompanied by a cassette.

Pegg, Bob. *Rites and Riots: Folk Customs of Britain and Europe*. Poole, England: Blandford Press, 1981.

Percy, Thomas. ed. *Reliques of Ancient English Poetry: consisting of Old Heroic Ballads, Songs, and other pieces of our Earlier Poets, together with some few of later date*. London, 1765. Reprint. New York: Dover, 1966.

Peterson, Richard A. *Creating Country Music: Fabricating Authenticity*. Chicago: University of Chicago Press, 1997.

Porter, James, and Herschel Gower. *Jeannie Robertson: Emergent Singer, Transformative Voice*. Knoxville, Tenn.: University of Tennessee Press, 1995.

Prendergast, Mark J. *Irish Rock: Roots, Personalities, Directions*. Dublin: O'Brien Press, 1987.

Price, William, and Chris Sharratt. "Harps, Bards, and Punks" in *World Music: The Rough Guide*. Edited by Simon Broughton, Mark Ellingham, David Muddyman, and Richard Trillo. London: Rough Guides, 1994.

Purser, John. *Scotland's Music: A History of the Traditional and Classical Music of Scotland from Early Times to the Present Day*. Edinburgh: Mainstream Publishing in conjunction with BBC Scotland, 1992.

Rammel, Hal. *Nowhere in America: The Big Rock Candy Mountain and Other Comic Utopias*. Urbana, Ill.: University of Illinois Press, 1990.

Ratcliffe, Sam D. "The American Cowboy: A Note on the Development of a Musical Image." JEMF Quarterly 20 (Spring-Summer 1984).

Reed, James. *The Border Ballads*. London: Athlone Press, 1973.

Reed, John Shelton. *One South: An Ethnic Approach to Regional Culture*. Baton Rouge, La.: Louisiana State University Press, 1982.

_____. *Southern Folk Plain and Fancy: Native White Social Types*. Lamar Memorial Lectures No. 29. Athens, Ga.: University of Georgia Press, 1986.

_____. *Whistling Dixie: Dispatches from the South*. San Diego, Calif.: Harcourt Brace Jovanovich, 1990.

Reilly, Charlie. *Ballads and Ballast*. Philadelphia: Clydewater Publishers, 1995.

Rimmer, Joan. *The Irish Harp*. Cork: Mercier Press, 1984.

Ritchie, Jean. *Singing Family of the Cumberlands*. New York: Oak Publications, 1963.

Ritson, Joseph, ed. *Scotish Song*. Glasgow: Hugh Hopkins, 1869.

Rosenberg, Neil V. *Bluegrass: A History*. Urbana, Ill.: University of Illinois Press, 1985.

Rosenberg, Neil V., ed. *Transforming Tradition: Folk Music Revivals Examined*. Urbana, Ill.: University of Illinois Press, 1993.

Ross, Betsy Marlene. "Writings about Scotland's Music: An Annotated Bibliography" (diss., Claremont Graduate School, 1993).

Sandburg, Carl. *The American Songbag*. New York: Harvest/Harcourt, Brace, Jovanovich, 1990.

Sargent, Helen, and George L. Kittredge. *English and Scottish Popular Ballads*. Boston: Houghton Mifflin, 1932.

Sawyers, June Skinner. "The Blues and the Greys: Songs of the Civil War." *Sing Out!* 36, vol. 3 (November/December 1991–January 1992): 2–13.

_____. *The Celtic Roots of Southern Music*. Booklet. Morgantown, W.V.: Unicorn Ltd., 1994.

_____. "Dougie Maclean: A Quiet Side of Scotland." *Sing Out!* 34, no. 4 (fall 1989): 11–19.

_____. "Faithful Hearts and Gentle Lovers: The Romantic Impulse in the Songs of Andy M. Stewart." *Scottish Tradition* 21 (1996).

_____. "A New Day Dawning: The Struggle for National Identity in Contemporary Scottish Song." *Scottish Tradition* 19 (1994): 1–23.

_____. "The pipes are calling: Charting the influence of the lastest musical hybrid, Celtic rock." *Chicago Tribune*, December 10, 1989.

_____. "Jean Redpath and the Soul of Scotland." *Come For To Sing* 11, no. 3 (Summer 1985): 16–18.

Scaduto, Anthony. *Bob Dylan: An Intimate Biography*. New York: Grosset, 1971.

Scarborough, Dorothy. *A Song Catcher in Southern Mountains: American Folk Songs of British Ancestry*. New York: Columbia University Press, 1937.

Schrier, Arnold. *Ireland and the American Emigration 1850–1900*. Chester Springs, Penn.: Dufour Editions, 1997.

Scott, Paul, ed. *Scotland: A Concise Cultural History*. Edinburgh: Mainstream Publishing, 1993.

Scott, Sir Walter. *Minstrelsy of the Scottish Border.* 3 vols. Kelso and Edinburgh, 1802–1803. Reprint. Edinburgh: Blackwood, 1902.

Scottish Music Handbook 1996. Glasgow: Scottish Music Information Centre, 1995.

Shapiro, Herbert D. *Appalachia on My Mind: The Southern Mountains and Mountaineers in the American Consciousness, 1870–1920.* Chapel Hill, N.C.: University of North Carolina Press, 1978.

Sharp, Cecil J. *English Folk Song: Some Conclusions.* Revised by Maud Karpeles, eds. Belmont, Calif.: Wadsworth, 1965.

Sharp, Cecil J., and Maud Karpeles, eds. *English Folk Songs from the Southern Appalachians.* 2 vols. London: Oxford University Press, 1932.

Shaw, Margaret Fay. *Folksongs and Folklore of South Uist.* Oxford: Oxford University Press, 1977.

Shepard, Leslie. *The Broadside Ballad: The Development of the Street Ballad from Traditional Song to Popular Newspaper.* Hatboro, Pa.: 1978.

Shuldham-Shaw, Patrick, and Emily Lyle, eds. *Greig-Duncan Song Collection.* Aberdeen: Aberdeen University Press, 1981.

Silverman, Jerry. *Songs of Scotland.* Pacific, Mo.: Mel Bay Publications, 1991.

Sinclair, Marion, ed. *Hebridean Odyssey: Songs, Poems, Prose, and Images.* Edinburgh: Polygon, 1996.

Slotkin, Richard. *Gunfighter Nation: The Myth of the Frontier in Twentieth-Century America.* New York: HarperCollins, 1992.

Smith, Henry Nash. *Virgin Land: The American West as Symbol and Myth.* Cambridge, Mass.: Harvard University Press, 1950.

Smith, Richard D. *Bluegrass: An Informal Guide.* Chicago: a cappella books, 1995.
_____. *Can't You Hear Me Callin': The Life of Bill Monroe, Father of Bluegrass.* New York: Little, Brown, 2000.

Smyth, Sam. *Riverdance: The Story.* London: Andre Deutsch, 1996.

Snyder, Robert W. *The Voice of the City: Vaudeville and Popular Culture in New York.* Chicago: Ivan R. Dee, 2000.

Spottswood, Richard K. *Ethnic Music on Records: A Discography of Ethnic Recordings Produced in the United States, 1893–1942.* Vol. 5. Urbana, Ill.: University of Illinois Press, 1990.

Stanley, David, and Elaine Thatcher, eds. *Cowboy Poets and Cowboy Poetry.* Urbana, Ill.: University of Illinois Press, 2000.

Stewart, Bob. *Where Is Saint George?: Pagan Imagery in English Folksong.* London: Blandford Press, 1988.

Synge, John Millington. *The Aran Islands.* Edited with an introduction by Tim Robinson. London: Penguin Books, 1992.

Thomas, Jean. *Ballad Makin' in the Mountains of Kentucky.* New York: Henry Holt & Co., 1939.

Thomson, David. *The People of the Sea: A Journey in Search of the Seal Legend.* London: Granada Publishing, 1980.

Thomson, Derick. *Why Gaelic Matters.* Saltire Pamphlets. New Series 5. Edinburgh: Saltire Society, 1984.

Thomson, Derick S., ed. *The Companion to Gaelic Scotland.* New York: Blackwell, 1987.

Thomson, William, ed. *Orpheus Caledonius: A Collection of Scots Songs Set to Music by William Thomson.* Edinburgh: Mercat Press, 1972.

Tichi, Cecelia. *High Lonesome: The American Culture of Country Music.* Chapel Hill, N.C.: University of North Carolina Press, 1994.

Tosches, Nick. *Country: The Twisted Roots of Rock 'n' Roll.* New York: Da Capo Press, 1996.

Travers, Raymond. "The Breton Accent" in *World Music: The Rough Guide.* Edited by Simon Broughton, Mark Ellingham, David Muddyman, and Richard Trillo. London: Rough Guides, 1994.

von Schmidt, Eric, and Jim Rooney. *Baby, Let Me Follow You Down: The Illustrated Story of the Cambridge Folk Years.* Garden City, N.Y.: Anchor, 1979.

Watson, J. Carmichael, ed. *Gaelic Songs of Mary MacLeod.* Edinburgh: Scottish Academic Press for the Scottish Gaelic Texts Society, 1982.

Watson, Roderick. *The Literature of Scotland.* London: Macmillan, 1984.

Wells, Evelyn K. *The Ballad Tree: A Study of British and American Ballads.* New York: Ronald Press, 1950.

White, John. *Git Along, Little Dogies: Songs and Songmakers of the American West.* Urbana, Ill.: University of Illinois Press, 1975.

Wiggins, Gene. *Fiddlin' Georgia Crazy: Fiddlin' John Carson, His Real World, and the World of His Songs.* Urbana, Ill.: University of Illinois Press, 1987.

Williams, William H. A. *'Twas Only an Irishman's Dream: The Image of Ireland and the Irish in American Popular Song Lyrics, 1800–1920.* Music in American Life series. Urbana, Ill.: University of Illinois Press, 1996.

_____. "Irish Traditional Music in the United States." In *America and Ireland, 1776–1976: The American Identity and the Irish Connection.* David Noel David and Owen Dudley Edwards, eds. Westport, Conn.: Greenwood Press, 1980.

Wilson, Charles Reagan, and William Ferris, co-editors. *Encyclopedia of Southern Culture.* Chapel Hill, N.C.: University of North Carolina Press, 1989.

Wimberly, Lowry C. *Folklore in the English and Scottish Ballads.* Chicago: University of Chicago Press, 1928.

Winch, Terence. *Irish Musicians American Friends.* Minneapolis, Minn.: Coffee House Press, 1985.

Winick, Steve. "Milladoiro: Between Fish & Chips." *Dirty Linen,* April/May 1993.

_____. "Songs that Bind Us: The Music of Tommy Sands." *Sing Out!* 36, no. 3 (November-December 1991/January 1992): 14–21.

Wittke, Carl. *The Irish in America.* 1956. New York: Russell, Russell, 1970.

Woliver, Robbie. *Bringing It All Back Home: Twenty-Five Years of American Music at Folk City.* New York: Random, 1986.

Wood, Nicola. *Scottish Traditional Music.* Edinburgh: Chambers, 1991.

Woods, Fred. *Folk Revival: The Rediscovery of a National Music.* Poole, Dorset, England: Blandford Press, 1979.

Wright, Robert L., ed. *Irish Emigrant Ballads and Songs.* Bowling Green, Ohio: Bowling Green Popular Press, 1975.

Index